CORRECTIONS *or* ALTERATIONS

to

LAND GRANTS

in

NORTH CAROLINA
-1714-1873-
and
TENNESSEE
-1778-1796-

Compiled by:
Dr. A.B. Pruitt

Southern Historical Press, Inc.
Greenville, South Carolina

Please direct all correspondence and book orders to:
www.southernhistoricalpress.com
or
SOUTHERN HISTORICAL PRESS, Inc.
1071 Park West Blvd.
Greenville, SC   29611

Southernhistoricalpress@gmail.com

Introduction

This book contains information about corrections or alterations to land grants in North Carolina and Tennessee. From their creation until about 1990, this material was filed in the Secretary of State's Land Grant Office. About 1988 or 1989, the papers were placed in a series of shucks (one petition or alteration per shuck). The work was performed by the author under the direction of Mrs. Martha Paskewich during the last years of the administration of Secretary Thad Eure and with his acquiescence. In 1990, papers in the Land Grant Office were moved to the North Carolina Archives. In the archives, the shucks are now in three boxes titled "State Land Office Petitions to Alter Patents (1780-1873)", series SS XII. The boxes are numbered 164 (Anson County through Johnson County), 165 (Jones County through Surry County), and 166 (Tyrrell County through Yancey County and Claiborne County, TN, through Wilson County, TN). While many of the papers are in good condition, a few are already in several pieces and two are extremely fragile.

The General Assembly passed an act in 1790 (chapter 26) [see NC State & Colonial Records vol. 25 p. 77 & 78] which allowed persons to petition their county pleas and quarter sessions court to correct errors in land grants. The error could have been made by the surveyor in his return (or survey) to the Secretary's office, or the error could have been a copying error in the Secretary's office as the grant was made out. The Secretary was allowed £0.4 for correcting a surveyor's error, but nothing for correcting an error made in the Secretary's office [evidently even when the error was made by a previous Secretary]. Thirty days prior to presenting his petition, the petitioner was required to notify adjoining landowners and anyone owning land described in the petition. A majority of the justices needed to be present to hear the petition. If the county court agreed that the grant needed to be corrected, they ordered the clerk to send the Secretary a description of the correction; for this the clerk was paid £0.5 by the petitioner. The opinion of the county court could be appealed to district superior court. The county court could also order the county surveyor and five "freeholders not interested" to examine and survey the disputed land, ascertain the lines, and make a report to the court; the petitioner paid the cost of the survey [resurveys were frequently ordered in Washington Co, TN]. The same method could be used to correct errors (made by Registers of Deeds) in recorded grants, "mesne conveyance, bill of sale, or other instruments of writing". When deeds were involved, the grantor of the deed had to be notified. The report would be sent by the clerk to the county Register of Deeds.

Also included in this book is information about some grants which were not found to be recorded in the Secretary's grant books. These grants were recorded due to another act of the Assembly in 1788 (chapter 23) [see NC State & Colonial Records vol. 24 p. 966 & 967]. When grants were not found in the Secretary's grant books, petitions were presented to the Governor and Council of State. If the grant appeared to be "fairly" obtained, the Governor & Council could order the Secretary to record the grant along with their order.   Some of these grant include: #180 granted in 1714, #54 granted in 1720, #147 & 442 granted in 1727, #443 granted in 1728, #205 granted in 1730, & #204 granted in 1760.   Item 205 includes a second grant even though no copy of the order from the Governor was located.

Also included in the book are two petitions, for alteration of a grant, made directly to the Assembly.   The Committee on Propositions & Grievances heard such petitions and presented a proposed resolution to the Assembly.   If the Assembly agreed, the Secretary was required to correct the grant.

Finally, this book also includes some receipts for land entry fees for land in Buncombe County.   These receipts were produced to remedy problems with original land entry taker for Buncombe County and his entry book [see items 103, 104, 105, & 112].

On the outside of each shuck is the name of the petitioner and county where the petition was filed.   For this book, an item number was assigned to each shuck; this number is used only in the index of this book. After the item number is the abstracted information from the petition. Sometimes the petition mentions a problem with only one or two lines of the survey or grant; sometimes there were multiple errors; sometimes a complete resurvey was made without describing the exact error. On the backs of petition, the Secretary usually noted that the grant was altered and indicated the date; but the Secretary mentioned the grant number only occasionally.   In the grant book, the Secretary usually made marginal comments above the corrections, but no changes were made to the warrant or survey.   An effort was made to identify the grant, indicate the grant book and page number, and indicate the shuck containing loose papers for the grant.   If the grant was identified, it is mentioned in brackets at the end of the item.

The author wishes to thanks to Mrs. Martha Paskewich & Mr. Earl Ijames for their help in the preparation of this book.

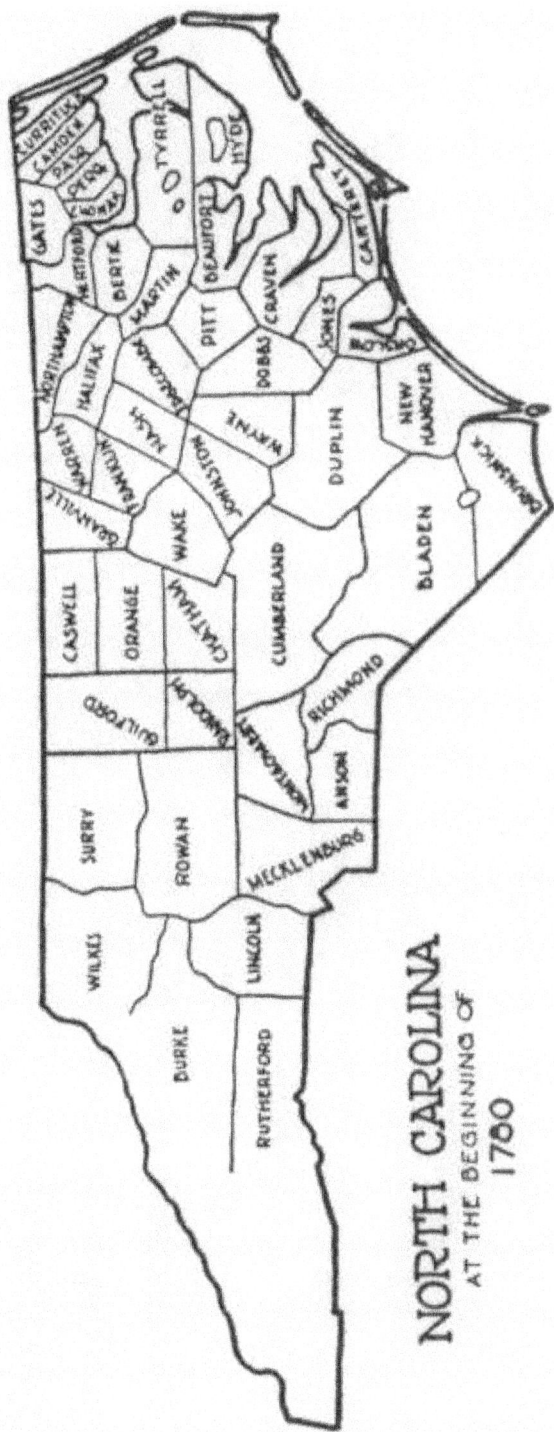

NORTH CAROLINA
AT THE BEGINNING OF
1760

Richard Grift's
patent

N10W 320 p

to beginning

S73W 102 p

S85E 202 p

S40W 170 p

S10W 200 p

E 160 p

S5W 210 p

S5W 315 p

S35E 44 p

S 46 p

S84W 132 p

S84W 132 p

385 ac

S19W 57 p

N20E 160 p

Willie Hall
Beaufort Co

to beginning

N60W 204 p

to beginning

N60W 292 p

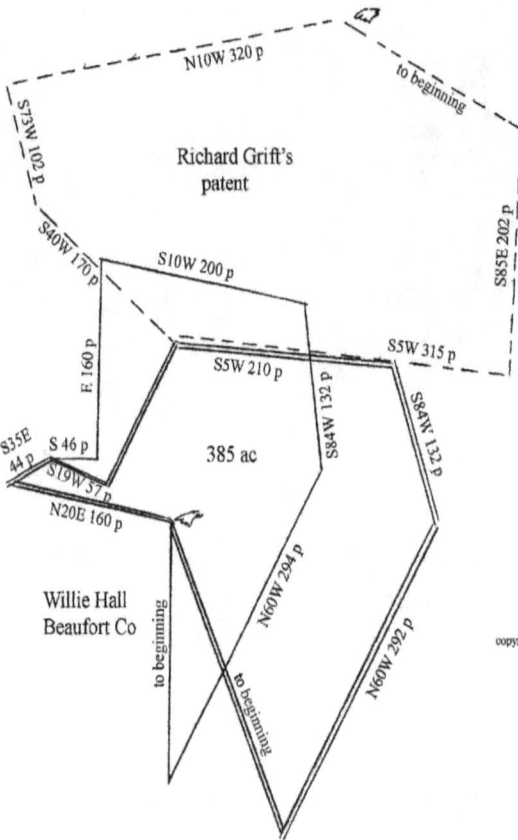

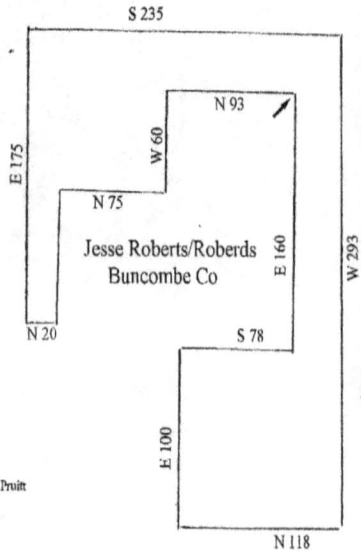

copyright 2002 A B Pruitt

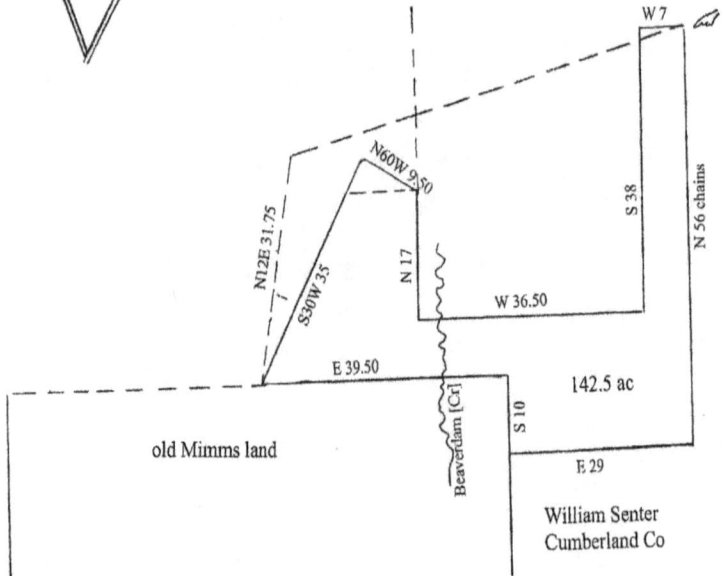

S 235

E 175

W 60

N 93

N 75

Jesse Roberts/Roberds
Buncombe Co

E 160

W 293

N 20

S 78

E 100

N 118

W 7

N60W 9.50

N12E 31.75

S30W 35

N 17

S 38

N 56 chains

W 36.50

E 39.50

Beaverdam [Cr]

S 10

142.5 ac

old Mimms land

E 29

William Senter
Cumberland Co

S24E 17

S78W 20.50

S28W 20.50

N87E 31.63

N79E 17

S12E 50.30

N8W 44

N87E 4.50

S3E 31.63

S45E 15

Cape Fear River

N89E 38.30

S82W 38

N8E 25

B

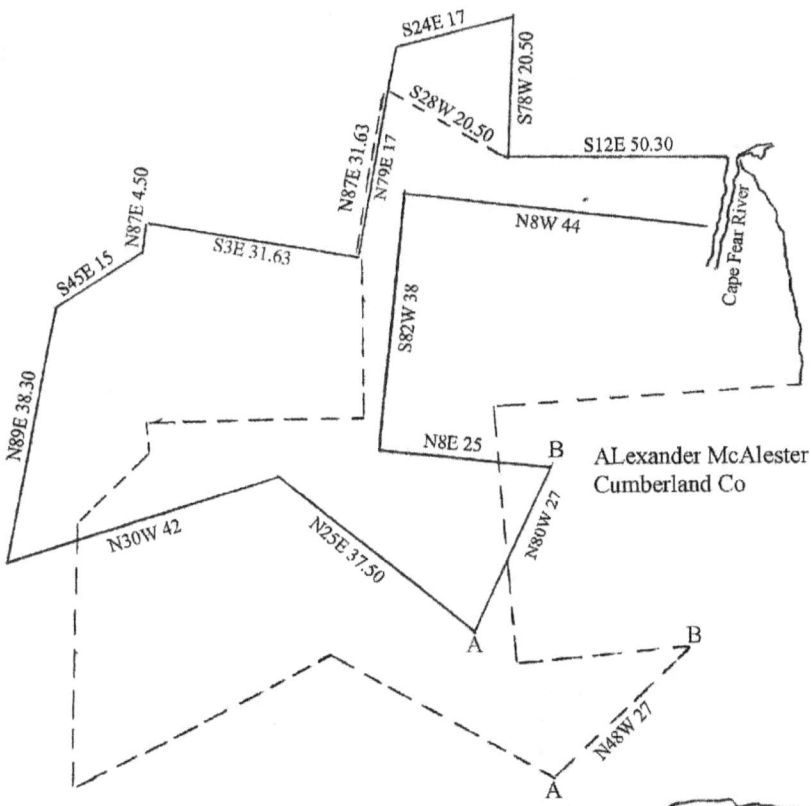

ALexander McAlester
Cumberland Co

N30W 42

N25E 37.50

N80W 27

A

B

N48W 27

A

copyright 2002 A B Pruitt

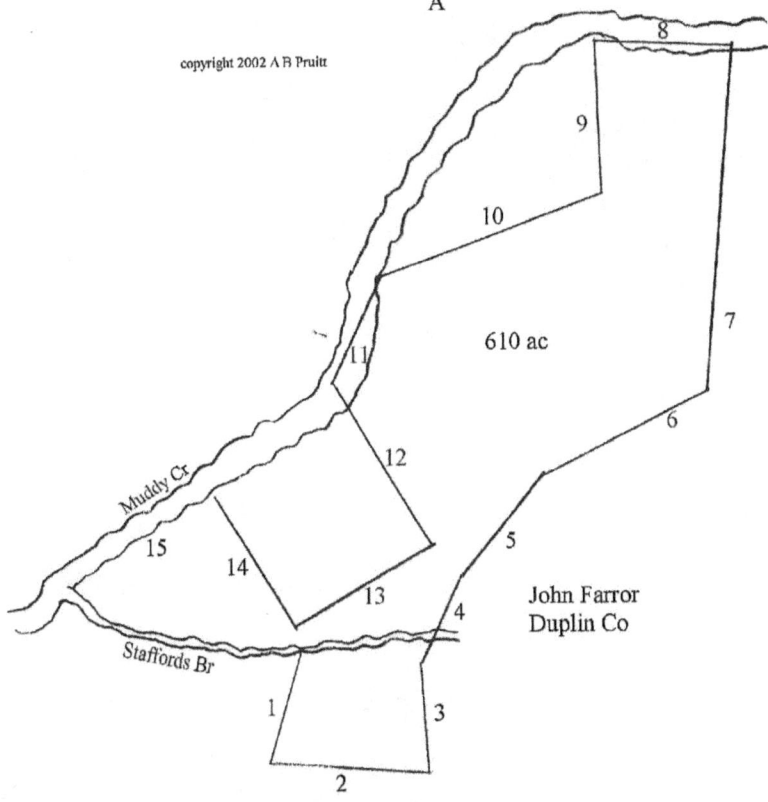

8

9

10

7

610 ac

11

6

12

5

Muddy Cr

15

14

13

4

John Farror
Duplin Co

Staffords Br

1

3

2

Adam Andrews
Jones Co

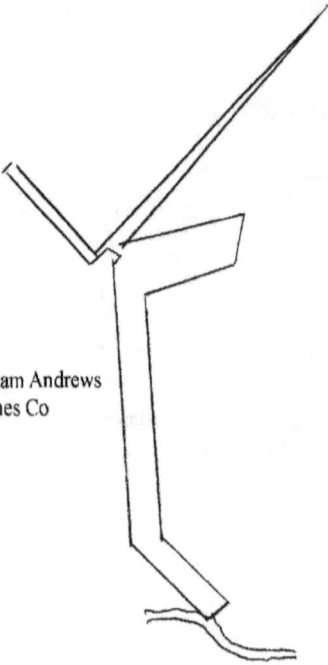

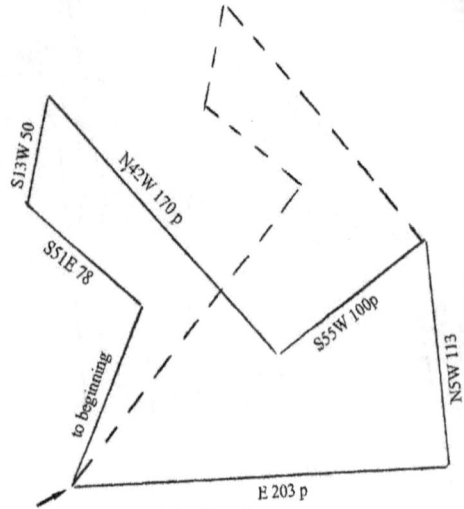

S13W 50
N42W 170 p
S51E 78
S55W 100p
NSW 113
to beginning
E 203 p

John Neagle
Lincoln Co

copyright 2002 A B Pruitt

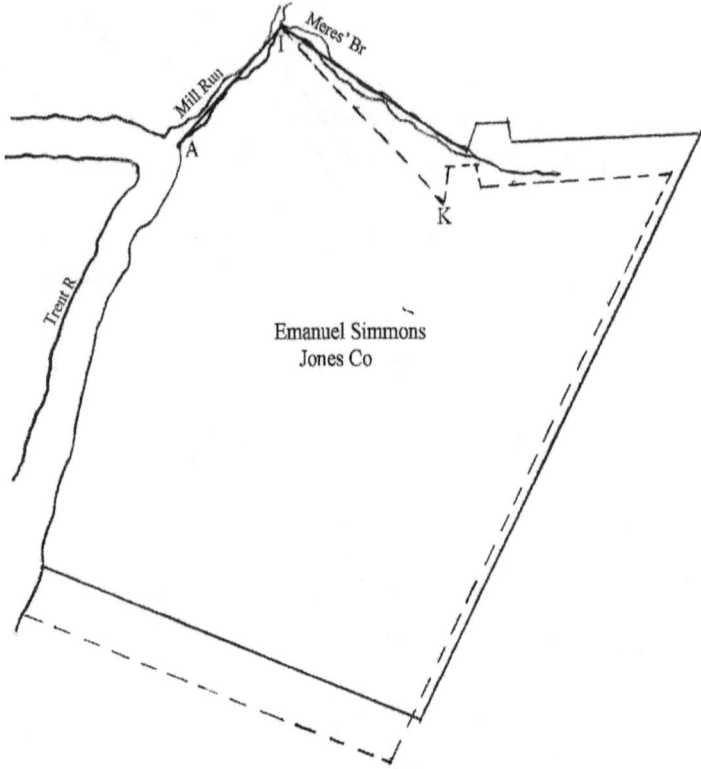

Meres' Br
Mill Run
I
A
K
Trent R

Emanuel Simmons
Jones Co

right line N40W "gives 320 p. on conclusion"

false line "gives 160 poles cocluding"

S30W 320 p

160 p

Hosea Lanier
Martin Co

B

A

40

N26W 268 p

S5W 256 p

William White
Mecklenburg Co

N80W 116 p

130 ac

N24W 54 p

N25E 51 p

to beginning

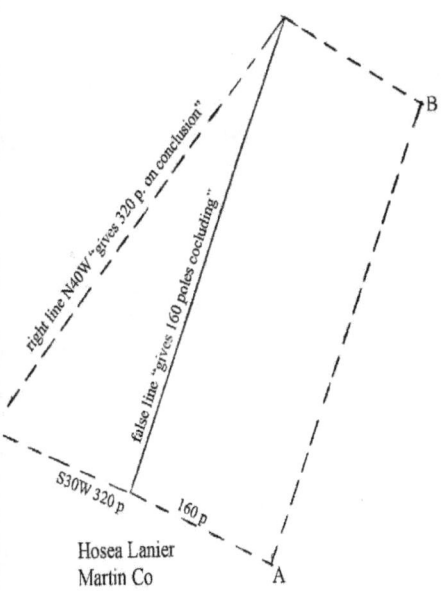

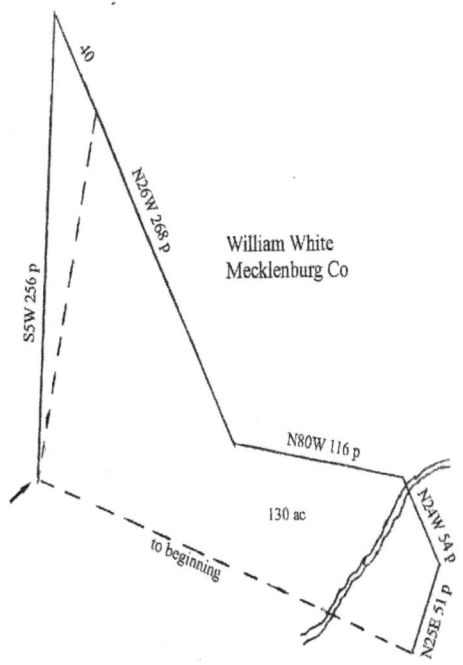

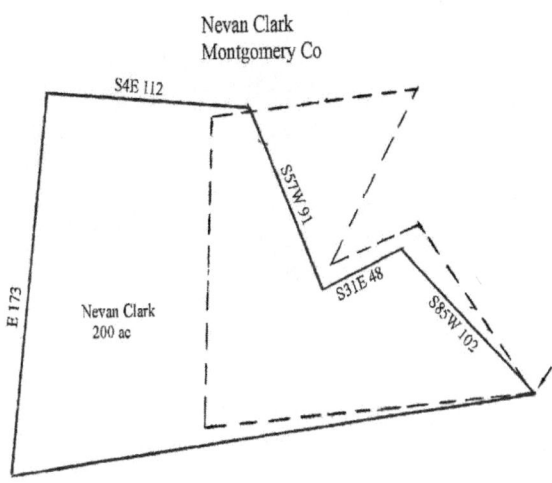

Nevan Clark
Montgomery Co

S4E 112

S5W 91

S31E 48

S8SW 102

E 173

Nevan Clark
200 ac

Thomas Sugg
Montgomery Co

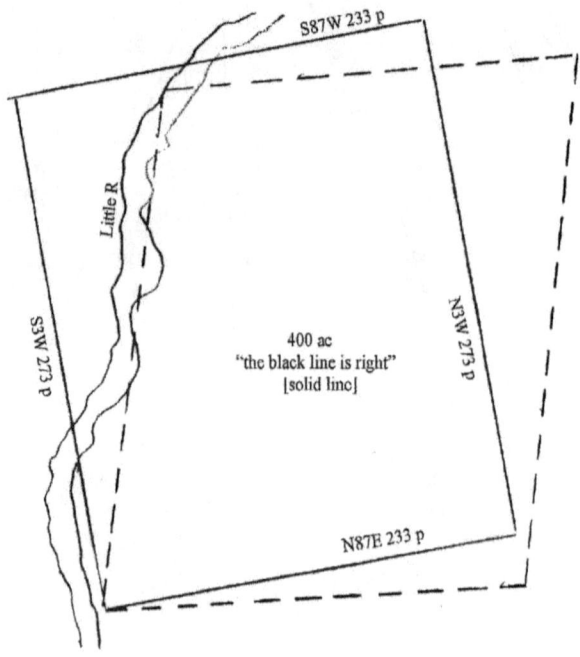

S87W 233 p

Little R

S3W 273 p

N3W 273 p

400 ac
"the black line is right"
[solid line]

N87E 233 p

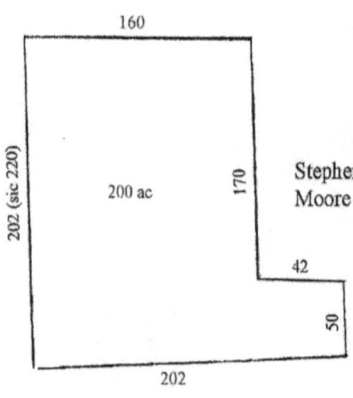

160

202 (sic 220)

200 ac

170

42

50

202

Stephen Collins
Moore Co

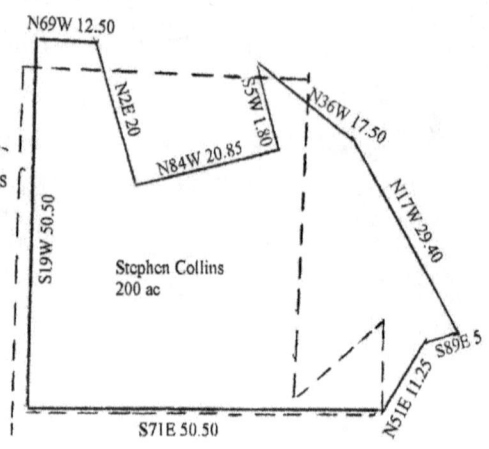

N69W 12.50

N2E 20

S5W 1.80

N84W 20.85

N36W 17.50

N17W 29.40

S19W 50.50

Stephen Collins
200 ac

S89E 5

N51E 11.25

S71E 50.50

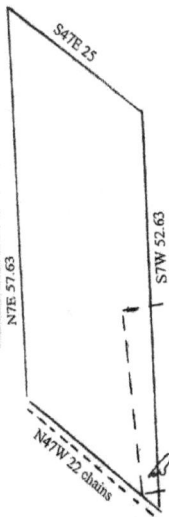

Archibald McLean
Moore Co

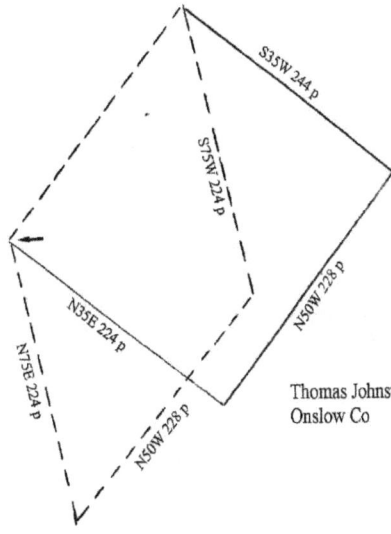

S47E 25

N7E 57.63

S7W 52.63

E 160

S 100

N47W 22 chains

Thomas Johnston
Onslow Co

S35W 244 p

S75W 224 p

N50W 228 P

N35E 224 P

N75E 224 p

N50W 228 P

copyright 2002 A R Pruitt

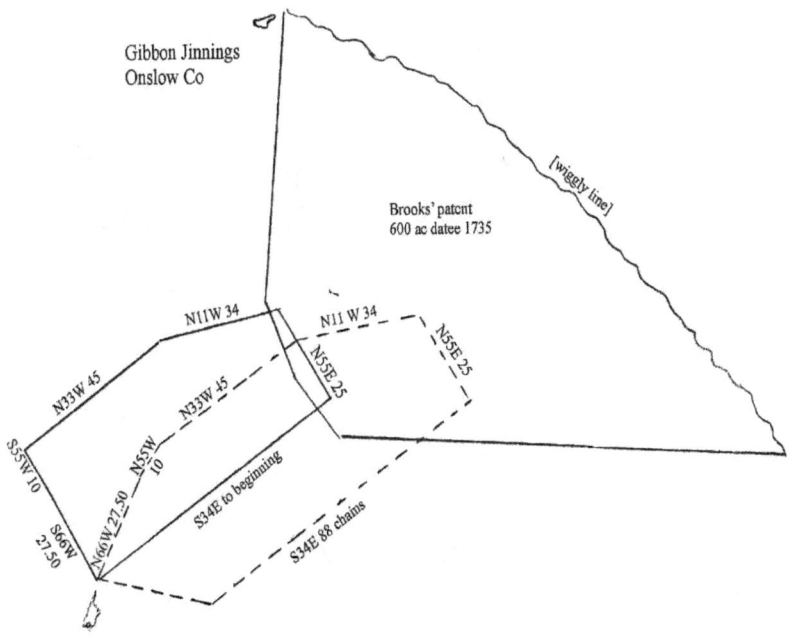

Gibbon Jinnings
Onslow Co

Brooks' patent
600 ac datee 1735

[wiggly line]

N11W 34

N11 W 34

N55E 25

N55E 25

N33W 45

N33W 45

N33W 45

N55W 10

S34E to beginning

S34E 88 chains

S55W 10

S66W 27.50

N66W 27.50

Archibald McEachern
Robeson Co

Haricane Bay

W 25

J Gilchrist
40 ac

S 16

E 25

N 16

J Gilchrist
40 ac

W 25

Long Swamp

Currie
120 ac

Daniel's
old field

Currie
50 ac

Currie
50 ac

S 97 p

N45W 99

S45E 52

S45W 152

S68E 147

N 94 p

Thomas Edgerton
Wayne Co

copyright 2002 A B Pruitt

Grants Cr

S5E 44 chains

N55W 37.5 chains

Martin Brandon
Rowan Co

E 41.5 chains

S70W
25.5 chains

Panther Run

S 15 chains

S 5.75 chains

E 34.5 chains

Great Road

W 13.5 chains

N 30.5 chains

S to beginning

E 5 chains

N 14 chains

S 37.75 chains

N5W 43 chains

Crane Cr

Jesse Bean
2,000 ac

German Cr

E 916 p

S 104

S 140

S54W 105

S 60

N 470 p

S 60   W 208

S 40

W 490 p

W 100

Jesse (George) Bean
Grainger Co, TN

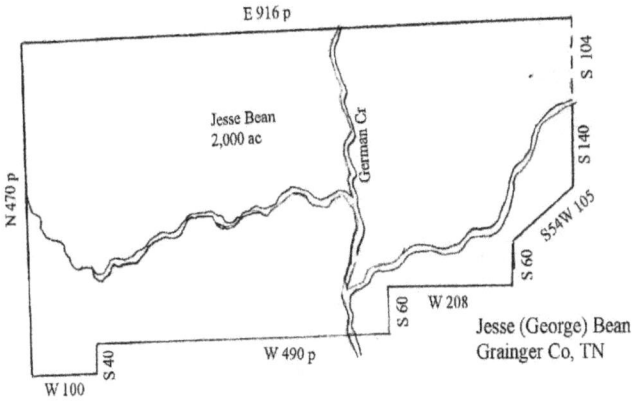

copyright 2002 A B Pruitt

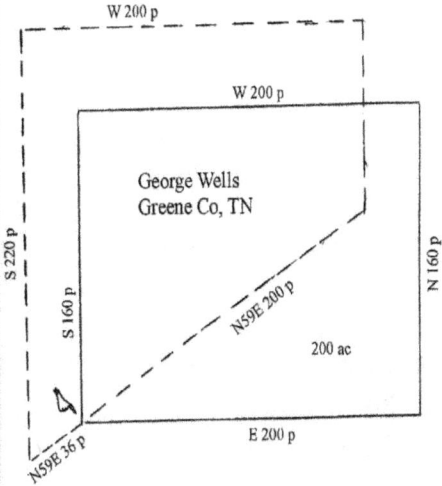

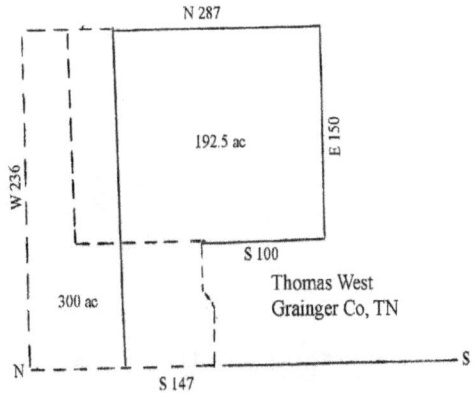

W 200 p

W 200 p

George Wells
Greene Co, TN

S 220 p

S 160 p

NS9E 200 p

N 160 p

200 ac

NS9E 36 p

E 200 p

N 287

192.5 ac

E 150

W 236

S 100

Thomas West
Grainger Co, TN

300 ac

N   S 147   S

Joseph Hardin
Greene Co, TN

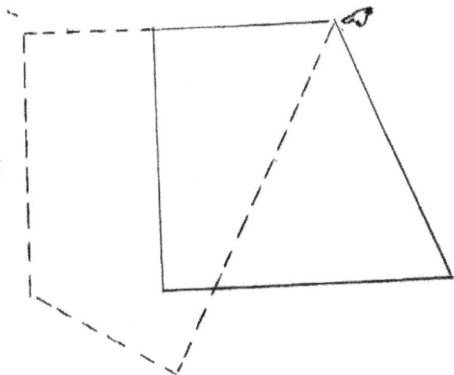

Mathew Cox
for Ben Goodwin
Greene Co, TN

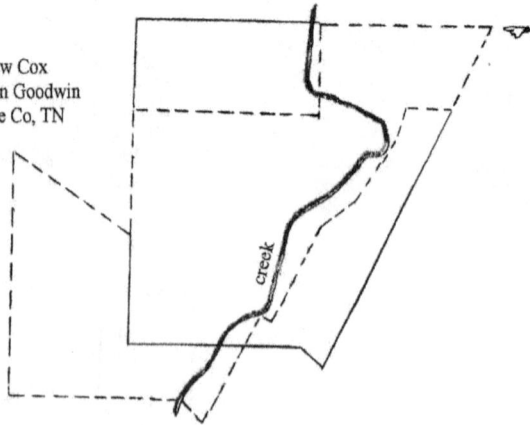

creek

William Kerr
Jefferson Co, TN

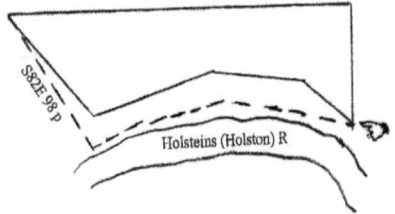

David Larkin
Hawkins Co, TN

N79W 280 p

S82E 98 p

Holsteins (Holston) R

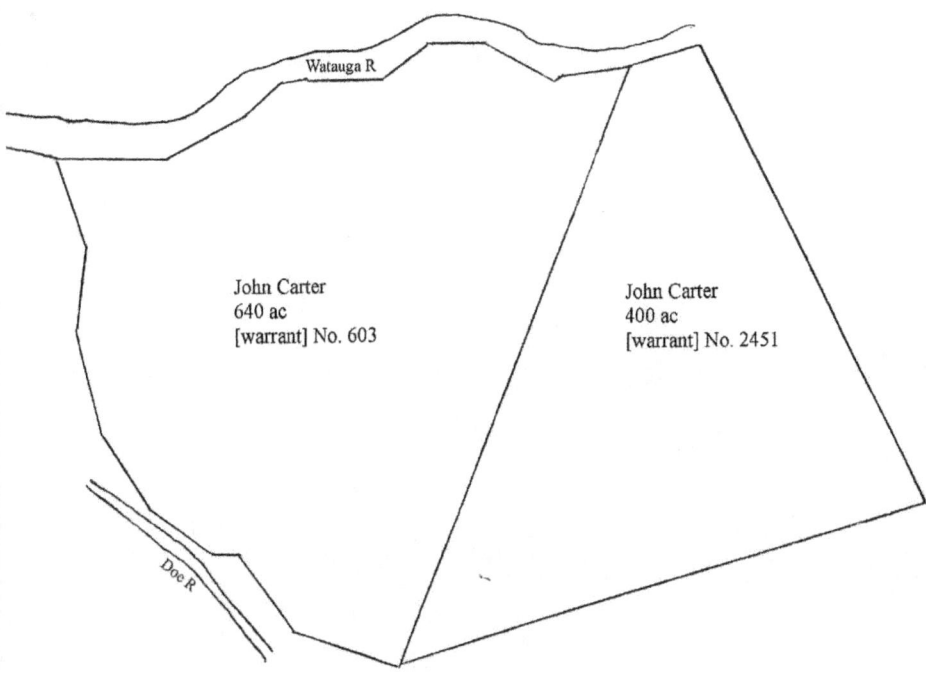

Watauga R

John Carter
640 ac
[warrant] No. 603

John Carter
400 ac
[warrant] No. 2451

Doe R

John Carter
Washington Co, TN
[in 2 shucks]
copyright 2002 A B Pruitt

Corrections/Alterations to Land Grants

1. Anson Co court Jan. 1796 James Boggan sr swears in sale of confiscated property in this county by Mr. Charles Bruce, commissioner, he bought 300 ac on Goulds Fork of Brown Cr and paid £120 full consideration money for land being sold as Robert Rainey's property; land was 205 ac (sic) on S side of Pee Dee [R], on Goulds Fork of Brown Cr, & below Gould's upper survey; begins at Zachariah Philips' corner pine, runs SW 120 poles to a small red oak near a marked pine in Gould's lower line, N70W 240 poles to a white oak, N8E 160 poles to a pine, & S61 E 250 poles along Philips' line to first station; he has applied by "his friend" to the Secretary for a grant agreeable to an act of Assembly, but a mistake which will manifestly appear by "a voucher" accompanying the grant came out of the office for a different piece of land--on both sides of Goulds Fork, late property of Robert Rainey, begins at a stake on E side of Goulds Fork & fourth corner of Gould's upper survey, runs N45W crossing the fork 220 poles to a stake, S45W 220 poles to a stake, S45E crossing the fork again 220 poles to a stake, & N45E 220 poles to first station; last described land is not land which was purchased by the petitioner; the former described land is actually the land the petitioner is entitled to; so he asks for relief. (signed) James Boggan sr.

Court ordered relief be granted to James Boggan sr in this case as act of Assembly has empowered the county courts to grant.

Sept. 13, 1796 Anson Co court office to "Sir" I certify the foregoing is a true copy from the minutes of an order of court respecting petition of James Boggan sr (signed) W W Strain, DC; [on back] #1541 James Boggan 205 ac 1795 pat. altered Sept. 13, 1796; [appears to be item #16 in Sales of Confiscated Land & Property in North Carolina; land was formerly Robert Rainey's; land sold Sept. 22, 1787 to Sampson Lanier who transferred to James Boggan; 6 grants to James Boggan in Secretary's grant files, but not No. 1541].

2. to Anson Co Court of Common Pleas, petition of Thomas Griffin: a patent for 300 ac was issued to William Barnes entered Feb. 27, 1800 & grant issued "same under date" 1803 in Anson Co No. 626; begins at a white oak by 2 hickory pointers on the bluff of Negro head Cr at or near Thomas Griffin's corner, runs S 35 chains with his line to a white oak near said creek by 2 hickories & a pine pointers, E 32 chains to a black gum in Gilchrist's line, S 96 chains with his line to a stake over said Negro head [Cr], N 114 chains to beginning; surveyed Feb. 8, 1802; chain men Stephen Trall & John Griffin; by examining the plat it is evident the tract never intended to run in manner laid down in the grant; Griffin asks for court to order alterations in the lines: beginning shall be as in the original, runs S 35 chains to a white oak aforesaid, E 32 chains to the gum as aforesaid, S28W 65 chains to a stake (instead of the due South line in original 96 chains long), W 27 chains 50 links to a post oak, N 91 chains to a stake, & to beginning (signed) Thomas Griffin;

Anson Co Jan. 1820 It appears to satisfaction of court there was an error in original grant of 300 ac to Wm "Barns"; it is ordered by the court that petitioner's request be granted & necessary alteration be made (signed) Tod Robinson, clerk;

[on back] Wm Barnes 300 ac Anson Co; order of court to alter patent;

1

Corrections/Alterations to Land Grants

altered Apr. 12, 1820 W H; [grant on entry #626 is grant No. 1821, grant book 118 p. 31, see shuck #5706 in Anson Co in Secretary's grant files].

3. To Anson Co Court of Pleas & Quarter Sessions Apr. term 1825: petition of David Brumbelow [Moses Culbertson--lined out] jr saying a grant was issued from state of North Carolina to him [David Brumbelow--lined out] for land in Anson Co on Buck Br; begins at Charles Coock's (sic) corner post oak, runs S 48 [chains] with his own line, E44 chains to a stake in his own   line, N42E 20 chains to a stake, N47W 55 chains to a stake, & to beginning; 100 ac; but land has been granted heretofore to other persons; the surveyor made an error in platting the land; the court ordered a resurvey which began at Charles Cook's corner post oak, runs with his own (Brumbelo's) line N48W 45 chains to a stake in his own line, S42W 20 chains to a stake, S47E 55 chains to a stake, N27E passing Cook's corner & to beginning for 100 ac surveyed Feb. 8, 1825; the petitioner says he will be greatly injured without alteration of the grant; he asks the clerk to certify to the Secretary of State the errors in the original grant (signed) Fabart(?), atto for "Sal"; [on back] David Brumbelo 100 ac Anson Co; petition for alteration of grant; altered Dec. 15, 1827 W H, received 5/ (sic) fee to alter the grant W H;

 Anson Co Apr. 1825 The petitioner has preferred to county court for alteration of grant to David Brumbelo; there appears to be a mistake in the original plat; an order of court first issued to Moses W Cuthbertson to resurvey the land; that was done so court orders the plats be directed to the Secretary of State [metes & bounds repeated] (signed) W Dismukes, clerk; [on back] received $0.50 my fee for altering the grant Dec. 14, 1826 (signed) Wm Hill;

 copy of survey Feb. 8, 1825 by Moses W Cuthbertson; chain carriers Michel Hanagar & David "Brumblo"; grant No. 1928 to David Brumblo; [metes & bounds repeated & plat included]; [7 grants to David Brumbeow or Brumloe, but not No. 1928 in Secretary's grant files, grant not identified].

4. Anson Co Court of Pleas & Quarter Sessions at court house in Wadesborough third Monday in July 1791: Petition of Benjamin Hinson: Benjamin Hinson (of Anson Co) swears he became the buyer of a grant to William Kemp by "his Majesties patent" dated Apr. 14, 1749 for 400 ac in Anson Co; begins at a gum, runs S89E 194 poles to a red oak, N68E 140 poles to a pine, N6W 160 poles to a pine, S 300 poles, & "direct" course to beginning; the petitioner shows the surveyor made a mistake in fourth line by directing "South" when it ought to be West coming within six (?) degrees of traversing the third line & does by no means include the land intended which appears by plat hereunto annexed; the court is empowered by act of General Assembly in such cases to order the Secretary to correct fourth line of the grant to West to agree with the marked lines of the land [not signed]; the court ordered the sheriff to notify "&c"; petition was continued from court to court until third Monday in Apr. 1792 when Benjamin Hinson by his attorney came and court ordered a certificate issue from the court to the Secretary directing him to correct the error. "a true copy" (signed) Wm Johnson, clerk [on back] Ben Hinson, peto. for alt patent done; [grant book 5 p. 317, see shuck #509 in Anson Co in Secretary's grant files].

Corrections/Alterations to Land Grants

5. Anson Co July session 1803: on petition of "Normon" McLeod & proof of notice being made of this petition, ordered by the court that original grant to John Corbo be "amended" agreeable to petition by altering "fith" line of the grant from N37E 90 chains 75 links to N88E 90 chains 75 links, and a copy of this order be transmitted to Secretary of State, to be amended agreeable to act of Assembly in such case made & provided, copy from the minutes (signed) Tod Robinson, clerk; [on back] this alteration cannot be made til the grant is forwarded proof [or] that it is destroyed (signed) W White; certificate for alteration of a grant in name of John Corbo; altered Dec. 7, 1804; Mr. Marshall wants a copy of the grant to be altered; [one grant to John Curbo, No. 151 issued Sept. 3, 1779, grant book 30 p. 314, see shuck #4113 in Anson Co in Secretary's grant files].

6. Anson Co Oct. court 1798: ordered the fifth line of a tract of 200 ac patented by Nathan Morris be altered from running S42W to run N42W; it appears to be a mistake in the surveyor, & the clerk to certify this order to the Secretary (signed) Wm Johnson, clerk; [on back] Nathan Morris order for alteration of a grant; alteration made Dec. 17, 1798; [4 grants to Nathan Morris but none for 200 ac in Anson Co in Secretary's grant files, grant not identified].

7. Anson Co Oct. 1802: ordered that the grant from the State to Solomon Townsend for 50 ac No. 432 be altered so as to correspond with lines of "said" survey, from the minutes (signed) Tod Robinson, clerk; [grant issued Oct. 24, 1782, book 49 p. 238, see shuck #4272 in Secretary's grant files];
    survey attached: surveyed Oct. 23, 1802 by Ezra Bostick, DS & Prossear; John Benbrook & Wm Liles, chain carriers; 50 ac: begins at beginning white oak of Solomon Townsin's 300 ac tract, runs N65E 94 poles to a state amongst a white oak a hickory a pine pointers, N25W 60 poles to a stake amongst 4 black jack pointers, S65W 110 poles to a stake amongst a white oak & a pine pointers, S25E 62 poles to a stake a pine & a red oak pointers, & N65E 23 poles to beginning; [on back] cert. for alteration of a grant in name of Solo. Townsend; altered Nov. 23, 1803; [plat included].

8. Ashe Co, NC: to Secretary of State, it has been made to appear to us that Joseph Hendon, Wilkes Co surveyor, made an error in the certificate of survey for 200 ac for William Huff now conveyed to Wells Blevens on Helton Cr to wit: in third line he has said running N 140 poles to a white oak and in "like manner" a grant has issued for the same No. 713 greatly to the "enjury" of said grantee; whereas the truth & in fact said line aught to run N 160 poles to a white oak; we have directed said [page torn] the surveyor of said county of correct the certificate by making the line run N 160 poles instead of run N 140 poles; we certify the same to you in order that the grant & records of it may be corrected in your office agreeable to an act of Assembly in that case made & provided; witness John McMillan, clerk of said court at office Nov. 11, 1806 (signed) Jos Callaway, DC for Jno McMillan clerk; [on back] Wm Huff certificate for alteration of a grant; grant altered Dec. 9, 1806; [grant issued Sept. 22, 1785, grant book 59 p. 238, see

shuck #716 in Wilkes Co in Secretary's grant files];

[on second sheet] survey Oct. 14, 1806 for Wells Blevens 200 ac; begins at a "read" oak, runs N160 poles to a white oak, E 200 poles to a stake, S 160 poles to a stake, & to first station (signed) Jos Callaway, DS for Eli Clunlan [or Clerntan] CC; Mills Blevens & Wells Penington, chain carriers; [plat included]; [on back] "Wills Bleavim" plan & certificate 200 ac.

9. Second Monday of Aug. 1807 Ashe Co court to North Carolina Secretary: it has been made to appear to us that Robert Nall, late surveyor of said county, made an error in his certificate of survey for 150 ac to James "Blavins" and a grant issued for the same No. 1522; in the certificate it is said begins on a white oak "Petter" Hart's line, runs S 200 poles to a white oak "&c", E 120 poles to a stake, W 200 poles to a stake; in fact the first line ought to have said runs North, then to first station; we hereby certify the same to you in order that the grant & records of it in your office may be altered & the word North be inserted in place of West, agreeable to an act of Assembly in such case made & provided (signed) David Earnest, clerk; [on back] James Blevins certificate of alteration of a grant; altered Dec. 10, 1808; [2 grants in Ashe Co to James Blevins found, but not this grant number; no grants identified in Wilkes Co match either].

10. Ashe Co Court of Pleas & Quarter Sessions May term 1828: the court [ordered] an error be corrected in grant No. 1762 for 100 ac issued to Methias Carpenter; the error will be corrected by saying begin at a white oak "Buckey" & maple, runs N57W instead of N47W (signed) May 12, 1828 Thos Callaway, clerk; [on back] Matthias Carpenter 100 ac Ashe Co formerly Wilkes Co; order of court to alter grant; altered Dec. 2, 1828 (signed) Wm Hill, Sec; [grant issued Dec. 13, 1798, grant book 99 p. 66; see shuck #1526 in Wilkes Co in Secretary's grant files].

11. Ashe Co at Ashe Co Pleas & Quarter Sessions Court held at court house in Jefferson on fourth Monday in Nov. 1855 "being" Nov. 26: following justices presiding--George Bowen, Geo H Hamilton, & A B McMillan: following order made Jesse P Caudle ex parte petition to court errors in a grant: on hearing the petition & proof in this case, it is made to appear to the court "seven" magistrates being present that Solomon Jones, deputy surveyor for Ashe Co, in his certificate of a survey made Jun. 25, 1847 for 99 ac for the petitioner Jesse Caudle; a grant issued Nov. 29, 1848 on the survey & plat committed the following errors in making out the courses of the survey to wit: instead of the calls contained in the survey after the call for "South70West 94 poles to a stake" the calls should have been as follows South 70 poles to a stake, W 118 poles to a stake, & N to beginning "to the end thereof" that the Secretary of State may correct the error in the grant; it is ordered by the court that the facts be certified by the clerk of this court to the Secretary of State. Sept. 12, 1856 Robert Gamble, clerk of Ashe Co Pleas & Quarter Sessions Court, certifies the foregoing in a true copy in my office in above named case (signed) R Gamble, clerk per Jn(?) Gentry DC; [on back] Jesse "Cordill" 99 ac Ashe Co order of court to alter grant; altered Oct. 7, 1856

Corrections/Alterations to Land Grants

(signed) W Hill, Sec.

11. Ashe Co Nov. term 1828 Thos Collaway, clerk of Ashe Co court, certifies an error in a grant of 50 ac issued Jan. 27, 1822 to Aratham "Collans" be corrected by saying Rich hill Cr instead of Hich Cr (signed) Nov. 19 [or 15] Thos Callaway; [on back] Abraham Collins 50 ac Ashe Co; ordered of court to alter grant; altered Dec. 1, 1828 (signed) W Hill, Sec.

12. Ashe Co May term 1820 ordered by court that an error in a grant of 200 ac issued to Joseph Colwell #912 "entered" Mar. 15, 1815 [grant] issued Nov. 27, 1816 be corrected by inserting 70 poles E from a white oak bush the "4" corner from the beginning to a stake, N45W 160 poles to a chesnut, W 70 poles to a chesnut, S 20 poles to a white oak "the" corner of said survey "&c" (signed) May 9, 1820 Thos Callaway, clerk; altered Oct. 2, 1821; [on back] Joseph "Coldwell" 200 ac Ashe Co order of court to alter patent; altered Oct. 2, 1821 (signed) Wm Hill, Secry; [grant in book 130 p. 222; see shuck #1023 in Secretary's grant files].

13. Ashe Co court to Secretary of State: it has been made to appear to us that Eli Cleveland [or Cloueland], county surveyor, made an error in his certificate of survey for 150 ac for Joshua Cox on Kings Cr a branch of S fork of New R to wit in the first line he has said runs E 109 poles to a white oak & in a like manner the grant has issued for the same No. 541 greatly to the "enjury" of the grantee; in truth the line should run N 109 poles; we have directed the surveyor to correct the certificate by making the line runs North instead of running East; we certify the same to you so the grant & records of it may be corrected in your office agreeable to an act of Assembly (signed) May 14, 1806 Jos Callaway, DC for John McMillan clerk; [on back] Joshua Cox certificate for alteration of a grant; altered Dec. 9, 1806; [grant issued Sept. 30, 1805, grant book 119 p. 137; see shuck #547 in Ashe Co in Secretary's grant files];
     survey Oct. 18, 1806 surveyed for Joshua Cox 150 ac; begins at a white oak, runs N 109 poles to a white oak, E 20 poles to a locust, N 32 poles to a white oak, E 62 poles to a spanish oak, N 42 poles to a white oak, E 76 poles to a "read" oak, N70E 38 poles to a white oak in Colwell's line, S 116 poles to a stake, & to first station (signed) Jos Callaway, DS for Eli Cleveland [or Clwaland]; Joshua Cox & William Snow, chain carriers [plat included].

14. to Ashe Co court Nov. term 1804 petition of John Dick: he shows a state grant #1749 issued Dec. 13, 1798 to him for 400 ac; owing to an error or mistake of the surveyor, the grant doesn't contain the land actually run by the surveyor; the plat dated Oct. 30, 1804 annexed to the this petition & signed by Eli Cleveland county surveyor contains the true courses & distances run by the former surveyor and intended to be included in the grant; the petitioner is apprehensive he will be very much injured if the errors in the grant aren't corrected, so he asks the Secretary of State be ordered by the court to correct the errors so the grant agrees with the annexed plat which he asks to be taken as part of the petition [not signed]; Nov. term 1804 Ashe Co Pleas & Quarter Sessions Court: court ordered the prayer of

the petition be granted & Secretary of State amend the grant mentioned in the petition to agree with the annexed plat; the clerk to make a copy of this order for John Dick which is done (signed) Jno McMillan, clerk; [grant in book 99 p. 60, see shuck #1513 in Wilkes Co in Secretary's grant files];

survey Oct. 30, 1804 for John Dick 400 ac on S fork of New R; begins at mouth of Little Naked Cr a branch of said river, runs S44E 73 poles to a white oak, S33W 30 poles to a stake, S28E 80 poles to 2 chesnuts, N70E 52 poles to 2 white oaks, N28E 30 poles to a spanish oak on the river bank, down the river to a locust at mouth of a small drean, N 84 poles to a spanish oak, W 54 poles to a stake, S4W 172 poles to a spanish oak in William Walter's line, E 18 poles to a white oak, & to first station (signed) Eli "Cleveld" CS; David Roland & Michel Stucker, chain carriers; [plat included]; [on back] John Dick plan & certificate 400 ac order of court for alteration of John Dick's grant; altered Nov. 24, 1804.

15. Ashe Co Aug. term 1830: grant #671; ordered by the court that an error in a grant for 150 ac issued Dec. 6, 1809 to James Estep be corrected by beginning at a white oak in Stephen Ausborn's line, runs N 200 poles to a shuger tree, W 120 poles to a stake on the state line, S 200 poles with the state line to a stake, & to first station; (signed) Aug. 17, 1830 Thos Callaway, clerk; [on back] James Estep 150 ac Ashe Co; order of court to alter grant; altered Dec. 17, 1830 (signed) Wm Hill, Secry; [grant in book 126 p. 46, see shuck #795 in Ashe Co in Secretary's grant files].

16. Ashe Co Feb. term 1822 ordered by court that an error in a grant to Daniel Egger for 50 ac No. 589 be corrected by inserting runs West 63 poles from the second corner which is a chesnut to a stake, then N 126 poles to a stake, & to first station; this will correct error in the grant agreeable to the petition filed (signed) Feb. 12, 1824 Thos Callaway, clerk; [on back] Danl "Eggers" 50 ac Ashe Co order of court to alter patent; altered Nov. 24, 1824 (signed) Wm Hill, Sec; [grant issued Nov. 30, 1805, grant book 121 p. 16, see shuck #597 in Ashe Co in Secretary's grant files].

17. Ashe Co court to Secretary of State: it has been made to appear to us that Joseph Callaway, deputy surveyor, made an error in his certificate of survey for 100 ac for Daniel Egars on S fork of New R near the Raven Rocks to wit in second line he said runs West 160 poles crossing the river to a stake; in like manner grant #588 issued for the same greatly to injury of the grantee; in truth the line should run E 160 poles to a stake, S 100 poles to a stake, & to first station; we have directed said surveyor to correct the certificate by making the second line run East instead of West "&c"; we hereby certify the same to you so the grant & records of it may be corrected in your office agreeable to an act of Assembly in that case made & provided John McMillan, clerk (signed) May 14, 1807 Jno McMillan, clerk; [on back] Daniel Eggars certificate for alteration of a grant; altered Dec. 9, 1806; [grant issued Nov. 30, 1806, grant book 121 p. 16, see shuck #596 in Ashe Co in Secretary's grant files];

survey Oct. 12, 1806 for Daniel Eggars 100 ac on S fork of New R;

begins at a spanish oak in the East & West line on N line of land bought of Lenoir near the Raven Rock, runs N 100 poles to a bunch of chesnut oak bushes, E 160 poles to a stake, S 100 poles to a stake, & to first station (signed) Jos Callaway, DS for Eli Cleveland CS; Daniel Eggars jr & Jas Eggars, chain carriers; [plat included].

18. Ashe Co court to Secretary of State: it has been made to appear to us that Eli Cleveland, county surveyor, made a error in his certificate for 150 ac for James Fletcher when he said begins at 3 white oaks a little above a poll bridge, runs E 218 poles to a spanish oak bush, S 110 poles to a locust not far from said creek, W 218 poles to a chesnut oak, & to first station; it has been plainly made to appear to us that the above lines don't include the land specified in the location. The court ordered & we directed the surveyor to resurvey the land; the resurvey begins at a spanish oak on W side of Long Shoal Cr above a small bridge, runs S 176 poles to a red oak, E 136 poles to a chesnut oak & spanish oak near a small branch, N 176 poles down the branch to 3 white oak saplings, & to first station; these lines contain the land entered. We certify the same to you so the records of the grant in your office can be altered & made agreeable to the second survey agreeable to an act of the Assembly passed in 1790 John McMillan, clerk (signed) second Monday in Aug. 1806 Jno McMillan, clk [on back] certificate for alteration of a grant to Jas Fletcher for 150 ac; grant No. 610 issued Jul. 22, 1806; altered Sept. 29, 1806; [may be grant #510 issued Dec. 4, 1804, grant book 118 p. 420, see shuck #516 in Ashe Co in Secretary's grant files];

        survey Aug. 28, 1806 for 150 ac for James Fletcher [same metes & bounds as second survey above] (signed) Eli Cleveland, CS; Michel Stucker & "Petur" Eller, chain carriers; [2 copies of survey included].

19. Ashe Co Aug. term 1829 ordered by the court that an error in grant #994 issued to Saml "Griffis" for 50 ac be corrected by beginning at a locust "spraught" near N fork of New R, runs W 12 poles to a stake on the river bank, N 45E 80 poles down the river to a plum bush, S45E 12 poles to a white oak in Samuel Coxe's line, S60E 12 poles to a stake at Wm Griffith's corner, S 108 poles with said line to a stake, W 60 poles to a stake in Lewis' line, & to first station. (signed) Nov. 8, 1830 Thos Callaway, clerk; [on back] Saml Griffith 50 ac Ashe Co order of court to alter grant; altered Dec. 17, 1830 (signed) Wm Hill; [grant issued Dec. 10, 1818, grant book 133 p. 155, see shuck #1106 in Secretary's grant files].

20. Ashe Co Court of Pleas & Quarter Sessions May term 1850 Lowrey Grimsley ex parte petition to correct error in a grant; 7 justices present; it appears to satisfaction of court on petition & testimony of Solomon Jones, the former surveyor of said county, & Charles H Doughten the present county surveyor that there are mistakes in a survey & plat made by Solomon Jones due to land warrant No. 10754 for the petitioner Lowrey Grimsley & state grant No. 4545 in his name; said Grimsley is liable to be injured by the mistake; so court ordered the mistake be corrected by the Secretary of State and Charles Doughten to resurvey the land & make out 2 correct plats & "surtificates" and clerk of court ordered to inclose

the same together with the plat of Solomon Jones & grant No. 4545 and certified copy of this order & Secretary of State is ordered to correct the grant agreeable to the resurvey & and file a copy of this certificate of this order in his office; John Ray, clerk of Ashe Co Pleas & Quarter Sessions Court, certifies the foregoing is a correct copy of the records (signed) fourth Monday in May 1850 Jno Ray, clerk; [on back] Ashe Co order of court to alter grant to Lowrey Grimsley; altered Nov. 20, 1850 (signed) Wm Hill, Sec; [2 grants to Grimsley for 25 ac in 1840 & 1842, but no grant identified for 35 ac or grant for warrant #10754];

survey due to warrant #10754 issued Sept. 18, 1845; survey 35 ac May 28, 1850 for Lowery Grimsley on N fork of New R; begins at a water oak on E bank of the river, runs S 38 poles up the river to a white walnut at mouth of Porters Br, N75W 104 poles crossing the river to a chesnut in Ballows "bounty" line, N 45 poles with said line to a "Servis", # 82 poles to a stake on the river bank, & S25E to beginning (signed) C H Doughten, CS; Nathaniel Rice & James Porter, chain carriers.

21. Ashe Co Nov. term 1838 ordered by court that John Holsclaw have a resurvey on land entry No. 6900 & grant No. 1922 for 280 ac in said county; it's further ordered the Secretary correct the grant according to the resurvey (signed) Jno Ray, clerk; [on back] No. 1922 John "Holtsclaw" 280 ac Ashe Co order of court to alter grant; altered Dec. 21, 1841; grant dated Aug. 24, 1835; [grant issued Aug. 24, 1835, grant book 142 p. 14, see shuck #2024 in Ashe Co in Secretary's grant files];

survey Mar. 11, 1839 due to order of Ashe Co Court of Pleas & Quarter Sessions to correct error in grant #1922 issued on warrant No. 6900 for John Holtsclaw for 280 ac on Elk Cr; begins at a white oak on N side of the creek, runs N 220 poles across 2 branches to a chesnut, W 150 poles crossing 2 branches to a stake in his line, S 16 poles to his corner, W 70 poles to a birch, S 204 poles to a stake, E 92 poles to a stake, N 70 poles to a stake, E 36 poles to a stake, S 70 poles to a stake, & to beginning (signed) R Mast, CS; Alfred B Baird & Zerilda Baird, chain carriers [plat included].

22. Ashe Co court to Secretary of State: it has been made to appear to us that Robert Nall, late county surveyor, made an error in his certificate of survey for 100 ac for Parmenus Howard leaving out one line altogether and grant No. 364 has issued for the same; Parmenus Howard, by petition, had his land resurveyed by Eli "Clevland", the present county surveyor, begins at a hickory, runs N 22 poles to a spanish oak on a ridge, W 40 poles to a sugar tree, S 173 poles to a beach, E 100 poles to a stake, & to first station; this is correct courses and contains the land entered in entry taker's office per plan & certificate of Eli Cleveland; we certify the same to you so a new grant can be obtained for the land or the records of the old grant can be corrected in your office so complete justice can be done to the grantee agreeable to an act of Assembly passed in 1790 (signed) second Monday in AUg. 180 David Earnest, clerk; [on back] "Parmenious" Howard certificate for alteration of a grant; altered Nov. 30, 1808; [grant issued Dec. 17, 1802, grant book 116 p. 320, see shuck #372 in Ashe Co in Secretary's grant files];

survey Aug. 7, 1807 [same metes & bounds as above] (signed) Eli

Corrections/Alterations to Land Grants

Cleveland, CS; Rubin Smitheal & William Firman, chain carriers; [2 copies of survey included, but one copy of survey is very faint].

23. Ashe Co court to Secretary of State: it has been made to appear to us that Robert Nall, late Ashe Co surveyor, made an error in his certificate for survey for 200 ac for Parmenus Howard and grant No. 365 issued for the same; the third line it is said runs West where it ought to have been East as you will easily perceive by observing the plot & reading the certificate; we certify the same to you so the records of th grant can be corrected in your office by changing the word West in the third line to East agreeable to an act of Assembly in such case made & provided (signed) second Monday in Aug. 1807 David Earnest, clerk; [on back] Purmenious Howard certificate for alteration of grant No. 365 dated Dec. 1802; altered Nov. 30, 1808; [grant issued Dec. 17, 1802, grant book 116 p. 320, see shuck #373 in Secretary's grant files].

24. Aug. term 1801 justices of Ashe Co court to William White, Secretary of State: it has been satisfactorily made to appear to us that the surveyor made an error in making out the certificate for 50 ac No. 2057 for Joseph Keslar in said county of waters of "Baver" Cr; the surveyor said begins at NE corner when the beginning ought to be the SE corner; Jos Keslar petitioned us and our clerk is directed to certify the mistake to you so you can correct the grant & the records in your office making the beginning the SE corner; certified by John McMillan, clerk at office. (signed) Aug. 12, 1801 Jno McMillan, clerk; [on back] certificate to alter a grant; altered Nov. 16, 1801; [grant No. 2057 issued Nov. 14, 1800, grant book 108 p. 289, see shuck #1768 in Wilkes Co in Secretary's grant files].

25. Ashe Co Nov. term 1821 grant #1707; ordered by court that an error in a grant to James Langley Dec. 15, 1831 for 50 ac be corrected by saying South from the beginning corner instead of East, then South instead of East in the third line; (signed) Nov. 12, 1832 Thos Callaway, clerk; [on back] James Langley 50 ac Ashe Co order to be altered; altered Dec. 31, 1821 (signed) Wm Hill, Secy; [grant in book 139 p. 368, see shuck #1818 in Ashe Co in Secretary's grant files].

26. Aug. term 1801 Ashe Co justices to William White, Secretary of State: it has been satisfactorily made to appear to us that our county surveyor made an error in making out certificate of survey for 300 ac for William Lenoir No. 39 "now" in said county on S fork of New R at lower end of Elk Shoals; surveyor's error was saying after runs N 162 poles to a locust under the Round Knob then W 120 poles to a stake but the line out to be 220 poles long as laid down in the plat; William Lenoir has petitioned us so our clerk be directed to certify the mistake to you so you can correct the grant for said land and the records in your office so the line runs West 220 poles to a stake instead of 120 poles; certified by John McMillan, clerk (signed) Aug. 10, 1801 Jno McMillan, clerk; [on back] Wm Lenoir; altered Dec. 16, 1801; [grant issued Dec. 13, 1800; grant book 108 p. 397; see shuck #32 in Ashe Co in Secretary's grant files].

Corrections/Alterations to Land Grants

27. May session 1819 Ashe Co Pleas & Quarter Sessions Court petition to correct an error in grant No. 2095 for 640 ac to William Lenoir jr; it has been made to appear to our satisfaction that the survey made an error in his return of the plat & certificate of "another survey of equal number of acres" instead of returning plats & certificates for land actually surveyed. So it is ordered that Secretary of State correct the error by issuing a grant according to plat & certificate herewith transmitted. For 640 ac in Ashe Co: begins at a large red oak in a cove at head of left hand fork of Rich hill Cr of N fork of New R, runs E 300 poles to a chesnut near top of said ridge at head of right hand fork of the creek, S 341 poles to a stake, W 300 poles to a stake, & to first station; certified by Thomas "Calloway", clerk. (signed) May 14, 1819 Thos Callaway; [on back] Wm Lenoir jr 640 ac Wilkes now Ashe Co order to alter grant; altered Nov. 24, 1819 W H; [grant issued Dec. 13, 1800, grant book 108 p. 409, see shuck #1805 in Wilkes Co in Secretary's grant files];

        survey Jun. 17, 1802 for 640 ac for William Lenoir [same metes & bounds as above] (signed) Robt Nall, CS; David Roten & Charles Lewis, chain carriers; [plat included].

28. Ashe Co May term 1825 ordered by court that an error in grant No. 1111 to Daniel Lewis for 50 ac be corrected; begins at Johnson's corner chesnut, runs E 126 poles to a lynn tree, S 63 poles to a stake, W 126 poles to a stake in Whitenton's line, & to beginning; these "corses" & distance corrects the errors in the grant. (signed) Nov. 8, 1825 Thos Calloway; [on back] Daniel Lewis 50 ac Ashe Co order of court to alter patent; altered Dec. 7, 1825 (signed) Wm Hill, Sec; [grant issued Dec. 21, 1822, grant book 135 p. 359, see shuck #122 in Ashe Co in Secretary's grant files].

29. Nov. term 1825 Ashe Co; ordered by court for you to correct an error in grant No. 1203 issued to David May for 100 ac to wit: begins at second corner chesnut oak of said "Lusey", runs N 32 poles to an ashe, E10S 128 poles to a black gum, S140 poles to a black oak, W to his old line, N 160 poles with said line to a stake, & to first station; (signed) Mar. 6, 1825 Thos Calloway, clerk; [on back] Mr. Secretary Hill: Please correct the error in the grant agreeable to within certificate and "enclose" the same to me by mail to Ashe Court house in town of Jefferson (signed) David May "N B" your fee is enclosed within; altered Apr. 1, 1826 W H; [grant issued Dec. 15, 1824, grant book 136 p. 109, see shuck #1314 in Ashe Co in Secretary's grant files].

30. Nov. term 1841 Ashe Co; ordered by court that Secretary of State correct grant No. 2022 issued Dec. 5, 1835 to Adam Miller for 50 ac; that is to say from the third corner chesnut oak to "read East the place of West" 126 poles to a stake; certified by John Ray, clerk of said court (signed) [no date] Jno Ray, clerk; [on back] Adam Miller 50 ac Ashe Co order of court to alter patent; altered Nov. 23, 1844 (signed) Wm Hill, Sec; [grant issued Dec. 3, 1835, grant book 142 p. 218, see shuck #2224 in Ashe Co in Secretary's grant files].

Corrections/Alterations to Land Grants

31. Ashe Co John Ray, clerk of Ashe Co Pleas & Quarter Sessions Court certifies at Nov. session of said court, it was ordered that Secretary of State alter grant No. 1670 to Abner Nelson of Ashe Co for 50 ac so the grant agrees with within resurvey. (signed) Nov. 11, 1834 Jno Ray, clerk; [on back] survey Nov. 10, 1834 due to order of Ashe Co court for Abner Nelson 50 ac original survey being in part on other deeded land; warrant #6039 entered Mar. 16, 1824; begins at a dogwood saplin also a beginning corner, runs N10E 40 poles to a buckeye in drean, S45E [or S45W] 20 poles to a stake in Sutherlin's line, S30W 12 poles to a sugar tree, S25E 86 poles to a stake, W 110 poles with Egger's line to said Nelson's corner stake in Egger's line, N 26 poles with Nelson's line to his corner stake, & with said Nelson's line to beginning (signed) Thos Braver for N Ballow CS; Thos Brown & Thos "Sutherlan", chain carriers; [on separate sheet] order of court to alter grant; altered Nov. 24, 1834 (signed) Wm Hill, Sec; [grant issued Dec. 5, 1831, grant book 139 p. 282, see shuck #1781 in Ashe Co in Secretary's grant files].

32. Ashe Co Pleas & Quarter Sessions Court Aug. session 1837 ordered by court that Timothy Perkins have following alterations made in state grant No. 831 issued Dec. 23, 1813 to him for 50 ac in said county to wit: begins at a black walnut, runs N32W 46 poles to a white oak, N24E 32 poles to his corner hickory, N72E 67 poles to his corner white oak, S 130 poles to a stake, S72 W 60 poles to a stake, & to first station; John Ray, clerk, certifies foregoing order was made at Aug. session 1837 (signed) Sept. 9, 1837 Jno Ray; [on back] Timothy Perkins 50 ac Ashe Co order of court to alter grant; altered Sept. 16, 1837;

    attached is a survey Nov. 19, 1836 due to court order & warrant No. 831 on waters of Little Helton Cr [same metes & bounds as above] (signed) Thos Ballow, DS; Wm Rite & Johnson Perkins, chain carriers; [plat included];

    Aug. term 1837 Thomas Ballow, deputy surveyor, swears the attached survey & plat correct an error in grant No. 831 for 50 ac (signed) Aug. 28, 1837 Thos Ballow before Jno Ray, clerk; [grant issued Dec. 23, 1813, grant book 128 p. 229, see shuck #942 in Ashe Co in Secretary's grant files].

33. Ashe Co Pleas & Quarter Sessions Court May term 1839 court ordered a survey be "granted" to William Price for grant No. 1758 for 50 ac in Ashe Co that is to say first line in place of running W30S 133 poles to a stake in his own line to run W30N 130 (sic) poles to a stake in his own line; it's further ordered that Secretary of State correct the grant agreeable to above order; John Ray, clerk of court, certifies foregoing is a true copy from the records in my office (signed) Sept. 28, 1840 Jno Ray, clk; [on back] Wm Price 50 ac Ashe Co No. 1758; order of court to alter grant; altered Nov. 21, 1846 (signed) W H; [grant issued Nov. 29, 1832, grant book 140 p. 111, see shuck #1870 in Ashe Co in Secretary's grant files].

34. Ashe Co Pleas & Quarter Sessions Court Nov. term 1846 court ordered Secretary of State correct an error in grant No. 1736 to John Reeves for 50 ac in Ashe Co that is to say in second line to run N40E 80 poles to a stake instead of S40W; John Ray, clerk of said court, certifies foregoing order is an act of the court

with 3 lawful justices present (signed) Dec. 20, 1846 Jno Ray, clerk by H Ray DC; [on back] John "Reaves" 50 ac Ashe Co order of court to alter patent; altered Dec. 28, 1846 (signed) Wm Hill, Sec; [grant issued Dec. 22, 1831, grant book 139 p. 399, see shuck #1847 in Ashe Co in Secretary's grant files].

35. Ashe Co court to Secretary of State: it has been made to appear to us that Robert Nall, county surveyor, made an error in his certificate of survey for 100 ac for James Richardson on Poiny Cr to within third line he said runs W 77 poles to a stake and grant No. 7 issued in same manner greatly to injury of grantee; in truth the line "aught" to run N15W 62 poles to a white oak, W 120 poles to a stake "&c"; we have directed the surveyor to correct the certificate making the line run N15W instead of [due] West; we certify the same to you so the grant & records may be corrected in your office agreeable to act of Assembly in that case "maid" & provided; certified by John McMillan, clerk (signed) May 14, 1806 Jos Callaway, DC for Jno McMillan clk; [on back] altered Dec. 9, 1806;
    survey Oct. 15, 1806 for James Richardson for 100 ac on Poiny Cr; begins at a hickory in John Baldwin's line, runs E 60 poles to a stake in Lenoir's line, N17E 80 poles to a white oak & chesnut, N60E 60 poles to a red oak, N15W 62 poles to a white oak, W 120 poles to a stake, & to first station (signed) Jos Callaway, DS for Eli "Cliveland" CS; John Baldwin & Enoch Baldwin, chain carriers; [plat included]; [grant issued Dec. 5, 1800, grant book 108 p. 334, see shuck #7 in Ashe Co in Secretary's grant files].

36. Aug. term 1825 Ashe Co ordered by court that an error be corrected in grant No. 951 for 250 ac to James Richardson by running from the "5" corners South 170 poles to a stake in Richardson's old line with his old line to his corner, S 42 poles with his old line to his corner spanish oak, W 62 poles with his old line to his corner white oak, S 32 poles to his corner locust, W 100 poles to a stake, & to first station (signed) Aug. 12, 1825 Thos Calloway, clerk; [on back] James Richardson 250 ac Ashe Co order of court to alter patent; altered Oct. 10, 1825 (signed) Wm Hill, Secy; [grant issued Nov. 30, 1818, grant book 133 p. 26, see shuck #1063 in Ashe Co in Secretary's grant files].

37. Nov. term 1838 Ashe Co ordered by court that an error be corrected in grant No. 1801 issued Sept. 7, 1833 to Saml Sapp for 640 ac on waters of Richhill Cr due to fifth line being 80 poles longer that is called for in the field notes of survey and eighth line being left out of the field notes and eleventh line found to be 10 poles longer than is called for; the court of Pleas & Quarter Sessions has ordered Secretary be requested to make above correction agreeable to resurvey; John Ray, clerk, certifies foregoing is a true copy of records in my office (signed) [no date] Jno Ray, clerk; [on back] Saml Sapp 640 ac Ashe Co order of court to alter grant; altered Sept. 14, 1840 (signed) Wm Hill, Sec;
    survey Dec. 4, 1838 for Saml Sapp for 640 ac on Richhill Cr; begins at a chesnut tree on the dividing ridge between Richhill Cr & Roaring Fork waters of N fork of New R near Walling's old "Sang" Camp, runs E 100 poles to a hickory, S 20 poles to a chesnut, E 134 poles to a white walnut saplin in the line

of a 50 ac survey "of said Sapp's deeded to him" by Henry Graybeal, S40E 60 poles with said line to a chesnut on the line, S 280 poles to a white oak saplin on the bank of Richhill Cr, E 80 poles to a chesnut, S 106 poles to a birch across the creek, W 110 poles to 2 chesnut saplins on a ridge, N28W 74 poles to Alen Dougherty's corner large red oak, W 214 poles to a red oak saplin on Pleasant Eastridge's line, N 106 poles with said line to Eastridge's corner locust saplin on Ephraim Gentry's line of "the" green cove, N60E 62 poles with Gentry's line to Gentry's corner in head of a branch, N50W 53 poles with Gentry's line to a buckeye on said line, & to first station (signed) R Mast, CS; [no chain carriers mentioned]; plat shows 50 ac of "deeded land within this survey"; [grant issued Sept. 7, 1833, grant book 140 p. 389, see shuck #1903 in Ashe Co in Secretary's grant files].

38. Ashe Co Pleas & Quarter Sessions Court Feb. term 1847 it appears to satisfaction of the court there are 2 errors in grant No. 3045 to John Shearer for 40 ac to wit: the words "then West 38 poles to a stake" is omitted being fourth line of the survey & words "then N55E 32 poles to a stake" is omitted in sixth line; the court ordered the Secretary of State to correct the grant to read as follows: begins at a cucumber [tree], runs S 65 poles to a hickory, W 20 poles to a stake, N 22 poles to a stake, W 38 poles to a stake, N20E 53 poles to a stake, N55E 32 poles to a stake, E 106 poles to a sugar tree at a branch, S 30 poles to a stake in his line, & W with said line to beginning; John Ray, clerk, certifies foregoing is a true copy of records in my office (signed) [no date] Jno Ray, clerk; [on back] altered Sept. 25, 1847 (signed) Wm Hill, Sec;

      survey Oct. 14, 1844 due to warrant No. 9913 for John Shearer 40 ac on waters of Howards Cr; begins at his corner cucumber [remainder is same metes & bounds as above] (signed) R Mast, CS; John Shearer jr & Robert Shearer, chain carriers; [plat included]; [grant issued Nov. 18, 1844, grant book 149 p. 260, see shuck #3142 in Ashe Co in Secretary's grant files.

39. Nov. term 1838 Ashe Co ordered by court that an error be corrected in a grant to Conrod Smitteal for 50 ac as follows: begins at Smitteal's old corner chesnut & chesnut oak, runs S15W in place of running S15E; John Ray, clerk, certifies foregoing is a true copy from the records in my office (signed) Dec. 15, 1858 Jno Ray, clk; [on back] "Coonrod Smitteal" altered Dec. 21, 1838 (signed) Wm Hill, Sec; [may be grant #1912 issued Dec. 19, 1834, grant book 141 p. 386, see shuck #2014 in Ashe Co in Secretary's grant files].

40. Feb. term 1825 Ashe Co ordered by court that you are required to correct an error in grant No. 887 to More Stamper in the following words: begins at a white oak, runs E 24 poles to a hickory on N side of N fork of New R, 40 poles up said river to a spanish oak, W 180 poles to a poplar, N 100 poles to a maple, E 156 poles to a stake, & to first station. (signed) Feb. 7, 1825 Thos Callaway, clerk; [on back] grant No. 887 to More Stamper for 100 ac Ashe Co to Secretary Hill; altered Jan. 18, 1827 W H; [grant issued Nov. 30, 1815, grant book 129 p. 443, see shuck #998 in Ashe Co in Secretary's grant files].

41. Ashe Co ordered by court that an error be corrected in grant No. 1717 to Francis Stogell issued Dec. 15, 1831 for 45 ac by inserting his West corner instead of his NE corner in beginning corner. (signed) [omitted] 12, 1832 Thos Callaway, clerk; [on back] Francis "Sturgill 25 ac" order of court to alter grant; altered Dec. 31, 1832 (signed) W H; [Francis Stogell received grants in Ashe County but none numbered 1717].

42. Nov. term 1819 Ashe Co court ordered an error be corrected in grant No. 964 issued Nov. 30, 1818 to Jno "Tator"; the error will be corrected by running N 98 poles from the beginning to Jno Potter's corner burch tree, W 25 poles to Potter's corner beach, S 152 poles to Potter's corner beach, W 100 poles to a stake in Potter's line, S 40 poles to a stake in Bowers' line, E 125 poles to a stake in Charls. "Talar's" line, & to first station. (signed) Nov. 8, 1819 Thos Callaway, clerk; [on back] John Taylor 50 ac order of court to alter grant; altered Dec. 18, 1819 (signed) Wm Hill, Secy; [grant issued Nov. 30, 1818, grant book 133 p. 30, see shuck #1076 in Ashe Co in Secretary's grant files].

43. Jno "Toliver" filed his petition in Ashe Co court to rectify errors in grant No. 615; ordered by court that the courses be made as follows: begins at a chesnut near Evin's line, runs E 126 poles to a white oak, N 126 poles to a red oak, W 126 poles to a stake, & to first station; certified to Secretary's office without delay (signed) [no date] David Earnest, clerk; [on back John Toliver grant No. 615 issued Nov. 27, 1806 order for alteration; altered Dec. 14, 1809;
    survey Nov. 10, 1808 for John Toliver 100 ac on waters of Fighting Cr [metes & bounds same as above] (signed) Eli Cleveland; Barnabas Evins & David Tatferd(?), chain carriers; [plat included]; [grant in grant book 121 p. 339, see shuck #616 in Ashe Co in Secretary's grant files].

44. Nov. term 1829 Ashe Co to Mr. William Hill, Secretary of State: agreeable to order of Ashe Co court you are required to alter & correct errors in grant No. 109 issued Dec. 4, 1821 to David Waganer; the error will be corrected by running from the beginning pine N83E 120 poles to a stake, N63W 240 poles to a stake, S63W 134 poles to a stake, S 250 poles to Ramis' corner buckeye, E 169 poles to his own corner maple, & to first station. (signed) Nov. 17, 1829 Thos Callaway, clerk; [on back] altered Dec. 17, 1830 (signed) W H; [grant issued Dec. 4, 1821, grant book 135 p. 205, see shuck #1192 in Ashe Co in Secretary's grant files].

45. to Ashe Co court petitioner shows Jno Allin Woodruff obtained a survey by Robt "Noll" for 200 ac in said county agreeable to intent of said Wooduff; but when the grant issued from the state the plat of survey was all wrong as appears from the grant dated Jan. 1, 1798; the survey should have been returned: beginning at a chesnut, runs S 160 poles to a spanish oak, W 40 poles to a black gum, N62W 114 poles to 3 chesnuts, N 120 poles to a white oak & chesnut, N62E 306 poles to a stake, & to first station; the petitioner asks the grant be altered agreeable to an act of Genl. Assembly in such case made & provided (signed) Aug. 3, 1807

Corrections/Alterations to Land Grants

John Allin Woodruff; I certify the above petition was granted by the court & ordered certified to Sec. of State (signed) David Earnest, clerk Aug. term 1807; [on back] altered Dec. 5, 1807; [grant not identified].

46. Nov. term 1827 Ashe Co Thos Callaway, clerk of court, certifies the court ordered an error in grant No. 798 issued Nov. 24, 1813 to Jno Allen Woodruff by striking out the word in his old line which is twice in the certificate & the grant (signed) Oct. 5, 1827 Thos Callaway, clerk; [on back] altered Dec. 5, 1827 (signed) Wm Hill, Sec; [grant issued Nov. 24, 1813, grant book 127 p. 520, see shuck #907 in Ashe Co in Secretary's grant files].

47. Aug. term 1837 Ashe Co ordered by court that Logans Woody have a resurvey on grant No. 1528 for 200 ac in Ashe Co; it is further ordered the Secretary of State correct the grant according to the survey (signed) Aug. 8, 1849 (at Jefferson) John Ray, clerk; [on back] altered Oct. 12, 1852 (signed) Wm Hill, Secretary;
    survey Sept. 25, 1838 by court order of grant No. 1528 200 ac on Laurel Fork of Cramberry Cr above the old ford; begins at a chesnut, runs S 56 poles to a locust, S65E 180 poles to a white oak, E 100 poles to a stake, N 175 poles to a stake, & to first station (signed) Baker Ballow, for M Ballow CS; Michael Miller & Willson Wooddy, chain carriers; [plat included]; grant issued Nov. 20, 1830, grant book 158 p. 418, see shuck #1639 in Ashe Co in Secretary's grant files].

48. Beaufort Co Sept. term 1801 Nathan Bonner vs Henry S Bonner petition to alter a patent granted Mar. 12, 1780 to James Bonner jr for 502 ac; it is ordered in this case that the clerk certify to Secretary of State it has been manifestly made to appear there was a mistake by the surveyor in making out the certificate of survey on which the grant issued; mistake is in second & sixth lines of the survey: second line ought to be N34E instead of N64E and sixth line ought to be S4E instead of N4W; certified by Alderson Ellison, clerk (signed) Sept. 6, 1801 by Ald Ellison; [on back] altered Oct. 1, 1803; [grant #51 issued Apr. 12, 1780 (sic), grant book 31 p. 182, see shuck #916 in Beaufort Co in Secretary's grant files].

49. Beaufort Co Pleas & Quarter Sessions Court Nov. term 1822 on Monday next before last Monday in Aug. 1822 Thomas Ecklin "by" Wright C Stanley esq his attorney brought his petition to court as follows: to justices of Beaufort Co court petition of Thomas Ecklin--on Oct. 28, 1782 a grant issued to Christopher Ecklin for 250 ac; the boundaries in the grant are on S side of Pamplico R & W side of Blounts Cr, begins at Darby Haggin's corner, runs S30W 50 poles with said Haggin's line to a pine, S14W 30 poles to a pine, S20W 34 poles to a pine, S52W 72 poles to a pine on Joshua Ecklin's line, S50W 154 poles with said line to a pine, N10W 260 poles to a pine, & E 260 poles to first station; the petitioner alleges & is ready to prove the surveyor made an error in platting the land; in truth the patent ought to run to contain land in following boundaries: begins at a small branch at a red oak, runs S30W 202 poles, N56W 153 poles, N11W 265 poles, & S59E 324 poles to beginning; the petitioner asks the court to direct the clerk to certify the facts to the Secretary of State and grant further relief as needful; the petitioner

Corrections/Alterations to Land Grants

"omitted to state" he is presently the lawful owner of the land (signed) W C Stanley for pettr. On hearing, it is ordered copies & notices issue to John Gray Blount, Jno W Potts an infant by his guardian Joseph B Hinton, Omend Ecklin, Christopher Ecklin, Joshua Hill, & Thomas Yeates an infant by his guardian Joseph Pearce. On Monday next before last Monday in Nov. 1822 the parties came; it was made to appear to the court, all the parties interested in the proposed alteration of the grant [were present ?], and an error had been made by the surveyor in grant issued Oct. 7, 1782 to Christopher Ecklin; the courses should have been begins at a red oak in a swamp of Blounts Cr, runs S30W 202 poles to a pine, N56W 153 poles to a post oak, N11W 265 poles to a small pine, & S59E 324 poles to beginning; it is ordered that clerk certify above facts to Secretary of State. Nov. 28, 1822 Thomas Smaw, clerk, certifies foregoing is tru copy from the records of the court (signed) Tho Smaw; [on back] altered Nov. 29, 1823 (signed) Wm Hill, Secy.

50. Beaufort Co Pleas & Quarter Sessions Court Sept. 1839 petition of Zion Flowers alleging a mistake in description of a tract in said county in a state grant in his name; Flowers asks for relief & 7 judges were present; court ordered the clerk to certify to Secretary of State following facts in Flowers' petition and Flowers is liable to be injured: Zino Flowers obtained a state grant Sept. 21, 1838 for land in Beaufort Co described as follows: on S side of Pamlico R & in district of Goose Creek; begins at John G Blount's NW corner, runs N 28 poles, N45W 35 poles, N13W 120 poles with Warner's line to Eastmost Cr, N75E 70 poles "towards" mouth of Posters Gut, S23E 203 poles, & W 100 poles to beginning; the grant issued to Lewis Flowers but the real name of the intended patentee is Zion Flowers; the mistake in the patentee's name is the Secretary of State's; Zion Flowers is liable to be injured by the mistakes of the county surveyor & Secretary of State. Pursuant to directions of the court Will C Eborn, clerk, certifies the same. (signed) Sept. 6, 1839 Will C Eborn; [on back] Zion Flowers certificates of Beaufort Co court; order of court to alter patent; altered Sept. 24, 1839 (signed) Wm Hill, Sec; [grant #1124 issued Sept. 21, 1838, grant book 143 p. 658, see shuck #1973 in Beaufort Co in Secretary's grant files].

51. Beaufort Co Pleas & Quarter Sessions Court to Secretary of State: Willie Hill "et als lately" exhibited their petition in writing before this court stating John Hill, Willie's father, obtained a grant from North Carolina on Oct. 13, 1783 for 259 ac in Beaufort Co on S side of Pamplico R; begins at Reading Blount's corner pine, runs N10E 160 poles to Benjamin Grist's corner pine, S35E 44 poles with Grist's line to a pine, S 46 poles to Lewis Blount's corner pine, due E 160 poles with said Blount's line to Richard Grist's corner pine, S10W 200 poles with said Grist's line to a pine on N side of Piney Pocoson, S84W 132 poles to a stake, N60W 294 poles to a pine in Reading Blount's line, & with his line to beginning. The petitioners say the surveyor made a mistake in the plat to wit: in third line from beginning the course & distance of the line as S 46 [poles] to Lewis Blount's corner but the true course from a pine at end of second line was S19W 57 poles to Lewis Blount's corner; fourth line calls from Lewis Blount's corner E 160 poles to Richard Grist's

16

corner pine and real course should be from Lewis Blount's corner S61E 130 poles to Richard Grist's line; next course calls S10W 200 poles with said Grist's line but real course is S5W 210 poles with Grist's line to a pine on N side of Piney Pocoson. The petitioners say the owners of adjoining land "might be noticed" to appear before the court and show cause why the courses in John Hill's grant shouldn't be altered to run from third corner S19W 57 poles to Lewis Blount's corner, S61 E 130 poles with his line to Richard Grist's corner pine, S5W 210 poles with his line to a pine on N side of Piney Pocoson, S84W 132 poles to a stake, N60W 290 poles to Reading Blount's line, & with his line to first station. The court heard the allegations & inspected the survey made by county surveyor; it appears to their satisfaction that lines in John Hill's grant are wrong and it was the surveyor's error; it is right for the error to be corrected; so they ordered the clerk to certify the facts to Secretary of State so he can alter the grant to John Hill; certified by Thomas Smaw, clerk (signed) Aug. 28, 1819 Thos Smaw, clk; [on back] filed Oct. 3, 1820 for Willie Hall et al; altered Oct. 3, 1820 (signed) W Hill, Secretary;

survey included; surveyed Dec. 23, 1817 by "McNaurry"; [no chain carriers mentioned]; Richard Grist's "patten" shown adjoining 385 ac (sic) tract; [no grant identified in Beaufort Co to John Hill, one grant to "Wiley" Hill for 100 ac in 1820 see shuck #1860].

52. Jun. term 1796 petition of Wylle Kennedy for amendment of a grant from office of [Gov.] Richard Dobbs Spaight to him for 200 ac on N side of Pamplico R & W side of Bonners Mill Swamp; it appears to us the surveyor erred in making out the plat & certificate to the Secretary; it should have been begins at Bronoch Owens & Henry Snoad Bonner's beginning pine, runs N48E 104 poles to Floyd's corner pine, S25E 151 poles with his line to Floyd's corner oak, N56E 102 poles with Col. Henry Bonner's line to a pine on Newman's line, N60W 56 poles with his line to Newman's corner pine, N35E 66 poles with his line to his other corner pine, S51E 82 poles to a pine, N46E 47 poles to a pine in "the" dismal, N55W 260 poles to Owens' line, S26 1/2E 232 poles to beginning; copy from the minutes (signed) Thos Smaw for Henry Ellison clk; [on back] Willie "Cannday" 200 ac "Beaufert" No. 388 issued Jun. 19, 1793; [grant No. 388 issued Jun. 27, 1793 to Kennedy, grant book 80 p. 429, see shuck #1263 in Secretary's grant files].

53. trial docket Mar. term 1795 "E H" Jonathan Perkins vs "W K" John Muse caveat & suspension "7 con" verdict returned & exceptions taken thereto motion for a new trial by court; jury "impanneled" & sworn find a verdict for the defendant; Sept. 9, 1802 Henry Ellison, clerk of Beaufort Co court certifies above is a true copy of the record in suit by Jonathan Perkins vs John Muse (signed) Henry Ellison, clk; [on back] filed Sept. 19, 1804; [on separate sheet] Jun. 16, 1787 [entry] No. 512 John Muse 113 ac in Beaufort Co on N side of Bay [or Buy] R & W side of Bear Cr, joins Bennet Cr & his home land, a true copy from record (signed) Sept. 12, 1801 Reading Blount, ET; [grant suspension, not a correction].

54. to James Glasgow, Secretary: you are directed to record in your office a grant

for 800 ac issued to Thomas Jackson of Bath Co but now Beaufort dated Nov. 15, 1723 agreeable to "advice & council of state" & an act of General Assembly in 1788. (signed) Feb. 26, 1794 Richd Dobbs Spaight; [see grant #157 in book 82 p. 157 and shuck #1300 in Beaufort Co or shuck #182 in Bath Co; law may be chapter 24 in 1788 see State & Colonial Records vol. 24 p. 966; grant issued Nov. 15, 1720; grantee paid £8 for 800 ac in Bath Co on N side of "Pamticough" R & E side of mouth of North Dividing Cr, begins at a pine on the river side, runs N10E 320 poles to a pine, N30W 78 poles to a pine, N45W 330 poles to 3 pines on Roger Monteagues Cr, then with "windings" of the creek & Pamticough R to first station (signed) Wm Reed, J Lovich, C Gale, R Sanderson, & T Pollock; grant recorded Feb. 26, 1794 by James Glasgow due to order of governor; governor's order dated Feb. 26, 1794 repeated on p. 158 (signed) Richd Dobbs Spaight].

55. Mar. term 1805 Bladen Co court petition of "the subscriber" shows she has a grant for 67 ac on E side of White Marsh "in name of Daniel Shipman "granted to her" Nov. 3, 1797; there appears to be a mistake in second corner of the grant so land is plotted quite different to the location as shown in above plats the black line shows the mistake and dotted lines shows intended location; petitioner asks for relief allowed by General Assembly in such cases to run courses from second corner "viz" begins at a maple, runs S25E 25 chains 70 links, N65E 25 chains 70 links, N25W 25 chains 70 links, & S65W 25 chains 70 links to beginning resurveyed [no date] by Daniel Campbell (signed) Mary Amis; [plat shows 2 tracts side by side, second line in incorrect plat runs N65W 25 chains 70 links]; [on back] Mar. term 1805 James S Purdie, clerk of Bladen Co Pleas & Quarter Sessions Court, "makes known" within is a copy of the petition heard in this term & ordered the clerk to transmit a copy of Secretary of State with certificate that facts were satisfactory to the court (signed) J S Purdie, clk; altered Dec. 2, 1805; [Shipman has several grants, this one may be No. 2136 issued Nov. 3, 1797, grant book 94 p. 123, see shuck #5036 in Bladen Co].

56. Feb. term 1819 Bladen Co Pleas & Quarter Sessions Court petition of Ervin Andres, guardian: he shows on Dec. 11, 1810 Abraham Jessop obtained a grant from the State for 100 ac on E side of Busby Lake; since then said Abraham died leaving his children Susan, Amos, Jonathan, Young, Eday [or Edry], & William his heirs; the petitioner is guardian of Abraham Jessop's minor children; Andres says there is an error by the surveyor in description of the land by which the interest of his wards are likely to be injured; he asks the following courses be substituted in place of those in the grant so "mischiefs" can be avoided: begins at a pine now Jessop's own corner 50 poles SE of "the" drain, runs S34E 24 chains 77 links to a small pine 3 pointers, N56E 15 chains to a stake in Turnbull Marsh, N10W 17 chains 30 links to a stake, N73E 10 chains to a stake, S17E 3 chains to a stake, N73E 20 chains to a stake, N17W 28 chains 50 links to a stake, S73W 20 chains to a stake, S17E 23 chains 50 links to his own line, & with his own line to beginning (signed) James J McKay for petitioner. Aug. term 1819 petition of error [by] Andres, Guardian, describing error in grant to Abraham Jessop for 100

ac; ordered the grant be altered; William J Cowan, clerk certifies foregoing is correct copy of petition (signed) Mar. 15, 1820 Will J Cowan, clk; [on back] altered Mar. 18, 1820; [grant #3374, grant book 124 p. 391, see shuck #6211 in Bladen Co in Secretary's grant files].

57. Bladen Co court petition of heirs of late John Andres sr deceased: John Andrew obtained a grant for 150 ac, but there appears to be a mistake in surveyor's certificate shown in above plat; the double line shows intention of original survey as appears by marked lines & single line shows attitude of mistake shown in the certificate; following are true courses: in "liew" of N41E is S41E, in lieu of N36W is N36E, in lieu of S41W is N41W, then direct line to beginning; petitioners ask the court to consider the case & grant relief allowed by General Assembly in such cases; resurveyed & examined Feb. 16, 1805 by A Sellers, DS; [on back] James S Purdie, clerk of Bladen Co Pleas & Quarter Sessions Court, certifies within is copy of the petition heard in this term; ordered the clerk transmit a copy to Secretary of State since facts alleged appear to our satisfaction (signed) Mar. term 1805 J S Purdie, clk; altered Sept. 13, 1805 W W; [the 2 plats shown are side by side; grant #3154 issued Dec. 3, 1806, grant book 121 p. 244, see shuck #6025 in Bladen Co in Secretary's grant files].

58. May term 1796 Bladen Co petition of William H Beatty esq; respond by ordering following errors be corrected in grant issued Nov. 2, 1764 to Beringer Moore for land on South R: instead of N59W 20 chains it should be N42W 22 chains & instead of N71W 57 chains 40 links it should be N76W 68 chains 75 links; Secretary of State is authorised to correct said errors according to act of Assembly; a true copy from minutes (signed) J S Purdie, clk; [on back] filed Jan. 4, 1800; [Moore received 2 grants on this date No. 8 in grant book 18 p. 73 see shucks 1636 & 1741 and No. 9 in grant book 18 p. 73 see shucks 1637 & 1742].

59. [Bladen Co] May term 1797 petition of William H Beatty esq; respond by ordering following errors be corrected in grant in 1753 to George Moore for land on South R: instead of S22E 56 chains 57 links to a pine in a pont it should be N22E 56 chains 57 links to a pine in a pond; the Secretary of State is authorised to correct the error according to act of Assembly; true copy from the minutes (signed) J S Purdie, clk; [on back; alter a patent to Geo Moore 320 ac; filed Jan 4, 1800; [grant #282 in grant book 2 p. 57 see shuck #425 and in grant book 10 p. 376 see shuck #1135].

60. petition of William H Beatty setting forth an error was committed by Bladen Co surveyor in laying warrant No. 713 about Apr. 4, 1794 for 50 ac "by" William H Beatty and a grant was issued to said Beatty Dec. 17, 1796; error was in first line: instead of S38W he should have said S88W 41 chains to a pine; Beatty asks for an alteration according to act of Assembly in such cases which was granted; ordered the clerk certify the mistake to Secretary of State so petitioner's request can be granted; I certify foregoing is correct copy from minutes of Bladen Co Pleas & Quarter Sessions Court Nov. term 1823 (signed) Nov. 7, 1823 Alexr

Corrections/Alterations to Land Grants

McDowell, clerk; [on back] altered Mar. 25, 1824 W H; [grant #2067, grant book 90 p. 120, see shuck #4964 in Bladen Co in Secretary's grant files].

61. to Justices of Bladen Co court: "sometime ago" the petitioner entered 250 ac & paid publick fees thereon & obtained a warrant; surveyor surveyed the same "your petitioner expected it was done according to his wish"; but a resurvey finds the surveyor platted the wrong land to the disadvantage of the petitioner; lower plat has longest dotted line and shows land as granted which laps on an older surveyor of the petitioner for 250 ac "discribed" by the black lines; petitioner "looses" nearly a third of his latest entry; so he asks the clerk be directed to certify to Secretary of State so he can alter the grant according to above plat having longest black lines instead of saying "begins at his own corner pine & runs W 53 chains" and so on he can say "begins at his own corner pine & runs N 20 chains, W 53 chains, S 109 chains, S75E 25 chains, N15E 12 chains 50 links, N75W 12 chains to his own corner, N 80 chains along the line of said land, & E 35 chains 35 links to beginning" (signed) John Chancy; [on back] court heard petition of John "Chansey" to alter a grant; ordered the clerk to send the petition to Secretary of State to correct the erros (signed) Sept. term 1805 J S Purdie, clk; altered Nov. 20, 1805; [grant #2914 issued Nov. 23, 1804, grant book 120 p. 301, see shuck #5887 in Bladen Co in Secretary's grant files].

62. Bladen Co court petition of Colin Conoly: he has grant #507 issued Feb. 28, 1789 for 50 ac but the surveyor's certificate has a mistake which "goes near to rob" him of the whole benefit of the entry; mistake is in distance of second "corner & from the third": from second corner S10E 60 chains, N40E 80 chains 50 links, & N70W 50 chains to beginning; but S10E 8 chains from second corner, S80W 50 chains, S66E 10 chains, N80E 30 chains, & N40E 17 chains to beginning corresponds to the survey & marked lines; the other courses except about 5 o 6 ac on the petitioner's old granted land are not supported by a marked tree or boundary; the first line is conformable with what was really run; so petitioner asks for relief allowed by act or acts of Gen. Assembly in such case [note at bottom of page] No & date must "alude" to No & date of entry as that is it in the grant sent to be altered, grant is No. 2110 issued Dec. 17, 1796 W W; James S Purdie, clerk of Bladen Co Pleas & Quarter Sessions Court, certifies above is a copy in this term of court & ordered the clerk to transmit a copy to Secretary of State since facts appear to satisfaction of the court (signed) Dec. 7, 1803 James S Purdie, clerk; [on back altered Mar. 22, 1804; [grant #2110 issued Dec. 17, 176, grant book 90 p. 138, see shuck #5007 in Bladen Co in Secretary's grant files].

63. Jun. 7, 1803 to Bladen Co court "prayers" of James & Alexander Cromartie: they have grant #2010 for 640 ac issued Jun. 4, 1799; there appears to be a mistake in first course in surveyor's certificate by calling S68E whereas S68W corresponds to the survey; so petitioners ask the court to consider the case & grant them relief allowed by General Assembly (signed) James Cromartie & Alexander Cromartie; James S Purdie, clerk of Bladen Co Pleas & Quarter Sessions Court, certifies above is a copy of petition heard at this term & ordered the clerk transmit to

Corrections/Alterations to Land Grants

Secretary of State a copy since facts alleged are satisfactory to the court (signed) Jun. 8, 1803 James S Purdie; [on back] grant altered Jun. 6, 1804; [grant #2519 issued Apr. 16, 1802 on entry #2010, grant book 114 p. 401, see shuck #5449 in Bladen Co in Secretary of State's grant files].

64. to Bladen Co Pleas & Quarter Sessions Court petition of Robert Dowey: a grant issued Nov. 29, 1803 to Robert Dowey for 600 ac on NE side of NW River, begins at a hickory stake central to 4 young red oaks a dogwood a sweet gum called John Clayton's corner, runs S41W 141 chains to a gum in a branch, S47W 41 chains to a pine on Brown's line, N41E 32 chains to a stake, N12W 23 chains 50 links to a sassafras pine & black jack on a branch, N17E 71 chains to the river, & down the river to beginning; includes part of 3 tracts designated by "the" black lines; includes the plantation where James Dowey lives & land known as Beverly Hill lands; instead of NE side of the river it should have been SW side of NW River; the petitioner prays, agreeable to act of Assembly in such case made, for the court to direct the clerk to certify to Secretary of State an error as stated so it can be corrected (signed) Robert Dowey; [on back] James S Purdie, clerk of Bladen Co Pleas & Quarter Sessions Court, certifies within is a copy of petition heard this term & ordered the clerk to transmit a copy of facts which appear to satisfaction of the court (signed) Sept. term 1806 J S Purdie, clk; grant #2806 altered Dec. 22, 1809; [grant #2806 issued Nov. 29, 1803, grant book 117 p. 100, see shuck #5697 in Bladen Co in Secretary of State's grant files].

65. Bladen Co Pleas & Quarter Sessions Aug. term 1836 petition of Benjamin Evans asking to correct an error in a grant: grant issued Jul. 6, 1809 for 640 ac, begins at a small pine SE of Lyan Swamp being "senteral" to several marked pine pointers near Larkins' corner, runs S30W 40 chains to a stake, N60W 25 chains, S30W 25 chains, S60E 50 chains, N30E 20 chains, S60E 93 chains 12 links, N30E 45 chains, & a direct line to beginning; error was made by surveyor in filling out certificate to the Secretary's office; it appears to satisfaction of court from testimony introduced that alteration in petition is true and it appears Benjamin Evans, patentee, is liable to be "ingered"; so courses specified in the grant should be reversed to read: begins at a small pine NE of Lyon Swamp central to several marked pine pointers near Larkin's corner, runs N30E 40 chains to a stake, S60E 25 chains, N30E 25 chains, N60W 50 chains, S30W 20 chains, N60W 93 chains 12 links, S30W 45 chains, & a direct line to beginning; court ordered David Lewis, clerk, to certify above facts to Secretary of State (signed) Oct. 1836 David Lewis, clk; [on back] record altered Nov. 24, 1836 Wm Hill, Secy; [may be grant #3473 issued Jul. 6, 1812 and entered Jul. 6, 1809, grant book 176 p. 375, see shuck #6375 in Bladen Co in Secretary's grant files].

66. to Justices of Bladen Co Pleas & Quarter Sessions Court May term 1854 petition of Solomon Faircloth: he entered land Oct. 8, 1849 & obtained a grant Feb. 12, 1852 from the State; a copy of the survey is annexed marked "A"; but surveyor omitted the courses as follows vis: "the other" line N45W 9 chains and also N88E 34.5 chains being third & seventh lines; surveyor marked the lines in

the plot but didn't name them in "the calls"; it has not been 3 years since the grant issued & petitioner didn't know of the mistake until he received the grant; he will be very much injured & aggrieved by the mistake; no one else claims the land; so petitioner asks for mistakes to be corrected in third & seventh lines [not signed]; [on back] altered Dec. 25, 1854;

survey [marked "A" & no date] 80 ac for Solomon Faircloth; begins at his own corner pine & pine pointers of a 50 ac survey being "the Big" corner granted to Pope (sic), runs N42E 8 chains with that line to the corner, S85E 15 chains 85 links "the other line" to the corner, N45W 9 chains "the other" line, N85W 5 chains the other line to the corner, N12W 9 chains the other line to a line of another 50 ac survey, S60E 18.5 chains with that line to a corner, N88E 34.5 chains, S 14 chains to Melvin's line, S80W 47 chains with his line to his corner, & with his own line to "the Big"(signed) M Momoe; Thos & W Fort, chain carriers; [plat included]; [grant #4885 issued Feb. 12, 1852, grant book 165 p. 464, see shuck #7798 in Bladen Co in Secretary's grant files].

67. petition to Bladen Co court: grant #2808 issued for 200 ac with 2 "palapable" errors: one says second line is N65W which throws location entirely on old patented land belonging to Mr. Anderson by which it was intended to be bounded as surveyor's evidence will show requiring a reversal of second line to S65E; other error is that second line is 32 chains 61 [links] only amounting to 195 ac but extension of it to "32.80" will cover the quantity granted; petitioner asks for help under act of 1790 to alter the Secretary to alter the grant (signed) Jun. term 1804 J R Gautier; Jun. term 1804 court considered petition of J R Gautier for alteration of grant #2808 and are satisfied with the facts of surveyor's error; clerk ordered to certify to Secretary of State that first line of grant #2808 for 200 ac is right S25W 61 chains, second line should be S65E 32 chains 80 links, third line is N25E 61 chains, & without remedy petitioner will sustain injury (signed) Jun. 6, 1804 J S Purdie, clk; [on back] altered Sept. 16, 1804; [grant issued Nov. 29, 1805, grant book 117 p. 101, see shuck #5699 in Bladen Co in Secretary's grant files].

68. "prayer" of subscriber to Bladen Co court: Lazarus Hall obtained grant No. 767 on Mar. 4, 1775 for 200 ac; there appears to be a mistake in surveyor's certificate in beginning corner calling to begin on lower side of Green Sea Br but it is found to begin on upper side of said branch to correspond to marked trees; so petitioner asks the court to consider his case & grant such relief as allowed by General Assembly in such case; land was granted to Lazarus Hall who sold to Saml Bozman who sold to the subscriber (signed) Willi Bozman; resurveyed & examined [no date] by Archibald Sellers, surveyor; James S Purdie, clerk of Bladen Co Pleas & Quarter Sessions Court, certifies the above petition was heard this term & copy ordered to be transmitted to Secretary of State because facts alleged are satisfactory (signed) Dec. term 1804 J S Purdie, clk; [on back] altered Nov. 21, 1805; [grant #767 issued Mar. 4, 1775, grant book 25 p. 169, see shuck #2406 in Bladen Co in Secretary's grant files].

69. Bladen Co Pleas & Quarter Sessions Court held at court house in Elizabeth

Corrections/Alterations to Land Grants

Town first Monday in Aug. 1833 7 magistrates on the bench; petition of heirs of Josiah Hendon for alteration of grant; petition was heard and it appears to satisfaction of court that in 1765 300 ac were surveyed for Josiah Hendon: begins at a scrub oak near Cheshire's upper back corner "said to be" near or on Harnet's line, runs S45E 21 chains 27 links to a stake by a marked scrub oak on Ishamar Singletary's line, S45W 70 chains "with it" to a stake between a marked pine & a scrub oak, S45E 23 chains 23 links with his other line & John Wilkinson's to a scrub oak, S45W 44 chains 50 links to a stake by a marked pine, & N45E 103 chains 96 links to beginning; grant issued Apr. 26, 1767 to Josiah "Harden" instead of Hendon as will appear by a certified copy of the survey & grant; before his death Josiah Hendon possessed the land & no such person as Josiah Harden ever laid claim to the same; from the facts, court believes a mistake was made in issuing the grant; so petitioners ask for an alteration; court ordered clerk to certify foregoing facts to Secretary of State so mistake can be corrected if it is found; Patrick Kelly, clerk, certifies foregoing is true copy from the court records (signed) Aug. 26, 1833 P Kelly, clk; [on back] altered Sept. 9, 1833 (signed) Wm Hill; [grant in book 18 p. 352, see shuck #1828 in Bladen Co in Secretary's grant files].

70. petition of Richard Holmes to Bladen Co Pleas & Quarter Sessions Court: the petitioner owns 100 ac on E side of White Marsh Swamp patented in name of John Cohoon; there appears to be a surveyor's error which will injure the petitioner if not remedied; so he asks the court to order the clerk to certify the error to Secretary of State agreeable to an act of General Assembly passed in 1790 in that case made (signed) Richard Holmes. James S Purdie, clerk of Bladen Co Pleas & Quarter Sessions Court, certifies above is true copy of petition heard this term & ordered the clerk to send a copy to Secretary of State since the facts are satisfactory to the court (signed) Sept. 8, 1803 James S Purdie, clk; [on back] altered Nov. 23, 1803; [2 grant possible: #96 in grant book 34 p. 253 see shuck #3048 in Bladen Co and #528 in grant book 49 p. 322 see shuck #3521 in Bladen Co in Secretary's grant files];

survey attached: on E side of White Marsh Swamp granted to James Cohoon; surveyed Dec. 21, 1788 by James Sample; error in surveyor's certificate in first line S80W instead of S80E; lines in red [no red visible] are agreeable to the marked lines & those in black the courses of the grant; surveyed Apr. 10, 1803 (signed) D Schaw; begins at a stake on a ditch, runs S80W 31.62, S10W 31.62, N80W 31.62, & to beginning [lines overlap].

71. Committee of Propo. & Grievances report on petition of Richard Holmes (of Bladen Co) asking Secretary of State alter a record in his office: the committee believes from representations made to them it would be "common justice" to grant the prayer and interference of Legislature ought to be extended to his relief; so they recommend following resolution: Resolved that Secretary of State is directed to alter a "certain record" in his office in James Lyon's name for 500 ac granted in 1735 to make it conformable to the patent (signed) Alex Martin, chairman. Dec. 6, 1804 in Senate read & resolved this house concurs (signed) Jo Reddeck

Corrections/Alterations to Land Grants

SS & M Stokes, clk; [on back] Dec. 7, 1804 in House of Commons resolved this house concurs (signed) S Cabarrus Sp & J Hunt, clk; altered Dec. 20, 1804 W W; [grant recorded twice book 9 p. 20 shuck #689 and book 3 p. 386 shuck #46 in Bladen Co in Secretary's grant files; grant issued Sept. 9, 1735 for 500 ac on E side of White Marsh, includes part of the marsh, joins S side of Joseph Sool's land, begins at Godfrey's corner gum, runs W 126 poles to a stake in the marsh, N50E 58 chains to another stake in the marsh, S75E to a gum, same course 50 chains to a black oak, & S 10W 26 chains to first station; grantee to pay £0.40 yearly quit rent, cultivate 3% of the land is 3 years, & record grant with Auditor's office (Legislative resolution not mentioned)].

72. William James Cowan, clerk of Bladen Co Pleas & Quarter Sessions Court, certifies at Feb. term 1820 John Jones sr & Jesse Moore presented a petition that an error was made by the surveyor for 200 ac granted Nov. 11, 1779 to Cornelius Ferell, begins "according to grant" at Solomon Lewis' corner black jack, runs N25W 179 poles with his line to a stake & 3 pines, N65W 179 poles to a small pine, S25E 175 poles to a stake & 3 pines, & S65W 179 poles to beginning; petitioners ask that line running N65W 179 poles be altered to N65E 179 poles; court considered the same & believe a mistake was made & ordered the clerk to take the necessary measures affecting alterations (signed) May 3, 1820 Will J Cowan, clk. Aug. term 1824 Jesse Moore swears the grant is lost or mislaid (signed) Aug. 2, 1824 Alexr McDowell, clk; [on back] altered Dec. 3, 1824 (signed) Wm Hill, Secry; [grant #55, grant book 34 p. 212, see shuck #3007 in Bladen Co in Secretary's grant files];

    [on a small sheet] "representation" of platts--red lines [which appear faint] is agreeable with "the courses" & black lines is way the marked trees "is"; (signed) F Green, surveyor; [faint line doesn't close on itself; black lines enclose 200 ac in a square].

73. Mar. term 1806 to Justices of Bladen Co Pleas & Quarter Sessions Court petition of Richard M Lewis: a grant for 400 ac on S side of Thomas Bryan's Swamp issued Nov. 11, 1779 to William "Ruding" and by "mesne conveyances" is now the petitioner's property; due to an error in the grant, the petitioner is injured; courses in the grant are begins at a fore & aft pine in Thomas Simpson's line, runs S29W 34 chains 73 links along & beyond said Simpson's line to a pine, S61E 89 chains 46 links to a stake, N29E 44 chains 73 links to a stake, N61W 89 chains 46 links to a stake, & S29W 10 chains to beginning; petitioner asks grant be altered to following courses begins at a fore & aft pine in Thomas Simpson's line, runs S29E 34 chains 73 links along & beyond Simpson's line to a pine, N61E 89 chains 46 links t a stake, N29W 44 chains 73 links to a stake, S61W 89 chains 46 links, & S29E 10 chains to beginning (signed) Richd M Lewis. James S Purdie, Bladen Co clerk, certifies petition was heard this term & ordered the clerk to certify to Secretary of State the facts are satisfactory (signed) Mar. term 1806 J S Purdie, clk; altered Dec. 2, 1807; [on back] survey for land granted Nov. 11, 1779 to William Reading; surveyed [no date] by Wm Hendon, DS [no chain carriers mentioned]; [no grant identified].

Corrections/Alterations to Land Grants

74. to Bladen Co court "prayer" of heirs of David Lock sr deceased: David Lock obtained grant #87 for 640 ac; there appears to be a mistake in the surveyor's certificate which will turn the land "quite the reverse" of the intended location & survey as shown in plats [at top of page] calling S68E 56 chains 50 links "will be found" N22E 113 chains 50 links, N22E 113 chains 50 links should be N68W 56 chains 50 links and N68W 60 chains 50 links should be S22W 113 chains 50 links & a direct line to beginning; the petitioner asks the court to consider the case and grant "them" relief allowed by General Assembly; Mar. term 1804 [not signed]. James S Purdie, clerk of Bladen Co Pleas & Quarter Sessions Court certifies above is a copy of petition heard at this term & ordered the clerk to send a copy to Secretary of State because facts appear satisfactory to court (signed) J S Purdie, clerk; [on back] altered Sept. 14, 1804; [plat shows 2 adjoining tracts]; [grant in book 34 p. 244, see shuck #3039 in Bladen Co in Secretary's grant files].

75. petition to Bladen Co court: the petitioner obtained a state grant for 100 ac; but he finds the surveyor made a mistake in first line which runs N50W 20 chains 20 links but ought to be 22 chains 50 links to second line and word "West" in second line ought to be "East"; so petitioner asks to have the error corrected agreeable to act of Assembly in such cases (signed) Dec. 7, 1801 Matthew McEwin. James S Purdie, clerk of Bladen Co Pleas & Quarter Sessions Court, certifies above petition was heard this term & ordered the clerk to send a copy to Secretary of State because the facts appear satisfactory to court (signed) Dec. term 1801 J S Purdie, clk; [on back] altered Nov. 22, 1806; [2 possible grants: #1388 issued May 18, 1789, grant book 70 p. 28, see shuck #4453 in Bladen Co OR grant #186 issued Dec. 20, 1791, grant book 78 p. 79, see shuck #4808 in Bladen Co in Secretary's grant files].

76. Bladen Co Pleas & Quarter Sessions Court Feb. term 1819 petition of Archibald McMillan: on Dec. 20, 1791 Thomas Fitzgerald "regularly" obtained a grant for 200 ac on N Side of Brown Marsh Swamp; the petitioner says the surveyor made an error in describing the land which is likely to injure the petitioner; land begins at a red oak, runs N7W 25 chains to a pine, S83W 80 chains to a stake, S7E 25 chains to a stake near Sarah Graves' corner, & a direct line to beginning; but land intended to be "appropriated" isn't included; petitioner says following are the true courses: begins at a red oak, runs N80W 25 chains to a pine, S10W 80 chains to a stake, S80E 25 chains to a stake in Sarah Grave's line, & N10E 80 chains with her line to beginning; petitioner says he is legal owner of the land by "proper" mesne conveyances; so he asks for alteration of description of land agreeable to an act of Assembly in such cases (signed) James J McKay for petitioner. Appearance docket Feb. 1819 "M K" Archd McMillan vs Duncan McColl petition for alteration of grant ordered the courses & distances be altered agreeable to prayer of petitioner; William J Cowan, clerk, certifies foregoing is correct copy of petition & transcript of appearance docket of the court (signed) Mar. 15, 1820 Will J Cowan, clk; [on back] altered Mar. 18, 1820; [grant #1743 in grant book 78 p. 31, see shuck #4665 in Bladen Co in Secretary's grant files].

77. petition of Frederick Miller to Bladen Co Pleas & Quarter Sessions Court: an error was committed in a grant issued May 23, 1757 for 200 ac to Thomas Vince; error was by surveyor in the plat OR by the Secretary in issuing the grant; the first line runs S60W instead of S45W which the second line "would strike" Gill's line which appears by the plat of third line to have been intended as boundary of the tract; so petitioner asks the court to direct the clerk to certify the error to the Secretary so the error can be corrected agreeable to an act of Gen. Assembly in such cases (signed) Frederick Miller "a true copy" (signed) James S Purdie, clk. Court heard petition to correct an error in grant for 200 ac issued May 23, 1757; court ordered clerk to issued a certificate stating the error in first line runs S60W instead of S45W "which appears by description of third line which cals for Gill's line to have been intended" "copy" J S Purdie, clk. James S Purdie, clerk, certifies petition was heard this term & ordered for clerk to transmit a copy to Secretary of State because it appears to court that facts are satisfactory (signed) Sept. 4, 1804 J S Purdie, clk; altered Nov. 20, 1804; [grant in grant book 15 p. 234, see shuck #1455 in Bladen Co in Secretary's grant files].

78. petition of Hugh Murphy to Bladen Co Pleas & Quarter Sessions Court: a grant issued Mar. 6, 1799 to Hugh Murphy for 150 ac on Big Colly [R], begins at a black oak [runs] S63E 54 chains 78 links to a stake, N28E 27 chains 39 links to a stake, N62W 54 chains 78 links to a stake, S28W 27 chains 39 links to beginning oak; instead of these, the grant calls for begins at a black oak, runs S62E 54 chains 78 links to a stake, S28W 27 chains 39 links to a [omitted], N62W 54 chains 78 links to a stake, & a direct line to beginning; petitioner asks, agreeable to act of Assembly in such cases, the court to direct the clerk to certify the error to Secretary of State so they can be corrected. (signed) Hugh Murphy; Jun. 1803 Hugh Murphy swears there is no land adjoining above except his own land (signed) James S Purdie, clk. James S Purdie, clerk, certifies above petition was made this term & ordered the clerk to send a copy to Secretary of State because facts are satisfactory to the court (signed) Jun. 6, 1803 James S Purdie, ccc; [on back] altered Oct. 21, 1803; [grant #2264, grant book 103 p. 265, see shuck #5138 in Bladen Co in Secretary's grant files].

79. Bladen Co Pleas & Quarter Sessions Court Aug. term 1829: ordered that clerk certify to Secretary of State there is an error in grant #3969 issued Jan. 2, 1828 to Charles Oliver for 100 ac; error injures the grantee; in describing beginning of land on N side of Lyon Swamp it should be on N side of Buckel Swamp; P Kelly, clerk of said court, certifies foregoing is a copy from the minutes. (signed) Nov. 5, 1829 P Kelly, clk; [on back] altered Dec. 7, 1829; [grant issued Jan. 3, 1828 (sic), grant book 137 p. 240, see shuck #6882 in Bladen Co in Secretary's grant files].

80. petition of Nicholas Parker to Justices of Bladen Co Pleas & Quarter Sessions Court on first Monday in June 1801: in 1784 John Suggs obtained a patent from the state for 100 ac in Bladen Co in forks of David Gans [or Gam] Br, begins at a

large pine, runs N 40 chains to a stake, W 25 chains to a stake, S 40 chains to a stake, & E 25 chains to beginning; the petitioner is now the owner of the land; the petitioner obtained a state grant on Dec. 17, 1796 for 50 ac on E side of Turnbull [Swamp], begins at NE corner stake of John Sugg's 100 ac survey "described above", runs W 15 chains 82 links on that line to a stake, S 31 chains 63 links to a [blank], E 15 chains 82 link to a stake, & N 31 chains 63 links to beginning; the petitioner says there is a mistake by surveyor or Secretary in the 50 ac grant which puts it within the 100 ac tract because it begins at NE corner of the 100 ac survey instead of NW corner as it should have; petitioner hopes this will be clear by seeing surveyor's field book & "other testimony in due time"; petitioner asks the court to have the 50 ac grant altered as follows: in lieu of begins at NE corner of Sugg's 100 ac survey that it begin at a stake & 4 pines by John Sugg's NW corner, runs W 15 chains 82 links to a stake, S 31 chains 63 links to a stake, E 15 chains 82 links to a stake, & direct line to beginning; thereby the petitioner will obtain relief agreeable to act of General Assembly in such cases and agreeable with surveyor's field book "a true copy" (signed) J S Purdie, clk.   James S Purdie, clerk, certifies above petition was heard this term & ordered the clerk send a copy to Secretary of State because the facts appear satisfactory (signed) Jun. 1801 J S Purdie, clk; [on back] altered Nov. 17, 1801 W W; [grant #2383 issued Dec. 5, 1800, grant book 108 p. 322, see shuck #5190 in Bladen Co in Secretary's grant files].

81. Bladen Co Pleas & Quarter Sessions Court Aug. term 1836 petition of Sarah A Purdie, John Purdie, & Thomas J Purdie, heirs of James B Purdie by their guardian Anna Maria Purdie & James Smith "grantees" of Richard Salter [or Solter] heir of James Salter grantee of J Ellis: there is a mistake in grant #1801 issued Dec. 20, 1791 to James White, John White, & David L White for 350 ac on E of Jones' Cr, begins at W White's corner old dead pine, runs S32E 70 chains, S50W 50 chains, N32E 70 chains, & to beginning; they ask the grant be altered to begin at W White's corner old dead pine, runs S32E 70 chains, N50E 50 chains, N32E 70 chains, & to beginning; request was granted; court ordered David Lewis, clerk, to certify above facts to Secretary of State & to county register so the mistake can be corrected in grant & mesne conveyances.   David Lewis, clerk certifies above is true copy from the minutes (signed) David Lewis, clk; [on back] record altered Nov. 4, 1836; [grant issued Dec. 20, 1791, grant book 78 p. 51, see shuck #4723 in Bladen Co in Secretary's grant files].

82. petition to Justices of Bladen Co court: the petitioner obtained a grant for 6 ac on S side of Whites Cr, W of Rays Br, & on both sides of the main road, begins at Malcom Shaw's corner stake "centrial" to 3 pines, runs N52W 7 chains 30 links to said Ray's own corner post oak, S3W 10 chains 50 links t a pine in John Blue's line, S82W 6 chains 24 links to a stake, & to beginning; there is an error in the first line; the word "West" should be "East"; the petitioner asks for relief allowed by law (signed) Jun. 13, 1806 Duncan Ray "copy" J S Purdie, clk.   James S Purdie, clerk, certifies above petition was heard this term & ordered the clerk send a copy to Secretary of State because facts are satisfactory to the court (signed)

Corrections/Alterations to Land Grants

Jun. term 1806 J S Purdie, clk; altered Nov. 18, 1806 "N B" the record stands right without alteration W W; [plat included]; [grant #3053 issued Nov. 27, 1805, grant book 119 p. 181, see shuck #5822 in Bladen Co in Secretary's grant files].

83. petition of Rehum Redding to Justices of Bladen Co Pleas & Quarter Sessions Court: the petitioner obtained grant #1889 Dec. 20, 1791 from the state for 200 ac on both sides of Hester's Mill Swamp & on Great Swamp; there is a "material" difference between courses in the patent & courses actually run; lines actually run contain 200 ac; petitioner is likely to be "meterially" injured by mistake, so he asks for grant to be altered as follows: (a) distance in first line should be 10 chains 50 links in lieu of 5 chains 50 links, (b) seventh line should be S80W 24 poles to a stake in lieu of N36W 60 chains to a stake, (c) eighth line should be N13W 58 chains to a stake in lieu of N 40 chains, (d) ninth line should be a direct line to beginning in lieu of N53E 38 chains (signed) Rehum Reading.   James S Purdie, clerk, certifies above petition was heard this term & ordered the clerk send a copy of Secretary of State because the facts appear satisfactory to the court (signed) Jun. 6, 1804 J S Purdie, clk; altered Nov. 23, 1804 W W; [grant in book 78 p. 81, see shuck #4811 in Bladen Co in Secretary's grant files].

84. petition of Saml N Richardson to Bladen Co court Aug. term 1825: the petitioner obtained a grant Nov. 26, 1799 for 100 ac entered Aug. 14, 1795 on E side of Harrisons Cr, begins at a stake & 3 small sweet gums marked as pointers in S edge of White oak Swamp in Mary Johnston's line, runs N6W 44 chains with her line "&c"; but agreeable with survey the line should be N6W; so grant & survey don't correspond; there is another error: the grant says begins on SE side of White oak Swamp instead of SW side of said swamp; so petitioner is likely to be injured; so he asks the court to direct the clerk to certify necessary facts to Secretary of State so errors can be corrected (signed) "Wright" for petitioner. Aug. term 1826 Samuel N Richardson vs Bernard "Laspayere" petition for alteration of a grant: court heard testimony of plaintiff & defendant; court ordered prayer of petitioner be granted & clerk certify error so alteration can be made. Alex McDowell, clerk, certifies foregoing is true copy from records in my office (signed) Sept. 28, 1826 Alex McDowell, clk. survey included: errors are (a) begins on SE side of White oak Swamp which should have been SW side & (b) runs N6W wth Mary Johnston's line to her corner pine should have been N60W; resurveyed Jan. 20, 1825 Aaron Lewis [no chain carriers mentioned]; [plat included, land in shape of triangle, runs N60W 44 chains, S20E 60 chains, & N43 E 40 chains]; altered Apr. 5, 1827 W H; [may be grant #2255 in grant book 105 p. 77, see shuck #5181 in Bladen Co in Secretary's grant files].

85. petition of John Scriven to Justices of Bladen Co Pleas & Quarter Sessions Court May term 1819: the petitioner owns a tract granted in 1757 to John Scriven; there was a mistake in second line in making out the grant which runs N45W but cals for North "only"; he asks the court to correct the second line to N45W agreeable to the marked line made by the surveyor; court agreed & ordered clerk to take necessary measures to have alteration made; William J Cowan, clerk,

certifies the above is correct transcript from the minutes (signed) May 7, 1819 Will J Cowan; altered Dec. 8, 1820 Wm Hill, Sec; [grant recorded twice book 2 p. 155 see shuck #544 in Bladen Co & book 16 p. 94 see shuck #1557 in Bladen Co in Secretary's grant files].

86. "prayers" of Jonathan Singletary to Bladen Co "now sitting": the petitioner "has" grant #142 issued Nov. 11, 1779 for 200 ac; it appears there is an error in the surveyor's certificate: "from begins at first corner from second corner to third corner & from fourth corner to beginning" from the beginning runs N 179 poles, W 179 poles, S 179 poles, E 179 poles, & N "60" to beginning; but it will be found following corresponds to survey & marked lines: N70W 95 poles, due N 179 poles, S70E 179 poles, due S 179 poles, N70W 84 poles to beginning; the other course runs "all but" 86 ac on old patent land and doesn't have any marked line except beginning; so petitioner asks the court to consider his case & grant him relief allowed by General Assembly Mar. term 1804 [not signed]. James S Purdie, clerk, says above is a copy of case heard this term & ordered clerk to send a copy to Secretary of State because facts are satisfactory to the court (signed) [no date] J S Purdie, ccc [plat included at top of page]; [on back] certificate for alteration of grant to Edward Harrison; altered Nov. 24, 1804; [grant in grant book 34 p. 299, see shuck #3094 in Bladen Co in Secretary's grant files].

87. petition of Richard & John Singletary to Bladen Co court Jun. 1801: in 1790 Daniel Shaw esq surveyed 101 ac; but an error was made in making out the plat: second line ran N40W where it should have run S50E, fourth & last line ran S40E but should have run a direct line to beginning; the courses in the plat are different than those run & "the whole" appears to be a surveyor's error; petitioners ask the court to order the errors be corrected as per act of Assembly (signed) Richard Singletary & John Singletary (witness) J S Purdie, clk. James S Purdie, clerk, says within is copy of petition heard this term & ordered the clerk send a copy to Secretary of State because facts appears satisfactory to court (signed) Jun. term 1801 James S Purdie, clk; [on back] altered Dec. 12, 1801; [may be grant #1992 issued Aug. 27, 1795 for 100 ac, grant book 87 p. 444, see shuck #4891 in Bladen Co in Secretary's grant files].

88. Bladen Co Pleas & Quarter Sessions Court Nov. term 1827: ordered clerk certify to the Secretary following statement: on examination before the court, it was found grant #3747 issued May 18, 1818 to Ezekiel Suggs contains an error to injury of grantee viz second line runs N62E when it should be N63W; true copy from minutes (signed) Nov. 3, 1829 P Kelly, clk; [on back] altered Dec. 9, 1829 (signed) Wm Hill, Secy; [grant in grant book 132 p. 217, see shuck #6657 in Bladen Co in Secretary's grant files].

89. petition to Justices of Bladen Co Pleas & Quarter Sessions Court: "some time" in 1779 "one" Robert Stockey obtained a grant for 200 ac on Mile Branch Dismal "in which" the word "West" is written instead of "North" as seen in the plat; through a "great many transfers" of the land the petitioner is now last purchaser

Corrections/Alterations to Land Grants

& present owner; so he asks the court to order the grant be corrected by changing word to "North" in place of "West" (signed) Samuel Swindal by his attorney J A Manthly.   Herman H Robinson, clerk, certifies above is a true copy of petition filed in my office (signed) Nov. 12, 1846 H H Robinson, ccc.   Bladen Co Pleas & Quarter Sessions Court Aug. 1845: it appears to the court that an error was made by the Secretary in grant to Robert Starker: the word "West" was written instead of "North" in second line; court ordered clerk to certify the fact to Secretary of State so error can be corrected. Herman H Robinson, clerk, certifies foregoing is correct transcript from records in my office (signed) Nov. 12, 1846 H H Robinson, ccc; [on back] altered Nov. 17, 1846 (signed) Wm Hill, Secy; [grant #332 issued Nov. 12, 1779, grant book 30 p. 380, see shuck #2816 in Bladen Co in Secretary's grant files].

90. Bladen Co court Nov. term 1810: the petitioner owns 200 ac granted Jun. 7, 1799 to Sarah Wilson on E side of NW River, joins Council & Overler; a resurvey of land shows surveyor made a mistake in the plat of grant which says begins at Council's upper corner gum, runs N43W 109 chains to a holley, sassafras, & white oak, S47W 28 chains 25 links to a stake, N48W 25 chains to a stake, N47E 38 chains to a stake in Ray's line, S43E 134 chains with said line to the river, & down the river to beginning; the lines should be begins at Council's upper corner gum, runs N48E 109 chains to a holley, sassafras, & white oak, S47E 28 chains 25 links to a stake, N43E 25 chains to a stake, N47W 38 chains to a stake in Ray's line, S43W 134 chains to the river, & down the river to beginning; so petitioner asks for clerk be directed to tell the Secretary of State about the mistake & direct him to alter the grant agreeable to the last courses in this petition (signed) Joseph Thames.   James S Purdie, clerk of Bladen Co Pleas & Quarter Sessions Court, says above is a copy of a petition heard this term & ordered that clerk send a copy to Secretary of State because facts appear satisfactory to the court (signed) Nov. term 1810 J S Purdie, clk; [on back] alteration of grant No. 2214 to Sarah Wilson; altered Dec. 22, 1810; [grant in grant book 103 p. 25; see shuck #5113 in Secretary's grant files].

91. petition of Archibald White to Bladen Co Pleas & Quarter Sessions Court: a grant issued Oct. 26, 1767 to Edmund Russ for 200 ac on Crawley Swamp, begins at an oak, runs S45W 35 chains 11 links to a pine, S45E 44 chains 73 links, N45W 44 chains 73 links, & direct line to beginning; but it should have been begins at an oak, runs S43W 35 chains 11 links to a pine, S47E 44 chains 73 links, N43E 44 chains 73 links, N4;7W 44 chains 73 link, & a direct line to beginning; the petitioner asks the court to direct the clerk to certify the error to Secretary of State agreeable to an act of Assembly made in such cases (signed) Archibald White. Dec. term 1803 James S Purdie, clerk, says above is a copy of a petition heard this term & ordered the clerk send a copy to Secretary of State because the facts appear satisfactory to the court (signed) Dec. 5, 1803 James S Purdie, ccc; altered Nov. 24, 1804; grant #198 in grant book 23 p. 116; see shuck #2330 in Bladen Co in Secretary's grant files].

Corrections/Alterations to Land Grants

92. petition of Isaac Wright asking for alteration of grant Dec. 18, 1797 to James Moorhead for 100 ac; the court heard the testimony to support the allegations, considered, & adjudged an error was made by the surveyor in second line [of survey]; instead of N55E 25 chains to a stake as in the surveyor's return and transferred by the Secretary to the grant, it should be S55W 25 chains to a stake; the petitioner claims under patentee James Moorehead & is liable to be "prejudiced" by the error; the court ordered the clerk to certify these facts to Secretary of State so the error can be corrected in the grant & records in his office. P Kelly, clerk of Bladen Co Pleas & Quarter Sessions Court, certifies foregoing is true transcript from court minutes & the error does exist (signed) P Kelly, clk; [on back] altered Nov. 20, 1828 (signed) Wm Hill, Secy; [grant #2147 in grant book 95 p. 55; see shuck #5047 in Bladen Co in Secretary's grant files].

93. petition of Richard Docher to Brunswick Co court: Jonathan Swain deceased in his lifetime entered 100 ac in Brunswick Co between Judah Cr & Dutchmans Cr called Judahs Island; a grant has issued for the land in name of Joseph Swain; the petitioner asks the court to consider the same & instruct that it be altered to Jonathan Swain's name (signed) "Ribert" Docher. Oct. 1793 Bruswick Co the above appeared in court & ordered the clerk to certify the same to Secretary of State or that entry was made for & money paid by Jonathan Swain and "right" does not appear to belong to anyone buy Jonathan Swain (signed) Pat Bacot, ccc; [on back] No. 73 patent altered alter record Oct. 1793; [grant #73 issued Oct. 27, 1784; grant book 56 p. 1; see shuck #224 in Brunswick Co in Secretary's grant files].

94. petition of Joseph Hewit to Brunswick Co Pleas & Quarter Sessions Court held second Monday in Apr. 1794: a "pattent" issued Sept. 24, 1754 to Jonathan Swain for 200 ac in Fraziers Neck; there is a mistake in the courses as will appear by comparing the plat & pattent; so petitioner asks the court to order the Secretary to alter the grant as follows: first line N7E and third line S7W agreeable to the platt (signed) Joseph Hewit.   above petition was heard & ordered the Secretary alter the courses (signed) Pat Bacot, ccc; [on back] entered on the minutes by M Hankins DPCC; "done"   1794; [on a small sheet] ordered that clerk certify to Secretary of State that the court "are" satisfied of mistake described in the petition by Joseph "Heut" & recommend alteration; [no grant identified for this date].

95. John Gause jr, clerk of Brunswick Co Pleas & Quarter Sessions Court, to William White, Secretary of State: the court at Apr. term 1809 ordered me to certify to you a correction of a grant as follows: at "present term" Alfred Moore sr esquire filed his petition asking the line in a grant issued in 1743 to John Davis for 1,000 ac on Livingstons Cr "now" said Alfred's property be altered as mentioned in his petition; it appears to satisfaction of court that errors "complained of" by the petitioner originated in a surveyor's mistake; all persons interested in the premises have been properly notified & served with a copy of the petition; court adjudged & ordered the grant be corrected as in the petition or begins at a red oak instead of running S65E 320 poles as erroneously stated in the

patent should be N77E 320 poles and instead of N25E 60 poles the course should be N22E 60 poles and instead of E 240 poles it should be N77E 340 poles and instead of S 180 in should be S32E 180 poles and instead of W 60 poles it should be S22W 60 poles and instead of N65W 320 poles it should be S77W 320 poles and instead of N37W 252 poles to beginning it should be N32W 10 poles to beginning; pursuant to order of court, I certify to you the condition herein stated so "pattent" & "several" mesne conveyances can be corrected agreeable to act of Assembly made in such cases. (signed) Apr. 27, 1809 Jno Gause jr, clk; [on back] altered Jul. 5, 1809; [may be grant in grant book 5 p. 261, see shuck #236 in Bladen Co (sic) in Secretary's grant files].

96. Brunswick Co Pleas & Quarter Sessions Court Apr. term 1806 to William White, Secretary of State: on second day of said term, Joseph Watters asked the court to correct an error committed by the surveyor in a platt for a survey made Jul. 31, 1752 for a grant to Joseph Watters "the elder" grandfather of the petitioner; grant issued [blank] 1775 (sic) for 400 ac; resurvey was produced and it appears the surveyor made an error in first line described as running S60E instead of N60E and third line N60W instead of S60W; it is ordered I certify to you, the Secretary of State, the surveyor's error in the platt so it can be corrected agreeable to act of Assembly made in such cases; so I certify the same (signed) May 2, 1806 John Gause jr, clk CP; [Joseph Waters has several grants in Bladen Co files in Secretary's grant files].

97. Jan. [April--lined out] session 1798 Bruncombe Co petition of Job Braughton [or Broughton]: there is an error in a grant for 200 ac which "might be rectified April session"; after hearing testimony and "being sensible" that there actually is an error in the grant which greatly injures the claimant, the court ordered the clerk certify to Secretary of State that following error exists: third line of survey calls for 140 poles to a stake but from testimony of surveyor it ought to call for 254 poles "equve" with first line, the grant calls for 200 ac, courses & distance as mentioned in the platt includes no more that 155 ac 20 poles, so the claimant is much injured; if third line is extended from 140 poles to 254 poles, the claimant will have 200 ac as called for in the grant (signed) certified Jul. 13, 1798 by D Vance, clk; [on back] altered agreeable to the order Nov. 30, 1798; [grant #302 issued Jul. 10, 1797, grant book 91 p. 607, see shuck #331 in Buncombe Co in Secretary's grant files].

98. petition of James Bridges to Buncombe Co Please & Quarter Sessions Court Jul. session 1810: there is a mistake by the surveyor in his plat of grant #1604 issued Dec. 20, 1806 to the petitioner; mistake is in description of first line stated in grant as runs "with Miller's line" W 210 poles but it ought to say runs with "said Cooper's line" W 210 poles; the grant is correct except for inserting "Miller's" instead of "said Cooper's"; so the petitioner asks the court to order his grant be amended agreeable to acts of Assembly made in such cases (signed) R Ruffin, pltfs atto. Oct. session 1810 on hearing foregoing petition, it appears from information & testimony "adduced" the requisites of the law have been complied

with & proofs of error are entirely sufficient; so it's ordered that patent be amended & "rectified" agreeable to petition as the law directs in such cases (signed) D Vance, clk; [on back] grant altered Dec. 13, 1810; [grant in book 121 p. 402; see shuck #1574 in Buncombe Co in Secretary's grant files].

99. Buncombe Co Oct. session 1797: it appears to court, on oath of Moses Thompson a deputy surveyor, that the claimant "in part" is misnamed and there is an error in the certificate & grant issued to Abraham Castleman which ought to be Abm Castleman (sic) for 100 ac; so court ordered the clerk certify to the Secretary that grant & certificate be amended in following manner: instert name of Abraham instead of Alexander and "stricking" out words "crossing said creek to the beginning" instead thereof the words "a stake" (signed) D Vance, clk, to James Glasgow, Secry; [on back] No. 997 100 ac "altered agreeably"; [no grant to A Castleman identified in Buncombe or Burke Counties].

100. petition of William Davidson to Justices of Buncombe Co court: the petitioner employed Gabriel Ragsdale as deputy surveyor under John Patton to run 100 ac on a branch of Raccoon Cr; the petitioner obtained a grant Aug. 31, 1798 for the land with lines run as follows: begins at a large hickory, runs S30E 160 poles to a stake, N60E 100 poles to a stake, N30W 160 poles to a stake, & S60W 100 poles to beginning; the petitioner shows the surveyor should have platted it N30W 160 poles to a stake, N60E 100 poles to a stake, S60E 160 poles to a stake, & to beginning; due to the error the petitioner is deprived of land intended to be covered by his survey; so he asks the mistake be amended under rules & regulations in an act of Assembly by altering the courses as described. (signed) Jul. 20, 1807 William Davidson. Jul. session 1807 on hearing the petition, it appears from information & testimony "adduced" that requisites of the law have been complied with & proofs of error are entirely sufficient; so it's ordered that patent be amended & rectified agreeable to petition as the law directs in such cases (signed) Sept. 8, 1807 D Vance, clk; [grant #451 in grant book 98 p. 286, see shuck #598 in Buncombe Co in Secretary's grant files].

101. petition of John M Greenlee to Buncombe Co court Jan. 1808: William Davidson obtained a grant for 200 ac which by surveyor's mistake "or otherwise" is represented as on W side of French Broad R and begins at a black oak on W bank of the river, runs N70W 96 poles to a black oak by a mountain, N70E 420 poles with the mountain to a stake, S70E [no distance] to a stake on W bank of the river, & up meanders of the river to beginning; but the land surveyed & marked is on E side of the river & begins at a black oak on E bank of the river, runs N70E 70 poles to a black oak, N20W 420 poles to a stake, S70W 96 poles to the river, & up the meanders of the river to beginning; the petitioner asks the court to have [correction made of] the errors or mistakes in the grant & deeds of mesne conveyance from William Davidson to John Greenlee and from John Greenlee to John Greenlee jr as registered in Register's office of said county "or counties where they may be" according to act of Assembly made in such cases. (signed) John M Greenlee. Jan. session 1810 on hearing the petition, it appeared from

information & testimony adduced that requisites of law have been complied with & proofs of error are sufficient; so it's ordered that grant be amended & rectified agreeable to petition (signed) first Monday in Jan. 1810 D Vance, clk; [on back] altered Dec. 13, 1810; [may be grant #80 issued Sept. 1, 1800 to W Davidson & Joseph Henry, grant book 109 p. 234, see shuck #826 in Buncombe Co in Secretary's grant files].

102. Buncombe Co Pleas & Quarter Sessions Court held third Monday in Jan. 1805 at court house in Asheville present Lambert Clayton, Wm Brittain, & Joshua Williams esquires: petition of John Giles that a grant issued Jun. 7, 1799 to the petitioner for 100 ac "entered to comprize" the Long Bottom; by a surveyor's mistake the grant doesn't comprise Long Bottom "or the creek"; the petitioner shows the first course in the grant is wrong which calls for running S 160 poles to a stake but was actually run W 160 poles to a stake, then S 100 poles, E 160 poles, & N to beginning; the petitioner asks the court to rectify the error agreeable to acts of General Assembly made in such cases (signed) John Giles. Apr. session 1805 on hearing the petition, it appears from information & testimony adduced that requisites of th law have been complied with & proofs of error are sufficient; it's ordered that grant be amended & rectified agreeable to petition (signed) D Vance; [on back] altered Nov. 26, 1805 (signed) W W; [only grant to J Giles in Buncombe Co is in 1802 see shuck #1005 in Buncombe Co in Secretary's grant files].

103. Jul. session 1796 Austin Hackworth came to court & swore he paid the purchase money for Gabriel Keith to Thomas Davidson, entry taker Buncombe Co for 100 ac entry on White oak Br; warrant on which the grant is "claimed" was fairly obtained without fraud (signed) at office at Morristown D Vance; [not grant alteration; receipt for fees for grant #469 issued Sept. 28, 1798 due to entry #300 made Aug. 11, 1793; grant book 97 p. 153; see shuck #438 in Buncombe Co in Secretary's grant files].

104. Jul. session 1796 Austin Hackworth came to court & swore he paid purchase money for Gabriel "Kieth" to Thomas Davidson, Buncombe Co Entry Taker, for 300 ac on N side of Ivey R & on Gabriels Cr; warrant on which grant is claimed was obtained fairly without fraud (signed) at my office at Morristown D Vance, clerk; [on a small sheet] May 11, 1793 received of "Gabrel Kith" fees & "secetery" money for 300 ac on N side of Ivey R & on Gabriels Cr begins near the mouth of a small branch, runs down the creek, & includes Kieth's improvement (signed) T Davidson, ET [on back] Jul. session 1796 sworn in open court (signed) D Vance, clk; [not grant alteration; receipt for fees for grant #272 issued Dec. 21, 1792; grant book 91 p. 498; see shuck #316 in Buncombe Co in Secretary's grant files].

105. Jul. session 1796 Austin Hackworth came to court & swore he paid purchase money to Thomas Davidson, Buncombe Co Entry Taker, for 2 entries: (a) 100 ac on White oak Br includes said Hackworth's improvement and (b) 100 ac on said

branch, begins at Ainsworth's upper line, & runs up the branch; the warrants on which the grants are claimed were obtained fairly & without fraud. (signed) at my office at Morristown D Vance, clk; [on a small sheet] May 11, 1793 received of Austin "Heckworth" all fees & "Secetery" money for 100 ac on White oak Br, includes said Hackworth's improvement where he lives (signed) Thos Davidson, ET, and May 11, 1793 received of Austin Hockworth all fees & Secetery money for 100 ac on White oak Br, begins at "Hainsworth's" upper line, & runs up the branch (signed) T Davidson, ET, July session 1796 sworn in open court (signed) D Vance, clk; [not grant correction; receipt for fees on (a) grant #256 issued Dec. 21, 1796 due to entry #213 dated Jul. 10, 1793 in grant book 91 p. 491 see shuck #300 in Buncombe Co AND (b) grant #264 issued Dec. 21, 1796 due to entry #271 dated Jun. 10, 1793 grant book 91 p. 495 see shuck #308 in Buncombe Co in Secretary's grant files].

106. Jul. session 1808 petition of John Halcombe (of Buncombe Co): on Oct. 20, 1795 he entered 100 ac on S side of big Ivey [R] in Buncombe Co Entry Taker's office; the same was surveyed by Robert Love who made following error: "begins at a white oak on William Whitson's line, runs N 30 poles to a corner white oak of said Halcombe's other survey" but the survey should have begun at said white oak & run S 30 poles to a stake; the petitioner asks that his grant be amended accordingly (signed) John Halcombe.   Jul. session 1808 on hearing the petition, it appears from information & testimony adduced that requisites of the law have been complied with & proofs of the error are sufficient; court ordered the grant be amended & rectified according to petition as law directs. (signed) at office first Monday in Jul. 1808 D Vance, clk [David Vance]; [on back] No. 511 issued Dec. 13, 1798; altered Dec. 15, 1809; [may be grant #551 in shuck #520 or grant #544 in shuck #513 in Buncombe Co in Secretary's grant files].

107. Oct. session 1792 petition at "last" July session of Joseph Henry & William Davidson to correct an error in a patent; petition was considered & ordered that clerk certify the facts to Secretary of State.   I certify that there's an error in a deed No. 614 "or patent" granted to Joseph Henry & William Davidson for 250 ac on both sides of a large creek that empties into French Broad R on E side; error is in first course of the plat which says run S 50 chains when it should be E 50 chains; second course in certificate says S 50 chains [correct course not mentioned] which is "plainly" inconsistent averting the courses round the plat "will clearly point out the error" (signed) Oct. 17, 1792 D Vance, cc, to James Glasgow, Secry; [on back] Henry & Davidson 250 Rutherford No. 614; "done" Oct. 17, 1792; [grant #614 to Davidson & Henry not found in Buncombe Co in Secretary's grant files].

108. petition of Joseph Henry & William Davidson to Jan. session 1796 Buncombe Co court: court ordered the clerk certify to Secretary of State an error in a stake grant to said Henry & Davidson for 49 ac; I David Vance, clerk, certify an error in seventh line of a certificate annexed to the grant; the line mentions runs N30W when it should say N30E; the error will be easily perceived by observing the platt or diagram (signed) D Vance, clk, to James Glasgow, Secretary of State;

Corrections/Alterations to Land Grants

[on back] pat. No. 66 date 1794; [grant issued Jul. 7, 1794; grant book 85 p. 8; see shuck #149 in Buncombe Co in Secretary's grant files].

109. to Justices of Buncombe Co Pleas & Quarter Sessions Court petition of William Gudger, guardian & next friend of John Gooch & Benjamin Gooch, miners under age 21 & heirs of Jonas Gooch deceased: the petitioners show Jonas Gooch in his lifetime obtained a survey for 200 ac "then" in Burke Co on W side of French Broad R & on both sides of Fall Cr and includes the fork, a white oak, & pointers about 20 poles E of the creek, runs W 160 poles crossing the creek below the fork to a pine, S 200 poles crossing main fork to a stake, E 160 poles to a stake, & N crossing the fork to beginning; grant was obtained Aug. 7, 1787; the petitioner shows the Secretary made a mistake in the grant by inserting Jonas Going instead of Jonas Gooch and said orphans, John & Benjamin Gooch, are liable to be injured; so William Gudger, in behalf of the orphans, asks to inquire into the facts & order the Secretary to correct the error (signed) William Gudger. Oct. session 1801 on hearing the petition, it appears from testimony adduced that requisites of the law have been complied with & proofs are sufficient; so it's ordered that patent be amended & rectified agreeable to petition as law allows (signed) D Vance, clk; [on back] altered Nov. 18, 1801 (signed) W W; [grant #939 in grant book 65 p. 366; see shuck #937 in Burke Co in Secretary's grant files].

110. to Justices of Buncombe Co court: the Burke Co surveyor made a mistake in surveying land for Gabriel Hackworth on French Broad R; the land is "truely" in Buncombe Co and lines are in the grant now laid before the court; lines don't include the intended land; so he asks the court to order the "land" be rectified agreeable to "the corner called for in the grant" (signed) Lewis Bull, for Gabriel Hackworth. Oct. session 1803 on hearing the petition, it appeared from information & testimony adduced that requisites of the law have been complied with and proofs of error are sufficient; so court ordered the patent be amended agreeable to petition as law allows and agreeable to distances mentioned in an accompanying plat (signed) D Vance, clk; [on back] altered Nov. 24, 1803; [only shuck is #0504 (no grant) in Buncombe Co in Secretary's grant files];
 survey: begins at a sugar tree near mouth of Buck Br on S side of French Broad R, runs S73E 106 poles to a dogwood, S78E 74 poles to a hickory, N53E 199 poles to a stake, & a direct line to beginning; [plat included, land in shape of triangle].

111. petition of Richard Hightower & David Miller to Buncombe Co court: a grant issued Nov. 27, 1789 to them for 300 ac in Rutherford Co "now" Buncombe on both sides of a small creek that runs into French Broad R through the land then claimed by Plumbley "as stated in the grant"; "sundry" mistakes appear manifest in the grant & certificate; they ask the grant be amended in following manner: insert name of David Miller in 2 places with name of said Hightower after words "to have & to hold", inserting in the grant 3 courses & distances which are in the plat annexed to the grant to wit "W 200 poles, S 220 poles, E 240 poles to beginning" which words were left out by mistake in the grant (signed) Jan. 23,

36

Corrections/Alterations to Land Grants

1799 David Miller & Richard Hightower. Notice to issue to sheriff to notify William Wilson esq & Samuel King [esq--lined out] to show cause why the grant should not be awarded in manner requested (signed) W Avery, atto. I William Wilson admit notice in due time of intention of moving for & filing the petition (signed) William Wilson. I Samuel King admit notice as above in due time (signed) Sam King's mark [backward "S"] (witness) D Vance. Oct. session 1799 on hearing the petition it appears from testimony adduced that requisites of the law have been complied with & proofs of error are sufficient; it's ordered that patent be amended agreeable with petition as law directs (signed) D Vance, clk; [on back] record altered Nov. 27, 1799 (signed) W W; [Hightower & Miller have 4 grants on this date in Rutherford Co see shucks #536, 538, 539, & 544].

112. Oct. session 1796 William Hunter came into court & swore he paid purchase money & other fees for Solomon Lewis to Thomas Davidson, Buncombe Co Entry Taker, for 50 ac; warrant on which grant is claimed was obtained fairly & without fraud (signed) at my office at Morristown D Vance, clk; [on a small sheet] received of Solomon Lewis "twenty-one and 8" pence for 50 ac entered (signed) Thos Davidson, Oct. session 1796 sworn to in open court D Vance, clk; [on back] please "transfair" 50 ac in Wm Hunter's name and in so doing you will greatly oblidge me (signed) Solomon Lewis; [not grant alteration; certificate for fees paid for grant #271 issued Dec. 21, 1796 due to entry #270 issued Jun. 10, 1793; grant book 91 p. 497; see shuck #315 in Buncombe Co in Secretary's grant files].

113. Jan. session 1828 Buncombe Co Pleas & Quarter Sessions Court: John Miller, clerk, certifies about petition of John Laning filed with the court and 7 justices present: a grant was obtained Dec. 15, 1802 by said Laning for 55 ac; courses & distances follow: begins at a leaning white oak on the point of a ridge at said Laning's SE corner, runs N12E 63 poles crossing a branch to a poplar in head of a hollow, N78W 20 poles to a red oak on S side of a hill, N12E 20 poles to a red oak & white oak on a ridge, S48E 140 poles to a stake, S 200 poles to a stake, & to beginning; in fourth line of the grant & surveyor's certificate it was stated runs S48E 140 poles but should be N48E 140 poles; he will suffer injury by this mistake; evidence was shown about the same; Laning asked for an order directing clerk to certify the facts to Secretary of State as required by act of Assembly in such cases. (signed) Jan. 10, 1828 Jno Miller, clk; [on back] John "Lanning" 55 ac Buncombe Co; altered Dec. 1, 1828; plat on a small sheet; [grant #1062 issued Dec. 15, 1802; grant book 116 p. 138; see shuck #1024 in Buncombe Co in Secretary's grant files].

114. Haywood Co Dec. term 1820 William Mahaffy's petition for alteration of grant #1207 for 70 ac: the cause was heard & it appears to satisfaction of court that facts in the petition are "treu"; patentee is likely to be injured; courses & distances in plat & grant are erroneous; courses & distances should be begins at a white oak Lewis' old corner, runs N 26 poles to a spanish oak Gooch's corner, N45W 96 poles to a white oak, S64W 20 poles to a white oak, N44W 119 poles to a stake on the river, S78W 54 poles with the river to Rice's corner poplar, S13E

Corrections/Alterations to Land Grants

40 poles to a stake & black oak, N76E 13 poles to a stake, S35E 112 poles to a stake, S70E 70.75 poles to a pine, S20E 29.25 poles to a red oak in Lewis' old line, N74E 60 poles to beginning; John Gooch's land joins William Mahaffy's land; Gooch came to court & consented to the alteration; it's ordered that request is granted & clerk to certify to Secretary's office the courses & distances in this decree along with 2 plats of the same surveyed & made out by Thomas Lenoir; Secretary to alter the grant to William Mahaffy as law requires; I certify foregoing is true copy from records in my office (signed) Jul. 24, 1820 Rt. Love, C Hd HCC; [on back] Buncombe Co now Haywood Co; altered Dec. 4, 1820 (signed) Wm Hill, Secry; [grant may be shuck #1154 in Buncombe Co, but more likely shuck #18 in Haywood Co in Secretary's grant files];

[one copy of plat included; same metes & bounds on plat; indicates survey contains 102 ac 2 roods & 3 poles].

115. Jan. session 1822 Buncombe Co Pleas & Quarter Sessions Court: Edwin Poor [or Coor] exparte petition to amend grant #485 issued Nov. 26, 1789: the case was heard; petitioner's exhibits & evidence was adduced; it's ordered that clerk to certify to Secretary of State that petitioner Edwin "Pore" claims land now in "Buncomb" Co which was granted Nov. 26, 1789 to "Waitstell" Avery grant No. 485 in "a part" of Rutherford Co now Buncombe Co; it appears to satisfaction of court that land intended to be in grant was improperly described in the grant due to surveyor's mistake; first line omitted length from first to second station; certificate should have been made out in following words: begins at a chesnut, runs S60E 100 poles along Elijah Williamson's line to a stake & pointers, S196 poles crossing Mill Cr to a chesnut, W 200 poles to a chesnut, N 134 poles to "the" river, & down the river to beginning; Edwin Pore is likely to be injured by the error; the court believes grant should be altered so length of first line is mentioned as 100 poles. John Miller, clerk, certifies this is true copy of record (signed) Jan. 10, 1822 Jno Miller, clk; [on back] altered Sept. 15, 1823 (signed) W H; [grant in book 71 p. 349; see shuck #521 in Rutherford Co in Secretary's grant files].

116. Buncombe Co due to warrant from M B Patton, entry taker, for entry #3236 entered Sept. 18, 1829, surveyed 200 ac for Jesse M Roberts on head of Flat Cr; begins at a chesnut, runs N 93 poles to a poplar & hickory, W 60 poles to 2 poplars, N 75 poles to a small "B" oak on side of a mountain, W 80 poles to a stake in Roberts field near a small drain, N 20 poles to a stake, E 175 poles to a stake, S 235 poles to a stake, W 293 poles to a stake, N 118 poles to a stake in Roberts line, E 100 poles with the line of "the same" to a corner of the same, S 78 poles with a line of the same to a corner of the same, E 160 poles with the same to beginning; certified Aug. 24, 1830 D Vance, DS; Joshua Roberts & Wm Chambers, chain carriers; Apr. 20, 1832 D Vance before N Blackstouk swears above plat is correct (signed) D Vance & N "Blackstock"; [grant in book 139 p. 206; see shuck #2916 in Buncombe Co in Secretary's grant files];

Aug. session 1833 Buncombe Co Pleas & Quarter Sessions Court Jesse "Roberds" exparte petition to amend an error in patent 2930 issued Sept. 20, 1831: on hearing the petition & testimony, ordered the clerk certify to Secretary of State the "fact" of the case; court is satisfied an error was made in original survey; the annexed plat shows courses & distances originally designed to be described in grant to Jesse Roberds founded on warrant #3236 (signed) Aug. 29, 1833 John Miller, clerk & N W Woodfin, DC; [on back] altered Sept. 16, 1833 (signed) W H.

117. Jul. session 1806 petition of Edmon Sams to Justices of Buncombe Co court: a patent & annexed plat are erroneous and don't agree with explanation of original grantee James McDowell; the land now belongs to said Sams; the petitioner asks the court to order an amendment of the grant agreeable to act of Assembly made in such cases; courses of the grant follow: surveyed 20 ac for James McDowell on W side of French Broad R near mouth of Swananoa [R], begins at a stake on the river bank, runs N70E down the river 306 poles to a walnut about 3 poles from the water, N 60 poles to 3 white oaks, W 287 poles to a stake, & S to beginning; alteration requested follows: second corner walnut to be made the beginning, then as the grant states N 60 poles to 3 white oaks, W 287 poles to a stake, S [blank] poles to a stake on the river bank, & with the river to beginning which will cover the intended land (signed) Edmon Sams. Oct. session 1806 on hearing foregoing petition, it appears the requisites of law have been complied with & proofs of error are sufficient for the court; court ordered the grant be amended agreeable to last courses in the petition. (signed) third Monday of Oct. 1806 D Vance, clk [David Vance]; [on back] altered Nov. 30, 1808 (signed) W W.

118. Oct. session 1806 petition of William Sharpe & John McKnitt Alexander to Buncombe Co court: grant No. 518 issued Nov. 16, 1790 and includes a surveyor's error to wit: first course was intended to be S 180 poles & third course was intended to be N 180 poles; these lines were marked by the surveyor, but by mistake he called first course N 180 poles and third course S 180 poles; the grant was consumed by fire while in possession of one of the petitioners; they ask to have grant amended agreeable to act of Assembly (signed) Wm Sharpe & John McKnitt Alexander. Jan. session 1807 foregoing petition was heard & it appears requisites of law have been complied with & proofs of error are sufficient; court ordered grant be amended agreeable with petition. (signed) Sept. 3, 1807 D Vance, clk [David Vance]; received my fee 5/ (signed) D Vance; altered Nov. 30, 1808 "J Harris esq is to do this service for Jno McK Alexander"; [plat on back of sheet] begins at a pine, runs S 180 poles to a stake, E 360 poles to a stake, N 180 poles to a stake, & W 360 poles to beginning; land shown on both sides of Big Br surveyed in 1790 by Abner Sharpe & error now rectified by court Jan. 1807 (signed) "Fish"; [no grant of this number identified in Buncombe or Burke Co to Sharpe & Alexander; but they did receive several grants in Burke Co].

119. petition of Nathan Smith to Buncombe Co Court Apr. session 1807: he entered land #8301 on Jan. 21, 1801 with John Henry, Buncombe Co Entry officer, on S fork of Dicks Cr, begins about 0.25 miles above a wolf pen at a white oak on a ridge, runs down "the" branch, & includes both sides of the branch; the surveyor made an error in the certificates by putting date & location of another entry & survey of the petitioner No. 8557 dated Jul. 21, 1801; grant No. 1230

Corrections/Alterations to Land Grants

issued to Nathan Smith for 100 ac on W side of French Broad R, joins SE line of
the tract where said Smith lives & runs along said line; the petitioner asks for grant
to be amended: instead of location in the grant insert following: by virtue of
warrant No. 5301 from Joseph Henry, Entry Taker, entered Jan. 21, 1801 I have
surveyed for Nathan Smith 100 ac on S fork of Dicks Cr, begins about 0.25 miles
above a wolf pen at a white oak on a ridge, runs down the branch, & includes both
sides of the branch, from the white oak on a ridge runs N 127 poles to a white oak,
E 127 poles to a white oak, S 127 poles to a stake, & W to beginning (signed)
Nathan Smith.   Jul. session 1807 petition was heard & it appears requisites of
law have been complied with & proofs of error are sufficient for the court; so it's
ordered that grant be amended agreeable to petition (signed) Sept. 5, 1807 D
Vance, clk [David Vance]; [on back] altered Nov. 30, 1807; [grant in book 117 p.
418; see shuck #1177 in Buncombe Co in Secretary's grant files].

120. Oct. session 1804 petition of John Thomas to Justices of Buncombe Co court:
he obtained a grant for 550 ac Dec. 15, 1801; there is a surveyor's error in the
grant which omitted the land intended by the entry and a "considerable" part of
land is taken by an older grant; so he asks to begin at fifth station where line
extends S 200 poles but ought to extend N 132 poles to David McCarson's line,
W 150 poles, S 175 poles, E 190 poles, S 160 poles, & E to beginning; the
petitioner has complied with act of Assembly in giving notice to adjoining land
owners; he asks for an order "as is provided" in his behalf to correct the errors
(signed) John Thomas.   Oct session 1805 petition was heard & court ordered the
request be granted since it appears notice was served on "several" person who
own adjoining land & evidence of true courses of the land follow: begins at a
white oak on George B Greer's line in a ridge, runs N 68 poles to a white oak, N
50 poles, W 286 poles to a black oak, S 50 poles to a chesnut, W 160 poles to a
spanish oak, N 132 poles, W 150 poles, S 175 poles, E 190 poles, S 160 poles, &
E 340 poles to beginning; reference made to "late" resurvey (signed) D Vance,
clk; [on back] altered Nov. 21, 1805; [no grant for 550 ac identified to John
Thomas in Buncombe Co in Secretary's grant files];
     survey on separate sheet with metes & bounds written along the plat.

121. Apr. session 1805 Burke Co petition of Waightstill Avery for amendment of
grant No. 1149 issued May 18, 1789 for 100 ac on Three mile Br; on hearing
petition, court ordered the grant be amended by Secretary of State to begin at a
spanish oak, runs N 40 chains to a spanish oak, W 25 chains to a stake by a spanish
oak, S 40 chains to a white oak, & E 25 chains to beginning. James Erwin, clerk,
certifies above is true copy from the records (signed) May [Apr.--lined ot] 6, 1805
J Erwin, clk; [on back] grant No. 1149 issued May 18, 1789 altered Sept. 26, 1806;
[grant in book 71 p. 40; see shuck #1148 in Burke Co in Secretary's grant files].

122. Apr. session 1803 Burke Co: court ordered the clerk to certify to Secretary
of State to alter grant No. 356 issued Oct. 28, 1782 to James Burke for 200 ac on
both sides of Drowning Cr; in third line say "West" instead of "East". (signed)
Apr. 27, 1803 J Erwin, clk; [on back] altered Sept. 24, 1803; grant in book 44 p.

Corrections/Alterations to Land Grants

135; see shuck #355 in Burke Co in Secretary's grant files].

123. Oct. term 1796 Burke Co petition of John Connelly esq asking for "benefit" of an order to Secretary of State to amend grant #1793 to John Connelly for 400 ac; there is a surveyor's error in the certificate of survey in third course: N 172 poles to a post oak to be inserted; ordered Secretary to proceed to amend the same agreeable to act of Assembly. (signed) Oct. 26, 1796 at Morganton J Erwin, clk; [grant in book 85 p. 94; see shuck #1827 in Burke Co in Secretary's grant files].

124. Apr. session 1807 Burke Co petition to amend grant No. 1599 to John Hinde for 100 ac as follows: begins at a chesnut tree, runs W 31 chains 62 links to a stake in Nalor's old line, E 31 chains 62 links to a stake, & S to beginning; court ordered Secretary of State to alter the grant as follows: begins at a chesnut tree his West corner, runs W 31 chains 62 links to a stake, N 31 chains 62 links to a stake in Nalor's old line, E 31 chains 62 links with said line to a stake, & S crossing the creek to beginning. (signed) May 4, 1807 J Erwin, clk; [on back] grant altered Dec. 21, 1809; [grant in book 80 p. 55; see shuck #1628 in Burke Co in Secretary's grant files].

125. to Secretary of State: you are directed by order of Burke Co court Oct. term 1791, after oath made by William White D Surveyor in court that he surveyed 300 ac on Lower Cr joining James Blair for Fredrick Hisaw, but he mistook & named Henry instead of Fredrick; so alter the name of Henry to Fredrick in grant for 300 ac. (signed) Nov. 23, 1791 Alex Erwin, clk; [no grant identified to Hinsaw in Burke Co].

126. Burke Co Joseph D Ferree, clerk of Burke Co Pleas & Quarter Sessions Court, certifies at "late" court term Jul. term 1845 with 7 justices present, the court ordered the clerk to certify to Secretary of State an error was made by county surveyor in running lines of entry made Apr. 2, 1842 by Rebecca Lail; entry was on waters of Rock Cr in Burke Co, joins Michael Huffman & Thomas Walker and contains 100 ac; survey made Oct. 28, 1842; fourth line was said to be S 108 poles but should have been N 108 poles; this certificate made pursuant to court order so Secretary of State can correct the grant (signed) Sept. 18, 1847 J D Ferree, clerk; [on back] No. 6121 altered Oct. 12, 1847 (signed) Wm Hill, Secry; [grant in book #147 p. 76; see shuck #5471 in Burke Co in Secretary's grant files].

127. Jul. session 1806 Burke Co Pleas & Quarter Sessions Court: petition in behalf of Thomas Smith, Joseph Dobson, & Brice Collins; ordered by the court that grant No. 2488 be amended as follows: number of warrant purporting to be No. 537 be altered to 536; and grant to said petitioners No. 2489 be amended as follows: number of warrant purporting to be No. 536 be altered to 537; it was made to appear to satisfaction of court that a mistake was made in above numbers and they ought to have stood as they are here ordered to be amended; clerk to certify this order to Secretary of State and he is to amend them accordingly. (signed) Sept. 24, 1806 J Erwin; [on back] altered Nov. 18, 1806; [grant #2488 in book 101 p.

41

Corrections/Alterations to Land Grants

50 see shuck #2699 in Burke Co and grant #2489 in book 101 p. 50 see shuck #2700 in Burke Co in Secretary's grant files].

128. Burke Co Oct. session 1802: petition of Isaac Thompson to amend a grant as described in petition & notices to parties owning adjoining land served & proved in open court; ordered the prayer of petition be granted; so court ordered clerk to certify to Secretary of State that it has been proved that Isaac Thompson made a location in Burke Co with the entry taker for 200 ac on both sides of a fork of Hunting Cr; a warrant of survey was obtained for the same; warrant issued Sept. 12, 1791 to county surveyor; survey begins at a red oak called a black jack on Browning's line, runs N20E 166 poles to a post oak, N54E 136 poles to a post oak, S 107 poles to a white oak, S3W 237 poles to a stake, & N65W to beginning; but the surveyor made a mistake as follows: begins at a black jack in Browning's line, runs S 120 poles to a post oak, E 190 poles crossing the fork to a black oak, N84E 50 poles to a pine, N110 poles to a hickory, & W 240 poles to beginning; Secretary of State ordered to alter the grant recorded in his office according to true courses of survey (signed) J Erwin, clk; [on back] altered Nov. 16, 1802;
survey included [no date] by Wm W Erwin, surveyor [no chain carriers mentioned]; [plat included]; [maybe grant #1597 issued Nov. 27, 1792 in book 80 p. 55 see shuck #1626 in Burke Co in Secretary's grant files].

129. Cabarrus Co Pleas & Quarter Sessions Court Oct. term 1810: at said court held at the court house on third Monday in Oct. 1810 Paul Barringer esq petitioned the court: in 1807 he obtained a grant for 60 ac issued Nov. 24, 1807; but Elisha Spears, deputy surveyor, made a mistake in the certificate putting E side of Dutch Buffalow Cr instead of W side of the creek; it has been made to appear to satisfaction of court that the error was made; Secretary of State is directed to alter the grant agreeable to act of Assembly made in such cases. (signed) Nov. 6, 1810 George Phifer CCC; [on back] grant No. 350 altered Dec. 13, 1810; [grant issued Nov. 24, 1807 in book 124 p. 3, see shuck #370 in Cabarrus Co in Secretary's grant files].

130. Cabarrus Co Jul. session 1808: I certify that county court at this term ordered Secretary of State to correct a mistake in a grant from William White's office "at present secretary": a line in the location omitted 100 poles, the course of said line is S53E; grant issued to Peter Isahour (signed) Rd Brandon, clk; [on back] grant No. 267 dated 1802 altered Nov. 30, 1808; [nearest is grant #276 issued Dec. 8, 1802 in book 116 p. 330, see shuck #280 in Cabarrus Co in Secretary's grant files].

131. Cabarrus Co Pleas & Quarter Session Court held at the court house in Concord third Monday in Jul. 1828; petition of Aaron Redenhour: petitioner shows the court he purchased 7.5 ac which was granted Dec. 17, 1825 to Martin Rendleman; there is an error in the grant in misnaming one of the courses; it should have been an East line but calls for a West course; error was committed by surveyor; so the land granted lies in the petitioner's old deeded land; the petitioner will "bring forward" witnesses to prove the facts in the petition; so he asks for a

hearing & to have error corrected (signed) Aaron Rendenhour. Court examined John Barnhart about the allegations in the petition and made following order: ordered on Dec. 17, 1825 Martin Rendleman "took out" a patent for 7.5 ac which contained a surveyor's mistake; West course should be East course as proved on trial of petition of Aaron Redenhour "the purchaseor" by testimony of John Barnhart; so clerk of court is to certify these facts to Secretary of State according to act of Assembly in 1790 chapter 326 (sic) (signed) James G Spears, clerk Aug. 25, 1828; [on back] altered Nov. 18, 1828 (signed) W H.

132. Elisha P Miller, clerk of Caldwell Co Pleas & Quarter Sessions Court, certifies Daniel Crump filed a petition to correct an error in platt No. 95 surveyed Jun. 15, 1842 and grant No. 42 issued Dec. 19, 1842; error was proved by oath of surveyor to be "the last call calling from a stake 20 poles South to beginning" but it should be from a stake 20 poles North to beginning (signed) Oct. 24, 1844 E P Miller, clk by R C Miller D C; [on back] altered Nov. 25, 1844 W Hill, Sec of State; [grant in book 148 p. 189, see shuck #42 in Caldwell Co in Secretary's grant files].

133. petition of Enoch Sawyer to Camden Co court: there is an error in a grant for 600 ac on North River Swamp from Crooked Cr to "the" Indian line; the present course by the grant is N78W but the real course should be N61W which would be agreeable to the grant to heirs of Thomas Sawyer deceased and line marked & established "between us"; so Enoch asks the court to order his grant be taken to Secretary of State so error can be corrected (signed) Aug. 7, 1799 Enoch Sawyer "for himself & others concerned". Aug. term 1799 on order of Enoch Sawyer, executor of Demsey Sawyer deceased, ordered grant No. 45 to Demsey Sawyer (sic) be taken to Secretary's office and Secretary correct an error in the course of the grant in line from Crooked Creek to wit N78W "as now by grant" to N61W which will make the line conform to patent No. 46 issued to heirs of Thomas Sawyer deceased (signed) Aug. 6, 1799 (sic) Malachi Sawyer, ccc; [on back] filed Nov. 24, 1799; [no grant to Dempsey Sawyer found in Camden or Pasquotank Co; grant to Thomas Sawyer may be in book 1 p. 75 see shuck #103 in Pasquotank Co in Secretary's grant files].

134. Camden Co court Nov. term 1795 Thos P Williams et un. et als to the court petition to correct error in patent: petition of Thomas Pool Williams & wife Elizabeth and Peter Dauge & wife Margaret for themselves and William Scarbrough & wife Lucy coheirs of Thos Sawyer deceased: court has heard the evidence as to truth of allegations in petition; ordered clerk of court certify to Secretary of State that it appears to satisfaction of court that there is a manifest error in first course of grant No. 46 to heirs of Thomas Sawyer deceased for 650 ac in this county issued Dec. 21, 1785; course in patent runs N78W 136 chains to a cypress in the Indian line, but it should run N61W to a line of marked trees "to" the Indian line; foregoing is a copy from Camden Co records (signed) Nov. [county seal on top of date], 1795 Malachi Sawyer, ccc; [may be grant (no number) in book 1 p. 75 see shuck #103 in Pasquotank Co in Secretary's grant

Corrections/Alterations to Land Grants

files].

135. petition of Joseph Borden to Justices of Carteret Co court May term 1803: Arthur Mabson received a grant Apr. 20, 1745 for 400 ac begins at a pine on W of Newport R near James Wainwright's bounds, runs N15E 253 poles to a pine, S75W 253 poles, S15W to Wainwright's bounds, & S75 W along the bounds to first station; the land was "regularly conveyed or descended" to William Mabson, son of Arthur, and from William Mabson to William Borden, father of the petitioner who sold to the petitioner; an error was made either by surveyor in platting the land or Secretary in the grant: second or "head" line of the grant was in fact N75W 253 poles not S75W 253 poles as the grant represents erroneously; because of this error the petitioner is in danger of being materially injured and losing all of the land since the grant will be for different land from that intended & paid for; George Bell, Abner Bell, Malachi Bell, & Abner Quin are the only persons having adjoining land or who "pretend to claim title" to land described in the petition; so petitioner asks court to summon George, Abner, Malachi [Bell], & Abner Quinn and all other persons who may be interested in the premise so they can have an opportunity to be heard against the petition; case to be heard third Monday in Aug. "next"; petitioner asks court hear the case & if he is likely to be injured then clerk to certify the facts to Secretary of State so error can be corrected; court can order a survey of land if needed or make any other order as needed (signed) Joseph Borden, by Edward Graham his attorney "a true copy" (signed) Geo Read, cc. Aug. term 1803 Carteret Co Pleas & Quarter Sessions Court to Secretary of State: at this term petition of Joseph Borden was heard concerning error in grant Apr. 20, 1745 to Arthur Mabson; defendants came to court & admitted allegations in petition; court examined evidence and are satisfied an error was made; land should be 400 ac begins at a pine on W side of maid branch of Deep Cr & N side of Newport R near James Wainwright's bounds, runs N15E 253 poles to a pine, N75W 253 poles, S15W to Wainwright's bounds, & S75W along his bounds to first station; certified by George Read, clerk at Beaufort Aug. 16, 1803 (signed) Geo Read, cc; [on back] grant ought to accompany this in order to be altered as well as the record (signed) W W; [may be grant recorded twice issued Aug. 20, 1745 in book 5 p. 306 see shuck #131 and book 10 p. 146 see shuck #234 in Carteret Co in Secretary's grant files].

136. Carteret Co Pleas & Quarter Sessions Court May term 1803 to Secretary of State: at this term Caleb Bell petitioned the court about a surveyor's error in certificate to Secretary's office for grant issued Jul. 10, 1788; petitioner asked to have error corrected; court examined witnesses, depositions, & other documents produced by petitioner to support allegations and "objections & testimony" of John McKane & others "the defendants"; court believes errors was made; following is true description of land: 200 ac near head of Deep Cr begins at Abner Quin's back & eastermost corner, runs N13W 200 poles to a pine, crosses Deep Creek N50W 256 poles to a pine on W side of Deep Cr, S13E 200 poles to a pine, & S50E 256 poles to first station as shown on annexed certificate; certified by George Read, clerk of court at Beaufort May 19, 1802 (signed) Geo Read, cc;

Corrections/Alterations to Land Grants

May term 1799 Carteret Co Pleas & Quarter Sessions Court; petition of Caleb Bell: he made an entry & obtained a grant for 200 ac; but the surveyor misrepresented the land as follows: 200 ac near head of Deep Cr begins at Abner Quin's back line & eastermost corner pine, runs N 200 poles to a pine, W 160 poles to a pine on W side of the creek, S 200 poles to a pine, & E 160 poles to first station; but land should be as follows [same as first set of metes & bounds]; so the petitioner's grant would be thrown on the property of others and cover land of no value; Bell filed his petition by his attorney William Slade in this court to discover the error & notices Joseph Hatch & Needham Whitfield who Bell thought were "only" owners of adjoining land; but due to inaccuracies in the petition, John McKean claims adjoining land; so Bell "discontinued" his petition so he could "renew the same" and notify the above people; McKean was notified but continues to "daily pillage" the land and "resists the fair title" of Bell; in addition William Gardiner, Abner Quin, & [blank] Gabriels were notified who are "the whole" of persons who own or pretend to own adjoining land; Bell asks for assistance and an order for clerk to certify error to Secretary of State so error can be corrected (signed) Daniel Carthy & Edwd Graham, atto for petitioner "a true copy" (signed) Geo Read ccc;

survey included [same metes & bounds as first mentioned] (signed) William W Taylor, survr Feb. 26, 1787; May 9, 1796 I certify above plat & courses are agreeable to survey I made and the plot is an "intire mistake" (sic) and will not cover the land intended by me at the day I surveyed it; a true copy from my field book (signed) Wm W Taylor [but courses are first (or correct set) not second (or incorrect set) mentioned in petition]; [on back] altered Sept. 24, 1802; [grant #235 in book 68 p. 171, see shuck #874 in Secretary's grant files].

137. May term 1794 Carteret Co Jacob Cannady & William Borden "inform" the court there is an error in a grant held by them on S side of Newport R issued May 22, 1740 to James "Winright" "enrolled" Apr. 4, 1743; error is in 2 lines which should be reversed: first line & course from N10E to S10W and fifth line from S45W to N45E; [court] grants prayer of petitioners and orders clerk to certify same to Secretary's office so record can be altered (signed) May 22, 1794 at Beaufort Benja Fulford, cc; [on back] 375 May 1740 pat. altd. alter record; [grant in book 5 p. 144 see shuck #106 and book 4 p. 192 see shuck #78 in Carteret Co in Secretary's grant files].

138. Justices of Carteret Co Pleas & Quarter Sessions Court May term 1820 to Secretary of State: at this term petition of William Fisher was heard; Fisher claims a tract under grant issued Apr. 6, 1745 to Newell Bell for 200 ac on SW side of Newport R near David Sheppard's line "Reed Neck"; but a mistake was made by Secretary of State in the courses in the grant; third line was N45E 170 poles "almost half to a pine" but grant indicated S45E 170 poles almost half to a pine; court examined grant & annexed plat and are satisfied mistake was made; so court ordered clerk to certify same to Secretary of State for correction of third line of grant from S45E to N45E (signed) Geo Read, clk; [on back] altered Sept. 28, 1820 (signed) Wm Hill, Sec; [grant to "Nevil" Bell in book 10 p. 141 see shuck #232

Corrections/Alterations to Land Grants

and book 5 p. 302 see shuck #129 in Carteret Co in Secretary's grant files].

139. petition of Thomas Goulding to Carteret Co court Aug. term 1804: court is satisfied errors mentioned in petition were made in grant issued Mar. 28, 1755 to the petitioner for 300 ac opposite the thoroughfare of Cedar Island begins at a "parsimmon" on S side of Long Bay Cr his former corner, runs N18E 292 poles, N34E 185 poles, S50E 55 poles, S3W 100 poles, N82W 156 poles, N50W 60 poles to head of Cardugana Cr his former corner, & S62W 530 poles along his own line to first station; line N82W 156 poles ought to have been N82E 156 poles and line N50W 60 poles should ave been S50E 60 poles; clerk ordered to certify the same to Secretary of State so he can correct courses in the patent & records in his office (signed) Geo Read, cc; [on back] grant altered May 31, 1806; [grant in book 2 p. 123 see shuck #150 in Carteret Co in Secretary's grant files].

140. petition of Samuel Smith to Carteret Co Pleas & Quarter Sessions Court May term 1807: petition filed last term stating an error in a grant [date blank] to David Bailey under which Smith claims; error made by surveyor or by Secretary to great damage of Smith; fourth line in grant is S12E 160 poles but should be S53E 266 poles; petition was heard & court is satisfied error was made; true location is begins at "&c" runs N52W 100 poles, N40W 80 poles, N10E 360 poles, S53E 266 poles, S18W 290 poles, & S60W 80 poles to beginning; court ordered clerk to certify the same to Secretary for correction of grant & records in his office (signed) Geo Read, cc; [on back] altered Nov. 27, 1807; [may be grant issued Mar. 1, 1719 in book 8 p. 204, see shuck #368 in Pasquotank Co in Secretary's grant files].

141. to Caswell Co Pleas & Quarter Sessions Court Oct. term 1807 petition of David Hodge, Isaac Hodge, & Samuel Hodge, heirs at law of John Hodge "late" of Caswell Co deceased: petitioners ask to have error corrected in grant issued Dec. 20, 1779 to John Hodge for 225 ac begins at a pine in Charles Stephens' old line, runs N 25 chains to 2 pointers, W 15 chains to a post oak, N 16 chains 75 links to a dogwood, E 63 chains to a stake on Hugh Dobbins old line, S 41 chains 75 links with his old line to a stake, W48 chains with Charles Stephens' line to first station; court heard allegations & supporting testimony; court ordered clerk to certify to Secretary of State there appears to be an error, to court's satisfaction, in survey sent to Secretary's office on which the grant issued; so grant needs to be amended as follows: begins at a white oak on Nathaniel Comer's line, runs S2 1/2E 66 chains 84 links with his line crossing Reedy fork of Hico [R] to a post oak, S88W 32 chains 45 links to a poplar on William Stephens' line, N 2 1/2W 29 chains 50 links with his line & Benjamin Stephens' line crossing the creek to a beech, W 10 chains 20 links to a white oak, N 38 chains to a dogwood & white oak on "said" Stephens' line, & E 41 chains 25 links to beginning or 225 ac; certified Nov. 10, 1807 by Archibald Murphey, clerk (signed) Ad Murphey, cc; [on back] altered Dec. 2, 1807; [grant is #179 in book 41 p. 172, see shuck #181 in Caswell Co in Secretary's grant files].

Corrections/Alterations to Land Grants

142. Chatham Co Nov. term 1797; order to correct error in grant #1235 to Lewis Ashman for 150 ac; correction due to his petition & act of Assembly provided in such case; instead of Lewis Ashborn as it is now on the grant Lewis Ashman be inserted; clerk to this court to certify the same to Secretary of State; Aug. 28, 1795 (signed) John Ramsey, cc; [on back] pat. altered; [closest is grant #1235 in shuck #1331 issued to Ashborn in Chatham Co in Secretary's grant files].

143. Chatham Co Feb. session 1795: petition of Levi Johnson to rectify mistake in survey granted to Levi Johnson; ordered clerk to certify to Secretary of State to alter grant #1116 for 150 ac to 265 ac; it appears to the court to be a mistake of the surveyor (signed) John Ramsey, ck; [grant in book 82 p. 251, see shuck #1211 in Chatham Co in Secretary's grant files].

144. Cherokee Co Pleas & Quarter Sessions Court Jun. term 1856; present N G Howell, J R Dyche, Stephens Rhea, Harmon Lovinggood, R B Chambers, Wm A Wigans, & E M Kilpatrick justices; petition of Alfred White: he had 88 ac surveyed by Wm McConnell on waters of Gumlog [Cr]; he paid the State & a grant issued; but surveyor made a mistake in the survey: begins at a black oak corner of No. 149, runs N18E 126 poles with line of No. 149 & Green's preemption to a small hickory on top of a ridge, W 112 poles to a corner hickory of No. 166, S78W 126 poles to a white oak, & E 112 poles to beginning; but survey as made was different: begins at a corner black oak of No. 149, runs N18E 126 poles to a small hickory on top of a ridge, E 112 poles to a stake on line of No. 166, S72W 126 poles with the line of the same to a white oak, & W 112 poles to beginning; grant is No. 2300 issued Sept. 28, 1855; because of mistake the grant is on land owned by William White due to a purchase from the State; unless the mistake is corrected, the petitioner will be seriously injured and his title to land defective; so he asks that clerk certify mistake to Secretary of State so grant can be corrected and allow other relief that "nature of the case" might require (signed) Alfred White Jun. 5, 1855 & Drury Weeks, clk; Jun. 5, 1856 Wm McConnell, surveyor, swears facts in petition are true and he made a mistake in the plat (signed) Wm McConnell & Drury Weeks, clk.   It appears to satisfaction of court that mistake was made in plat; court ordered clerk to certify the same to Secretary of State.   Drury Weeks, clerk, certifies this is true copy from records (signed) Aug. 1, 1856 Drury Weeks; [on back] alteration made Aug. 12, 1856;
　　　survey included due to certificate from agent for collection of Cherokee Bonds: 88 ac surveyed Sept. 5, 1851 for Alfred White in District No. 3 on waters of Gumlog Cr; includes his improvement [metes & bounds same as second metes & bounds above] (signed) N M Moore, Cs by B Wm McConnell DS; Thos Waldrope & C White, chain carriers; [grant in book 161 p. 137 see shuck #1132 in Cherokee Co in Secretary's grant files].

145. Chowan Co court Jun. term 1794 petition of William Bains jr to correct grant to John Wilkins sr for 200 ac issued Mar. 5, 1744; court examined the grant & find facts in petition are true; William Bains jr is entitled to remedy provided in act of General Assembly passed in 1790 at Fayetteville; ordered clerk to certify

the same to Secretary of State to error can be corrected (signed) Jos Blount, Clk;

petition of William "Baines" jr: there is an error in a grant for 200 ac issued Mar. 5, 1744 to John Wilkins sr; Baines purchased the land and found error upon surveying it: first line runs S65W instead of S65E which omits the land intended in the grant where Baines lives; so Bains asks the court to direct Secretary of State to alter grant to begin at same place at a water oak, runs S65E 104 poles, N44E 50 poles, N70W 76 poles, N47W 90 poles, N20W 33 poles, S48W 230 poles, S30E 97 poles, & N48E 200 poles to first station or 155 ac; there will be less land, but the petitioner believes he will be much benefitted & no one will be injured; George Baines sr owns all land that will be "convised" by the grant as altered (signed) William Baines jr;

survey included on W side of Beaverdam [Cr] of head of Yawpim River Swamp [metes & bounds same as second metes & bounds above, but edge of page missing]; former survey made Jan. 27, 1743 by Richd McClure, dep. surveyor & "newly" surveyed by George "Bains" sr, D surveyor; [on back] pat. altered; [grant not identified, John Wilkins did receive a grant (not this date) in Pasquotank Co].

146. Chowan Co court Dec. term 1800 petition of William Bennett (of Chowan Co): court finds Secretary of State made an error in 2 grants to William Bennett issued Apr. 18, 1794 for 2 lots in town of Edenton known as #16 & 17; William Bennett was required to register the grants in "Teyrrel" Co Register's office but by laws of the state, all grants should be registered in county where land is or Chowan Co in this case; the mistake may prove injurious to William Bennett; so it's ordered that clerk certify facts to Secretary of State so errors can be corrected agreeable to act of General Assembly in such cases (signed) Norfleet, clk; [on back] altered Nov. 18, 1801 W W; [only one grant found #536 in book 62 p. 314, see shuck #1119 in Chowan Co in Secretary's grant files].

147. Chowan Co court Jun. term 1791 petition of Malachi Halsey: on Oct. 21, 1789 Mr. John Norcom, county surveyor, surveyed for the petitioner "a piece" of land and gave a certificate which was used to obtain a grant Dec. 10, 1790 for 176 ac; there are 2 mistakes in the certificate: (a) saying includes 100 ac held by a grant to John Jones but it should be a grant to John Robinson and (b) saying date of old patent was 1727 when it should be 1714; court has hear testimony of John Norcom, examined the patent, & find the facts in the petition are true; Malachi Halsey is entitled to remedy provided by act of General Assembly passed in 1790 at Fayetteville allowing county pleas & quarter sessions courts to direct Secretary of State to correct grants when surveyor's or Secretary's errors are found; court ordered clerk to certify the errors to Secretary of State so the same can be rectified (signed) Jos Blount, clk; [on back] "dated Dec. 10, 90 done"; [grant in book 73 p. 281, see shuck #1130 in Chowan Co in Secretary's grant files].

148. [Columbus Co] Pleas & Quarter Sessions Court petitioner shows on Apr. 19, 1823 320 ac was granted to him Prosper Forney Duval on W side of Waccamaw Lake; but plat mentioned East instead of West [side of lake] (signed) Prosper Forney "Duvall"; Aug. term 1824 Columbus Co court ordered Secretary alter his

Corrections/Alterations to Land Grants

records of Forney Dugal's grant to read West instead of East & above alteration [to be made] in Register's office (signed) Chs Baldwin, clk; [on back] altered Apr. 5, 1825 (signed) Wm Hill, Sec; [grant to Prosper "Forneyduall" in book 135 p. 388, see shuck #358 in Columbus Co in Secretary's grant files].

149. Columbus Co Pleas & Quarter Sessions Court Nov. term 1858: it appears to satisfaction of court, due to petition of Warren Haynes & "proofs", that the surveyor made a mistake in grant No. 1629 issued Dec. 2, 1857 to Warren Haynes; the survey says begins at a large short straw pine Wm G Smith's corner, runs N47E 4 chains 25 links to a stake, S52W 18 chains, N50W 19 chains, & N20W 24 chains to beginning; court ordered following correction be made: begins at a large short straw pine William G Smith's corner, runs N47E 4 chains 25 links to a stake & "S50E 45 chains" is to be added to the courses; William M Baldwin, clerk, certifies within court order relating to Warren Haynes' grant (signed) Feb. 2, 1859 W M Baldwin; [grant in book 162 p. 258, see shuck #1631 in Columbus Co in Secretary's grant files].

150. petition of Ithemore Hudson to Columbus Co Pleas & Quarter Sessions Court: about 2 years ago, he had 300 ac surveyed by Josiah Powell, deputy surveyor; when the grant issued, he finds an error in the plat: "South, West, North, & East to beginning" when it should be due West from beginning, then North, then East, then to beginning; land was surveyed Sept. 30, 1818 (signed) Ithemore Hudson's mark "X". Aug. term 1820 Columbus Co Josiah Powell came to court & swore there is an error in Ithemore Hudson's plat "runs South, West, North, & East" when it should run due West 77 chains 44 links, N 38 chains 72 links, E 77 chains 44 links, & to beginning for 300 ac (signed) Josiah Powell DS; Aug. 14, 1820 I certify Josiah Powell was deputy surveyor & was sworn; ordered that above alterations be made in Secretary's office (signed) Eli Nichols, clk; [on back] altered Dec. 8, 1820 Wm Hill, Sec; [grant is #305 in book 133 p. 161, see shuck #304 in Columbus Co in Secretary's grant files].

151. petition of Frederick Sasser, guardian of John Harper a minor of George Harper deceased to Columbus Co Pleas & Quarter Sessions Court Mar. term 1835: George Harper deceased entered 300 ac in 1807 in Bladen now Columbus Co; John H White was deputy surveyor at that time & surveyed the 300 ac and made following mistake in plat to Secretary: instead of beginning & running from a white oak S24W 36 chains to a small pine, S74W 14 chains to a stake, N84W 13 chains to a small pine, S66W 74 chains to a stake near Wm Floyd's line, N38E 135 chains to a stake, S2W 44 chains 76 links to a small white oak, & N88E 22 chains 36 links to beginning; it should run as follows: begins at said white oak, runs N24E 34 chains to a small pine, N74E 14 chains to a stake, S84E 13 chains to a small pine, N66E 74 chains to a stake near Wm Floyd's line, S38W 135 chains to a stake, N2E 44 chains 72 links to a small white oak, & S88W 22 chains 36 links to beginning; George Harper deceased's dwelling house is on the last mentioned 300 ac; the proprietor will be very much injured if grant is allowed to stand without correction; petitioner asks court to order clerk to certify mistake to

Corrections/Alterations to Land Grants

Secretary of State so grant can be corrected (signed) Frederick Sasser, guardian of John Harper; [on back] altered Dec. 11, 1835;

Charles Baldwin, clerk of court, certifies at Feb. term 1835 court heard petition of Frederick Sasser, guardian of John Harper minor of George Harper deceased; petition to rectify error made by John H White, deputy surveyor in 300 ac for said deceased in 1807 [correct & incorrect metes & bounds repeated] (signed) Nov. 10, 1835 at Whiteville Chs Baldwin, clk; grant in book 125 p. 194, see shuck #39 in Columbus Co in Secretary's grant files].

152. Columbus Co Pleas & Quarter Sessions Court Jun. term 1809 to Secretary of State: due to a court order, I certify Wm Sibbet came to court & petitioned to correct a mistake in distances in a grant issued Oct. 23, 1782 to John Padget under whom the petitioner claimed; correction will include the land called for; following fact appear to satisfaction of court: the surveyor made an error in certificate to Secretary of State; lines fall short of known & established corners and include 203 ac instead of 250 ac called for in grant; first line should be 147 poles instead of 140 poles, second line 274 poles instead of 232, third line 147 poles instead of 140, & fourth line 274 poles instead of 232; court directs me to certify the same to Secretary of State so grant can be corrected (signed) Jun. 6, 1809 Job Goodman, clk; [on back] grant No. 550 issued Oct. 23, 1782 altered Dec. 22, 1809; [grant in book 47 p. 217, see shuck #3298 in Bladen Co in Secretary's grant files].

153. Craven Co court Sept. term 1801 Samuel Chapman and James Bryan & wife Rachel vs. John C Bryan & "others": petition to alter a patent; seven magistrates on the bench; petition was read & it appears that adjoining land owners were notified and no one appeared to defend; a grant issued Mar. 10, 1750 to William Herritage for 520 ac which the petitioners own; grant was produced & examined; surveyor made a mistake in eleventh line of the grant which is said to run N40W 34 chains 25 links but should "as by plat" run N4W 34 chains 25 links; ordered that clerk certify this mistake to Secretary of State so it can be corrected; I certify the same at office at Newbern Sept. 19, 1801 (signed) Saml Chapman, cc; [on back] grant to Wm Herritage dated 1758 (sic) altered Oct. 18, 1801; [grant issued in 1758 and in book 2 p. 186 see shuck #668 in Craven Co and book 16 p. 180 see shuck #2175 in Craven Co in Secretary's grant files].

154. Craven Co Pleas & Quarter Sessions Court Jun. term 1791; petition of John Dubberly read; a grant issued May 14, 1772 for 300 ac in Craven Co on S side of Glade Swamp; second course in the grant is S20E 160 poles instead of N20E 160 poles due to surveyor's mistake in platting the survey; the petitioner is much injured & asks for relief agreeable to act of Assembly made in such cases; John Allen esq is proprietor of adjoining land and has been notified agreeable to law; Allen appeared in court & consented to the alteration; ordered Mr. Secretary to have notice accordingly (signed) Saml Chapman, cc; [grant in 1772 not identified in Craven Co].

155. Craven Co Pleas & Quarter Sessions Court Nov. term 1831 present John P

Corrections/Alterations to Land Grants

Daves, Silvester Brour, John Reel, Joseph J Fowler, William B Perkins, Frederick P Latham, George Wilson, & Harely Whitferd esqs; petition of Hardy L Jones: he is legal owner of 290 ac granted Jun. 30, 1758 to Thomas Lovick; but surveyor omitted sixth course in certificate attached to grant: after the course S 150 poles "N82E 278 poles to a pine in Rutledge's line"; the court of 8 above justices heard testimony and are satisfied "N82E 278 poles" was omitted and petitioner is liable to be injured; so court ordered this fact be certified to Secretary of State. certified by James G Stanly, clerk at New Bern Nov. 17, 1831 (signed) J G Stanly; altered Jan. 7, 1832 (signed) Wm Hill, Secy; [grant in book 16 p. 202, see shuck #2195 in Craven Co in Secretary's grant files].

156. petition of Edward Nelson to Craven Co court: he wants an alteration to his grant because there is a mistake in the number of poles in the survey: line is N50E where it says 150 poles it should be 250 poles to make the compliment of acres in the grant; the plat is correct but the right number of poles is not put in as it stands. (signed) Jun. 13, 1796 Edward Nelson. "Endorsed granted". Foregoing is copy of original petition of Edward Nelson & endorsement of clerk filed in clerk's office (signed) Aug. 18, 1820 J G Stanly, cc; [on back] altered Aug. 25, 1820 (signed) Wm Hill, Secy; [grant in book 85 p. 322, see shuck #4506 in Craven Co in Secretary's grant files].

157. surveyed for William Pugh "above lines" being granted to Simon Bryan begins at a red oak on the pocoson supposed to be William Bryan's last corner "but is not", runs S30E 120 poles to the river, N50E 220 poles to a maple in the pocoson, N83W 380 poles to William Bryan's other corner "which course is wrong" but N57W 405 poles runs to said corner called for in patent which course N83W 380 poles is what your petitioner wishes the court to alter to that of N57W 405 poles which course the land intended appears in black line of plan & dotted line crosses the river is wrong [not signed];

 petition of William "Pow" to Craven Co Court: he is owner & proprietor of 300 ac granted Nov. 22, 1771 to Simon Bright; land is on N side of Neuse R & begins at William Bryan's red oak now John Allen's line, runs S30E 220 poles to the river at an oak on the river bank, N50E 220 poles to a maple in the pocoson, N51W 380 poles to said William Bryan's corner, S24E 219 poles with his line to another of his corners, & with another of his lines to beginning; the petitioner shows a surveyor's mistake was made in third line of certificate of survey; instead of N83W it should be N51W to William Bryan's corner; petitioner is liable to suffer due to the mistake; so he asks court to order clerk to certify mistake to Secretary of State according to the act in such cases (signed) E Harris, for petr. Sept. term 1802 Craven Co court present Levi Dawson, William M Herritage, Lewis Bryan, George Lane, Lewis Fonville, Thos A Green, & Sacker Dubberly; foregoing petition was read & ordered clerk certify error appears satisfactory to the court and line should be N57W 405 poles to Bryan's corner instead of N83W 320 poles; I certify the same to Secretary of State so error can be corrected (signed) Saml Chapman, cc; [on back] Wm Pew vs Sacker Dubberly altered Dec. 6, 1803; costs docketing petition £0.10, 3 continuances £0.9, entering decrees of

Corrections/Alterations to Land Grants

court £0.7.6, record copy & seals $0.7 [total] £1.13.6; [no grant identified in 1771].

158. Craven Co Pleas & Quarter Sessions Court Jun. term 1815; on second Monday in Dec. 1813 Moses Arnold, by Edward Graham his attorney, came before the justices to present his petition against David Whitford; on Nov. 17, 1743 a grant issued to John Hill for 100 ac joins his own line, begins at a pine on W side of John James' Br, runs N80E 140 poles, N40E 162 poles to a hickory, N45E 80 poles to a pine by the swamp, & to first station; there is a surveyor's error in description of plat or Secretary's error in grant; third course instead of N45E was actually run N65W; so claimants & proprietors of the land are injured & liable to be "ousted" from a greater part of the intended land; by a "regular chain of descents, devises, & conveyances" Arnold owns all the land in the grant; said Whitford is the only adjoining land owner; Whitford was notified; Arnold ask court to hear the testimony and rule in the case (signed) Moses Arnold by Edwd Graham his attorney. Subponas issued from the court to David Whitford to attend court Friday Dec. 17 "next" & signed James G Stanly, clerk second Monday in Sept. 1813 and issued Nov. 13, 1813. Subpoena was served by Reuben P Jones, sheriff who reported to Dec. 1813 court that he served subpona Nov. 17, 1813 to Whitford. Dec. 1813 court ordered a survey and case continued until second Monday in Jun. 1815 when following judges were present: John Snead, William P Moore, Hasten Dixon, John S Nelson, Isaac Wingate, Claiborne Ivey, & William M Herritage; petition was read & evidence heard; judges ordered clerk to certify an error was made in third line of the described grant; error is to be corrected so it runs N45W 80 poles instead of N45E 60 poles; so the clerk certifies to Secretary of State that there is error in third line of the grant; certified Apr. 18, 1849 by James G Stanly, clerk (signed) J G Stanly; [on back] altered Apr. 23, 1849 (signed) W Hill, Sec; [grant in book 5 p. 166 see shuck #194 and book 10 p. 15 see shuck #1022 in Craven Co in Secretary's grant files].

159. Craven Co Jun. term 1796 petition of William Phipps: the surveyor made a mistake in first course in "within" mentioned patent which says 72 degrees West but should be S72W; "the same" was examined; court ordered Secretary of State rectify the mistake & make course S72W (signed) Saml Chapman, cc by George Vulteius; [on back] altered Nov. 27, 1799; [3 grants to Phipps in Craven co in shucks 4617, 4337, & 3877 in Secretary's grant files].

160. Cumberland Co Pleas & Quarter Sessions Court Dec. 1820 petition of Richard Avera, executor of Richard Ryals deceased, to alter the courses of grant #760 for 200 ac; it appears to court that courses in the grant don't cover the premises surveyed & marked; ordered that Secretary of State alter the courses of the grant & record in his office as follows: begins at a gum in Black R, runs E 44 chains to a pine, S 55 chains to a stake, W 30 chains to a gum in Black River Swamp, & up the river to beginning; "from the minutes" John Armstrong Dec. 22, 1820 (signed) Jno Armstong, clk; [on back] altered Oct. 5, 1821 (signed) Wm Hill, Secy; [grant in book 72 p. 115, see shuck #2520 in Cumberland Co in

52

Corrections/Alterations to Land Grants

Secretary's grant files].

161. 115.5 ac granted to James Booker as 150 ac; begins at a red oak where Mimms' line & Chatham County line intersect, N30E 49 chains on the county line to a black jack in Drake's old line now James Booker's, S60E 26 chains 50 links on that line to a pine, S30W 34 chains to a stake in old Mimms' line, & W 31 chains on that line to beginning; above courses agreeable to lines run & marked by James Dyer, formerly Cumberland Co surveyor, for James Booker to cover 150 ac "as they supposed" granted Nov. 6, 1784 to said Booker but no resurvey only 115.5 ac found (signed) Dec. 15, 1802 Jas Atkins, D Surv; Daniel Booker & William Duffle, chain carriers; [plat shows two adjoining tracts 150 ac and 115.5 ac];

Cumberland Co Feb. 6, 1806 petition to court: petitioners ask court to order Secretary of State to alter the courses of a grant to James Booker, one of the petitioners, for 150 ac issued Nov. 6, 1784: begins at Mimms' corner in Chatham Co line, runs N34E 54 chains 77 links to a black jack on William Drake's line formerly now one of the petitioner's, then instead of running with that line as grant calls for run "into Chatham Co" N60W 27 chains 38 links, S30W 54 chains 77 links, & to beginning; this throws the land "altogether" into Chatham County contrary to intent of grant; courses run agreeable to old lines "on the other side" of 115.5 ac which is what the petitioners want [metes & bounds same as in survey]; "N B" James Atkins, one of petitioners is now proprietor of the land by sale from James Booker the other petitioner (signed) Jas Atkins & James Booker's mark "X". Jun. term 1806 Secretary of State is directed to alter lines of grant issued Nov. 6, 1784 to James Booker for 150 ac; certified by Robinson Mumford, clerk (signed) at Fayette Jun. 17, 1806 Robinson Mumford; [no grant this early identified for James Booker in Cumberland Co].

162. petition of John Campbell sr & John Campbell jr to Justices of Cumberland Co court: about Jun. 20, 1794 John Campbell, then county surveyor, & James McNeill, his deputy, surveyed "into the settlement" where your petitioners reside; the deputy surveyed 25 ac for John Campbell jr and the county surveyor laid off 25 ac for John Campbell sr; they made out their returns to Secretary's office for land of John Campbell sr in description of grant No. 1628 to John Campbell jr "and vice versa" put location for John Campbell jr's land in John Campbell sr's grant No. 2075 without mentioning senior or junior in returns; so petitioners ask court to direct Secretary of State to alter grant No. 1628 after "25 ac of land" strike out "beginning" in fifth line of plat & insert "between his own line & Hector McKinnon's line near Juniper Pond entered Sept. 1, 1791"; and alter grant No. 2075 after "county" in third line strike out "beginning" in seventh line & insert "by virtue of warrant No. 586 on waters of Puppy Cr near a black pond on S side of his plantation entered Aug. 27, 1793"; from foregoing statement, the surveyor's error will be visible; so they have no doubt they will meet with a speedy & effectual remedy (signed) John Campbell sr & John Campbell jr. a true copy in Aug. term 1802 (signed) Robinson Mumford, clerk. Aug. term 1802 petition was heard & court ordered prayer granted & Secretary directed to alter grants

Corrections/Alterations to Land Grants

(signed) Aug. 13, 1802 Robinson Mumford; [grant #2075 in book 107 p. 427 see shuck #3819 & grant #1628 in book 99 p. 207 see shuck #3369 in Cumberland Co in Secretary's grant files].

163. Cumberland Co Court of Pleas & Quarter Sessions Dec. term 1810: seven justices present, court ordered Secretary of State be directed to alter courses of 640 ac in grant No. 783 issued Nov. 27, 1789 to Gilbert Eccles; [alteration] agreeable to a plot made Dec. 3, 1810 by John Black as follows: begins at "A", runs N 38 chains 75 links to "B" at a pine on N side of big swamp, N65E 113 [chains] to "C" a stake, S 15 chains to Elliot's line, S36W 38 chains with said line to "E", S 25 chains to "F", then along the river to "A" 614 ac (sic) including 50 ac belonging to Neill McNeill; Robinson Mumford, clerk, certifies above is true extract from the minutes. (signed) Jun. 15, 1811 at Fayetteville Robinson Munford; [on back] altered Jun. 17, 1811;
       survey included; surveyed Dec. 3, 1810 by John Black [no chain carriers mentioned] of 640 ac granted to Gilbert "Ecles" on Lower Little R; [metes & bounds same as above]; "dotted line from Elliot's line to 'D' is distance the patent would have gone if it had been continued S to the river which would make 631 ac besides 50 ac belonging to "McNeill"; plat shows Big Swamp & "L Little" R; [grant in book 71 p. 251, see shuck #2199 in Cumberland Co in Secretary's grant files].

164. Cumberland Co Pleas & Quarter Sessions Court Dec. term 1808: petition of Robert Grice was heard; court ordered Secretary of State correct an error in grant No. 1563 issued Aug. 31, 1798 to Robert Grice for 200 ac by striking out the word "Harrisons" [Cr] in the grant & plat and inserting "Sandy" [Cr] in lieu thereof; Robinson Mumford, clerk, certifies above is true copy from the minutes. (signed) Dec. 12, 1808 at Fayetteville Robinson Mumford; [on back] altered Dec. 14, 1808; [grant in book 98 p. 241, see shuck #3308 in Cumberland Co in Secretary's grant files].

165. Cumberland Co Pleas & Quarter Sessions Court May term 1803: petition of Samuel Johnston was heard asking to correct an error in grant No. 67 issued Apr. 10, 1761 to Richard Adams; court ordered the clerk to certify to Secretary of State to alter he first course of the grant & records: after the word "beginning" instead of S20W insert N20E and in third line in place of N20E insert S20W being conformable to the marked lines; Robinson Mumford, clerk, certifies above is true copy from the minutes. (signed) May 12, 1803 at Fayetteville Robinson Mumford; [on back] altered Nov. 23, 1803; [grant in book 13 p. 274 see shuck #146 and book 15 p. 348 see shuck #304 in Cumberland Co in Secretary's grant files].

166. Cumberland Co Pleas & Quarter Sessions Court May term 1803: petition of Samuel Johnston was heard asking to correct a grant; court ordered Secretary of State alter the courses of grant No. 1850 issued Nov. 6, 1799 to Samuel Johnston for 50 ac: after the word "beginning" obliterate all the courses of the grant and insert N20W 22 chains 36 links to a stake, S70W 22 chains 36 links, S20E 22

54

chains 36 links, & to beginning being conformable to the marked lines; Robinson Mumford, clerk, certifies above is true extract from the minutes. (signed) May 12, 1803 at Fayetteville Robinson Mumford; [on back] altered Nov. 23, 1803; [grant in book 103 p. 163, see shuck #3552 in Cumberland Co in Secretary's grant files].

167. Cumberland Co Pleas & Quarter Sessions Court Sept. term 1810: ordered that Secretary of State is directed to alter second line of a grant for 500 ac issued May 18, 1787 to John Lee: on Black Pungo [to be altered] from N25E to S25E; it has been made to appears to the court that land was run & marked agreeable to intended alteration; Robinson Mumford, clerk, certifies above is true copy from the minutes. (signed) Sept. 7, 1810 at Fayetteville Robinson Mumford [on back] altered Apr. 19, 1811; [may be grant #475 issued May 18, 1789 in grant book 72 p. 7, see shuck #2237 in Cumberland Co in Secretary's grant files].

168. above plat represents 250 ac granted Dec. 31, 1801 to Alexander McAlester surrounding 80 ac granted Jun. 2, 1802 to him; it appears there is an error in plotting following courses of the surveyor's plat & certificate as is plainly seen by plating the courses of the grant which is represented by the dotted line in above plan & also by lines marked by surveyor in laying off the land: second line instead of S28W should be S78W, third line S79E should be S24E, line from "A to B" N28W should be N80W; plotted & examined May 26, 1806 (signed) Dunn. McIntyre, DS;

   petition of Alexander McAlester to justices of Cumberland Co: petitioner shows he obtained a grant for 250 ac on E side of Cape Fear R joining his own lines; the grant issued Dec. 31, 1801; by running courses & distances of the grant, second & third courses are different from the survey and eleventh line represented in annexed plan as "A to B" [is in error]; so petitioner prays the 3 lines be corrected: second line to runs S78W, third line to run S24E, & eleventh line N80W instead of S28W, S79E, & N48W; petitioner also prays court will direct an order to Secretary of State to correct the grant (signed) Alexr McAlester;

   Cumberland Co Jun. term 1806: grant No. 2303 issued Dec. 31, 1801 to Alexander McAlester for 250 ac; by his petition McAlester represents there is an error in courses of the grant & surveyor's plat; 7 justices present & court ordered Secretary of State to correct the figures in second line from S28W to S78W, in third line from S79E to S24E, & eleventh line from N48W to N80W; Robinson Mumford, clerk, certifies above is true copy of th minutes. (signed) Jun. 17, 1806 at Fayetteville Robinson Mumford; [4 grants issued to Alexander McAlester on this date, see shucks 4094, 4099, 4100, & 4102 in Cumberland Co in Secretary's grant files].

169. Cumberland Co Pleas & Quarter Sessions Court May term 1802: petition of John McDaniel was heard asking to rectify an error in a grant; court ordered Secretary of State to correct grant issued Dec. 2, 1768 to Richard Lyon for 400 ac by inserting after termination of first line & distance following course & distance "then S45W 63 chains 25 links to a stake & 3 pine pointers"; Robinson Mumford, clerk, certifies above is true extract from the minutes. (signed) May 27, 1802 at

Corrections/Alterations to Land Grants

Fayetteville Robinson Mumford; [on back] altered Nov. 16, 1802; [grant in book 23 p. 318, see shuck #1526 in Cumberland Co in Secretary's grant files].

170. Cumberland Co Pleas & Quarter Sessions Court Sept. term 1831: petition of Archibald McKellar to alter a grant; it appeared to satisfaction of court that surveyor made an error in a certificate of survey viz: N32E 24 chains as represented in the plat; court ordered that it be certified to Secretary of State that the error exists and needs to be corrected. (signed) Sept. 27, 1831 D "McDiamia", clerk; [on back] Archd "McKeller" altered May 12, 1832 (signed) Wm Hill, Secry; [A McKeller received 7 grants in Cumberland Co].

171. Cumberland Co Apr. term 1800: at this term Hector McNiell presented his grant for 200 ac; but 250 ac were actually entered, paid for, & surveyed but only 200 ac were granted; court ordered the clerk to certify the same to Secretary of State's office so error can be corrected [grant] No. 1708 issued Jun. 7, 1799; Robinson Mumford, clerk certifies above is true extract from the minutes. (signed) Nov. 7, 1800 at Fayetteville R Mumford; [on back] altered Dec. 10, 1802; [grant in book 102 p. 148, see shuck #3449 in Cumberland Co in Secretary's grant files].

172. Cumberland Co Jul. term 1794: court ordered clerk to certify to Secretary that grant No. 1204 issued to Hugh McRanie contains an error in second line which should be 160 poles "in room" of 108; copy from minutes (signed) John Ingram, cc; [on back] Hugh McRanie dated 1754; [grant not identified in Cumberland or Bladen Counties].

173. Cumberland Co Pleas & Quarter Sessions Court Dec. term 1808: petition of John Peterson heard by 7 justices; petition asks that words "a small pine on E side of Little Creek" in the plat & grant No. 2127 issued May 14, 1800 to John Peterson for 100 ac be struck out and in place insert words "large pine E of head of a small branch of Little Creek deemed in or near Alexander Graham's upper line"; court ordered it be certified to Secretary of State to alter aforesaid [grant] & record in his office; a true copy from minutes. (signed) Robinson Mumford, clerk; [on back] altered Nov. 12, 1810; [grant is book 107 p. 449, see shuck #3871 in Cumberland Co in Secretary's grant files].

174. Cumberland Co Nov. 20, 1805 surveyed agreeable to old lines & marked by James Dyer, former surveyor, 142.5 ac on Beaverdam [Cr] that was surveyed for William Senter for sai Dyer as 150 ac due to courses from Secretary's office: begins at a large red oak in Hayes' line formerly Senter's, runs W 7 chains to a stake in old Elkin's line, S38 chains with that line to a corner post oak, W36 chains 50 links as "the other" line crossing Beaverdam [Cr] to a corner post oak, N17 chains to a pine in Hays' (sic) line formerly Drake's, N60W 9 chains 50 links as that line to James Atkins' corner pine formerly Booker's, S30W 35 chains with that line to a stake on old Mimms' line, S39 chains 50 links with that line crossing Beaverdam [Cr] to a corner hickory, S 10 chains with the other line to James Atkins corner of his 380 ac survey, E 29 chains with his line to his corner pine, N

56 chains with "his other" line & past the corner to beginning (signed) Jas Atkins, D Surveyor; [old Mimms' land indicated beside 142.5 ac on plat];

Feb. 6, 1806 Cumberland Co court: the petitioner prays the court will order the Secretary of State to alter a grant issued Nov. 6, 1784 for 150 ac to William Senter and insert courses agreeable to plat on other side [of this sheet] as these courses "is" agreeable to lines marked round the land by the surveyor; [metes & bounds repeated]; 142.5 ac found instead of 150 ac (signed) Jas Atkins "his" [attorney ?] Wm Senter's mark "X".   To Cumberland Co court: Please grant the prayer of within petition since it does not concern me although it joins 3 of my lines (signed) Owen Juton's mark "P".   Cumberland Co Jun. term 1806 Secretary of State is directed to alter lines of a grant issued Nov. 6, 1784 to William Senter for 150 ac agreeable to petition of William Senter & James Atkins; Robinson Mumford, clerk, certifies above is true extract from the minutes and he certifies attached surveyor's pot and petition are true copies from originals in office. (signed) Jun 17, 1806 Robinson Mumford; [grant in book 55 p. 309, see shuck #1903 in Cumberland Co in Secretary's grant files].

175. Cumberland Co Pleas & Quarter Sessions Court Jun. term 1810: petition of Daniel Smith heard; 7 justices present; petition asks to correct an error in a grant issued Dec. 6, 1809 to "him" for 50 ac; court ordered Secretary of State in "last place" where patentee's name is mentioned in the grant alter the word or name "May" and insert word or name "Smith" to make the patent "perfect" in name of Daniel Smith; Robinson Mumford, clerk, certifies above is true copy from minutes. (signed) Oct. 31, 1810 at Fayetteville Robinson Mumford; [on back] altered Dec. 4, 1810; [Daniel Smith received 2 grants on this date see shucks #4497 & 4498 in Cumberland Co in Secretary's grant files].

176. Cumberland Co Oct. session 1798: court ordered Secretary of State alter record of grant issued Nov. 6, 1784 to Isaac Williams in third line "from" S58W 36 chains 75 links with Smith's line "to" S25W 33 chains with David Smith's line to Williams' corner red oak AND record of a grant issued Nov. 27, 1789 to said Isaac Williams for 100 ac in first line "from" S10E "to" S10W (signed) R Mumford, cc; [on back] grants altered Dec. 27, 1799; [first grant in grant book 55 p. 334 see shuck #1978 and second grant in book 71 p. 296 see shuck #2207 in Cumberland Co in Secretary's grant files].

177. Currituck Co Mr. No. 15 Jun. 9, 1787 Edward Doughty enters 200 ac of juniper & gum swamp, begins at a cypress tree in line of Messrs Doughty & Haymon's entry "viz" about 7 miles from Moyock Mill in said county a South course 25 East 80 chains along said line to a juniper, S0E 40 chains to a maple, "northerly" 40 chains to a bay, N25W 80 chains to a loral, & to first station (signed) Thos Younghusband, ET; ordered for survey Oct. 8, 1787; copy (signed) Wm Taylor Dy. CCC;

Currituck Co Aug. term 1796: present "the justices": court ordered Samuel Ferebe be appointed surveyor to correct a survey Josiah Nicholson made for Mr. Edward Doughty dated Oct. 10, 1788 (signed) Wm Taylor, Dy CCC;

Corrections/Alterations to Land Grants

survey Nov. 12, 1796 for 200 ac of swamp land entered Jun. 9, 1787 by Mr. Edwd Doughty as by copy of entry No. 15 and surveyed Oct. 15, 1788 by Josiah Nicholson which contains following errors: he says begins at a cypress in the Virginia line at a corner of Edwd Doughty & Hayman's patent it is nearly 2 miles from Virginia line, then he goes round "right title" the distance in fifth course where he says 95 chains but it is only 80 chains, then he says being West which is wrong "if" he had said East, but I say N45E 20 chains to beginning; I certify the errors by order of Aug. court 1796 (signed) S Ferebee, Dy Cy Surv; [metes & bounds indicated on plat: S25E 80 chains along Doughty & Hayman's line to juniper, S60E 4 chains to gum, S45W 20 chains to maple, N60W 40 chains to a bay, N25W 30 chains to a laurel, & N45E 20 chains];

Nov. term 1796 present the justices: court ordered the clerk send to Secretary of State a copy of surveyor's return of errors in grant to Edward Doughty dated Nov. 13, 1790 (signed) Wm Taylor, Dy CCC; [on back] altered agreeable to within order Oct. 13, 1797 (signed) Wm Hill, D Sec; [may be grant in book 74 p. 181, see shuck #474 in Currituck Co in Secretary's grant files].

178. Currituck Co court Nov. term 1819: Thomas C Ferebee petition to court to correct errors in a grant issued Oct. 29, 1782: cause was heard and grant & survey exhibited; court decreed following errors are in the patent: (a) the patent contains 1 rood 24 poles less than the survey, (b) the course W 60 chains in the patent is W 10 chains in the survey, & (c) the course W 10 chains in the patent is W 60 chains in the survey; ordered the clerk certify the errors to Secretary of State; it is proved to satisfaction of court that Thomas C Ferebee is entitled to the premises in his petition; Thomas Baxter, clerk, certifies foregoing decree is true from minutes of Nov. term "last" (signed) Dec. 8, 1819 T Baxter, ccc; [on back] altered Dec. 19, 1820;

petition of Thomas Cooper Ferebee to Currituck Co Pleas & Quarter Sessions Court May term 1819: William Ferebee entered land & "samp" and had the same surveyed by Josiah Nicholson, county surveyor, Oct. 22, 1779; following are courses in the survey the petitioner is ready to produce: 497 ac 1 rood & 24 poles begins at a gum in the fork, runs N45E 20 chains, N26E 15 chains, N13W 45 chains to a corner gum in Gregory's line, W 10 chains to Hutchins' line, N 80 chains along his line, W 60 [chains] to a maple, & S23 1/4E 182 chains to first station; William Ferebee applied to Gov. Alexander Martin & J Glasgow, Secretary of State, for a "correct & regular" patent for the land according to law; patent was issued Oct. 29, 1782 which the petitioner is ready to produce; there are following mistakes by the Secretary in description of land in the grant: there is 1 rood & 24 poles more land in the survey since patent calls for 497 ac only, a line of survey calls for W 10 chains to Hutchins' line but is W 60 chains to Hutchins' line in patent, another line is survey is W 60 chains to a maple but is W 10 chains to a maple in patent; the patentee is injured; William Ferebee devised the land by will dated Jul. 1, 1783 to the petitioner and James Ferebee "another of his sons" as tenants in common; the will was "duly proved"; due to deed dated Jun. 7, 1795 James Ferebee sold his moiety to John Humphries (of Currituck Co); by his will dated Dec. 19, 1795 John Humphries devised "among other things" that his

58

Corrections/Alterations to Land Grants

executors sell the land; on Jun. 18, 1796 executors Joseph Ferebee & Samuel Ferebee sold Humphries' interest to the petitioner and "obtained a deed" dated Nov. 24, 1798; petitioner is ready to produce the wills & deeds; he asks court to examine the patent & rectify the errors (signed) Thomas C Ferebee [no date] a true copy (signed) T Baxter, CCC; [on separate sheet] Thomas Baxter, clerk, certifies annexed is true copy of original petition of Thomas C Ferebee before May 1819 court (signed) Dec. 8, 1819 T Baxter, CCC; grant in book 48 p. 243, see shuck #376 in Currituck Co in Secretary's grant files].

179. Currituck Co Feb. term 1798 present "the justices"; court ordered, on petition of John Northern esq to rectify an error in a patent issued Dec. 20, 1748 to Saml Bright, that county surveyor survey the patent & correct the errors & make return to next court (signed) Wm Taylor Dy CCC;

    Currituck Co Aug. term 1799 present the justices; petition of John Northern esq was heard about error in grant issued Dec. 20, 1748 to Samuel Bright; court ordered clerk to certify to Secretary of State alter the course & distance of the grant "where they may not agree with course & distance" of "ennexed" plat returned by surveyor to this court agreeable to act of Assembly made in such case (signed) J Baxter, Dy CCC. Aug. term 1799 I certify Samuel Ferebee esq is lawful surveyor qualified in open court (signed) J Baxter Dy CCC;

    survey: 660 ac surveyed Sept. 10, 1748 by Richd McCluer for Samuel Bright: courses of patent follow: begins at a poplar in Light Swamp "so called", runs S35W 34 chains to Richard Bright's corner gum, S15W 51 chains along hs line to Ephraim Bright's corner sowerwood, S73W 47 chains along his line to a beach [in] Ephraim Bright's & Henry Bright's line, S14E 18 chains along Henry Bright's line to an oak, S27W 14.5 chains to a gum, S 20 chains, E 23 chains, N51W "which is wrong" the true course N51E 106 chains along "in" Great Swamp to a holley in Joseph Haymen's line, N55W 6.5 chains along his line to his corner maple, N38E 7.5 chains to a beach, N70W 6.5 chains to an oak, N10W 18 chains to a gum, N29E 37 chains to a water oak in Light Swamp "above said", & to first station; I certify eighth course N51W is wrong and true course is N51E (signed) May 10, 1798 S Ferebee; [on back] altered Nov. 28, 1799; [grant in book 11 p. 75, see shuck #182 in Secretary's grant files].

180. Currituck Co Aug. term 1792 petition of Thomas Payne & "others" about errors in a patent: after hearing testimony at Aug. term 1792 about "the ruth" of allegations in petition, court ordered clerk to certify to Secretary of State that courses & distances of William Nicholson's patent issued Nov. 8, 1714 don't agree with courses & distances mentioned hereafter; Secretary to alter the grant: begins at a red oak, runs S60W 104 poles to a pine, S4W 50 poles to a maple, S37E 40 poles to a pine, S23E 116 poles to a red oak, S56 1/2E 120 poles to the main road, S38E 72 poles to a pine stump in Hosea Ball's "plantation", S37E 40 poles to a hickory stump in said "plantation", S15E 40 poles to a stake where a pine & hickory had stood, S25E 80 poles to a white oak, S27E 86 poles 10 links to an oak stump, S14E 9 poles 8 links to a white oak at Reedy Br, S 19 poles to a maple, S15E 31 poles to a gum, S35E 36 poles to a red oak, S20E 19 poles 9 links to a

pine stump, S25W 20 poles, S15E 40 poles, S60E 26 poles, S26E 42 poles, S35E 60 poles, N70E 96 poles to a pine on "Easteran" Swamp, & along said swamp to first station (signed) Hollo Williams, CCC; [on back] Paynes et al vs Ball et all; [grant in book 8 p. 245, see shuck #1292 in Secretary's grant files].

181. Currituck Co Feb. term 1797 present the justices: court ordered Thomas Poyner, county survey, "run the patten" of John Whitehead & correct errors in th patent issued Mar. 26, 1743 (signed) Wm Taylor Dy CCC;

Currituck Co May term 1797 present the justices: court ordered the clerk to "send up" to Secretary of State a copy of surveyor's return of errors in a grant issued Mar. 26, 1743 to John Whitehead (signed) Wm Taylor Dy CCC; [no description of correction in shuck]; [on back] altered agreeable to order Oct. 13, 1797 (signed) P Malone, DS; [grant in book 5 p. 88 see shuck #92 and book 4 p. 110 see shuck #84 in Currituck Co in Secretary's grant files].

182. Dobbs Co Jan. term 1794 petition of James Cannon (of Dobbs Co) was read; petition describes an error in certificate of survey for him returned by the surveyor for 400 ac on Sellars Br & waters thereof; mistake was inserting word "East" instead of "West" in first course; he prays the court to order the same altered in Secretary's office agreeable to act of Assembly made in such cases; court ordered Secretary be directed to make the record "conformable thereto" (signed) W Caswell, clerk; [on back] James Cannon, Glasgow [Co]; [grant in book 29 p. 347, see shuck #1291 in Dobbs Co in Secretary's grant files].

183. Dobbs Co Oct. term 1791 petition of James Taylor was read; petition describes mistake made by surveyor in plat for grant issued Nov. 16, 1790 to him for 41 ac; the petitioner asks for mistake to be rectified; court ordered Secretary be directed to make "such alterations" as necessary in the grant "which is" John Faircloth instead of William Faircloth (signed) W Caswell, clerk; [on back] Wy Taylor's order to alter a patent, Glasgow [Co]; [no grant to John Faircloth identified, only one grant to William Faircloth in 1782, see shuck #1942 in Dobbs Co].

184. Duplin Co Jan. term 1803: Samuel Evens came to court & "suggested" there was an error in grant No. 1626 issued Aug. 29, 1799 to him for 20 ac; court ordered the county surveyor to inspect the grant and "assertain" & report to court the error if any so the same can be rectified as law directs in such cases; Joseph Dickson esq, county surveyor, reported the plat & "body" of the patent contains an error where it says N62E but should say N62W which follows John Avers' line as set forth in grant and will cover land surveyed "signed" Joseph Dickson, surveyor. certified by order of court (signed) Wm Dickson, CC; [on back] altered agreeable to order Nov. 30, 1808 (signed) W W; [grant in book 103 p. 72, see shuck #3425 in Duplin Co in Secretary's grant files].

185. [plat shows land is 610 ac on Muddy Cr & Staffords Br] errors in line of "this" patent are by being all of them too long (sic) as set forth in figures above

Corrections/Alterations to Land Grants

[on plat, only numbers shown on plat, no compass directions] line1 is "instead of" 80 poles 96 poles, #2 is 125 poles instead of 108 poles, #3 is 92 poles instead of 80 poles, #4 is 80 poles instead of 60 poles, #5 is 106 poles instead of 60 poles, #6 is 146 poles instead of 122 poles, #7 is 278 poles instead of 220 poles, #8 is 106 poles instead of 80 poles, #9 is 124 poles instead of 112 poles, #10 is 184 poles instead of 140 poles, #11 is 100 poles instead of 80 poles, #12 is 177 poles instead of 80 poles, #13 is 127 poles "and is" 127 poles, #14 is 127 poles instead of 80 poles, & #15 is 150 poles instead of 100 poles. The above are all to be altered in the records agreeable to resurvey so land will correspond with location in certificate of original survey and will contain 610 ac instead of 330 ac as appears by an "accurate" resurvey on the premises Apr. 14, 1797 (signed) Joseph Dickson, surveyor. Duplin Co Apr. term 1797 clerk is to certify Joseph Dickson is lawful surveyor of Duplin Co & had an order of county court to make within resurvey (signed) Wm Dickson, CC; [on back] altered record agreeable hereto [no date]; [grant in book 17 p. 174 see shuck #815 in Duplin Co in Secretary's grant files].

186. Duplin Co Jul. term 1819 Stephen Miller sr came to court & petitioned for alteration of a word in a grant for 500 ac on W side of NE branch of Cape Fear R & SW side of Woodwards Chase Cr issued Sept. 21, 1741 to William McRee then in New Hanover Co; error in patent is S70W 339 poles to a black oak but on resurvey on "ancient" marked lines of original survey runs S50W 339 poles to a black oak "the" ancient marked corner tree of said 500 ac survey and "appears to be" the true ancient marked line of grant to William McRee now possessed by Stephen Miller; court considered the matter & judged the error was a "means of some misprission in filling up" the patent; it should have said S50W 339 poles instead of S70W 339 poles to a black oak; court ordered such alteration be made and clerk to certify the same so alteration can be done in Secretary's office instead of S70W say S50W 339 poles to a black oak with will "set the matter right" and enable the patent to cover the land as originally surveyed (signed) Wm Dickson, CC; [on back] altered Dec. 22, 1823 (signed) Wm Hill, Secy; [grant in book 9 p. 389 see shuck #854 and book 8 p. 95 see shuck #563 in New Hanover Co in Secretary's grant files].

187. Duplin Co Apr. 1805 Jesse George came to court & "suggested" there was an error in his grant No. 989 issued Jul. 11, 1788 for 50 ac; court ordered county surveyor to go to the premises & "assertain" the error if any & report to next court; certified by order of court (signed) Wm Dickson CC;

[on a small sheet] 50 ac in grant No. 989 issued Jul. 11, 1788 to him: Jan. 18, 1806 plotted & found there was an error in the third line of grant where it says "North" instead of "South" and then "the given" line agrees with the grant (signed) Jn Stallings, DS; [on back] Mr. Stallings will observe his certificate of survey is not full enough to return to Secretary's office & paper did not contain enough room for clerk's certificate, Mr. Stallings will please sign the certificate I have drawn above my own (signed) Wm Dickson;

[on large sheet] pursuant to order of Duplin Co court Apr. term 1805, I surveyed & examined lines of grant No. 989 issued Jul. 11, 1788 to Jesse George for 50 ac; I find survey contains 50 ac but there is an error in surveyor's return;

Corrections/Alterations to Land Grants

third line of survey & grant says N 150 poles which is wrong; it should say S 150 poles which will be agreeable to the survey & cover land intended; surveyed Jan. 18, 1806 [not signed]. Duplin Co Jan. term 1806 the above return made by John Stallings, deputy surveyor appointed by court, & "deemed" by the court; pursuant to directions of court I certify the same to Secretary of State Jan. 24, 1806 (signed) Wm Dickson, CC; survey begins at a pine, runs N30E 70 poles, N49W 136 poles, S 150 poles, & E 70 poles; [on back] altered Oct. 17, 1806; [grant in book 66 p. 331, see shuck #2834 in Duplin Co in Secretary's grant files].

188. Duplin Co Apr. 1797 pursuant to order of court in favor of John Goff sr directing Joseph Dickson, county surveyor, to examine the lines of patent No. 262 issued Apr. 1, 1780 to John Goff; Joseph Dickson reports he proceeded to examine the plat & grant and finds an error in fifth line of certificate of plat & the grant: the words "West 180 poles" are omitted & should be inserted to cover the land surveyed & granted; court has concurred with report & ordered clerk to certify the same to Secretary's office; certified Apr. 23, 1797 (signed) Wm Dickson, ccc; [on back] altered agreeably Apr. 23, 1797 (sic); [John Goff sr received 4 grants in Duplin Co (but no #262), see shucks #2053, 2130, 2876, & 2906 in Secretary's grant files].

189. Duplin Co Oct. term 1796 pursuant to order of court passed Apr. term 1796 directing Joseph Dickson, county surveyor, to make an accurate survey of 200 ac granted Dec. 21, 1763 to Jeremiah Hand on branches of Rockfish [Cr] joining Fairis' land; it is "suggested" there is an error in the patent; Joseph Dickson reports [the land] begins at a pine, runs N13E 25 chains to a pine "the second corner", N77W 45 chains the second line to center of 3 pines "note" this second line as copied from record "reads" N77W 25 chains which doesn't reach the corner or include the quantity of land; the error is in second line which if extended to 45 chains will come to original marked corner tree of the survey; all other lines agree with the record & will include the "just" quantity of 200 ac; it appears this mistake is either in the surveyor or Secretary; but patent & original plat are lost and it can't be assertained which (signed) Joseph Dickson, survr. The above is true "coppey" of county surveyor's report to county court and was filed in clerk's office and ordered certified to Secretary's office. certified Oct. 20, 1796 (signed) Wm Dickson, CC; [on back] altered Dec. 24, 1797; [grant in book 13 p. 44 see shuck #355 and book 17 p. 2 see shuck #732 in Duplin Co in Secretary's grant files].

190. Duplin Co Jul. term 1798: pursuant to order of said court in favor of John Munrow directing Joseph Dickson, county surveyor, to "assertain" lines of grant No. 671 issued Dec. 10, 1784 to William Mercer for 100 ac; it is suggested there was an error in lines of the land; Joseph Dickson reports: he resurveyed the lines of the 100 ac agreeable to original marks and found an error in thirteenth line by omitting words "N50E 20 poles" which should be inserted; by inserting those words, the plat will be made conformable to survey & cover land surveyed; court concurred with the report & ordered the clerk to certify the same to Secretary's office; certified Jul. 23, 1798 (signed) Wm Dickson, CC; [on back] altered Jul.

Corrections/Alterations to Land Grants

23, 1798 (sic); [grant in book 55 p. 171, see shuck #2818 in Duplin Co in Secretary's grant files].

191. Duplin Co Jul. term 1798: pursuant to order of said court in favor of Joseph Screws directing Joseph Dickson, county surveyor, to examine lines of grant No. 1536 issued Jan. 8, 1798 to Joseph Screws for 150 ac; Joseph Dickson reports he resurveyed the 150 ac agreeable to the plat & found an error in third & fifth lines of the plat: the word "Dog" is inserted instead of word "Buckhorn" [so] expunge the word "Dog" and insert "Buckhorn" which will "assertain" beginning of the land agreeable to the boundaries; court concurred with report & ordered clerk to certify the same to Secretary's office; certified Jul. 23, 1798 (signed) Wm Dickson, CC; [on back] altered Jul. 23, 1798 [sic]; [grant in book 95 p. 93, see shuck #3395 in Duplin Co in Secretary's grant files].

192. Duplin Co Jan. term 1808: it has been "suggested" to court by Frederick Smith that there is an error in grant No. 1329 for 159 ac on E side of NE River; court ordered county surveyor to examine the grant & report to court if there is any error; Basil Kornegay, county surveyor, pursuant to said order examined the grant & reports that on running grant #1329 for Frederick Smith for 150 ac the first line calls for N75E but it should run S75E agreeable to the marked line "signed" B Kornegay, survr; court ordered the clerk to certify the same so it can be rectified in records in Secretary's office; certified from the minutes (signed) Jan. 22, 1808 Wm Dickson, CC; [on back] altered Nov. 30, 1808;
   [on a small sheet] I certify that on running grant No. 1329 for Fredk Smith sr for 150 ac the first line "for" N75E should be S75E agreeable to the marked trees (signed) B Kornegay, survr; [grant in book 79 p. 487, see shuck #3213 in Duplin Co in Secretary's grant files].

193. Duplin Co Jul. term 1797: read petition of Andrew Thally asking for a resurvey of 640 ac on Maxwell Swamp "formerly & originally" granted to Eleazer Allen & now possessed by Andrew Thally; county surveyor was directed to resurvey the same & return the plan to this court so court can make such order as consistant with law; [request] granted; pursuant to order of court Joseph Dickson resurvey 640 ac originally granted to Eleazer Allen; on running the lines, he finds fourth lines is wrong on the "coppey" of the record which says S60E 3 poles but should be S60E 320 poles; then the whole survey would be right & land covered agreeable to original intention (signed) Jul. 20, 1797 Jo Dickson, survr; court ordered the clerk certify the same to Secretary's office so record can be made agreeable to surveyor's report; certified by order of court (signed) Wm Dickson, cc; [grant not identified in Duplin Co].

194. Duplin Co Oct. 1795: pursuant to order of court issued Jul. term "last" directing Joseph Dickson, county surveyor, to resurvey lines of grant to Joel Wilder for 300 ac; Joseph Dickson reports he resurveyed the land and finds a "manifest" error in the second line of the grant which says N45E 200 poles which is wrong and should be S45W 160 poles in order to cover the land surveyed for

Corrections/Alterations to Land Grants

the grant; the court concurred with the report & ordered the clerk to certify the same to Secretary's office; certified by order of court (signed) Wm Dickson, cc; [grant not identified in Duplin Co].

195. Duplin Co Jan. term 1802: William "Wilkings" came to court & "suggested" there was an error in grant No. 297 issued Apr. 1, 1780 to Absalom Langston for 191 ac; Wilkings is in possession of the grant; court ordered county surveyor to "assertain" the error if any & report the same to county court; Joseph Dickson, county surveyor, came to court & rendered his report of the grant for 191 ac: he inspected the grant & plat and finds the surveyor who returned the plat made an error in the certificate in first line; the true course is S25W 180 poles; the certificate & grant say S25E 180 poles to a stake; to make it right & make land agreeable to original survey the first line must read S25W 180 poles to a stake and "so on" in the certificate "signed" Jo Dickson, survr; court ordered the clerk send the above report to Secretary's office so error can be rectified; certified by order of court (signed) Jan. 23, 1802 Wm Dickson, CC; [on back] altered Jan. 28, 1802; [grant in book 41 p. 128, see shuck #2026 in Duplin Co in Secretary's grant files].

196. Duplin Co Jan. term 1803 Aaron Williams came to court & produced grant No. 1661 issued Apr. 14, 1800 to him for 100 ac; Williams "suggested" there was an error in the courses of the grant; court ordered county surveyor to examine the grant & report to court the errors if any and "assertain" the same so they can be rectified according to law in such cases; Joseph Dickson, county surveyor reported there are following errors in body of certificate of grant: in eighth line the platt says N70W but it should be S70W & in eleventh line it says 78 poles but should be 28 poles; these alterations, when made, will make land "right" as surveyed in original survey "signed" Joseph Dickson, county survr; certified by order of court (signed) Wm Dickson, CC; [on back] altered Dec. 17, 1804; [grant in book 106 p. 443, see shuck #3453 in Duplin Co in Secretary's grant files].

197. Duplin Co Jan. term 1804: John Winder came to court & "suggested" there was an error in grant #348 issued Nov. 22, 1771 to him for 200 ac in Goshen Swamp; court ordered county surveyor to inspect the same & report to the court; pursuant to above order, William Beck, county surveyor, inspected the grant & plat and reported the second line is wrong; it says S50W 200 poles but should say S50E 200 poles which will agree with the line of the survey & cover land surveyed for which patent was intended; court ordered the error rectified as law directs in such cases; certified Jan. 21, 1804 (signed) Wm Dickson, CC; [on back] altered Dec. 14, 1804;

survey: on running lines of 200 ac granted to John Winder on Goshen Swamp, second line is wrong; instead of S50E 200 poles it says S50W 200 poles which can be seen by observing "the original" (signed) B Kornegay, D Sur for Wm Beck sur; [plat shows survey runs N25E 110 poles from swamp to a pine, S50E 200 poles to a white oak, S25W 26 poles to a "W O", S55E 286 poles, S 60 poles, along swamp to beginning; [grant in book 22 p. 295, see shuck #1347 in Duplin Co in Secretary's grant files].

Corrections/Alterations to Land Grants

198. Duplin Co Pleas & Quarter Sessions Court Oct. term 1836: Burwell Williams to the court petition to alter a grant: on reading the petition, it was made to appear to satisfaction of court by testimony of Daniel Jones, county survey, & plat he returned that there was an error made by the surveyor in running land granted Mar. 5, 1746 to Robert Beverly; court ordered prayer of petition granted; clerk to certify to Secretary of State that an error in "the" course which reads N65E but should be S65W and course which reads S65W should be N65E. Duplin Co clerk's office to William Hill, Secretary of State: I James Dickson, clerk, certifies above is true copy of decree of court in suit of Burrell Williams to the court (signed) Mar. 10, 1837 James Dickson, clerk; [on back] altered Mar. 25, 1837 (signed) Wm Hill, Secy; [grant in book 5 p. 256 see shuck #279 and book 10 p. 98 see shuck #932 in New Hanover Co in Secretary's grant files].

199. Edgecombe Co: It has been made to appear to county court by Coburn Eason that he made a land entry and it was surveyed by Frederick Philips, county surveyor; there is a "very considerable" error in surveyor's return to the Secretary's office; for remedy Eason presented his petition asking for order to the Secretary to rectify the error; the prayer of petition was granted; following alterations to be made in the land grant "vizt" instead of "begins at Samuel Davis' corner pine in said Eason's line, runs E 13 poles along said line to Isaac Eason's corner pine, N 96 poles along said Eason's line to Samuel Davis' corner pine, W 103 poles along said Davis' line to his other corner pine, & to first station"; the courses should be "begins at Coburn Eason's own corner pine, runs E 103 poles to Isaac Eason's corner pine, N 96 poles along said Isaac Eason's line to a pine in Samuel Davis' line, W 103 poles along said Davis' line to said Davis' corner pine, & S to first station". (signed) Aug. term 1794 Edward Hall; [on back] No. 600 Coburn Eason 61 3/4 [ac] "Edgecomb" Co patent altered Jun. 5, 1795; [grant book 78 p. 504, see shuck #2896 in Edgecombe Co in Secretary's grant files].

200. Edgecombe Co Nov. term 1792: Andrew Greer vs Alexander Godwin, John Deloach, & Benjamin Farmer--petition: the cause was tried "this day" and court decreed prayer of petition be granted "vizt" ninth and eleventh lines of patent "set forth" in petition [be corrected by] Secretary; instead of words "Alexander Godwin" insert words "David Godwin" and also in plat instead of "Alexander Godwin" insert words "David Godwin"; it appears to court by sufficient testimony that allegations in petition are true and the same to be certified by the clerk of court to the Secretary; true copy of decree (signed) Edward Hall; [on back] Andrew Greer, altered 1793; [grant #340 issued Nov. 15, 1797, grant book 62 p. 158, see shuck #2830 in Edgecombe Co in Secretary's grant files].

201. Edgecombe Co Nov. term 1792: Laurance OBryan vs Alexander Godwin, John Deloach, Samuel Deloach, & James Barnes--petition: the cause was tried "this day" and court decreed prayer of petition be granted "vizt" ninth and eleventh lines of patent "set forth" in petition [be corrected by] Secretary; instead of words "Alexander Godwin" insert words "David Godwin" and also in plat

instead of "Alexander Godwin" insert words "David Godwin"; it appears to court by sufficient testimony that allegations in petition are true and the same to be certified by the clerk of court to the Secretary; true copy of decree (signed) Edward Hall; [on back] Laurence OBryan, altered 1793; [grant #333 issued Nov. 15, 1787, grant book 62 p. 151, see shuck #2829 in Edgecombe Co in Secretary's grant files].

202. Edgecombe Co May session 1797: ex parte John Sutherland jr: the cause was heard this term before Edgecombe Co justices with majority of justices present; the substance of "said John's" petition was that John Earl Granville, formerly one of Lords Proprietor of this state, granted on Mar. 25, 1749 to William Davis 221 ac in Edgecombe Co; John Earl Granville's secretary made a mistake in describing the land as follows: "begins at a pine in his (the said patentee's) other line on N side of Hendricks Cr, runs N45E 140 poles along his line to his corner red oak, N45W 260 poles to a live oak, S45W 140 poles to a white oak on the creek, & down the creek to the first station"; but grant only says "begins at a pine in his other line on N side of Hendricks Cr, runs N45E 140 poles along his line to his corner red oak, S45W 140 poles to a white oak on the creek, & down the creek to the first station" which omits the second corse N45W 260 poles to a live oak; the petitioner "regularly deduces" his title from said Davis, the patentee and charges that because of this mistake his title to land is in question and he may be subjected to "considerable" trouble, expenses, & eventually "real danger"; he asks for relief due to act of Assembly passed in 1790 Chapter 15; on hearing proofs & examining the grant & survey, it appears clear to us that John Earl Granville's secretary made a mistake in making out the grant by leaving out N45W 260 poles to a live oak and following course is correct [first metes & bounds above are repeated]; the patent should be rectified; court ordered clerk to certify true courses to Secretary of State of grant by John Earl Granville on Mar. 25, 1749 to William Davis on Hendericks Cr [first metes & bounds above repeated]; second course N45W 260 poles to a live oak was omitted in the grant; certified May 25, 1797 at Tarborough (signed) Edward Hall, cc; [on back] grant altered Jun. 1797; [grant book 11 p. 157 see shuck #1135 and grant book 11 p. 165 see shuck #1167 in Edgecombe Co in Secretary's grant files].

203. [petition & survey are in pieces] Edgecombe Co Nov. term 1791: Josiah Sugg & executors of will of William Sugg "late" of Edgecombe Co deceased "that is to say" Matthew Stockdale, Amos Johnston, & Beverly "Betcheler" presented a petition in court May term "last" that in Oct. 1761 Earl of Granville granted 700 ac in Edgecombe Co: "begins at Aquilla Sugg's line on N side of Crooked Cr, runs "S55" 80 poles up the creek to a poplar, S40W 370 poles to a pine, E 346 poles to a black oak in Aquilla Sugg's line, & with his line to first station"; the land has been peaceably possessed by Josiah Sugg until his death & from thence by William Sugg, his brother & heir, until his death which happened sometime in Dec. 1787; William Sugg devised the land: part to Josiah Sugg one of petitioners, another part to Matthew Stockdale another petitioner, & "residue" to be sold by executors the other petitioners; the surveyor made an error in the plat returned to

the office issuing the grant; error is in the fourth line [page torn for one line] but true course is W 264 poles; fifth line is said to run E 346 poles but true course is N432 poles; sixth line was run from end of "said" East line to beginning but true corse is from end of North line East 470 poles & then to beginning; true representation of land is shown in survey by Edgecombe Co surveyor made after giving 30 days notice to adjoining land owners; court is satisfied notice was give to Simon Harrel, Samuel Mayo, heirs of Richard Bolton, Lemuel Sugg son of Lemuel, Isham Humphrey for John Parker deceased, & Mary Sugg guardian of Redding Sugg; court examined the evidence & believes a mistake was made in fourth, fifth, & sixth lines of grant and seventh line was omitted; court ordered clerk to send Secretary of State the grant, copy of this order, & copy of late survey by county surveyor so error can be corrected; Nov. term 1792 I certify above is true copy from the records (signed) Edward Hall;

survey: 1,158.5 ac surveyed Sept. 27, 1760 as 700 ac for Josiah Sugg: begins at "the" old corner poplar & white oak on S prong of "the" creek in Aquilla Sugg's line, runs S55W 104 poles up the creek to a poplar & white oak on S prong of the creek, S41W 82 poles up said prong, S46W 144 poles up the prong to a pine one of the old [page torn], W 264 poles on the old line to another old marked corner pine, N432 poles along another old line to where it strikes Aquilla Sugg's old line and supposed to be where the old black oak stood, S10E 21 poles along Aquilla Sugg's line to the first station. Nov. 16, 1789 (signed) Benjamin Dicken, C surv; Joseph Howell & Simon Harrel, chain carriers; [grant book 11 p. 267 see shuck #1602 and grant book 11 p. 262 see shuck #1571 in Edgecombe Co in Secretary's grant files].

204. Franklin Co Mar. term 1792: return made by Thomas Person, surveyor, for 700 ac surveyed Sept. 23, 1760 for James Terrell; court finds an error in courses & in a deed dated Jul. 29, 1761; line running W 320 poles to a red oak was omitted; so Jepthah Terrell, present proprietor & petitioner, is liable to be injured; court ordered clerk to certify the same to Secretary of State; (signed) G Hill, cc; [grant not identified].

205. to James Glasgow, Secretary of State: you are directed to record a grant dated Apr 9, 1730 to Lewis Conner for 5,000 ac in Bath Co formerly & now Glasgow Co; grant was laid before Council of State Feb. "last" and they recommended it be recorded due to an act of Assembly; New Bern Apr. 5, 1794 Richard Dobbs Spaight & Frans Hawks, P Sec; [no metes & bounds mentioned]; [grant book 85 p. 348, see shuck #183 (empty shuck) in Bath Co in Secretary's grant files; land granted Apr. 9, 1730 by John Lord Carteret & other Lords Proprietor for £50 paid to Receiver General by Lewis Conner (of Virginia) for 5,000 ac in Bath Co on N side of Neuse R & S side of Coteckney Cr, begins at a pine above the fork not far from the old Chinking Fort, runs S20W 320 poles to a white oak by a little swamp, N70W 2500 poles to a pine, N20E 320 poles to a red oak on the creek side, & down the main creek "or water course" to first station pine "on a right line" (signed) Gov. Richard Everand, J Worley, Ed Moseley, Thos Polloch, Rd Sanderson, Ed Gale, & Robert West, recorded in Secretary's office by T Knight,

Corrections/Alterations to Land Grants

D Sec, & J Glasgow, Sec; (statement by Gov. R D Spaight repeated on p. 349);
another grant to Lewis Conner for 5,860 ac in grant book 95 p. 387, see shuck #183A (empty shuck) in Bath Co; grant recorded due to governor's order Jun. 13, 1798 (signed) W Hill, D Sec [no details of order in grant book]; land near head of NW branch of Neuse R, begins at a black oak on SW side of the river, runs S52W 275 poles to a pine, N52W 400 poles to a pine, W 400 poles to a red oak, "NW B N" 710 poles to a red oak, N 100 poles to a red oak by a branch, N75E 100 poles down the branch to a red oak, N52E 120 poles to the river side, N52W 325 poles up the river to a beech on NE side of the river, N 250 poles to a pine, S52E 378 poles to a red oak, N640 (poles) to a black oak, S52E 250 poles to "a" Beaverdam Cr, down various courses of the creek to the mouth, & down the river to first station.

206. Graham Co Aug. term 1873: it appears to satisfaction of court, on petition & affidavit of William Proctor, that there is an error in grant No. 3392 "tract" No. 1632 which indicated in Macon Co in the grant but should have been Cherokee Co; land is now in Graham Co; court ordered the clerk to certify the facts to Secretary of State who should file the same in his office & rectify the error in the grant and records in his office. certified by John G Tatham in Robinsville first Monday in Aug. 1873 and Aug. 14, 1873 (signed) John G Tatham, clerk of Graham Co Superior Court; [grant book 166 p. 322, see shuck #2902 in Cherokee Co in Secretary's grant files].

207. Greene Co [TN] Justices to Secretary of State: William Morrow petitioned the court about an error in courses of grant No. 135 to William Morrow and surveyed by Isaac Taylor; land was resurveyed by James Woods Lacky & plat laid before the court & [error] proved to court; we direct clerk to certify the same to you so error can be corrected (signed) Daniel Kennedy second Monday in Aug. 1796 [on back] altered [no date] No. 135 Oct. 21, 1783; [probably grant #528 issued due to entry #135 in shuck #526 in Greene Co, TN, in Secretary's grant files; W Morrow had 4 other grants in Greene Co, TN];
327 ac surveyed due to act of General Assembly to rectify mistake: begins at a post oak on Richland Cr, runs N43E 52 poles to a chesnut oak, S57E 82 poles to a white oak & hickory, N33E 28 poles to a white oak, N54E 170 poles to a dead red oak near a lick, E 19 poles to 2 white oaks, S70E 154 poles to a black oak, S 44 poles to a black oak, S78W 68 poles to a stake, S27W 150 poles to a black oak, S53W 87 poles to a white oak & poplar in a sink hole, S65W 131 poles to a black oak on the creek, & with the creek to beginning (signed) J W Lackey, DS; David Allison & Hugh Blake, chain carriers.

208. Guilford Co Pleas & Quarter Sessions Court third Monday in Feb. 1797: petition of John Smith about an error in a plat & grant: runs from corner of fifth line a persimmon E51S (sic) 56 poles to a plum tree but should be E51N to a plum tree and "so on throughout said deed"; where it says to "vary" South in the deed it should be North but the same distance "as far as the river"; the Secretary of State is required to make the alteration. (signed) May 12, 1797 John Hamilton, cc;

Corrections/Alterations to Land Grants

[on back] 418 ac grant dated Mar. 21, 1789, altered patent Mar. 26, 1799 (signed) W H, D Sec; [grant book 70 p. 50, see shuck #1656 in Guilford Co in Secretary's grant files].

209. Guilford Co: petition of James Wilson, executor of Allen Wilson deceased, about deficiency in a grant to Allen Wilson for 133 ac on waters of "Polecut" [Cr] in Guilford Co; Robert Brattain, D surveyor, made a mistake; the grant issued for 18 ac but should contain [not mentioned]; Secretary of State is required to make necessary alterations as shown in attached plan   certificate (signed) third Monday in May 1797 Z(?) Hamilton, cc;
    2 copies of survey: 151 ac surveyed Nov. 9, 1792 [Quaker style date] for Allen Wilson of waters of Polecat [Cr]; begins at a black oak on Abigail Wilson's line, runs N 80 poles on her line to a red oak, W 160 poles to a stone, N40 poles on Foster's line to a white oak grub, W 121 poles to a stake, S 64 poles to a gum in Reynolds' line, E 45 poles to a black jack, S20E 60 poles to a black jack, & to first station (signed) R Brattain; John Wilson & Jonathan Hodgson, chain carriers; [grant book 82 p. 98, see shuck #1773 in Guilford Co in Secretary's grant files].

210. Henderson Co Pleas & Quarter Sessions Court at Hendersonville first Monday after fourth Monday in Sept. 1860 present Henry T Farmer, Alexander Henry, & Jas M Paris: following petition filed--Sept session 1860 P S Brittain, "late" county surveyor; 90 ac was entered by James Garren and "laid" Apr. 19, 1855; grant No. 569 issued Feb. 1, 1858; an error was made in courses which should be: "begins at a locust at or near Garren's corner, runs N38E 130 poles with his line to a stake, S57E 115 poles to a stake, S38W 120 poles to a black oak, N57W 68 poles to a black gum, N24W 26 poles to a chesnut, & to beginning on waters of Hoopers Cr and joins said Garren's survey (signed) P S Brittain, surveyor; petition was heard & following order issued: petition of grant No. 569 issued Feb. 18, 1858; it appears to satisfaction of court that allegations of P S Brittain are true about his error in survey for Garren; copy of petition & this order are to be sent to Secretary of State for "amendment"; certified by R W Allen, clerk Dec. 10, 1860 (signed) R W Allen; [grant book 162 p. 318, see shuck #568 in Henderson Co].

211. Henderson Co Pleas & Quarter Sessions Court Apr. term 1841 seven justices present; court ordered error be corrected in grant No. 3753 issued Dec. 24, 1838 to Boyd McCrary & Charles De Choiseul; fifth line should be North 325 poles instead of West 325 poles; Secretary of State is directed to alter the grant & record (signed) Apr. 28, 1841 Elisha King, ccc "private seal there being no public seal"; [on back] 640 ac Buncombe Co, altered Dec. 9, 1841 (signed) Wm Hill, Sec; [grant book 145 p. 393, see shuck #3751 in Buncombe Co in Secretary's grant files].

212. Henderson Co Pleas & Quarter Sessions Court Apr. term 1840 seven justices present; court ordered error be corrected in grant No. 3003 issued Dec. 22, 1831 to Archibald Nelson for 200 ac; seventh line to read N40W instead of S40W;

Corrections/Alterations to Land Grants

Secretary of State is directed to alter the same & the record (signed) Apr. 27, 1840 Elisha King, ccc "private seal there being no public seal"; [on back] 200 ac in Buncombe Co, altered Dec. 9, 1841 (signed) Wm Hill, Secy; [grant book 139 p. 428, see shuck #3000 in Buncombe Co in Secretary's grant file].

213. Grant for land entry No. 122 for 116 ac of "Parcosin" land in Hertford Co to Jacob Reele is "rong"; the mistake is in the gentleman's name; there is no Jacob Keele instead of Jacob Reele in Hertford Co that entered land "to the best of my knowledge" (signed) Oct. 27, 1795 Godwin Cotten, cs; [on back] Jacob "Keele" patent altered [no date]; [grant to "Keele" in grant book 80 p. 517, see shuck #135 in Hertford Co in Secretary's grant files].

214. Hyde Co Pleas & Quarter Sessions Court May term 1821: at present term following petition was filed by Benjamin Foreman & Caleb Foreman "an" infant by his friend B Foreman (of Hyde Co): their father Benjamin Foreman, late of Hyde Co, entered 500 ac in said county on E side of Pungo R--begins at Morris Bell's beginning on N side of Broad Cr, runs E 221 poles along his home line to his corner & Blount's line, S5E 517 poles, N46W 350 poles to Jasper's line, N21E 270 poles on Jasper's line to Broad Cr, & to beginning; as shown in plat attached to grant No. 494 which issued to Dec. 10, 1803 to Benjamin Foreman the father; but Secretary of State made an error in second course of the grant; instead of S5E 517 poles, the grant calls for N5E 517 poles; so petitioners ask for error to be corrected; they are entitled to the land due to will of Benjamin Foreman the father (signed) J B Houghton, atty for the petitioners; court viewed the grant & heard petition and are satisfied the Secretary of State made an error; court ordered clerk to certify the same to Secretary of State so the mistake can be corrected (signed) last Monday in May 1821 John B Jasper, clerk; [on back] altered Nov. 29, 1821; [grant book 118 p. 204, see shuck #988 in Hyde Co in Secretary's grant files].
215. Iredell Co petition of Zachariah Beal to have his grant amended; it was discovered to satisfaction of court that surveyor made an error in the plat; instead of East 19 chains he said South 20 chains; court ordered the clerk to certify error to Secretary of State (signed) at Statesville Aug. 17, 1805 A Share, clk; [on back] grant altered Nov. 27, 1805;
   survey "Mr. Zachariah" begins at a stake on W side of Rocky Cr, runs S30E 17 chains to a post oak, S24E 25 chains to a "sychamore then begins the error" instead of E 17 chains "I have plotted" S 20 chains which has laid out the land in an older claim [rest of lines not described (signed) David Beal; [may be grant No. 470 in grant book 117 p. 162, see shuck #491 in Iredell Co in Secretary's grant files].

216. Iredell Co: at county court held third Monday in Aug. 1792 at Statesville petition of John Callahan was heard asking to correct an error in a grant agreeable to act of Assembly made in such cases; court is satisfied there is an error; court ordered clerk to certify error to Secretary of State: begins at John Bone's corner gum on "the" creek bank, runs N 30 chains to a post oak on said Bone's line, E 77 chains 50 links to Thomas Bone's corner "black", S 58 chains to a sasefras on

the creek bank, & along the creek to the beginning; but courses should be begins at James Bone's corner gum on the creek bank, runs S 58 chains to a "B O" on said Bone's line, E 77.5 chains to Thomas Bone's corner post oak, N 30 chains to a sasifras on the creek bank, & up the creek to beginning; certified Oct. 23, 1792 (signed) A Sharpe, clk; [on back] No. 82 John "Callihan" 1780 Rowan; [grant book 28 p. 463, see shuck #664 in Rowan Co in Secretary's grant files].

217. Iredell Co May session 1803 petition of George Gordon to correct error in grant to him for 100 ac in Iredell Co on waters of Third Cr & S Yadkin R joined on N by Thomas Lackey, on S by William Lackey, on W by my own land, on NW (sic) by John Patterson, & begins at a white oak, runs S25E 20 chains to a white oak on a branch, W 10 chains to a pine, S 30 chains to a pine in a glade, S40W 16 chains to a white oak, W 7 chains 50 links to a branch, N 84 chains to a pine, & E 19 chains to beginning; grant issued Jun. 30, 1797; testimony was heard; it appears to court there was an error in second line of surveyor's return; line surveyed was East 10 chains to a pine instead of West 10 chains to a pine; clerk is directed to certify the same to Secretary of State so the error can be corrected. (signed) A Sharpe, clk; [on back] altered Nov. 22, 1803; [grant book 93 p. 153, see shuck #226 in Iredell Co in Secretary's grant files].

218. Iredell Co Aug. session 1796: Samuel Harris (of said county) applied to court to "amend" an error in his grant; court considered the matter & ordered error be rectified; error is omission of following words: along his line S 19 chains to Carson's corner "B O" which will more plainly appear by comparing surveyor's plan & certificate; certified at Statesville Aug. 25, 1796 A Sharpe, clk; [on back] Saml Harris grant Rowan, patent altered Dec. 10, 1796; [2 grants to Harris: 400 ac in shuck #1004 and 193 ac in shuck #1952 in Rowan Co in Secretary's grant file].

219. Iredell Co Aug. session 1798 petition of Isaac Holman about an error in a grant issued Oct. 6, 1783 to him for 300 ac; there is a surveyor's error; court ordered Secretary to correct the error; instead of W 250 poles passing Butler's corner pine to Butler's beginning corner "B O" and East to beginning, grant needs to be altered to W 250 poles to a post oak, N 240 poles passing Butler's corner pine to Butler's beginning "B O" and East to beginning; (signed) Aug. 23, 1798 A Sharpe, clk; [on back] 300 ac Rowan Co]; [may be grant in grant book 51 p. 57, see shuck #956 in Rowan Co in Secretary's grant files].

220. Iredell Co court Feb. session 1795: surveyor made an error in his return to Secretary's office for grant No. 232 for 320 ac as seen by comparing plat & courses; the petitioner notified those "concerned" and asks for remedy allowed by law (signed) Chrisr. Houston.   Feb. 10, 1795 I certify I ran lines for above tract and find line calling N61E 266 poles but I found to be N70E (signed) Thos Prather, D Surv. Row Co; "to the above alteration" is to be added second line it should be S19W 154 poles to a pine agreeable to plat [not signed];
    Iredell Co May session 1795 due to act of General Assembly passed in

Corrections/Alterations to Land Grants

1790 and petition of Christopher Houston "herewith sent" to Secretary's office; court granted prayer of petitioner agreeable to mode prescribed by law & directed corrections to be made (signed) A Sharpe, clk; [grant book 51 p. 8, see shuck #849 in Rowan Co in Secretary's grant files].

221. Iredell Co Nov. term 1802: James Kerr vs James Houston--petition of plaintiff to correct errors in certificate & platt; court believes prayer of petition should be granted; court ordered errors in petition to be certified to Secretary of State; land was granted to Robert Patton in said county & surveyed as 640 ac; surveyor should have said begins at Alexr. McCorkle's corner black oak, runs S60E 76 poles to a spanish oak, S 290 poles to a post oak, W 300 poles to a pine, N 320 poles to a post oak, & to beginning for 640 ac; but surveyor omitted the first course: begins at a black oak, runs S 320 poles to a black oak, E 320 poles to a pine, N 320 poles to a post oak, & to beginning for 640 ac. certified at Statesville Apr. 2, 1803 (signed) A Sharpe, clk; [on back] altered Nov. 23, 1803; [grant book 67 p. 95, see shuck #2102 in Rowan Co in Secretary's grant files].

222. Iredell Co court Nov. term 1791 to Secretary of State: I am directed to ascertain to you an error in a grant obtained by Joseph McEwen from your office; to satisfaction of the court, the error is that grant says "from thence to beginning" but should say "up the meanders of the river to beginning"; you are directed to alter the grant. (signed) A Sharpe, clk; [on back] altered Dec. 8, 1791 Jos "McKown" No. 282, 640 ac; [grant to McKown in grant book 51 p. 32, see shuck #899 in Rowan Co in Secretary's grant files].

223. Iredell Co petition of George McIntosh asking to "amend" an error in his grant; error was that George McIntosh was misnamed in latter part of the grant as John McIntosh, but it should have been George McIntosh; court considered the matter & ordered the error to be certified to Secretary of State. certified at Statesville Nov. 25, 1796 (signed) A Sharpe, clk; [book 82 p. 274, see shuck #84 in Iredell Co in Secretary's grant files].

224. Iredell Co Pleas & Quarter Sessions Court at Statesville third Monday in May 1825: Eli Scott (of Iredell Co), by his attorney M L Hill esq (practicing attorney of said county), presents a petition: Scott bought land on waters of S Yadkin R granted Nov. 23, 1801 to David McKnight; in grant land joins Wm White on S, David McKnight's own land on W, James McGuity & Fergus Milligan on N, & begins at a post oak, runs N81E 7 chains to a black oak "the dividing line", N 60 chains with McGuinty's line to a s take, N83W 13 chains to a pine, S 7 chains to a black oak, W 46 chains to a black oak, S 30 chains to a maple, E 50 chains to a corner, & to beginning; disputes arose about the boundaries, so Scott had them resurveyed by one of the county processioners; report of the processioner & his jury shows the surveyor's error in the plat; it should begin at a post oak, run E 28 poles to a pine, N 233 poles to a stake, N 83W 46 poles to a pine, S 29 poles to a pine, W 106 poles to a stake, S2E 208 poles to a gum, & E 116 poles to beginning; persons interested in the boundary

Corrections/Alterations to Land Grants

are: John Hooper, William Robertson, James Brotherton, John "Feemester", William Harris, Allen McKinzey, Benjamin Guy, & John Scroggs who had due notice of the petition; Scott asks justices to certify error to Secretary of State so grant can be corrected (signed) Eli Scott by M L Hill, his atto. Seven judges present to hear petition; court ordered prayer of petition granted; clerk directed to certify a copy of proceedings to Secretary of State. certified by Robert Simonton, clerk (signed) Jun. 1, 1825 R Simonton, clk; [notes at end:} (no date) the grant must be sent with the order (signed) Wm Hill, Sec; (no date) the grant is enclosed (signed) R Simonton, clk; [on back] altered Oct. 1, 1825; [grant book 114 p. 11, see shuck #404 in Iredell Co in Secretary's grant files].

225. Iredell Co court at Statesville third Monday in Aug. 1792: petition of James Stewart (of Iredell Co) to rectify error in a grant to him; it appeared to court there were errors; court ordered clerk to certify errors to Secretary of State; surveyor's certificate follows: begins at a white oak on "the" river bank, runs S 45 chains to a pine on William Bell's line, E 44 chains to a pine on John Archibald's line, N 7 [chains] to said Archibald's corner pine, E 11 chains to a black oak on the river bank, & along the river to beginning; but surveyor should have said begins at a white oak on the river bank, runs S 52 chains to a pine on Thomas Bell's line, E 47 chains 75 links to a pine on John Archibald's line, N 7 chains to said Archibald's corner pine, E 11 chains 75 links to a black oak on the river bank, & along the river bank to beginning. certified Nov. 3, 1792 (signed) A Sharpe, clk; [on back] Jas Stewart Nov. 106, 170 ac Rowan; [no grant #106 found, grant #107 in grant book 35 p. 321, see shuck #688 in Rowan Co in Secretary's grant files].
226. Iredell Co: It has been made to appear to satisfaction of Iredell Co Pleas & Quarter Sessions Court at Statesville third Monday in Aug. 1804 that there is an error in a grant to George Walestate [or Wales tate] of Rowan Co; error says 10 degrees East but should be 10 degrees West as appears by papers accompanying this certificate. certified at Statesville Nov. 14, 1804 (signed) A Sharpe, clk; [on back] altered Nov. 22, 1804 George "Wealls" grant; [grant not identified in Iredell or Rowan Co].

227. Iredell Co Aug. session 1801: court ordered clerk to certify there is "a want of dates in a deed" granted to Joseph Wasson for 290 ac joining John McLain & Rocky face Mountain; the same to be certified to Secretary's office. (signed) A Sharpe, clk; [on back] done Dec. 8, 1801; [grant book 64 p. 436, see shuck #1856 in Rowan Co in Secretary's office].

228. Iredell Co Aug. session 1802: petition of William Young about an error in grant No. 2040 issued Dec. 20, 1791 at New Bern to him for 200 ac; land is described as begins at 2 white oak saplins, runs S15E 50 poles to a maple "&c"; court is satisfied above line is wrong; it should be altered agreeable to prayer of petition: begins at 2 white oak saplins, runs S62W 50 poles to a maple "&c"; court ordered a certificate be sent to Secretary of State so grant can be altered (signed) A Sharpe, clk; [on back] altered Nov. 16, 1802; [grant book 75 p. 245, see shuck #2755 in Rowan Co in Secretary's grant files].

229. Iredell Co Feb. session 1795: petition of Thomas Young to justices of Iredell Co; he has a grant for 640 ac on N side of Hunting Cr joins James McCord & Christopher Houston; there is a "manifest" error in grant after first line to a post oak it should be S83E 106 poles to a white oak on Kennedy's Cr, E 32 poles to a post oak, N70E 60 poles to a post oak, E 225 poles to a forked white oak, S320 poles crossing Bryans Br to Houston's corner spanish oak, S68W 170 poles with his line to a hickory at Flat Rock Ford on Hunting Cr, & up meanders of the same to beginning; then grant will correspond with the plat (signed) Thomas Young; [on back] No. 334, 640 ac patent altered (no date); [grant book 51 p. 55, see shuck #951 in Rowan Co];

     May session 1795 Iredell Co pursuant to act of General Assembly in 1790 & Thomas Young's petition herewith sent to Secretary's office; said county court granted prayer of petition & directed corrections mentioned therein to be made (signed) A Sharpe.

230. To Secretary of State: petition by Hardy Bryan to Johnston Co Pleas & Quarter Sessions Court Nov. term 1802: he received a grant for 40 ac on Marks Cr being the surplus of a tract surveyed by William Hinton; due to Secretary's mistake a line in grant runs S 280 poles to an old corner post oak but it should be 208 poles to the old corner post oak; "then" E 31 poles to a stake at first station but it should be E 31 poles to a stake & to first station as appears by copy of surveyor's return of original plat from Secretary's office; so Bryan asks court to direct clerk to certify alterations as allowed by act of Assembly (signed) Dec. 1, 1802 Hardy Bryan. Court ordered the error be corrected; I certify the same to you, the Secretary, so it can be done. Reuben Sanders, clerk, fourth Monday in Nov. 1803 (signed) R Sanders; [on back] altered Feb. 21, 1804; [grant not identified].

231. Johnston Co Nov. term 1795 to James Glasgow, Secretary of State: John Giles petitioned this term of Johnston Co Pleas & Quarter Sessions Court saying he owns 332 ac in Johnston Co; but county surveyor made an error in his plot & certificate in first line he inserted North 60 poles instead of North 160 poles agreeable to plan; so Giles asks court to direct clerk to certify error to Secretary's office so grant can be altered agreeable to act of Assembly in such cases. (signed) Dec. 2, 1795 B Martin "pro" John Giles. Court ordered that proceedings be certified to Secretary agreeable to petition & act of Assembly so error can be corrected. (signed) R Sanders, clk; [on back] No. 345--1779 patent altered [no date]; [grant book 42 p. 162, see shuck #1821 in Johnston Co in Secretary's grant files].

232. To Secretary of State: at Johnston Co Pleas & Quarter Sessions Court Feb. term 1798, John Rosser [or Roper], county surveyor, made a petition: one of his deputies made 2 surveys Mar. 22, 1796 for Labon Haislip; in the 200 ac survey the word "West" should have been "North" and "North" in last line should be "West"; in the 100 ac survey the word "East" in second course should be "West"

and "West" in fourth course should be "East"; so he asks court to issue an order agreeable to act of Assembly allowing county courts to order correction of grants. (signed) John Rosser. Court ordered the same certified to Secretary of State so errors can be corrected (signed) Dec. 19, 1798 R Sanders, clk; [on back] grants altered Jun. 16, 1799; [100 ac grant in book 90 p. 146 see shuck #2928 and 200 ac grant in book 90 p. 146 see shuck #2929 in Johnston Co in Secretary's grant files].

233. To William White, Secretary of State: at Johnston Co Pleas & Quarter Sessions Court Feb. session 1801 William Holliman petitioned as follows: Feb. 24, 1801 petition of William Holliman to Johnston Co court: he entered & obtained state grant for 290 ac on N side of Little R, joins Zacheraus Oneil deceased; the surveyor made a mistake in "one rong" course in third line of plat saying "South" instead of "North" which "thows" the survey where it wasn't intended; so Holliman asks to have grant altered (signed) William Holliman. Pursuant to order of Johnston Co court passed as "aforesaid" session, I certify the error to Secretary of State so the same can be corrected agreeable to petition and law provided in such cases (signed) May 23, 1801 R Sanders, clk; [on back] altered May 23, 1801; [10 grants to W Holliman, none for 290 ac, closest is 250 ac in book 81 p. 285, see shuck #2541 in Johnston Co in Secretary's grant files].

234. Johnston Co Pleas & Quarter Sessions Court: "matter" of James Stephenson-
-petition to correct error in land grant; petition of James Stephenson was heard & testimony considered; seven justices present & court ordered that clerk of court certify to Secretary of State that a mistake occurred in grant issued Feb. 22, 1797 to James Stephenson for 50 ac "inserting" the word "West" instead of "North" in third course of the grant & survey; Ransom Sanders, clerk of Johnston Co Pleas & Quarter Sessions Court, certifies above is true copy of original petition filed in my files (signed) Feb. 25, 1824 Rm Sanders, clk; [on back] altered Aug. 16, 1824 (signed) Wm Hill, Sec; [grant book 90 p. 149, see shuck #2933 in Johnston Co in Secretary's grant files].

235. to William White, Secretary of State: at Johnston Co Pleas & Quarter Sessions Court Nov. session "present", Arthur Talton, by Matthias Handy esq his attorney, made following petition: nov. session 1800 to Johnston Co court petition of Arthur Talton: on Dec. 6, 1779 Talton obtained a grant for 100 ac; in the survey & plat, the surveyor mentioned 100 ac but it should have been 150 ac as appears by plat & testimony of the surveyor; all of which "your worships" are authorized to certify to Secretary of State so error an be corrected; so petitioner asks "your worships" to order the clerk of court to certify "the errors" stated to Secretary of State so the petitioner can have the benefit of land entered & surveyed (signed) Arthur Talton by M Handy atto. Pursuant to order of court agreeable to petition, I certify said error to Secretary of State so the same may be corrected agreeable to law (signed) last Monday in Nov. 1800 R Sanders, cc; [on back] altered Feb. 14, 1801 (signed) W Hill, D Sec; [grant book 106 p. 303, see shuck #3326 in Johnston Co in Secretary's grant files].

236. to Jones Co Court petition of William Adams: he "hath" 14 ac [in grant] No. 504; the survey being on N side of Trent R and runs with his lines until it comes to the river again then "calls" down the meanders of the same to beginning "which is" up the river; the petitioner asks to alter it from down the river to up the river (signed) Wm Adams; [on back] (no date) J Giles acknowledges "lawful" notice of within alteration and am "nulling that it shall take place"; Aug. term 1798 Jones Co court William Adams' petition heard in court and granted; court ordered that Secretary be directed to make alterations agreeable to act of Assembly (signed) J N Bryan, cc; altered Dec. 2, 1798; [grant book 86 p. 124, see shuck #552 in Jones Co in Secretary's grant files].

237. Jones Co Sept. 26, 1788 survey for Adam Andrews 73 ac on S side of Trent R, begins at a lightwood stake in his own line, runs N40W 84 poles to his own corner, S50W 240 poles to beginning hickory of 2 surveys, N47E 222 poles with "given" line os his new survey to another of his corners, S80W 94 poles, N15E 36 poles to Mallard's corner, "the reverse" of his line N75E 70 poles, N 164 poles, N44W 66 poles, N53E 16 poles to a hickory on "the" side of Trent R, S44E 78 poles with Reasonover's line, S 190 poles, S55W 7 poles to Reasonover's dead pine corner, S60E 14 poles to another of his corners, N53E 22 poles, S40E 88 poles to a lightwood stump, & direct line to beginning (not signed & no chain carriers mentioned); [on back] Jones Co Aug. term 1794 read petition of Adam Andrews asking to correct grant No. 336 issued Nov. 16, 1790 to him for 100 ac because there is a total omission of one line; court ordered Secretary to correct the grant by inserting between third & fourth lines "S80W 94 poles" agreeable to within plan (signed) L W Bryan, c c; patent altered Nov. 15, 1790; [grant book 76 p. 10, see shuck #356 in Jones Co in Secretary's grant files].

238. Jones Co court Nov. term 1805: John Andrews, Thomas Webber, & Francis Webber vs Anthony Hatch--petition to alter a patent: petition of John Andrews, Thomas Webber, & Francis Webber was heard saying they are proprietors of "or claim title to" 135 ac on N side of Trent R now in Jones Co; land was granted Mar. 15, 1775 to Isaiah Wood; court heard evidence supporting allegations in petition & are satisfied that error stated in petition does exist & the same should be corrected "viz" second line should be S33W 278 poles from the gum to Trent R, third line should then be down Trent R to a cypress on the river side, fourth line should be N76E 70 poles down the river to John Cummins' corner hickory, fifth line should be N34E 102 poles to his corner stake on "the" swamp; following justices present: Frederick Haret, Durant Hatch, George Stephens, William Kinsey, Jonathan "Krey", Isaac Brown, & Joseph Sanderson on the bench; court ordered clerk to certify the same to Secretary of State so said errors can be corrected; true copy from Jones Co records Nov. 13, 1805 (signed) Wm Orme, cc; [on back] altered Nov. 21, 1805; [grant #1277 issued Mar. 14, 1775 (sic), grant book 25 p. 339, see shuck #3527 in Craven Co in Secretary's grant files].

239. Jones Co court Feb term 1796: read petition of Capt. John Becton asking us

Corrections/Alterations to Land Grants

to direct the Secretary to alter word "third" corner to "fourth" corner in grant No. 401 issued Nov. 26, 1793 to John Slade Becton for 50 ac; it's been certified to us that notice agreeable to law was given to adjoining land owners & "no objection"; prayer of petition was granted & Secretary is authorized to make before mentioned alteration; witness John T Bryan, clk at Trenton Feb. 9, 1796 (signed) J T Bryan; [on back] patent altered May 27, 1796; [entry #436 in shuck #036 (no grant) in Jones Co in Secretary's grant files].

240. Jones Co court May term 1796: heard petition of Isaac Brown: in a grant for 200 ac to William Randall "late" of Jones Co, the third course contains an error; it is "laid down" as S60W 45 chains; but by plat annexed to the grant, it appears it should be S30W 45 chains; court ordered the clerk to certify the mistake to Secretary of State, and he is directed to alter the patent & endorsement thereof according to true courses of annexed plat & due to act of Assembly provided in such cases; pursuant to court order, I John T Bryan, clerk of Jones Co court, certify the same to James Glasgow, Secretary of State; (signed) May 10, 1796 at Trenton J T Bryan; [on back] altered Sept. 9, 1796; [no grant for 200 ac found, only one grant to W Randall for 150 ac in Jones Co].

241. at Jones Co Pleas & Quarter Sessions Court at court house in Trenton Aug. 13, 1792, Abraham Dudley & Benjn Collins brought their complaint "by a petition": petition of Abraham Dudley & Benjamin Collins--they own land on NE side of White oak R & on Black Swamp; land was granted Jun. 30, 1738 to Thomas Dudley; they are "advised" there is an omission in record of the patent in Secretary's office; the original [patent] is "much obliterated"; but they believe "sufficient" remains so record can be rectified; so they ask for certificate to Secretary of State to amend the record of the grant as law requires in such cases (signed) W Slade, for petitioners. Copy of W W Taylor's deposition: sometime about Sept. 29, 1786, he was called on pursuant to an order of Carteret Co court to survey & divide a grant issued Jun. 30, 1738 to Thomas Dudley between heirs of "one" Christopher Dudley; he surveyed the grant & it was "all perfect & whole" at that time; plat No. 1 [not in shuck] hereunto annexed contains a true representation of the survey then made; he understands the grant has been since destroyed or so defaced as to not be legible; it has been discovered there is a mistake in the record of the grant in the Secretary's office; since the error was discovered, he made a survey from the record & dotted lines on plat No. 2 [not in shuck] hereunto annexed are true representation of the record; it appears there are two mistakes: second course is N45E 280 poles but by plat & grant it should be N45E 208 poles and third course in grant is N31W 168 poles but is left out of the record (signed) Wm Wilkins Taylor (witness) Abn Comron, JP; copy of papers in clerk's office of Superior Court at New Bern (signed) W Slade & Silas Cooke, CSCL.   New Bern Superior Court Mar. term 1796 Dudley & Collins vs Andrew West: from petition & depositions, it appears the court there is an error in record of grant in Secretary's office; second line is recorded N45E 280 poles but should be N45E 208 poles and third line N31W 168 poles is omitted; court directed that clerk certifies the same & send it to Secretary so record can be rectified. (signed)

Corrections/Alterations to Land Grants

Silas Cooke, CSCL; [on back] altered to within court order Jun. 1, 1797 W H; [grant book 8 p. 1, see shuck #154 in Carteret Co in Secretary's grant files].

242. To Jones Co court: John Eubank informs the court that the Secretary of State made a mistake in a line of a patent issued Apr. 6, 1793 to said Eubank; land joins Durant Hatch, Amos Simmons, & "within his" old boundaries; the error "operates much against" validity of the grant; so Eubank asks for grant to be corrected agreeable to plat returned by the surveyor as law directs Aug. 13, 1799 (signed) John Eubank [request] "granted".   Jones Co court Aug. term 1799, read within petition in open court & ordered Secretary of State to alter the patent & make it conform to plat & certificate of survey; witness John L Bryan, clerk Aug. 13, 1799 (signed) J T Bryan, c c; [on back] altered agreeable to within order [no details] Nov. 28, 1799; [only one grant found #698 issued Nov. 24, 1797 (sic), grant book 92 p. 259, see shuck #669 in Jones Co in Secretary's grant files].

243. Jones Co court May term 1803: heard petition of Edmund Hatch; proof was made that due notice was given, as required by law, to Thomas Murphy, Wm Gray, & Benjamin Parker Gray; following justices present: Fredk. Harget, Edwd Bryan, Durant Hatch, Levin Lane, Sampson Lane, George Stephens, & James Shine; it appears to satisfaction of court that surveyor made an error in certificate to Secretary for grant issued Aug. 15, 1798 to Benjamin Stanton for 60 ac; error is in fourth line of survey written as "N1W 42 poles" but should be "S1W 42 poles to Allcock's corner"; court ordered clerk to certify the same to Secretary of State so error can be rectified.   True copy from records of Jones Co court (signed) Jun. 6, 1803 at Trenton Wm Orme, c c; altered Nov. 21, 1803; [grant book 97 p. 82, see shuck #708 in Jones Co in Secretary's grant files].

244. Jones Co court Nov. term 1805: John Houston & wife Sarah vs Benja Simmons & N A Bray--petition to alter a patent: heard petition of John Houston & wife asking to alter a grant issued Mar. 11, 1775 to Joseph Trow; following justices present: Frederick Harget, Durant Hatch, Joseph Sanderson, Isaac Brown, Enoch Foy, George Stephens, & Edward Bryan on the bench; proof was adduced that due notice, as required by law, was given to Benjamin Simmons & Nicholas A Bray who are adjoining proprietors; court ordered that patent be altered according to prayer of petition "to wit" insert N65E 24 poles being the "last line but one" and omitted; clerk to certify the same to Secretary of State so error can be rectified (signed) at Trenton Nov. 13, 1805 Wm Orme, c c; [on back] altered Nov. 20, 1805; [grant #980, grant book 25 p. 238, see shuck #3446 in Craven Co in Secretary's grant files].

245. Jones Co Aug. term 1800: court ordered prayer granted for petition of Bazell Pritchard to alter a grant issued Aug. 15, 1790 for 75 ac; courses in grant to be altered as follows: begins at a black jack in Joseph Brooks' line, runs S73W 121 poles with the same to Bryan's corner pine, S27E 97 poles with his line to "bisection" of said line and his own line, N27E 99 poles with his own line to his corner at centre of 2 pines & water oak, & N60E 190 poles with his line [to

beginning ?]; clerk to give certificate for "registration" accordingly. True copy from minutes (signed) Wm Orme, clk "pro tem" continued from May term 1799 to present term; [on back] altered Dec. 18, 1800; [grant book 97 p. 86, see shuck #700 in Jones Co in Secretary's grant files].

246. Jones Co court May term 1803: heard petition of Isaac Ramsey: he "because" purchaser of land in Jones Co on Tuckahoe Swamp; land was in grant No. 776 issued Jul. 10, 1788 by Gov. Samuel Johnston to Jacob Turner for 107 ac; there is a mistake in the surveyor's first course in the grant "N70E 36 poles" instead of "N20E 36 poles" and third line "S4W" instead of "S86W; petitioner asks court to consider request and allow relief provided by law (signed) Nov. 9, 1802 Isaac Ramsey. Following justices present: Fredk Harget, Edward Bryan, Durant Hatch, Levi Lane, Sampson Lane, James Shine, & George Stephens; due notice, required by law, has been given; court ordered clerk to certify the error to Secretary of State so it can be rectified according to petition; true copy of record (signed) Jun. 6, 1803 at Trenton Wm Orme, c c; [on back] altered Oct. 1, 1805; [no grant identified to Jacob Turner, only grants to John Turner in Jones Co].

247. Jones Co court Feb. term 1806: Emanuel Simmons petitioned last term of court: on Mar. 9, 1736 John Simmons received a grant for 640 ac on S side of Trent R in Craven Precinct now Jones Co; land begins at Col. Thomas Pollock's corner pine, runs S40W 280 poles to a pine, N50W 80 poles to a red oak, N40E 100 poles, N55W 180 poles to a pine, W 180 poles to a pine, S67E 237 poles to a pine, & down the river to first station; but there is a manifest error in th description by the Secretary; in the fourth line instead of N55W 80 poles, it should be N55W 100 poles; sole interest in land has been "regularily transmitted to" and is vested in the petitioner; following justices present: Durant Hatch, Edward Bryan, John Isler, George Stephens, Abner Averet, Levin Lane, & Enoch Foy; court finds "all the matters" set forth are true as shown by surveyor's plat & "other" documents; due to error, petitioner is likely to sustain injury since grant doesn't contain land surveyed; due notice has been given 30 days prior to petition to Needham Simmons, Lemuel Hatch, Durant Hatch, & Edmund Hatch; court ordered facts in petition be certified to Secretary of State so error can be "errected"; true copy of records (signed) at Trenton Feb. 12, 1806 Wm Orme, clk; [on back] altered Nov. 26, 1806; [grant book 9 p. 207, see shuck #836 in Craven Co in Secretary's grant files];

a plat on Trent R, Mill Run, & Mevers' Br: explanation of black lines in survey: "I K" is the error in "various" courses up Mevers' Br to a red oak on S side of the branch or N56 1/2W 151 poles instead of N43W 151 poles as by surveyor's certificate; Jones Co court May term 1794 petition of Mr. Simmons; court ordered Secretary to alter grant No. 346 to Emanuel Simmons in second line from N43W 151 poles to N56½ W 151 poles (signed) Lw Bryan, c c; patent altered (no date); [grant book 76 p. 13, see shuck #369 in Jones Co in Secretary's grant files].

248. Jones Co court May term 1805: heard petition of Needham Simmons & Isaac

Corrections/Alterations to Land Grants

Kornegy: they are proprietors of 224 ac in Jones Co granted Dec. 6, 1799 to Amos Simmons and Hardy Mitchell; there is a manifest error in fifth course of the grant described as "S63E" but should be "S63W"; it appears to satisfaction of court that due notice of petition, required by law, was given to Abraham Kornegy sr, Robert Kornegy, Joseph Sanderson guardian of heirs of Daniel Kornegy deceased; following judges are present: Fredk Harget, Durant Hatch, Fredk Foscue, Jon Kay, Abner Averet, Joseph Sanderson, Enoch Foy, Edm Hatch, & Lavender Simmons; court finds error exists; clerk to certify the same to Secretary of State so it can be corrected (signed) at Trenton May 14, 1805 Wm Orme, c c; [on back] altered Nov. 20, 1805; [grant book 107 p. 147, see shuck #765 in Jones Co in Secretary's grant files].

249. Jones Co Pleas & Quarter Sessions Court May term 1803 at court house in Trenton second Monday in May 1805: on Tuesday, second day of the term, following justices on the bench: Fredk Harget, Durant Hatch, Edward Bryan, Levin Lane, Sampson Lane, Joseph Sanderson, & James Shine; heard petition of Needham Simmons and adduced his testimony; proof given that notice, required by law, was given to Emmanuel Simmons, Abraham Kornegy sr, & Abraham Kornegy jr; court ordered clerk to certify to Secretary of State that an error has been made to satisfaction of court; grant issued Nov. 26, 1793 to Needham Simmons; the Secretary made an error in the grant from surveyor's return; error is in seventh line by inserting "poles" after "N76"; word "poles" isn't in surveyor's return so grant is not consistant with surveyor's return; court ordered clerk to certify error to Secretary of State so it can be rectified; true copy from the records (signed) at Trenton Jun. 6, 1803 Wm Orme, c c; [on back] altered Nov. 21, 1803; [grant book 81 p. 361, see shuck #429 in Jones Co in Secretary's grant files].

250. Jones Co: heard petition of John Eubanks asking for alterations of grant issued Feb. 16, 1737 to David Turner in Carteret Co now Jones Co by Gov. Gabriel Johnston [grant number blank]; John Eubanks became purchaser of the land; it appears Secretary of State (sic) made an error in second line of the grant: S70E 15 poles but should be S70E 152 poles; it appears to satisfaction of court that due notice, required by law, was given; following justices present: Durant Hatch, Edward Bryan, Joseph Sanderson, Lemuel Hatch, George Stephens, Enoch Foy, & Benjamin Harrison; court ordered clerk to issue certificate to Secretary of State so error can be rectified; true copy from records (signed) May 21, 1804 Wm Orme, c c; [on back] "rectified" Nov. 20, 1804; [grant book 9 p. 246 in shuck #194 in Carteret Co and grant book 3 p. 420 in shuck #52 in Carteret Co in Secretary's grant files].

251. Lenoir Co to Secretary of State: agreeable to order of Lenoir Co court Jan. term 1795, you are required to alter the courses of a grant issued Apr. 25, 1785 to James Armstrong or 220 ac in Dobbs Co and make it & the record conform to annexed plat; witness Jan. 19, 1785 Winston Caswell (signed) W Caswell;
      survey Jan. 6, 1795: surveyed 220 ac for Thomas Armstrong on S side

of Southwest Cr & on Nobles Br; begins at mouth of Deep Bottom Br on Nobles Br at "Griffing" Jones' corner, runs S80E 160 poles with Griffing Jones' line, S25W 240 poles, S62W 105 poles, N45W 100 poles to Nobles Br, & down Nobles Br being Herritage's line to beginning (signed) Leml Byrd, surv; Robert Ivy jr & Charles Ivy, chain carriers; [on back] patent No. 64 altered; [only 2 grants to James Armstrong: #74 in shuck #1662 and #75 in shuck #1603 in Dobbs Co in Secretary's grant files].

252. Lenoir Co court: petition of Simon Bruton: he has a grant for 50 ac which covers the surveyed land; but he supposes the surveyor made a mistake by leaving out "the given" line in the surveyor's certificate; so he asks the court to order alteration of third line from S30E to S76E so as to establish the given line as it appears in the plat; there being no "inpropriety" in doing so without surveying it again; the petitioner owns the land all around the grant; or the court can do what is just & right (signed) Sn Burton; petition was read; court ordered prayer of petition be granted & clerk to certify the same to Secretary so alteration can be made (signed) May 29, 1800 Sn Bright, c c; [on back] altered Jun. 25, 1800;
plat on separate sheet; [2 adjoining triangles] S85W 65 poles, N1W 106 poles, S30E "error", S76E 126 poles [last line blank]; [may be grant to Benjamin Bruton, grant book 42 p. 341, see shuck #1415 in Dobbs Co in Secretary's grant files].

253. Jul. term 1794 Lenoir Co: petition of Nathan Bryan (of Jones Co) esq was read; he asks for order to Secretary to rectify a mistake in fourth line of a patent for 250 ac in Dobbs Co now Lenoir Co issued Mar. 4, 1775: make the distance 260 poles instead of 160 poles; it appears to court that Mr. Bryan took all steps required by law notifying "several" adjoining landowners; they have no objection to alteration; so prayer of petition is granted; court ordered clerk to certify the same to Secretary (signed) at Kinston Jul. 11, 1794 W Caswell, clk; [grant book 27 p. 85 see shuck #1103 and grant book 25 p, 64 see shuck #4024 in Dobbs Co in Secretary's grant files].

254. Lenoir Co Pleas & Quarter Sessions Court Jan. term 1818: petition of Thomas Cauley [or Cauby]; about 1773 Thomas Torrons obtained a grant for land on S side of Neuse R & N side of Southwest Cr, begins at Samuel Thomas' corner white oak, runs S28W 162 poles, N54W 142 poles, N13W 124 poles to Richard Caswell's corner pine, N75E 200 poles, & to first station for 200 ac; in grant & plat it is mistakenly described as on N side of Neuse R & S side of Southwest Cr; but it is on S side of Neuse R & N side of Southwest Cr; fourth line in the grant is mistakenly described as runs N75W 200 poles but it runs N75E 200 poles; the land joins Lott Croom of said county & Bartholomew "Cauly", an infant under guardianship of William Miller of said county; petition is "remediless without interportion" of the court; so he asks court to correct & "amend" the above errors & direct copies be served on Lott Croom & Bartholomew Cauley jr (sic) "forthwith"; land was bought by Roger Cauley from Thomas Torrons and half of tract "descended" to the petitioner from Roger Cauley; he asks court to make any

other order necessary (signed) Vine Allen, atto for petitioner. Nov. 13, 1820 Charles Westbrook, clerk, certifies prayer of petition was granted; adjoining land owners have no objection; court ordered clerk to certify the same to Secretary of State so alterations can be made (signed) C Westbrook; [on back] Dobbs Co 200 ac Thos Torrance; altered Dec. 20, 1822 (signed) Wm Hill Sec; [grant book 25 p. 64, see shuck #1024 in Dobbs Co in Secretary's grant files].

255. Lenoir Co court petition of John Cobb: he is proprietor of land granted Nov. 10, 1784 to Richard Nixon for 30 ac in Dobbs Co now Lenoir Co on SE side of Southwest Cr between 2 old grants (a) to John Williams "the older" & ?(b) to Cornelius Loftin "to the which" belonged to Richard Nixon at time of grant and now belong to petitioner; the 30 ac grant begins at his own "(Nixon's)" and Roberts' corner black oak, runs N88W 70 poles with his own line to his corner pine, N22E 153 poles with his other line to his line to his line of another survey, N70E 160 poles with that line to his beginning white oak of another survey, N43W 44 poles to the beginning red oak of an old survey, S65W 60 poles to last corner red oak of said survey, S22W 153 poles along his other line to his corner red oak, "69W" 80 poles along his line to his corner pine, S50E 150 poles with Harmon Cox's & Benoni Loftin's lines to Roberts' line, & along the same to beginning; from description it is manifest that the patentee intended to include the land between the two old patents and lines of Cox & Loftin; but courses and distances in plat are very different from those "laid down" by surveyor and form lines run; beginning and all courses are well known & established; but courses in grant don't agree with lines of the old grant although said to run with them & distances aren't correct but run into the old grants; petitioner will be injured if correction isn't made; Joseph Loftin, Leonard Loftin, John Cox jr, & Harmon Cox are interested in or claim lands adjoining land claimed by the petitioner; he gave them 30 days notice of the petition; he asks that case be examined & errors, if found, be corrected by certifying to Secretary of State; Oct. term 1803 (signed) Jno Stanly, atto for petitioner; [197 ac grant in book 22 p. 228 see shuck #795 and 200 ac grant in book 22 p. 228 see shuck #797 in Dobbs Co in Secretary's grant files];

John Cobb vs Joseph Loftin, Leonard Loftin, Harmon Cox, & John Cox: petition to alter grant; following justices present: Lazarus Pearce, Zachariah Davis, John Wooten, Allen Wooten, Bryan Whitfield jr, James Bright, "Pearott" Mewborne, & Frederick Jones; court ordered clerk to certify to Secretary of State there are errors in grant issued Nov. 10, 1784 to Richard Nixon; errors to be corrected by making "several of the grant" to run as follows: begins at Roberts' corner black oak, runs N70W 94 poles to his corner, N2E 120 poles along his line to his corner, N70E 160 poles with his other line to beginning of "said" survey, S79W 43 poles to beginning of another of his old surveys, S64W 67 poles to a line of his first old survey, S70W 50 poles along that line to his corner, S2W 120 poles along his line to his corner, S22W 6 poles to a corner of his other old survey, N68W 80 poles along his line of that survey to his corner, N55E 100 poles to Cox's corner & "with" his line to Cox's other corner, S60E 13 poles to Loftin's corner, S50E 75 poles along Loftin's line to Roberts' line, & to first station (signed) C Westbrook, clk; [on back] altered Mar. 22, 1804; [grant #541 issued

Corrections/Alterations to Land Grants

Nov. 10, 1784, grant book 57 p. 239, see shuck #1788 in Dobbs Co in Secretary's grant files].

256. Lenoir Co Apr. court 1801 Nathan Creel vs Saml Hardy sr, Joshua Taylor, & Joseph Wilson: petition to correct certificate & "filling up" of a grant to render them conformable to the plat; case was heard at Oct. term "last"; court ordered correction; but clerk did it imperfectly; so petitioner asks the court to correct clerk's error in making out the order; court ordered prayer of petitioner granted because they believe surveyor made an error in certificate to the plat; one whole line was omitted "in the 3 last" courses that read S18E 72 poles to his corner hickory, S17E 40 poles with his line "again" to a pine, & S12E 210 poles with his line again to beginning; but it should read S18E 72 poles to his hickory corner, S17E 40 poles with his line again to a pine, S12E 206 poles, & N84E 210 poles to beginning; clerk to certify error to Secretary so grant can be made conformable to plat (signed) at Kinston Apr. 15, 1801 C Westbrook, clk; [grant not identified in Lenoir or Dobbs Co].

257. Winston Caswell, clerk of Lenoir Co court, to Secretary of State: you are authorized & required, agreeable to order of said court, to alter last course "but one" of a grant and record issued Apr. 11, 1749 to John Irons for 300 ac from "N77E" to "S77E" (signed) at Kinston Jul. 3, 1793 W Caswell; [on back] Major Croom vs Job Hunter & John Herring; [grant not identified in Lenoir, Dobbs, Craven, or Johnston Co; maybe a Granville grant].

258. Lenoir Co Jul. term 1797 "the justices" present; court ordered the clerk to certify to the Secretary of State "information" given to them that there is an error in second course of a grant & record for 250 ac to John Dortch in Dobbs Co issued Mar. 4, 1775 No. 580; to be altered from N12E to N12W; I certify the above Secretary of State (signed) W Caswell, clk; [grant book 27 p. 103, see shuck #1124 in Dobbs Co in Secretary's grant files].

259. Lenoir Co Jul. court 1808 petition of David George to the court: he is proprietor of 100 ac in Lenoir Co on both sides of Tuckahoe Cr granted Jul. 16, 1795 to Zachariah Brown; grant is said to begin at a post oak on S side of Tuckahoe [Cr] but said beginning post oak is on N side of Tuckahoe [Cr]; he asks that error be inquired into & if found to exist the same be certified to Secretary of State so it can be rectified; the land joins Job Leary esq & no other person (signed) J Stanley, atto for petitioner. Petition was heard in presence of James Bright, Frederick Jones, Lamuel Byrd, John Wooten, William Croom, Major Croom, & Lazarus Pearce esqs.; court finds "defendant" was duely notified; on examining plat, grant, & "other" testimony, court believes error exists; so clerk ordered to certify the same to Secretary of State so the same can be made "conformable" agreeable to the law. I certify this is a true copy from court minutes in my office (signed) at Kinston Nov. 20, 1809 C Westbrook, c c; [on back] altered Nov. 19, 1810; [grant book 86 p. 457, see shuck #109 in Lenoir Co in Secretary's grant files].

Corrections/Alterations to Land Grants

260. Lenoir Co Oct. term 1792: petition of Moses Gooding for relief due to error in grant issued Jul. 25, 1774 to Daniel Gooding; following facts were shown & proved; Daniel Gooding entered land in Dobbs now Lenoir Co "sometime" in 1774 on S side of Vine Swamp, joins Thomas Bryan, begins at a pine in a branch, runs S64E 116 poles to a white oak in William Dean's line, N25W 150 poles to a pine corner of William Dean's land, E 156 poles to "the" South Br, N10E 256 poles "with or near" Bryan's line to a black jack, N68W 44 poles to a pine, & to beginning; land was surveyed by William Caswell, who made a mistake in plat returned to Secretary of State; error is in second line described to run N25E but real course is N25W; there is also surveyor's error in fourth line with distance of 156 poles but in fact it is 256 poles; also fifth line is wrong [error not described] and should be conformable to "above" description; all of which was clearly proved in court & conformable to Daniel Gooding's entry; it appears to the court that Moses Gooding is likely to be injured by the mistakes, since he is present legal owner of the land, unless the same is rectified by law; clerk is directed to certify all of this to Secretary of State; a true copy from the minutes (signed) W Caswell (no date); [on back] "done"; [grant not identified].

261. Lenoir Co Jan. term 1800 I certify petition of James "Engram" was read showing that an error exists in fourth line of a grant issued in 1767 to Cleverly Wetherington in "said" county: N66E to a red oak should be S69E 120 poles to a "proved" corner red oak; the petitioner was complied with act of Assembly and asks that course be made S69E 120 poles to "said" red oak; the court considered the same & ordered prayer of petitioner be granted (signed) S Bright, c c; [on back] altered Jan. 23, 1800; [grant not identified in Dobbs Co].

262. [Lenoir Co] Pleas & Quarter Sessions Court Jul. term 1819 petition of Jesse Isler (of said county); Jesse has "just & lawful" title to following land: begins at a gum in edge of Southwest Cr near mouth of Motts Swamp, runs S45E 297 poles to a black jack, E 134 poles to a red oak in John Cox sr's line "which latter course & distance" the petitioner discovered is incorrect; instead of E 134 poles it should be S77E 180 poles to said oak; whereby the petitioner is damaged; so he asks the court to "award" an order to rectify the error and do "other such matters & things in this behalf" as seems right & just to the court according to act of Assembly provided in such cases (signed) Richd B Blackledge, atto for petr. Charles Westbrook, clerk of Lenoir Co court, certifies within case was heard Jul. term 1820; case was investigated & found "incorrect" as stated in petition; court ordered clerk to certify case to Secretary of State so necessary alteration can be made (signed) at Kinston Dec. 14, 1820 C Westbrook, clk; [on back] Charles Markland 150 ac Craven now Lenoir Co, altered Dec. 19, 1820 (signed) Wm Hill, Sec; [grant book 18 p. 106 see shuck #2600 and book 17 p. 118 see shuck #2350 in Craven Co].

263. Lenoir Co Jul. term 1794: petition of John Patrick sr read asking for order to Secretary to alter a line of grant Nov. 10, 1784 to Joel Patrick on S side of great

Corrections/Alterations to Land Grants

Contentnea Cr, joins lines of patents formerly belonging to Minan Patrick, William Dry, & Isaac Pate; the present owners of [adjoining] land were "cited" to appear at present court to show cause why prayer of petition shouldn't be granted; they have failed to appear; court ordered clerk be directed to certify to the Secretary that this court agrees second line in grant to be altered from S73E to S23E (signed) at Kinston Jul. 8, 1794 W Caswell, clk; [on back] altered; [grant book 57 p. 239, see shuck #1789 in Dobbs Co in Secretary's grant files].

264. Lenoir Co Jan. court 1794 present "the justices"; read petition of Jacob Rhem for relief from error in patent issued to William White for 100 ac; court ordered the clerk to directed to issue a certificate to the Secretary to alter the grant & record as follows: second line to be S56W 178 poles, third line S34E 152 poles, fourth line N42E 95 poles, fifth line N65W 33 poles, & sixth line N31E 143 poles agreeable to surveyor's return & report of "the jury" (signed) W Caswell, clk. Agreeable to above order, Secretary is directed to alter the record & grant as described (signed) W Caswell, clk; [2 grants to William White, but none for 100 ac in Lenoir Co in Secretary's grant files].

265. Apr. court 1806 present Lazarus Pearce, John Jackson, Benja Hartsfield, Jas Bright, Wm Branton, Benja White, John Wooten, & Simon Bruton; petition of John Washington to alter a grant issued Nov. 26, 1757 to Thomas Dick for 193 ac in Dobbs now Lenoir Co on Atkin Br; petition was heard; court is satisfied first line in the grant is wrong saying S 164 poles but should be E 164 poles; court believes first line should be E 164 poles; court ordered clerk to certify the same to Secretary of State so error can be rectified in grant & record (signed) Apr. 7, 1806 C Westbrook, c c; [on back] altered Jun. 24, 1807; [2 grants in Craven Co, none in Dobbs, & none for 194 ac to Thomas Dick in Secretary's grant files].

266. Lenoir Co Oct. term 1801 court ordered clerk to certify to Secretary of State it appears an error was made by surveyor in his certificate to survey for grant No. 201 to James Wilson for 180 ac; instead of beginning at Armwell Herring's corner red oak it is said to begin at Samuel Loftin deceased's red oak which is wrong; grant needs to be altered (signed) C Westbrook, c c; [on back] altered May 10, 1802; [grant book 100 p. 316, see shuck #205 in Lenoir Co in Secretary's grant files].

267. Lenoir Co Pleas & Quarter Sessions Court held first Monday in July 1802: Robert White esq petitioned court: on Oct. 10, 1783 he obtained a grant for 190 ac; the surveyor made an error in plot & certificate; error is in second line S30E 385 poles to a maple on "the river side of Ash Br" but it should be S25E to the maple; court ordered sheriff to summon a jury & have a "tryal" on the premises & made a return to next court. Oct. term 1802 Robert White vs Philip Miller-- petition to alter a grant; there is satisfactory proof Philip Miller "& others" who own adjoining land mentioned in the petition have had due notice; court heard petition & examined chain bearers & "other" evidence; court believes surveyor made an error in second line of plat & certificate mentioned in petition; second

line should be S25E instead of S30E; court ordered clerk to certify the same to Secretary of State so the error can be rectified. I certify foregoing is true copy of records in my office Dec. 13, 1802 (signed) Jos Eliot, D clk for Chas Westbrook; [on back] altered Dec. 22, 1802; [grant #468 issued Oct. 13, 1783 (sic), grant book 50 p. 38, see shuck #1623 in Dobbs Co in Secretary's grant files].

268. Lincoln Co Apr. session 1793 petition of John McGauhey asking court to amend his grant for 500 ac; it appears to court that notice has been given according to law; court ordered clerk to certify to Secretary of State that grant be amended as follows: seventeenth course should be described as N40E 64 poles instead of N40W 64 poles; certified at office Apr. 5, 1793 (signed) Jno Dickson, c c; [on back] Jno McGauhey Nov. 500 for 500 ac "Nov 90" grant altered; [grant book 75 p. 71, see shuck #563 in Lincoln Co in Secretary's grant files].

269. Lincoln Co Oct. session 1805 heard petition of James Martin; court ordered prayer of petition be granted; clerk to certify the same to Secretary of State so he can alter a grant issued Aug. 7, 1787 to James Martin as follows: begins at a chesnut tree, runs N 200 poles to a black oak, E 200 poles to a stake, S 200 poles to a stake, & W 200 poles to beginning; these courses are wrong & should be: begins at a chesnut tree, runs W 230 poles to a chesnut stump, N 150 poles to a white oak, E 186 poles to a black oak, & to beginning which were the real courses run by the surveyor in original survey; Lawson Henderson, clerk of court, certifies above is true copy from court records (signed) first Monday in Oct. 1805 Lwn Henderson; [on back] altered Sept. 19, 1807; [four grants to James Martin, but none on this date in Lincoln Co].

270. James Glasgow, Secretary, to Lincoln Co justices: the Governor has suspended a grant to Jonathan Gullick due to complaint of Nathan Mendenhall; land is in Lincoln Co & joins James Masters, Joseph Henry, & his own lines; I certify the same to you so the matter can be determined agreeable to law (signed) at Raleigh Nov. 28, 1795 J Glasgow. Sept. 21, 1796 Secretary is notified that "we" Nathan Mendenhall & Jonathan Gullick have "compremised" our dispute; Mendenhall, the caveator, requests Secretary to issue a grant to Gullick (signed) Nathan Mendenhall; filed Sept. 21, 1796; [grant suspension, not alteration; Gullick received 5 grants in Lincoln Co, grant not identified].

271. Lincoln Co Pleas & Quarter Sessions Court held at court house in Lincolnton fourth Monday after "fourth" in Mar. 1822; petition of John Neagle, by Robert Henry esq, his attorney; grant #792 issued Nov. 18, 1793 to Joseph Beaty; the petitioner is "interested" in the grant; the surveyor & Secretary made a manifest error in courses & distances in certificate & grant: begins at a hickory on George Devenport's line, runs E 206 poles with John Neagle's line to a black oak sapling on Samuel Martin's line, N57W 104 poles with his line to Isaac Erwin's corner hickory, N42W 154 poles with his line to his corner pine, S13W 50 poles with another of his lines to a stake, S55E 67 poles with another of his lines to Geo Devenport's corner stake, & with his line to beginning; the error is that third

course is omitted in surveyor's certificate & the grant; error begins at end of second line runs N57W 104 poles and next line should be S55W 104 poles to Isaac Erwin's corner post oak "which is omitted"; petitioner asks court to direct clerk to certify the error to Secretary of State so it can be corrected (signed) Robt Henry, atto, and J Neagle. At next court following notice was filed by petitioner: Isaac Erwin is summoned to next Lincoln Co court third Monday in July next concerning grant No. 792 issued Nov. 18, 1793 to Joseph Beaty which land joins said "Erwine's" land (signed) Apr. 22, 1822 "from your friend" J Neagle; notice endorsed acknowledged Jul. 5, 1822 (signed) Isaac Erwine "sr" (witness) Isaac Erwine jr. At next session of court Oct. 1822 Samuel McKee, surveyor, filed plat & certificate: resurvey Oct. 19, 1822 for John Neagle of grant issued Mar. 10, 1792 to Joseph Beaty, black line represents lines in original plat with small difference in third line S55W 100 poles with Isaac Erwin's line to a post oak, with his other line to a pine, with Allison's, then Wagstaff's; dotted lines are lines in surveyor's certificate which would run from a hickory through Erwin's land & would leave out the land as shown by the plat; third corner hickory not found said to be rotten & gone, the rest all standing (signed) Samuel McKee [no chain carriers mentioned]. Court examined the papers & heard the evidence and are satisfied of error in petition; surveyor and Secretary made an error; court ordered clerk to certify the same to Secretary so grant & Secretary's books can be corrected agreeable to petition and act of Assembly; certified at office in Lincolnton Nov. 7, 1822 (signed) Vardry McBee, clk; altered Nov. 20, 1822 (signed) Wm Hill, Sec; [3 grants to J Beaty in Lincoln Co, but none on this date].

272. Petition of Michael "Reap" to Lincoln Co court: in 1787 he had 275 ac surveyed by David Ramsey; plat was returned to the Secretary so a grant could issue; grant issued Dec. 20, 1791; the grant calls grantee Michel Russ instead of Reep and "endorsement" of grant calls for Richard Reese instead of Michael Reep; petitioner suggests the 275 ac was surveyed & returned by the surveyor; but transcription of grants calls for only 225 ac; so petitioner asks court to order the "several" errors be rectified according to law (signed) Oct. 8, 1793 Michael Reep; petition granted (signed) Jo Dickson, C clk; [on back] altered No. 569; [grant book 75 p. 318, see shuck #634 in Lincoln Co in Secretary's grant files].

273. At Lincoln Co Pleas & Quarter Sessions Court held at court house in Lincolnton third Monday in Jan. 1825 before "the justices": petition of Henry Rhodes (of said county): Rhodes owns 220 ac in grant No. 1079 issued Dec. 11, 1797 to Frederick Havner; there are errors in first & third lines of the grant: first line calls for "begins at John Wilson's corner black oak, runs S42E 220 poles with his line to a pine" but should be "S84E 330 poles" to above mentioned pine "and" from Wilson's corner black oak; third line says "N85W 202 poles from a chesnut to a black oak" but should be "S85W 202 poles from the chesnut to the black oak"; petitioner is liable to be injured due to the errors; so he asks that clerk certify errors to Secretary of State so the Secretary can correct the grant and first line will be S84E 330 poles to a pine instead of S42W 220 poles to a pine and third line will be S85W 202 poles to a black oak instead of N85W 202 poles to a black oak

Corrections/Alterations to Land Grants

(signed) Henry Rhodes. Vardry McBee, clerk of court, certifies that at Apr. session 1825 prayer of petition was granted; court ordered clerk to certify the same to Secretary of State so the same can be corrected (signed) Jul. 2, 1825 Vardry McBee, cc; [on back] altered Sept. 23, 1825 W H; [grant book 92 p. 318, see shuck #1479 in Lincoln Co in Secretary's grant files].

274. At Lincoln Co Pleas & Quarter Sessions Court held at court house in Lincolnton third Monday in Jul. 1824 before "the justices"; petition of Joshua Roberts: a grant issued Dec. 14, 1808 to John Carruth for 70 ac on waters of Muddy Fork of Buffaloe Cr, joins Robert Weir & Ephraim Black, begins at Weir's corner white oak, runs N 60 poles with his line to a stake on said line, E 155 poles with another of Weir's lines to a stake in Ledford's line, S10W 138 poles with said line to a stake on Ephraim Black's line, N40E 130 poles with said line to Black's corner post oak, S50W 60 poles with his line to a stake, & to beginning; the land was sold Apr. 3, 1824 by John Carruth jr, the patentee, to said Roberts; Roberts is likely to be injured by "aforementioned" error in the grant; he asks court to direct clerk to certify error to Secretary of State so it can be corrected: fourth line shall be N40W 130 poles instead of N40E 130 poles (signed) Joshua Roberts' mark "X". At court held fourth Monday after "fourth" in Sept. 1824, it appears to court that adjoining land owners were notified but no person appeared or objected to alteration of the grant; court granted prayer of petitioner & following alteration to be made: fourth line to read "N40W" instead of "N40E" (signed) at Lincolnton Nov. 8, 1824 Vardry McBee, cc; [on back] altered Nov. 19, 1824; [grant book 124 p. 197, see shuck #2588 in Lincoln Co in Secretary's grant files].

275. Macon Co Pleas & Quarter Sessions Court Jun. 15, 1856 following justices present: Jonathan M Bryson, Joab L Moore, Henry G Woodfin, Jesse R Silver, George W J Moore, Isaac N Kenner, & Burch McHan; heard petition of Andrew Hodgins to alter a grant: petition of "A H" Huggins (of said county) saying John McDowell, county surveyor, surveyed 50 ac for the petitioner in Macon Co on waters of "Skaner" Cr, begins at a corner locust of N Carroll's lot, runs S 100 poles to a poplar, "E thence E" 80 poles to a poplar, N 100 poles to a stake in a line of "old" Carroll's lot, & W 80 poles to beginning; the surveyor made an error in his certificate and called: begins at a corner locust of N Carroll's lot, runs S 100 poles to a poplar, E 80 poles to a poplar, W 100 poles to a stake in a line of old Carroll's lot, & W 80 poles to beginning; certified Jun. 2, 1851; grant No. 1218 issued Jun. 28, 1858 including the error; so petitioner is liable to be injured; the grant won't cover land intended; he asks court to hear the testimony, judge the facts, & order the clerk to certify the same to Secretary of State so grant can be corrected (signed) R M Henry, atto. For petitioner. Jun. 14, 1856 A H Hodgins wears above facts are true to best of his knowledge (signed) A H Hodges & John Hall, clk. Court ordered prayer of petitioner granted & clerk to forward decree to Secretary of State with grant & copy of petition so grant can be altered (signed) John Hall, clk. Jun. 17, 1856 John Hall, clerk, certifies foregoing is true copy of records in his office (signed) John Hall, clerk; [on back] altered Jun. 24, 1856;

Corrections/Alterations to Land Grants

[grant book 157 p. 263, see shuck #1966 in Macon Co in Secretary's grant files].

276. Macon Co Pleas & Quarter Sessions Court petition of John H Ledford asking court to order "amendment" of grant No. 1598 so it will "show the honest meaning"; Ledford obtained the grant for 50 ac which contains an error which may injure Ledford i.e. beginning corner isn't names; petitioner asks for court to make necessary order to have grant corrected (signed) Sept. 9, 1856 John H Ledford.   Petition was granted as far as ordering Secretary to insert "beginning at a hickory".   John Hall, clerk, certifies foregoing is perfect copy of records of this case (signed) Nov. 10, 1856 John Hall, clk; [on back] altered Dec. 13, 1856 W Hill, Sec. of State; [grant book 160 p. 56, see shuck #2481 in Macon Co in Secretary's grant files].

277. Macon Co Pleas & Quarter Sessions Court present H G Woodfin chairman, Jacob Silver, J M Syln(?), A B Bell, G W J Moore, Wm R McDowell, Danl McCoy, J M Bryson, & J N "Keener"; heard petition of H W Nolin; he obtained grant No. 2087 for tract No. 7956; there is a defect in the grant; begins at a [blank], runs N45W "&c" but grant should begin at a chestnut tree, runs N45W "& so on"; due to the defect, he is liable to be "much troubled" in the future; so he asks court to order clerk to make a return of proceedings to Secretary of State to alter the grant (signed) H M Nolin.   Court granted prayer of petition & ordered clerk to send necessary document to the Secretary.   John Hall, clerk, certifies foregoing is a true copy of minutes (signed) Jul. 1, 1857 John Hall, clk; [grant book 163 p. 194, see shuck #3346 in Macon Co in Secretary's grant files].

278. Sam L Rogers, clerk of Macon Co Superior Court, certifies transcript of case of E P Norton & "others" ex parte Nov. 13, 1791 (signed) Sam L Rogers;
        E P Norton, John Norton, Martha Norton, Mary Bumgarner, Vielta Rices, & Salena Norton, heirs at law of Elias Norton: petition to correct error in grant No. 705: an entry was made for 100 ac & surveyed and grant No. 705 issued to the enterer, Elias Norton; the surveyor made an error by omitting beginning corner being "a white oak tree"; the other calls of the survey are correct; since the grant "and conveyance" has been made [to omitted]; so they ask court to order the grant be corrected (signed) K Elias, atty. for petitioners.   Superior Court Fall term 1890 foregoing petition read & from the evidence it appears to the court that petitioners are entitled to their prayer; court ordered prayer be granted & "a white oak tree" should be inserted as beginning corner of grant No. 705 issued to Elias Norton; clerk is directed to certify a copy of order & petition to Secretary of State so grant can be corrected and send a copy of order & petition to Macon Co Register of Deeds so he an record it in his books; cost of proceedings to be paid by petitioner (signed) Fred Phillips, presiding judge; rendered Oct. 4, 1890 (signed) Sam L Rogers, clerk; [grant book 151 p. 457, see shuck #1267 in Macon Co in Secretary's grant files].

279. J F Mosburn, J N Kener, Joseph Welch, Wm J McDowell, H R Kimsey, A W Bell, & J M Lyle present; petition of Francis Poindexter asking to correct mistake in a grant issued Dec. 15, 1856 to him; it appears to court that land is on

Otters Cr instead of Peters Cr; petitioner is liable to be injured by the error; court ordered that this order be certified to Secretary of State so mistake can be corrected. Jun. term 1859 Macon Co R C Slayle, clerk, certifies foregoing is true copy of court records (signed) Sept. 27, 1859 R C Slayle, cc; [on back] "it appears that record of the grant is correct"; [grant book 161 p. 504, see shuck #3057 in Macon Co in Secretary's grant files].

280. Martin Co Jun. court 1794: read petition of Hosea Lanier; court is satisfied that notice was given to all persons "concerned"; it appeared to court that surveyor made a mistake in return of a plat mentioned in petitioner's "sale by" Earl of Granville's agent; eighth line of grant calls for W30N 320 poles but it should be N40W 435 poles to first station as is evident from examination of the old survey & grant and comparing to a new survey annexed to te petition which the court believes is the true plat; court ordered above plat be certified to Secretary of State so mistake can be rectified agreeable to an act of Assembly made in such cases; a true copy from record (signed) Thos Hunter, cc; [on back] altered Jan. 27, 1798;
 survey: first line is right and second; but third line is a mistake and reads W30N but should be N40W "which will give" 320 poles to "finishing" line as intended; black line forming a triangle is false and gives only 160 poles but it should be 320 poles to beginning letter "A"; true copy of plat annexed to petition (signed) Thos Hunter, cc; [no grant to Hosea Lanier identified; several Granville grants to other persons named Lanier].

281. Mecklenburg Co Oct. session 1803: Samuel Black, county surveyor, came to court & swore he surveyed 30 ac Jul. 9, 1794 for John Greer; he made a mistake Cabarrus Co instead of Mecklenburg Co (signed) Saml Black before Isaac Alexander, CMC. Oct. term 1803 court ordered prayer of petition granted and Secretary directed to make required alteration as described in surveyor's deposition (signed) Isaac Alexander, CMC; [on back] altered Nov. 26, 1804; [grant book 83 p. 155, see shuck #399A in Mecklenburg Co in Secretary's grant files].

282. Commissioners were appointed by Mecklenburg Co court to examine an error in a tract belonging to heirs of William Wilson deceased on waters of Sugar Cr, joins Joseph "Hayse", Richard Sharpe, Thomas Kilpatrick, Allen Reed, Joseph Reed, & "his" own land; they were sworn according to law; they examined the witnesses & every circumstance they could "meet with"; they believe there is an error in line from beginning hickory; instead of running S14W 218 poles as represented by the dotted line in annexed plat; it should run S5W 256 poles to a dead post oak in corner of Thomas Kilpatrick's old field (signed) Aug. 26, 1808 Hugh Parks, Isaac Alexander, Jas Wilson, Jas Sprott, & William "Lees" (witness) John Black, cs;
 Aug. 26, 1808 surveyed 190 ac for heirs of William Wilson esq deceased on Sugar Cr, begins at a hickory near Joseph Hayes' line, runs S5W 256 poles to a dead post oak in Thoms Kilpatrick's old field, N26W 268 poles with Reed's line to a "w o" by "the" road, N24W 54 poles with said of a hill crossing the creek to

Corrections/Alterations to Land Grants

a stake, N25E 50 poles to a hickory on the stony nob, & to beginning (signed) John Black; William Wilson & Joseph Reed, chain carriers. Oct. term 1808 court ordered error in annexed plat & certificate be rectified in Secretary's office agreeable to act of Assembly (signed) Isaac Alexander, CMC; [on back] "deed" No. 820 dated Mar. 4, 1775, altered Feb. 4, 1809; [grant book 27 p. 140, see shuck #2584 in Mecklenburg Co in Secretary's grant files].

283. Montgomery Co Court of Pleas & Quarter Sessions Apr. term 1853: court ordered Lookey Simmons, county surveyor, "has leave" to correct a survey made by him Apr. 5, 1842 for George Allen for 100 ac on which grant No. 3329 issued Nov. 11, 1844 (signed) Apr. 5, 1853 John McLennon, clerk; [note at bottom] Mr. Wm Hill please correct plat "filld" since I have one annexed to grant; interline third line say "South 32 poles to a stake" (signed) L Simmons, c sr; [on back] altered Apr. 22, 1853 W Hill, Sec; [grant book 149 p. 250, see shuck #3006 in Montgomery Co in Secretary's grant files].

284. Montgomery Co Oct. session 1796: petition of James Atkins: Isham Harris, late Montgomery Co surveyor, made a mistake in surveying 300 ac due to warrant No. 721; so James Atkins is injured & liable to loose part of his land; court ordered clerk to certify to James Glasgow, Secretary of State, so grant can be altered agreeable to annexed new plat. To James Glasgow, Secretary of State, George Davidson, clerk, certifies above is a true copy of court order requiring you to alter a grant agreeable to new plat & act of Assembly (signed) Nov. 16, 1797 Geor. Davidson, CMCC; [on back] altered Nov. 27, 1799;

Apr. 2, 1797 surveyed 300 ac for James Atkins on SW side of "P D" River and on Long Cr, begins at a sweet gum in a drain at intersection of said Atkins' 161 and 150 ac tracts, runs W 68 poles with line of the 150 tract to its corner with his other line, S 219 poles to his third corner post oak, S55W 93 poles to Wm Kendall's corner sweet gum, N40W 46 poles with & beyond Boss' line to a hickory, N 70 poles to a pine, N40E 40 poles to a white oak, N 40 poles to a pine, N20E 46 poles to a large white oak, N15W 320 poles to a stake, N80E 64 poles to William Weaver's third corner "with" his second line, S10E 160 poles "reverse" to his corner with his other line, N80E 72 poles to said Atkins' corner "white", & with his line to beginning (signed) J Atkins, DS; William Weaver & Abra Atkins, chain carriers; [grant not identified].

285. Montgomery Co Apr. session 1806 court ordered that Secretary alter courses of grant to Benjamin Beard, John Smith, & David Smith for 200 ac agreeable to annexed certificate; it appears to court there is an error in first survey; land has been sold to Thomas Chiles esq (signed) Jno Davidson, ccc; [on back] altered Dec. 11, 1806;

Plat represents 200 ac on NE side of Pee Dee [R] and W side of Little R, begins at a white oak on W side of Little R bank near or joins fourth line of the other survey that's on NE side of the river, runs S62W 179 poles, S28E 179 poles, N62E 179 poles, & N28W 179 poles to beginning; surveyed Mar. 11, 1775 for Benjn Beard, John Smith, & David Smith (signed) Jas Chappell, surv; [mistake puts same size plat West and joins correct tract]; [grant not identified].

286. Oct. 14, 1806 Montgomery Co General Thomas Chiles before William Peacock, one of justices of peace, swears a grant for 200 ac issued to Benjamin Beard, John Smith, & David Smith on W side fo Little R then in Anson Co and now Montgomery Co; grant is lost or mislaid and can't be found (signed) Thos Chiles (witness) William Peacock, JP; [grant No. 1067 issued Mar. 11, 1775, grant book 27 p. 176, see shuck #3928 in Montgomery Co in Secretary's grant files; lost grant, not an alteration].

287. Oct. 14, 1806 Montgomery Co; General Thomas Chiles before William Peacock, one of justices of peace, swears a grant for 200 ac issued to Benjamin Beard, John Smith, & David Smith on W side of Little R then in Anson Co & now in Montgomery Co; grant is lost or mislaid & can't be found (signed) Thos Chiles (witness) William Peacock, JP; [grant #1067 issued Mar. 11, 1775, book 27 p. 176, see shuck #3928 in Montgomery Co in Secretary's grant files],

288. Montgomery Co Apr. session 1801 court ordered that clerk certify to Secretary of State to alter the courses of 200 ac in said county on Mountain Cr, patented by Nevin Clark, agreeable to plat hereunto annexed by resurvey & order of county court (signed Apr. 6, 1801 Jno Davidson, CMCC; [on back] altered Dec. 8, 1803;
    200 ac on Mountain Cr, begins at a white oak, runs S35W 102 poles to Murdoh Chisholm's line, S31E 48 poles with his line to a poplar, S57W 91 poles with said Chisholm's line to a spanish oak, S4E 112 poles to Baton's line, E 173 poles crossing Fayetteville Road to a pine, & to beginning; land formerly surveyed for "Nevan" Clark & granted Jan. 22, 1773 to him but contained only 100 ac as shown by dotted lines; resurveyed Oct. 27, 1797 by Thos Cotton, survr; Kenneth Clark & John Yarbrough, chain carriers; [grant book 22 p. 133, see shuck #2915 in Anson Co in Secretary's grant files].

289. Montgomery Co: I certify I "attended" & made actual survey of 100 ac granted to Thomas Ellis on Scaly bark Br and find beginning corner "the marked line" to bear S27W instead of S27E, then N63W, then N27E, & to beginning (signed) Andrew Wade, sury. Montgomery Co court Oct. session 1822: petition of Thomas Ellis; it is ordered by court that Secretary of State made above alterations in the grant (signed) Oct. 25, 1822 J B Martin, clk; [on back] Thos Ellis 100 ac grant No. 655 Montgomery Co, altered Nov. 7, 1822 Wm Hill, Secry; [grant book 80 p. 455, see shuck #670 in Montgomery Co in Secretary's grant files].

290. Montgomery Co Pleas & Quarter Sessions Court held at court house in Troy first Monday in Oct. [Jan.–lined out] 1852 or Oct. 4; present following justices: William Coggin, George Coggin, Thos J Forney, E G L Barringer, David Bruton, James W McRae, Anlsy McAulay, P C Sand [or Sanders], John M Worth, Nelson Harris, Spencer Haltom [or Haltone], Neill Gillis, James Batten, S H Christian, E

Corrections/Alterations to Land Grants

H Davis, & A Graham; William Hamilton ex parte petition to correct a patent; Oct. session 1852 it appears to satisfaction of court that William Hamilton made a certificate according to law of 100 ac on waters of Barnes Cr joins land of Leah [or Seah] Steed & "others"; on Nov. 12, 1850 land was surveyed by Thos J Bright, county surveyor, & Nelson Steed & Ira Hamilton "chs"; the surveyor in plating the land said begins at William Hamilton's own corner gum but he should have said begins at a gum on W bank of Barnes Cr "about middle of William Hamilton old McCulloch's line"; the petitioner is ready to show this and he is liable to be "put to expence & inconvinance of a low suit" and perhaps be disposed of his land; so petitioner asks court to hear testimony about the truth of the allegations and if it appears the surveyor's return will injure the petitioner due the said mistake he asks court to direct clerk to certify the facts to Secretary of State and request he file the same in his office & correct the patent & records in his office (signed) Peacock, for the petitioner.   John McLennan, clerk, certifies above is true copy of facts in the petition; and certifies above justices were on the bench. (signed) at Troy Oct. 4, 1852 John McLennan, clerk; [on back] altered Nov. 18, 1852 W Hill, Sec. of State; [grant book 153 p. 683, see shuck #3224 in Montgomery Co in Secretary's grant files].

291. Montgomery Co Pleas & Quarter Sessions Court Jan. session 1835; petition of Myrick Harwood was heard; court ordered that Secretary of State alter courses of 50 ac in third line from S 26 chains 50 links to E 8 chains 75 links (signed) J B Martin, clk; [on back] Myrick "Harward" 50 ac Montgomery Co, altered Nov. 16, 1835 Wm Hill, Secretary; [grant book 140 p. 402, see shuck #2642 in Montgomery Co in Secretary's grant files].

292. Montgomery Co Jul. session 1801 heard petition of William Hunt to amend a grant to John Smith by extending third line from 18 to 180 poles; heard proof that error or mistake was made by surveyor and due notice has been served on "the person" whose land joins the petitioner; court ordered that clerk certify to Secretary of State that he amend the grant agreeable to petition and register alter registration to make it conformable to "wish" of petition (signed) Jul. 7, 1801 Jno Davidson, CMCC; [on back] altered Nov. 16, 1801 W W; [8 grants to John Smith in Montgomery Co].

293. Montgomery Co Pleas & Quarter Sessions Court Jul. session 1833; court ordered that Secretary of State alter courses of 130 ac granted to John Layton agreeable to survey made by Joseph Coble; John B Martin, clerk, certifies foregoing order is a true copy from records in my office (signed) Oct. 22, 1833 J B Martin, clk; [on back] John "Laton" 130 ac Montgomery Co, altered Dec. 6, 1833 W Hill, Secry;
    Jun. 28, 1833 plat represents 130 ac granted to John Laton agreeable to courses & distances of grant but it is found in running first line N60W the course given, it will not run with Mason's line as called for in the grant neither is Mason's corner post oak [present], Mason's corner is found to be North 43 poles of beginning corner of Laton's tract "a due West course and 58 poles in distance"

will reach the second [third—lined out] mentioned in the grant (signed) Jos "Couble"; [grant book 126 p. 347, see shuck #1898 in Secretary's grant files].

294. Montgomery Co Apr. session 1792 petition of Edmond Lilly who purchased 200 ac of Jacob Bankston on waters of Long Cr surveyed Nov. 17, 1779 by Joseph McClester, then deputy county surveyor; land was granted to Jacob Bankston Sept. 24, 1785; petitioner says there were errors in surveyor's certificate and in the grant whereby he is injured; I certify that on examination of grant, "the works", & surveyor's return, it was considered & found by court that second line of the tract ought to run N46W instead of N46E as surveyor certified; court ordered clerk to certify the same to "Honnerable" James Glasgow, Secretary of State, so the same can be altered as stated above agreeable to act of General Assembly made in such cases (signed) Dec. 6, 1793 Geo Davidson, CCC; [on back] No. 314 Nov. 24, 1785; [grant book 59 p. 48, see shuck #310 in Montgomery Co in Secretary's grant files].

295. Montgomery Co Oct. session 1807 it appears to justices of pleas & quarter sessions court that there was an error in lines of grant #792 issued Jul. 15, 1795 to Christopher Lyoley; court ordered that clerk issue an order to Secretary of State to alter the grant & make it agreeable to the annexed plat from James Chappell, county surveyor; John Smith, clerk, certifies James "Chappel" is county surveyor (signed) Oct. 12, 1807 J Smith, ccc; [on back] altered Nov. 10, 1807;
  I certify black lines includes land that was surveyed agreeable to marked trees "all round" from which there can be good proof "off", begins at a post oak by a red oak & post oak pointers, runs N85E 127 poles to a post oak by a post oak, S5E 127 poles, S85W 127 poles, N5W 127 poles to first station or 100 ac Sept. 5, 1807 (signed) Jas Chappell [no chain carriers mentioned, dotted line in shape of rectangle also drawn on plat]; [grant book 87 p. 292, see shuck #805 in Montgomery Co in Secretary's grant files].

296. Montgomery Co Jan. session 1807 ordered by court that Secretary of State alter grant No. 842 issued Jul. 15, 1795 to Phinehas Nixon as follows: begins at a pine on N side of Dutch Road, runs S45E 169 poles to a pine & post oak, E 250 poles to & with Walker's line crossing Long Cr to Hewet Weeks' corner post oak, N 90 poles with & beyond his line to a white oak in Rogers' line, W 120 poles with his line to his corner post oak, N 29 poles to a small red oak, & W 266 poles to beginning (signed) Jno Davidson, ccc.   I certify the above is true copy of order of court (signed) Jan. 9, 1807 Jno Davidson, ccc; [on back] altered Dec. 1, 1807; [grant book 87 p. 316, see shuck #855 in Montgomery Co in Secretary's grant files];
  Jan. 8, 1807 surveyed 200 ac by court order for Phenhas Nixon on SW side of Yadkin R & both sides of Long Cr [metes & bounds same as above] (signed) J Atkins, DS; Wm Walker & Frederick Rogers, chain carriers.

297. Montgomery Co Pleas & Quarter Sessions Court petition of William Peacock, present owner of 200 ac granted Dec. 20, 1791 to John Roe; last or

closing line of grant was omitted "to wit" from the creek to beginning corner; court ordered that Secretary made the necessary alterations to the grant agreeable to act of Assembly (signed) Jan. 25, 1822 J M Martin, clk; [on back] record & survey altered the grant not presented Dec. 10, 1822 W Hill, Secry; [grant book 79 p. 185, see shuck #668 in Montgomery Co in Secretary's grant files].

298. Montgomery Co Jan. session 1797 petition of Josiah Right: he was injured by error made by James Cotten, county surveyor, and he is liable to "loose" 10 ac out of the 100 ac surveyed by said James Cotten; allegations & testimony heard; court ordered clerk to certify to "Honnerable" James Glasgow, Secretary of State, to alter lines of the "land" and make out a new grant agreeable to new platts hereunto annexed to say begins at a beach at mouth of Little Mountain Br, runs N10E 118 poles to a spanish oak in Fry's line, W 86 poles with said line to Joseph McLester's line, S25W 60 poles, W 40 poles, S 50 poles, E 40 poles, S40E 62 poles to a black oak on the river bank, & up the river to beginning (signed) Apr. 13, 1797 Geo Davidson, CMC; [on back] altered Nov. 30, 1796;
    survey Jan. 5, 1797 agreeable to order of Jan. 1797 court; land sold by Josiah "Wright" to James Cox to find whether there is 100 ac or not: begins at a beech at mouth of Little Mountain Br in Fry's line, runs W 86 poles with said line to Joseph McLester's line, S25W 60 poles "but McLester's line said S15W", S 50 poles to a stake in Ledbetter's line, S40E 46 poles "but when measured was 62 poles" to a black oak on the river bank, & up the river to beginning which includes only 87 ac; for compliment I added 13 ac begins at fourth corner, runs N 40 poles, S 50 poles, & E 40 poles (signed) Isham Harris; Josiah Wright & Wm Cox, chain carriers; [2 copies of survey in shuck]; [grant book 76 p. 377, see shuck #584 in Montgomery Co in Secretary's grant files].

299. Montgomery Co Oct. session 1802 court ordered Secretary of State to alter patent No. 416 to John Randle surveyed May 24, 1785 by Edmond Lilly containing 300 ac to "inclosed platts" due to an act of General Assembly made in such cases due to error of former surveyor that "throughs" land on other patented land and leaves out land first intended (signed) Nov. 5, 1803 Jno Davidson, clk; [on back] altered Sept. 12, 1808;
    survey 300 ac on SW side of Pee Dee R & on waters of Jacobs Cr, begins at a white oak on W side of the creek, runs N57W 71 poles to a red oak, W 70 poles to a stake among 3 pines, S20W 69 poles to a pine, W 30 poles to a hickory in Upchurch's line, S14W 64 poles with said line to said Upchurch's corner pine, N76W 96 poles to a small corner red oak in Upchurch's line, S 202 ples to a corner red oak, N78E 194 poles, & N32E 262 poles to beginning; surveyed Mar. 25, 1803 for John Randle (signed) Thos Cotton, sur, Isham Harris, D S; Wilson Randle & Wm Randle, chain carriers; [2 copies of survey in shuck]; [grant book 65 p. 290, see shuck #425 in Montgomery Co in Secretary's grant files].

300. Montgomery Co Apr. session 1801 court ordered clerk to certify to Secretary of State to alter second course in a grant for 150 ac on Beverdam Cr granted to Jams Cotton now property of Samuel Reaves; grant to be altered agreeable to plat

filed in Secretary's office by a resurvey & court order (signed) Apr. 6, 1801 Jno Davidson, CMCC; [on back] altered Dec. 18, 1801;

Montgomery Co Jul. session 1799 court ordered that county surveyor resurvey 300 ac for Samuel Reaves according to his first intention to have the land run (signed) Jno Davidson, ccc;

agreeable to court order to me, resurveyed 300 ac for Samuel "Reeves" on Reynolds' fork of Beaverdam Cr; begins at a white oak between 4 white oak pointers, runs N6E 220 poles, S84E 220 poles, S6W 220 poles, & N84W 220 poles to beginning (signed) Oct. 22, 1799 Thos Cotton, survr; John Taylor & Jesse Reeves, chain carriers; [on back] this cannot issue the claimant ought to have got an order for the alteration of his grant, recd. Enclosed with this 6 shillings 6 pence W W; [may be grant in book 26 p. 56, see shuck #3516 in Anson Co; no 300 ac grant to J Cotton in Montgomery Co in Secretary's grant files].

301. Montgomery Co Jul. session 1809 it appears to court of pleas & quarter sessions that there is a mistake by the surveyor in courses of grant #78 in the Secretary's office; court ordered Secretary to alter the courses agreeable to annexed plan & issue a new grant for the same (signed) first Monday in Jul. 1809 J Smith, ccc.   Jul. session 1809 it appears to court that there is an error in grant No. 78 issued Jul. 1, 1758 to Thomas Sugg [no more information];

Jul. session 1809 on motion of Mr. Thos Sugg it appears to county court that there is error in grant No. 78 issued Jul. 1, 1758 in the Secretary's office; court ordered clerk [certify the same] to the Secretary so grant can be altered agreeable to annexed plan & new grant can issue (signed) first Monday in Jul. 1809 J Smith, ccc;

Feb. 20, 1808 I believe there is a surveyor's mistake in first line of plot of this land; old plat leaves out the river which anyone can see was intended to be in the survey; the dotted lines are the mistake; begins at a red oak, runs N87E 233 poles to a pine, N3W 273 poles, S87W 233 poles to a stake, & S3W 273 poles to first station; surveyed for Johnston & Semore Spencer (signed) Jas Chappell, surv; [no chain carriers mentioned]; [new survey on both sides of Little R]; [on back] altered Apr. 4, 1810; [grant book 2 p. 206, see shuck #500 in Anson Co in Secretary's grant files].

302. petition of Jesse Bean to justices of Moore Co court: about Jun. 2, 1795 Niell McLeod, surveyor, surveyed 50 ac for the petitioner "Wt" of McLendons Cr, begins at a stake 2 pines & a black jack pointers Samuel Dunn's corner, runs N48E 27 chains 50 links, N20W 20 chains, & S70W 36 chains to beginning; in the certificate, surveyor said third line was S70W 36 chains instead of S40W 36 chains; so the petitioner asks that the error in the patent can be rectified "as it" includes more land that the marked line "and" the petitioner's "enterd"; Archibald McBryde, clerk, certifies above is true copy of original petition filed in his office; at Feb. court "last" the prayer of petition was granted (signed) Nov. 17, 1804 A McBride; [on back] altered Nov. 21, 1805; [grant #1543 issued Dec. 5, 1800 due to entry #351, grant book 108 p. 311, see shuck #1593 in Moore Co].

Corrections/Alterations to Land Grants

303. Moore Co Pleas & Quarter Sessions Court May 1797 court ordered courses of 50 ac granted May 18, 189 to Christian Bethune be altered from beginning line N60W 80 poles to a pine, S30W 100 poles to a pine, S60E 80 poles to a hickory, & N30E 100 poles to beginning TO begins at a holly in a branch of S side of "the" improvement, runs N50W 15 chains to Allan Martin's corner red oak, N 10 chains to a pine black jack & gum pointers, N70E 14 chains to a small sourwood in Campbell's line, "then as it" S60E 27 chains 50 links, & S65W 28 chains to beginning; I certify above is true copy from minutes (signed) Jun. 2, 1797 Arch McBryde, clk; [on back] altered agreeable to within order Feb. 7, 1798 W H; [only one grant to C Bethune in Moore Co in 1822].

304. Petition of Jacob Carringer to May session 1798 Moore Co Pleas & Quarter Sessions Court: on Sept. 2, 1762 Ferquhard Campbell, surveyor, surveyed 200 ac for the petitioner in Cumberland Co now Moore on W side of Deep R, begins at a red [white—lined out] oak between William Morgan & Leonard Hart, runs S15E 134 poles along Hart's line to a pine, E 179 poles to a pine, N 130 poles to a stake, & W 218 poles to beginning; the surveyor made an error in platting the certificate to the Secretary's office as follows: begins at a red oak between William Morgan & Leonard Hart, runs S 179 poles to a pine, W 179 poles to a pine, N 179 poles to a stake, & E 179 poles to beginning; about [blank] term of court, the petitioner asked to have the courses altered alleging they should have been: begins at a red oak between William Morgan & Leonard Hart, runs N 179 poles to a pine, E 179 poles to a pine, S 179 poles to a stake, & W 179 poles to beginning; the court "afterwards" ordered "the same" accordingly & patent was altered according to the order; "afterwards" the petitioner discovered there is a mistake in alteration of the patent; so at [blank] term, he petitioned again to county court "among other things" saying he was mistaken in two of the courses in alteration of patent: first course & third course which should have been as originally in the patent before it was altered; so he asks to alter the patent "back" accordingly; court ordered "the same accordingly"; last mentioned order has not been certified to Secretary nor has patent been altered pursuant to last order; petitioner has discovered the first course instead of running South as in the patent was surveyed & should have been S15E and first distance instead of 179 poles as in the patent should have been 134 poles along Hart's line and third course instead of South as in alteration should have been North as "originally" and distance in third line should have been 130 poles instead of 19 poles and distance in fourth line instead of 179 poles as in patent should be 218 poles; Christopher Yew, John Gardner, Lewis Gardner, & George Carringer are all the people who have adjoining land to the patent; petitioner asks that last mentioned order to amend the first mentioned order be amended and courses of the patent be altered thus: begins at a red oak between William Morgan & Leonard Hart, runs S15E 134 poles along Hart's line to a pine, E 179 poles to a pine, N 130 poles to a stake, W 218 poles to beginning; then the mistakes aforesaid can be rectified pursuant to act of General Assembly made in such cases. Aug. session 1798 prayer of foregoing petition was granted (signed) Nov. 20, 1798 Murdoch McKenzie; [on back] altered Dec. 22, 1798;
petition of Jacob Carringer to Moore Co Pleas & Quarter Sessions Court

Corrections/Alterations to Land Grants

[same information as first part of above petition, same neighbors mentioned]; Nov. term 1794 Jacob Carringer vs Christopher Yew & "others" petition; ordered petition be taken "pro confesso" and patent be rectified; I certify foregoing is true copy of petition (signed) Dec. 7, 1796 Archd McBryde, cc; [on back] No. 60 patent altered; [grant #60 issued Dec. 21, 1763 due to entry #152, grant book 17 p. 28 see shuck #450 and grant book 18 p. 22 see shuck #630 in Cumberland Co in Secretary's grant files].

305. Moore Co Pleas & Quarter Sessions Court Aug. term 1826 Richard Cheek vs Richd Street, Wm Dowd, & George Stewart petition to rectify error in grant: in this case court ordered Secretary of State to alter courses & distances of lines of grant issued Nov. 11, 1807 to Richard Cheek as follows: begins at Shearing's corner post oak, runs E 40 chains, S 22 chains with "the" second line, E 55 chains 55 links to a stake 3 pines "pinters", N 71 chains 15 links to & with Carrell's line to a stake 2 pines pointers White's corner, W 22 chains to a stake, S 32 chains 30 links to & with Murly's line to his corner on the bank of Lick Cr, W 50 chains "as it" to a stake among 3 pines, N23 chains with another of Murley's lines, S 40 chains, & "direct" to beginning; Cornelius Dowd, clerk, certifies above is decree of the court in above case (signed) Oct. 26, 1826 Corn. Dowd, clk; [on back] altered Jan. 15, 1827; [grant No. 1941 issued Nov. 11, 1807, grant book 122 p. 384, see shuck #1978 in Moore Co in Secretary's grant files].

306. Moore Co Pleas & Quarter Sessions Court Nov. term 1825: petition of Kenneth Clark asking to correct errors in a grant for 100 ac to Wm Dunn and in a deed by Wm Dunn "and" Richd Cheek to said Clark for land in the grant; court ordered Secretary of State alter the grant to read as follows: [no beginning mentioned] N72E 25 chains, S18E 40 chains, S72W 25 chains, N18W 40 chains to beginning; register of Moore County to alter his records in "both cases" and make them conformable to above courses & distances.   Cornelius Dowd, clerk, certifies above is true transcript of records in his office (signed) Dec. 2, 1825 Corn. Dowd, clk; [on back] altered Dec. 9, 1825 Wm Hill, Secry; [Dunn has 2 grants for 100 ac in Moore Co: grant book 74 p. 78 see shuck #245 and grant book 102 p. 285 see shuck #1310 in Moore Co in Secretary's grant files].

307. petition of Stephen "Colins" to Moore Co court: petitioner shows that dotted lines in annexed plot represent courses of a certificate for original survey; black lines represent original survey as it was "run off" which shows an error in original plat & certificate; he asks court to order that survey be rectified agreeable to act of Assembly made in such cases (signed) Stephen Collins; [on back] Feb. term 1804 Moore Co court ordered that lines of 200 ac that's property of Stephen Collins be altered according to prayer of petition and said petition not be filed but returned to petitioner; Archibald McBryde, clerk, certifies above is true copy from court minutes, within is petition which was presented on which above order was obtained (signed) Sept. 20, 1804 A McBryde;

     survey Dec. 20, 1785 for Thomas Egerton for 200 ac due to warrant No. 506; on Dunnams Cr; begins at a pine, runs S70E 202 poles to a pine, N20E 5

Corrections/Alterations to Land Grants

poles to Alston's corner, S70W 70 poles to a stake, N20E 170 poles to a stake, N70W 160 poles to a stake, & S20W 202 poles to first station (signed) J Henson, DS; Ralph Davis & Wm Seal, chain carriers;

another survey [no date] 200 ac begins at a pine, runs N71E 50 chains 50 links to a stake, N51E 11 chains 20 links to Alston's corner red oak, S89E 5 chains with his line to a stake, N19W 29 chains 40 links to a stake in James Davis' line, N36W 17 chains 50 links to a stake in Yarborough's line, S5W 11 chains 80 links with it to a pine, N84W 20 chains 75 links to a lightwood stump, N2E 20 chains to a stake, N69W 12 chains 50 links to a stake, & S19w 50 chains 50 links to beginning; [dotted line also shown on this plat; plats of the 2 surveys don't match]; [on back] alteration of grant to Thomas "Eagerton" for 200 ac, altered Feb. 11, 1805; [grant #19 issued May 15, 1787, grant book 65 p. 171, see shuck #27 in Moore Co in Secretary's grant files].

308. Petition of Archibald Dalrymple on behalf of his wife Mary to Moore Co Pleas & Quarter Sessions Court: in right of his wife, the petitioner owns "most of" 100 ac granted to John Dobbins; the surveyor made an error in plotting the same in his return to the Secretary's office by describing land as follows: on a branch of Little R called Bear Cr, begins at a pine, runs N20W 127 poles to a pine, N70W 127 poles to a stake, S20E 126 poles to a pine, & N 70E 127 poles to beginning "intended" to contain 100 ac; but it should have been: begins at a white oak, runs N20W 127 poles to a pine, S70W 127 poles to a stake, S20E 127 poles to a pine, & N70E 127 poles to beginning; John Dobbins sold the land to Charles Walker who sold to Henry Garter sr deceased; the petitioner is one of heirs at law of said Henry in right of his wife Mary; the error runs through all the conveyances of the land; he asks for an order to Secretary of State & Register through whose offices the conveyances have passed to rectify the errors; the only persons owning adjoining land are Jacob Garter & the petitioner [not signed] Feb. session 1807 a true copy of original filed in my office (signed) A McBryde, clr. Feb. 1807 I certify this term the prayer of above petition was granted (signed) Mar. 1, 1807 A McBryde; [on back] altered Dec. 5, 1807; [only one grant in Moore Co to J Dobbins for 50 ac].

309. Petition of Archibald "Darymple" on behalf of himself & his wife Mary to Moore Co Pleas & Quarter Sessions Court: they own land in Moore Co as one of heirs at law of Henry Garter [or Gaster] sr deceased by right of the wife Mary; land was entered by said Henry & surveyed by J Hinson, deputy surveyor, Dec. 6, 1785; surveyor made an error in his return to Secretary's office by describing land: on a branch of Little R, begins at Mr. Dalrymple's corner black jack, runs N30W 140 poles to a pine, S50E 94 poles to a pine, N 60 poles, W 80 poles, S 120 poles, E 80 poles, S50E 110 poles to his own corner pine, S30E 94 poles with his own line to a pine, N50E 13 poles to first station "intended" to contain 100 ac; but lines should have been described: begins at Mr. Dalrymple's corner black jack, runs N32W 35 chains 20 links to a red oak, S50W 5 chains 50 links to a stake, S20W 3 chains 40 links to a stake, S20W 3 chains 40 links to a white oak, N70W 1 chains 50 links to a stake, S43W 11 chains 50 links to a pine, S 3 chains

Corrections/Alterations to Land Grants

75 links to a stake among pines in Dobbins' line, N70E 18 chains "as it" to a large pine, S20E 21 chains 50 lines, & to beginning; petitioner shows only persons owning adjoining land are himself, James Dalrymple, William Dalrymple, & Jacob Garter; petitioner asks court to order Secretary of State & Register of this county to rectify errors [not signed] Feb. session 1807 a true copy from original filed in my office (signed) A McBryde.   Feb. session 1807 I certify this term the prayer of petitioner was granted (signed) Mar. 1, 1807 A McBryde; [on back] altered Dec. 14, 1807 [following lines out] the grant ought to be brought forward to be made conformable to the record W W; [may be grant in book 65 p. 189, see shuck #99 in Moore Co in Secretary's grant files].

310. Aug. session 1804 Moore Co Pleas & Quarter Sessions Court petition of John Dalrymple, Arcibald Dalrymple & "other" heirs of John Dalrymple deceased: about Jun. 7, 1799 John Dalrymple sr obtained a grant for 100 [1,000--lined out] ac in Moore Co joins his "other" land; land is described, by mistake, in grant as follows: begins at a pine at intersection of Miller's & Garter's lines, runs S30W 25 chains to a red oak & 2 black jacks pointers, N60W 41 chains, N30E 25 chains, & to beginning; but courses intended and marked were: begins at a pine at intersection of Miller's & Garter's lines, runs S30W 25 chains to a red oak, S60E 41 chains, N30E 22 chains to Miller's line, & "as it" to beginning which are the true courses; petitioners ask that courses inserted by mistake be altered and made conformable to last mentioned coursed and that Secretary of State be ordered to make the alteration; petitioners ask that "usual process" issue to Alexander McIver the only person who has adjoining land except the petitioners [not signed]. At Moore Co Pleas & Quarter Sessions Court foregoing petition was heard; court ordered prayer of petition be granted; Secretary of State is requested to alter the grant (signed) Dec. 5, 1802 Archd McBryde & M McKenzie; [on back] altered Dec. 10, 1804; [grant #1256 issued Jun. 7, 1799, grant book 102 p. 279, see shuck #1304 in Moore Co in Secretary's grant files].

311. Moore Co court Nov. term 1825 petition of James Dalrymple asking to correct errors in a grant to Willis Oliver for 100 ac in Cumberland now Moore Co; court ordered that Secretary of State alter the grant to read as follows: begins at a dead red oak in Fordham Blackman's line between pointers, runs S52W crossing Midoltons Br to a stake near where a scrub oak stood, N38W 44 chains 60 links across Fall Cr to a stake & pointers, N40E 13 chains 78 links to a stake & pointers in Thomas Coxe's line, S49E 46 chains "as" that line to beginning; court ordered Register of Cumberland Co & Moore Co to correct their records where the grant or any conveyance is registered & make records conformable to above courses & distances.   Cornelius Dowd, clerk, certifies above is true transcript of the records in his office (signed) Dec. 2, 1825 Corn. Dowd, clk; [on back] altered Dec. 9, 1825; [grant book 69 p. 91, see shuck #2184 in Cumberland Co in Secretary's grant files].

312. Moore Co Pleas & Quarter Sessions Court Feb. term 1807 petition of Samuel Darke: about 1796 Archibald Ray, deputy county surveyor, surveyed land for the

petitioner; land was "run out" & lines marked as follows: begins at Sarah Runnels' corner, runs S42E 22 chains 50 links to a stake in Whitford's line, N60E 17 chains 50 links to Whitford's corner, S30W 22 chains 65 links to a post oak hickory black jack & red oak pointers, N30E 37 chains to a post oak, S32W 27 chains 25 links to Johnston's corner stake, S44W 35 chains to Johnston's corner pine, N23E 5 chains to said Johnston's corner, W 10 chains with Johnston's line to a stake among a hickory black jack & post oak pointers, N28W 13 chains to Jackson's [Johnston--lined out] 50 ac tract, S77W 20 chains to Jackson's other corner, S30E 24 chains, N70E 25 chains with Sarah Runnells' (sic) line to her corner, S31W 47 chains with her other line to beginning; but surveyor made a mistake in his plat & return to Secretary's office as follows: begins at Sarah Rynalds corner, runs S42E 22.50 [chains] to a stake on Whitford's line, N60E 17.50 [chains] to Whitford's corner, S30W 22.65 [chains] to a post oak, N75E 55 chains, N30E 40 chains, & S75W 78 chains to beginning; these courses run into land granted to other persons "many years ago" and covers "but" a small part of land laid off for the petitioner; petitioner says adjoining land owners are Jeptha Rynalds, James McDonald, & Carnaby Stevens; petitioner asks court to order Secretary of State to alter lines of the grant & make them conformable to courses first set forth in this petition (signed) Samuel Darke; Archibald McBryde, clerk, certifies foregoing is true copy of original petition in my office; prayer of petition was granted by the court (signed) Feb. 24, 1807 A McBryde; [on back Dec. 2, 1807; [grant book 101 p. 1, see shuck #1060 in Moore Co in Secretary's grant files].

313. petition of John Dowd (of Chatham Co) to Moore Co court: about Apr. 14, 1785 William Finley surveyed land for Moses Oliver on Fall Cr, begins at his own corner stake, runs N48E 38 chains 78 links to a stake by a black gum a white oak & spanish oak, N42W 41 chains to a post oak by 2 spanish oaks, N48E 34 chains to a stake by 3 red oaks, E 20 chains to a pine by 2 pines, S42E 22 chains to a stake by 3 pines by Underwood's second line, S51W 22 chains "as his line" to a hickory [stake by 3 pines--lined out] by a post oak pine & 3 red oaks & 2 hickories Underwood's third corner, S44E 20 chains as his line to a small sassafras between 3 red oaks on Murchison's line, S35W 30 chains as his line to a black jack by a hickory red oak & 2 black jacks Murchison's corner, S55E 25 chains as his second line to a red oak by a post oak a pine red oak & sassafras, S84 1/2W 24 chains to a stake by 3 pines Middleton's corner, N88W 27 chains 60 links to a spanish oak by 3 spanish oaks Willis Oliver sr's first corner of 100 ac, & N50W 10 chains to beginning; said Finley made a mistake in the certificate to the Secretary's office as follows: begins at his own corner stake, runs N48E 277 poles as his own line to a black oak by his other line, N42W 127 poles to a p;ost oak, E 250 poles to a pine, S 200 poles to a pine, S57W 150 poles by Murchison's line, W 241 poles "to the plan of beginning"; petitioner shows land has since become property of Judith Dowd of Chatham Co, mother of the petitioner; he asks court to rectify error by inserting first courses in the patent instead of latter courses; he shows Willis Oliver sr, Willis Oliver jr, George Underwood, & John Shepherd jr are only adjoining land owners; petitioner asks for an order consistent with equity & justice & agreeable with prayer of petition (signed) Feb. 22, 1798 John Dowd.   Moore

Corrections/Alterations to Land Grants

Co May session 1798 I certify foregoing is true copy of original petition filed in my office Feb. session last; copies were issued to adjoining land owners; deputy sheriff certified at this term he delivered the copies to the persons; court granted prayer of petition & ordered Secretary to rectify mistake and make grant conformable to petition; witness Arcibald McBryde, clerk (signed) May 26, 1798 to A McBryde; [on back] altered patent & record Jun. 19, 1798; [grant No. 101 issued May 15, 1787, grant book 65 p. 195, see shuck #109 in Moore Co in Secretary's grant files].

314. Moore Co Pleas & Quarter Sessions Court May 1800 Robert Edwards presented a petition asking to correct a mistake in a grant for 250 ac to him: first line as written in certificate annexed to grant be altered from S18E 27 chains 50 links to S18E 37 chains 50 links which will correspond with the plat of the land annexed to grant; adjoining land owners were present & "content"; this court ordered alteration be made according to prayer of petition & clerk to certify the same to Secretary of State; "Archibald", clerk, certifies above is true copy from records of said court (signed) Jun. 4, 1800 A McBryde; [on back] altered agreeable to within other Nov. 28, 1800 "L M"; [may be grant book 20 p. 385, see shuck #862 in Cumberland Co in Secretary's grant files].

315. Moore Co Pleas & Quarter Sessions Court Nov. term 1801 William Feagin vs William Fry & "others" petition to rectify errors in a grant: court ordered errors in grant mentioned in the petition be rectified so courses & distances are conformable to following: 250 ac begins at a pine in Joseph Fry's line, runs N20W 12 chains 50 links to Benjn Fry's line of 40 ac, N29E 5 chains to Benjn Fry's corner, N14W 44 chains to Benjn Fry's other corner, S69W 7 chains 75 links with Benjn Fry's line to Glascock's line, N 25 chains "as it" to William Feagin's corner red oak stump, N87E 10 chains to a stake 2 hickories & a post oak pointers, S50E 9 chains 12 links to William Feagin's corner on 2 black oaks, S50E 26 chains 88 links to Richardson Feagin's corner post oak, S5E 60 chains to Richardson Feagin's line, N80W 6 chains 50 links to Joseph Fry's corner, & with Joseph Fry's line to beginning; Archibald McBryde, clerk, certifies foregoing is true copy from the court records (signed) Nov. 19, 1801 A McBryde; [on back] altered Nov. 23, 1803;

 2 copies of survey made pursuant to court order Nov. term 1801 obtained by William Feagin to correct errors in grant No. 287 [same metes & bounds as above] (signed) Arck Ray, surveyor [no date & no chain carriers mentioned]; [grant No. 287 issued Nov. 24, 1790, grant book 74 p. 248, see shuck #295 in Moore Co].

316. Moore Co Pleas & Quarter Sessions Court May session 1803 William W Folsom vs Gressy Carmachael--petition to rectify errors in grant issued Sept. 24, 1749 to Philip Miller for 200 ac: petition was heard and court ordered lines of the grant stand at present on W side of "NW of NW" branch of Cape Fear R & on a branch of Little R beyond head of Lick Cr, begins at a white oak by a fork of the branch, runs N17E 27 chains to a white oak, N50W 70 chains to a pine, S17W 32

chains to a pine, & to first station; lines to be altered by Secretary of State as follows: on both sides of Lick Cr begins at a white oak on E side of the creek, runs N55W 27 chains to a white oak, S17W 70 chains to a pine, S55E 32 chains to a pine, & a "direct" course to first station; the last are true lines run by the surveyor; court ordered clerk to certify the same to Secretary of State; Archibald McBryde, clerk, certifies above is true copy of court order (signed) Dec. 3, 1803 A McBryde; [no grant identified in Cumberland Co to P Miller].

317. May session 1798 petition of Richardson Feagin to justices of Moore Co Pleas & Quarter Sessions court: about Apr. 16, 1785 William Fily surveyed 150 ac for the petitioner on Kellets Cr begins at a white oak on William Feagin's line, runs S40W 80 poles to a pine, N50W 60 poles to a post oak on Wm Feagin's line, S40W 60 poles to a pine, S8W 194 poles to a stake on Strickling's line, S80E 22 poles with said line to said Strickling's corner dead white oak, S43E 53 poles to his own beginning post oak of an old 100 ac survey, N10E 127 poles with fourth line of said survey to a stake by his corner 2 hickories, S80E 32 poles with his other line to a small pine, N30E 170 poles to beginning; surveyor made an error in his certificates to Secretary's office as follows: begins at a white oak in William Feagin's line, runs S40W 80 poles to his corner pine, N50W 60 poles along his line to a pine, N 60 poles by Wire's line to a post oak, S10W 140 poles to his own line, N 250 poles with said line to a pine, E 160 poles to a pine, & S 135 poles to beginning; these courses are wrong; so petitioner asks the court have latter courses & distances altered and made conformable to former [lines] agreeable with act of Assembly made in such cases; the petitioner is only adjoining land owner; petitioner asks court to make such order concerning above land as is consistent with justice & equity and agreeable to petition (signed) May 21, 1798 Richardson Feagin.   May session 1798 I certify foregoing is true copy of Richardson Feagin's petition filed this term & prayer of petition was granted by court; Secretary of State is requested to alter the grant conformable to first described courses (signed) Murdock McKenzie, DCC; altered Dec. 22, 1798; [no grant identified for Feagin in Moore Co].

318. Moore Co Nov. session 1798 court ordered grant No. 920 issued to Malcolm Gilchrist for 150 ac be amended by inserting words "and fifty" after word "hundred" and before word "acres"; a true copy from minutes (signed) Nov. 26, 1798 Murdock McKenzie DCC; grant to M Gilchrist esq Moore Co No. 20 Dec. 18, 1797, altered Dec. 15, 1798; [no grant identified for Gilchrest in Moore Co].

319. Moore Co Pleas & Quarter Sessions Court May session 1809 petition of Stephen Gilmore to the justices: "abought" May 1787 John "Burgainer" obtained a grant for land in Moore Co; surveyor made an error in describing land as follows: begins at a white oak [page torn] corner, runs S20W 100 poles by Millar's line to a black oak, S20E 80 poles to a post oak in "Harganier's" line, S20E 100 poles "by it" to a pine, & N70W 80 poles to beginning; in fact the surveyor ran & marked 50 ac as follows: begins at Carmichal's corner white oak, runs S20W 100 poles by Millar's line to a black oak, S70E 80 poles to a post oak in Bargarner's

line, N20E 100 poles by it to a pine, & a direct line to first station; the land is now the petitioner's property; he asks court to correct the error and direct Secretary of State to alter the courses of the grant & insert last mentioned courses and that Register of Moore Co alter records in his office as aforesaid; following are only adjoining land owners: John Sheppard, Andrew Brown, John Gunter, Mathew Watson(? page torn), Grissa "Cirmikel", Alexd Carmikel, & Patrick Carmikel. Aug. term 1809 it appears to court that adjoining land owners were legally notified & made no objection; court ordered prayer of petition be granted.   Sept. 1, 1809 I certify foregoing are true statements from the records (signed) Corn. Dowd, CC; [on back] alteration of grant to John Bargonear jr, altered Sept. 26, 1809; [no grant identified for Bargonear in Moore Co].

320. Nov. session 1806 petition of John Henly, son of Jesse Henly deceased, to Moore Co justices: Jesse Henly in his will devised land in Cumberland now Moore Co formerly granted to David Ergo who sold to William Ergo who sold to Jesse Henly; land is on waters of Deep R; in plat, the surveyor began at a white oak on the river bank near Trap's line, runs N45E 276 chains 38.5 links to a white oak, N45W 54 chains 77 links to a hickory, S45W 27 chains 38.5 links to a stake, & a direct line to first station; but the plat doesn't leave a foot of land; so petitioner asks for order to amend the grant as follows: begins at an ash [white oak--lined out] in Trap's line on the river bank, runs N45E 25 chains 50 links to a white oak, S45E 54 chains 77 links to a stake, S45W 21 chains to the river, & up the river various courses to beginning which are the true courses & distances intended (signed) John Henly; a true copy from original filed in my office A McBryde, CC. Feb. session 1807 I certify at this term prayer of above petition was granted (signed) Mar. 1,1807 A McBryde; [on back] altered Dec. 2, 1807; [no grant identified for Ergo or Argo in Cumberland Co].

321. Moore Co Aug. session 1791 court ordered lines of a patent to Duncan Johnston be altered; instead of words "on a prong of Long Br" insert "on S side of Little R on the swamp"; and another grant instead of "in the marsh by Long Br" insert "near mouth of Meadow Br on N side of Little R"; copy from minutes (signed) Arch McBryde, cc; [on back] Duncan Johnston 247 in 1789 and 220 in 1789; [grant 220: grant book 74 p. 69 see shuck #228 in Moore Co and grant 247: grant book 74 p. 83 see shuck #255 in Moore Co in Secretary's grant files].

322. Moore Co Nov. session 1797 following plot & petition was presented to court: [2 plats for 100 ac each in shape of rectangles side by side] petition of Phill Johnston to Moore Co Pleas & Quarter Sessions Court: about Apr. 3, 1796 [written over 1786], John Hinson surveyed 100 ac in Cumberland Co for the petitioner; land begins at a stake between a hickory saplin & white oak, N70E, N20W, S70W, & S20E; in making out the certificate to Secretary's office, he described the land by mistake as follows: begins at a stake between a hickory saplin & white oak, runs N70E, S20E, S70W, N20W, & a direct line to beginning; the petitioner asks the court to have latter courses altered and made agreeable to dotted lines which are the true courses run agreeable to act of Assembly; all

Corrections/Alterations to Land Grants

adjoining land is vacant; the petitioner asks court to issue an order concerning land described [order] to be consistent with justice & agreeable to this petition (signed) Nov. 22, 1797 Phill Johnston.   I certify foregoing is true copy of original filed in clerk's office (signed) Archd McBryde, cc.   Nov. session 1797 court ordered prayer of Phill Johnston's petition for altering a grant be granted and courses to be altered & made conformable to tenor [prayer—lined out] of petition filed.   True copy from the minutes (signed) Nov. 23, 1797 Arch McBryde, cc; [on back] Phillip Johnson 100 ac No. 46 dated 1787 patent altered; [grant book 65 p. 178, see shuck #54 in Moore Co in Secretary's grant files].

323. Moore Co Pleas & Quarter Sessions Court Aug. term 1827; it has been proved to satisfaction of court that surveyor made a mistake in first line of 100 ac surveyed for George Kennedy in grant No. 2344 issued Nov. 21, 1813; surveyor described first line to run S50W but in fact the land should have been S20W; court ordered Secretary of State to alter said line from S50W to S20W and make record of the grant in his office conformable to the alteration (witness) Cornelius Dowd, clerk, third Monday in Aug. 1827 (signed) Corn Dowd; [on back] altered Jan. 5, 1828 W Hill, Secry; [grant book 132 p. 351, see shuck #2382 in Moore Co in Secretary's grant files].

324. Moore Co Pleas & Quarter Sessions Court Feb. 1801; on Apr. 10, 1794 Neill McLeod, surveyor, surveyed 100 ac for the petitioner on Grassy Cr South of Deep R; certificate contains a "great" quantity more than 100 ac by mentioning S 46 chains but it should be S 28 chains and N 46 [chains] to beginning; the petitioner asks the court to order Secretary to alter second line to run S 28 chains (signed) David "Kannedy" a true copy.   Petition of David Kennedy was heard asking for courses of a 100 ac grant to be altered; court ordered prayer of petition be granted & Secretary of State is directed to make the alteration accordingly; Archibald McBryde, clerk, certifies above is true copy of petition of David Kennedy "esq" and order of court thereon (signed) Feb. 13, 1802 A McBryde; [on back] altered Dec. 1, 1802 D Caswell;

Moore Co Pleas & Quarter Sessions court Feb. 1825; petition of David Kennedy, "Bradly" Garner, & John Manes: on Apr. 10, 1794 Neill McLeod, Moore Co surveyor, surveyed land for David Kennedy who sold it to Bradley Gardner who has sold it to John Manes; land is 10 ac on Grassy Cr South of Deep R; the petitioners are injured by a mistake in the certificate; it should read begins at a white oak at intersection of Pennington & Huntsucker's line [on] SE of Grassy Cr, runs S60W 35 chains with Huntsucker's line, S 28 chains, E 30 chains, & N 46 chains to beginning; by certificate & grant land is "represented" to run S46 chains but it should be S 28 chains; petitioners ask that an order be issued to alter the grant so it reads as "above stated" and should read; petitioners represent Bradley Gardner, John B Kelly, & Alexander Kennedy own adjoining land (signed) David Kennedy, Bradley Gardner, & John "Manes".   May term 1825 on a "full" hearing of the petition, court ordered that prayer be granted & Secretary of State is directed to make the grant conformable to the petition that is to say as follows: begins at a white oak at intersection of Pennington's & Huntsucker's line

Corrections/Alterations to Land Grants

SE of Grassy Cr, runs S60W 35 chains with said Huntsucker's line, S 28 chains, E 30 chains, & N 46 chains to beginning [in the margin: granted Apr. 9, 1799]. Cornelius Dowd, clerk, certifies preceding is true statement from the records (signed) Jun. 23, 1825 Corn Dowd; [on back] altered Jul. 23, 1825 W H; [grant book 104 p. 242, see shuck #1462 in Moore Co in Secretary's grant files].

325. Moore Co Pleas & Quarter Sessions Court May term 1823; petition of Alexd McIntosh asking that errors in a grant, hereunto annexed, be rectified; court ordered that Secretary of State alter the courses of the grant & make them conformable to following courses: S6W 15 chains, S71W 6 chains, W 23 chains, N30E 8 chains, N60W 20 chains, N30E 9 chains 50 links, S55E 22 chains, & with McLeod's line to beginning. Cornelius Dowd, clerk, certifies above is true statement from records in my office (signed) Nov. 15, 1823 Corn Dowd, clk. Above order was attached to grant No. 1314 issued Jul. 19, 1799 to Alexander McIntosh for 50 ac which is altered Dec. 3, 1824 (signed) Wm Hill, Sec.; [on back] altered Dec. 3, 1824; [grant book 104 p. 235, see shuck #1446 in Moore Co in Secretary's grant files].

326. Moore Co court Aug. term 1835; petition of Malcom Shaw, surveyor, in behalf of Alexander McIntosh to Moore Co Pleas & Quarter Sessions Court: said surveyor made a mistake in making out plat & certificates for 50 ac "by" warrant No. 1499 for Alexander McIntosh; Secretary of State has issued a grant accordingly; the surveyor at a "subsequent time" discovered, through mistake, he inserted words N41W in first course contrary to his intention & survey made but it should be S41W which was run & marked at time land was surveyed; the patentee is owner of adjoining land and asks the court to instruct Secretary of State to make foregoing alteration in the grant & record kept by him in his office. Moore Co court Aug. term 1835 Malcom Shaw, surveyor in behalf of Alexr McIntosh vs [blank]; petition to alter courses of a grant; prayer of petition was granted & court ordered a copy of petition issue to Secretary of State. Alexander C Curry, clerk, certifies foregoing is true copy of petition filed in my office & true transcript of record of the court (signed) nov. 9, 1835 A C Curry ccc; [on back] altered Dec. 2, 1835 W Hill, Secy; [grant book 155 p. 36, see shuck #2554 in Moore Co in Secretary's grant files].

327. Moore Co Pleas & Quarter Sessions Court May term 1823; petition of Alexd McIntosh asking for alteration of errors in annexed grant; court ordered that Secretary of State be directed to alter courses of the grant & make them conformable to following courses: S30W 25 chains, S60E 20 chains, N30E 25 chains, & N60W 20 chains to beginning. Cornelius Dowd, clerk, certifies above is true statement of records in my office (signed) Nov. 15, 1823 Corn Dowd, clk. Above order was attached to grant No. 1325 issued Jul. 19, 1799 to Christian McIntosh for 50 ac in Moore Co; grant & record altered agreeable to the order Dec. 3, 1824 (signed) Wm Hill, Secretary; [on back] altered Dec. 3, 1824 Wm Hill, Sec; [grant book 104 p. 240, see shuck #1457 in Moore Co in Secretary's grant files].

Corrections/Alterations to Land Grants

328. Moore Co Pleas & Quarter Sessions Court Aug. term 1826; Alexander McIntosh vs Miles Kelley petition to rectify error in a grant: in this case, court ordered Secretary of State to alter a grant issued Dec. 17, 1810 to Alexd McIntosh for 50 ac so fifth line reads as follows: S47W 25 chains. Cornelius Dowd, clerk, certifies above is the decree of the court in above case (signed) Oct. 26, 1826 Corn Dowd, clk; [on back] altered Dec. 15, 1831 Wm Hill, Sec; [grant #2053, grant book 125 p. 364, see shuck #2089 in Moore Co in Secretary's grant files].

329. Moore Co Pleas & Quarter Sessions Court May 1800; court ordered lines of a "tract" of Duncan McIver's be altered; instead of words "begins at a stake by 3 sweet gums & a hickory in Archd Buie's line" the following words be inserted "begins at a stake by 3 sweet gums & a hickory in Duncan McIver's line"; clerk to certify the same to the Secretary. Archibald McBryde, clerk, certifies above is true copy of records in my office (signed) Jun. 4, 180 A McBryde; [on back] grant altered Nov. 25, 1800; [Duncan McIver received 18 grants in Moore Co; grant not identified].

330. Moore Co Feb. session 1798 Murdoch McKenzie petitioned court asking to have an error rectified in a grant about 1761 to Richard Burton; court ordered second line from beginning shall run West across Drowning Cr instead of running East as grant & plat annexed direct; copy from the minutes (signed) Archd McBryde, cc; [on back] altered Dec. 1, 1802 D Caswell; [no grant in 1761 found for Richard Burton, only grant in 1762 in following petition].

331. Moore Co court Feb. session 1797; petition of Murdoch McKenzie: there is an error in courses of a plat for a grant to Richard Burton & surveyed Feb. 3, 1761; plat is as follows: begins at a pine on E side of Drowning Cr, runs S 200 poles to a white oak & hickory, W 140 poles, N 200 poles, & E 140 poles which are the true courses; but courses written in certificate are: begins at a pine on E side of Drowning Cr, runs S 200 poles to a whit oak & hickory, E 140 poles across Drowning Cr to a pine, N 200 poles to a pine, & E 140 poles across said creek to first station containing 150 ac and includes the improvement "he" bought of Natahaniel Dennis; the petitioner notified all adjoining parties agreeable to law in order to have benefit of act of Assembly to correct errors in patents; the petitioner hopes the court will correct the same as the plat runs and have the same transferred to Secretary of State according to law (signed) Murdoch McKenzie. Court ordered that second line from beginning shall run West instead of East as grant & plat direct; copy from the minutes (signed) Arch McBryde, cc; [on back] patent granted to Richd Burton in 1762, altered Dec. 27, 1797 [not signed]; grant book 13 p. 344 see shuck #1544 in Anson Co or grant book 15 p. 420 see shuck #2039 in Anson Co in Secretary's grant files].

332. The red "one" describes the West side of Duncan Buie's land; the red dotted line describes NE side of Augus McDugald's old survey; the black dotted "line" describes courses in a patent for a new 100 ac survey issued to Augus McDonald showing an error in the survey; the black "lines" describes last mentioned survey agreeable to original survey as may be proved by Mr. Duncan Buie; [colors in plat

not evident]; [petitioner asks] the court to rectify error in survey agreeable to law "viz" begins at a white oak at or near his own line, runs N47W 22 with said line to his own corner, N7E 52 chains 63 links, S47E 25 chains, S7W 52 chains 63 links with Buie's line to where said McDugald's old line intersects Buie's line, & with [blank] own line to beginning (signed) Archibald McLean. Aug. session 1805 from the minutes: petition of Archd McLean about lines of land was filed; prayer of petition was granted & copy to go to the Secretary. I certify foregoing is true copy of petition of Archibald McLean filed at last Aug. session & order thereon (signed) Archd McBryde, cc; [on back] altered Feb. 2, 1806; [grant book 65 p. 185 see shuck #83 OR grant book 111 p. 149 see shuck #1661 in Moore Co in Secretary's grant files].

333. Moore Co petition of Archibald McLean to justices of Moore Co Pleas & Quarter Sessions Court: about May 16, 1793 Niel McLeod, Moore Co surveyor, surveyed 300 ac for Willis Agarton; land is now the petitioner's property; land is on waters of Governors Cr, begins at William B Whitford's corner stake, runs S58W 44 chains 75 links "as" his line to a stake by a pine, N32W 44 chains 75 links as his other line to a large stooping pine said Whitford's & Charles Herd's corner, S58W 34 chains to a stake, S32E 61 chains, S62E 26 chains, & a direct line to beginning; but surveyor in the plat & his return to Secretary's office made a mistake as follows: begins at William B Whitford's corner stake, runs S58W 44 chains 75 links as his line to a stake by a pine, N32W 76 chains as his other line, S88W 34 chains, S32E 61 chains, S62E 60 chains, N58E 44 chain 75 links, & direct line to beginning; last mentioned courses are not the true ones or those run by surveyor; they include upwards of 100 ac which was granted to Archibald McNiel of Cumberland Co "many years" before the petitioner's land was entered; the petitioner shows the first mentioned courses were the courses run by the surveyor; they are the true courses of the land as appears from the plat filed in Moore Co clerk's office; the petitioner shows only adjoining land owners are William Rhodes, John Cameron, & said Archibald "McNiell" of Cumberland Co; the petitioner asks that court direct the Secretary of State to alter the grant & make it and the books in his office conformable to first courses mentioned herein; the court can make other or further orders as consistent with justices [not signed]. Aug. session 1798 Archibald McLean vs William Rhodes & "others"; petition to alter courses of land was read and prayer was granted; a copy from minutes (signed) Nov. 5, 1798 Murdock McKenzie, DCC; [on back] alter patent of Willis Agerton No. 811 for 300 ac dated Aug. 1797, altered agreeable to the same Dec. 15, 1798 (not signed); [grant #811 issued Aug. 19, 1797 to Willis "Agerton", grant book 92 p. 61, see shuck #859 in Moore Co in Secretary's grant files].

334. Moore Co Pleas & Quarter Sessions Court petition of Niell McLeod: on Sept. 30, 1807 the petitioner surveyed 250 ac for himself in Moore Co on Persimmon Glade, begins at a stake "having 2 black & a post oak" pointers Charles Shearing's fourth corner of 200 ac, runs E 25 chains with his third line to Niell McLeod's sixth corner of 100 ac, S 20 chains with his fifth line to his fifth corner "&c"; but when certificate was written, he omitted to "certify" fourth line of the plan "viz"

after words "Cheeks line (South 7 chains 50 links to a stake 3 pine pointers thence)"; courses & distances of fourth line were omitted; the omission is within the parenthesis & makes quantity less and next line will run into an older survey; adjoining land belongs to William Martin & Niell McLeod; the petitioner asks that "2 blanks in a deed" from John McLimron to Niel McLeod be filled up and Moore Co Register be directed to fill up records of said deeds in proper places; first blank to be filled with "20" and second blank with "5"; when blanks are filled up that part of the deed will read "on 20th day of Aug. 1805"; petitioner asks that omissions be inserted in the grant & blanks in the deed agreeable to an act of Assembly made in such cases (signed) Niel McLeod. I certify at May term 1808 prayer of above petition was granted (signed) Mar. 12, 1809 Corn Dowd, cc; [on back] 20/3 due clerk, altered May 12, 1809 [not signed]; [grant book 123 p. 90, see shuck #1989 in Moore Co in Secretary's grant files].

335. Moore Co Pleas & Quarter Sessions Court Feb. term 1808: at this term Niell McLeod filed a petition to rectify errors in a grant to David Davidson for 50 ac in Moore Co East of Bear Cr, begins at an elm in Wm Manos' line, runs S17E 40 chains, N17W 34 chains 5 links to Nall's line, & S56W 32 chains 50 links "as it" to beginning; at May term petition was read & service notice was proved by William McLennon on Shadrick Meshack & William "Manous"; court ordered original grant & mesne conveyance of land mentioned in petition be amended & altered agreeable to "priar" of the petition "that is to say" the courses & distances of land to be altered as follows: begins at an elm in William Manos' line, runs S67E 40 chains, N71E 34 chains 50 links to Nalls' (sic) line, S40W 25 chains 50 links, & N77W 49 chains "thence" to beginning. Jul. 15, 1808 I certify foregoing statement is correct (signed) Corn Dowd, cc; [no alteration date mentioned]; [grant No. 1392 issued Nov. 26, 1799, grant book 105 p. 104, see shuck #1479 in Moore Co in Secretary's grant files].

336. petition of Allan Morrison to justices of Moore Co Pleas & Quarter Sessions Court: about Apr. 18, 1789 Niell McLeod, Moore Co surveyor, surveyed land for the petitioner in Moore Co on NW of Living [or Swing] Cr, begins at a black oak NW of the creek in Key's line, runs S7W 32 chains with his own line to his other corner spanish oak, W 20 chains with his other line to a maple in the bank of the creek, S45E 13 chains to a stake in Newton's line, S5E 12 chains 50 links with Newton's line, E 34 chains to Waddel's line, & N20W 58 chains to beginning; but surveyor made an error in his certificate annexed to the plat by inserting fifth line "17 chains" but it should be "34 chains" as will appear by measuring the line & the plat annexed to the patent with the scale of the plat "was protracted or laid down and also" run by the surveyor as distance of 17 chains which was inserted in certificate, but mistake doesn't include much more than half the land the petitioner should have which was surveyed by the surveyor for the petitioner "by his extending" the above fifth line 34 chains but originally surveyed, protracted, & laid down in the plat but not in his certificate; the petitioner asks court to make an order to extend & alter fifth line in patent to 34 chains agreeable to way it was originally surveyed instead of 17 chains which was inserted wrong in certificate

annexed to the plat; the petitioner is only land holder joining said land except Murdoch McAulay to whom the petitioner has given lawful notice (signed) Feb. 18, 1799 Allen Morrison. Feb. session 1799 foregoing is copy of Allen Morrison's petition filed this term; court ordered prayer of petition be granted (signed) at Carthage Feb. 20, 1799 M McKenzie, DCC; [on back] altered Jun. 13, 1799; [Allen Morrison received 2 grants in Moore Co; this grant not identified].

337. Moore Co petition of Simon Rubottom: about 1799 he entered 49 ac in Moore Co, begins at Wm Barret's corner pine, runs S50W 16.50 [chains] to a stake in Ferquhard Campbell's line of 200 ac, N8W 48 chains 50 links with & "by" it, S35E 44 chains 20 links to & with Donald McQueen's [line], & a direct line to beginning; but surveyor made a mistake in describing land as follows: begins at Wm "Barrett's" corner pine, runs S59W 16.50 to a stake in Farqd. Campbell's line of 200 ac, S8W 48.50 with & by it, S35E 44 chains 20 links to & with Donald McQueen's line, & to beginning; last mentioned courses are wrong & include land not intended to be entered & not includes in the petitioner's lines; the petitioner shows Donald McQueen, Jesse Rellar(?), & James Halcomb are only adjoining land owners; petitioner asks that Secretary of State be directed to alter last mentioned courses & make them conformable to first mentioned courses; "usual proofs" to issue to Donl McQueen, Jesse "Rettar", & James Halcomb giving them notice of this petition (signed) S "Rhubottom". Aug. session 1803 Archibald McBryde, clerk, certifies above is taken from the original [petition] & prayer of petition is ranted (signed) Dec. 9, 1804 A McBryde; [on back] Simon "Reubottom" certificate to alter a grant, grant altered Jun. 18, 1805; [grant book 102 p. 290, see shuck #1323 in Moore Co in Secretary's grant files].

338. to Moore Co Court: the "orator" examined a grant "brot me" from Raleigh; he discovered a mistake made by the deputy surveyor; so orator asks the court to order the Secretary of State to insert word "fifty" afer "one hundred" (signed) David Sears.   I certify above is true copy of original petition filed in my office; I also certify at last Nov. court for Moore Co, the prayer of petition was granted (signed) May 24, 1806 A McBryde, cc; [on back] grant dated Dec. 19, 1804; altered Oct, 2, 1806 [not signed]; [grant book 118 p. 388, see shuck #1881 in Moore Co in Secretary's grant files].

339. petition of John Shepherd: there are several mistakes in courses & distances in a grant accompanying this petition; the petitioner asks the court to make an order to alter the mistakes by the surveyor in "the former" certificate agreeable to following courses & distances: due to warrants No. 288 & 346 surveyed 400 ac for John Shepherd on both sides of Carrs Cr, begins at John Watson's third corner of 400 ac patented by Christopher Yew between 4 pines, runs S60W 62 chains 50 links with his third line to a stake among 3 post oaks, N50W 22 chains 40 links to a pine by a pine & 2 black jacks, then instead of N40W 29 chains 80 links that it be altered to N20W 24 chains 80 links to a stake & 4 red oak pointers in John Watson's line of 100 ac granted to "Hayes", E 22 chains 50 links with that line to a pine, N59E "instead" of 40 chains to be altered to 46 chains to a pine, instead of

Corrections/Alterations to Land Grants

N it be altered to S58E 27 chains to a pine, next line again instead of N "course nor distance" to be altered to run E 33 chains to David Allison's line, instead of S4W that it be altered to S34W 46 chains, & S30W 26 chains 40 links to beginning; the petitioner informs the court it was his intention to have the grant for above courses; it interferes with no persons land "only what is" the petitioner's (signed) Feb. 17, 1806 John Shepherd. Moore Co Mar. 24, 1806 Archibald McBryde, clerk, certifies within is true copy of original filed in my office & prayer of petition was granted at Feb. 1806 court (signed) A McBryde; [on back] altered Dec. 12, 1806; [grant book 102 p. 295, see shuck #1329 in Moore Co in Secretary's grant files].

340. Nov. session 1797 petition of John "Shephard" to Moore Co Pleas & Quarter Sessions Court: about Nov. 15, 1780 James Dyer surveyed 200 ac for the petitioner in Cumberland Co "running towards" Dry Cr, begins at a hickory in his own line, runs S70W 44 chains 75 links to a stake near his other old line, S15E 60 chains to a stake, N52E 19 chains 40 links to his line of 100 ac, N5E 16 chains "as" said line to his corner black gum, S85E 5 chains 25 links as his other line of 100 ac to first corner white oak of Andrew Shepherd's 300 ac survey, & N5E as said line of 300 ac to beginning; in plotting & making the certificate to Secretary's office, he described land, by mistake, as follows: begins at a hickory in his old line, runs S70W 44 chains 75 links as "that" to a stake near his other line, N15W 44 chains 75 links as that to a stake, N70E 44 chains 75 links to a stake between pointers, & a direct line to beginning; the petitioner asks the court to have latter courses altered & made conformable to former "which are the true courses" run by the surveyor agreeable to act of General Assembly; petitioner is only holder of adjoining land; petitioner asks court to make such order concerning the described land as consistent with justice & agreeable with the petition (signed) Nov. 22, 1797 John Shepherd "Moore"; Nov. session 1797 I certify within is true copy of original petition filed in my office (signed} Arch McBryde, cc; Nov. session 1797 court ordered prayer John Shepherd's petition to alter courses of a land grant [be granted] & grant be altered & made conformable to tenor of petition; I certify foregoing are true copies of records in my office (signed) Nov. 25, 1797 Archd McBryde, clk ct; on back) John Shepherd jr 200 ac No. 169 dated 1784, patent altered [no date & no signature]; [grant to John Shepherd "jr" in grant book 55 p. 335, see shuck #1981 in Cumberland Co in Secretary's grant files].

341. petition of John Shepherd to Moore Co Pleas & Quarter Sessions Court: about Dec. 1795 John Matthews, a deputy surveyor of Moore Co, surveyed 100 ac for the petitioner on waters of Lick Cr, begins at a hickory in his own line of 150 ac, runs S29E 45 chains to a red oak 2 pines 2 red oak pointers, N70W 22 chains 36 links to a stake by 2 pines, N29E 45 chains to a red oak at 2 red oaks & a pine pointers, & direct line to beginning; but surveyor made a mistake in plat of the land & certificate by describing as follows: begins at his own corner white oak, runs N4E 43 chains to a stake in his own line, N72E 25 chains, S14W [or S4W] 43 chains to a persimmon, & direct line to beginning; last mentioned courses aren't the true courses & will include other land than that laid off; the

petitioner asks that his grant be altered and first mentioned courses be inserted; he asks the court to make such order "in the premises" as is consistent with justice & the law (signed) "McBryde", atto for petitioner. May session 1800 John Shepherd presented his petition asking that lines in a tract described be altered; it appears to court that owners of adjoining land had sufficient notice of the petition; it appears to satisfaction of court that the alteration should be made; court ordered prayer of petition be granted & clerk certify same to the Secretary; I certify above is true copy of John Shepherd's petition & court order thereon witness Archibald McBryde, clerk (signed) May 31, 1800 A McBryde; [on back] grant altered Nov. 25, 1800; [may be one of 5 grants on Lick Cr to John Shepherd, see shucks 1330, 1336, 1337, 2372, & 2376 in Moore Co in Secretary's grant files].

342. petition of John Sheffield to Moore Co Pleas & Quarter Sessions Court: about Mar. 10, 1772 Robert Edwards surveyed 100 ac for John Sheffield in Cumberland Co on Bear Cr South of Deep R, begins at a white oak by a black oak on upper bank of "said" by upper line of his old survey, runs N68W 31 chains 63 links to a stake among 2 black oaks & 2 hickories, S22W 31 chains 63 links, S68E 31 chains 63 links, & direct line to beginning; surveyor made a mistake in platting & making out return to Secretary's office describing land as follows: begins at a white oak by a black oak on upper side of said creek by upper line of his old survey, runs S68W 31 chains 63 links to a stake among 2 black oaks & 2 hickories, S22E 31 chains 63 links, N68E 31 chains 63 links, & direct line to beginning; courses & distances run by surveyor on the land are agreeable to first mentioned [lines]; latter was platted by mistake & takes land that wasn't laid off in the survey and runs on an old survey that it begins at; the lines are marked "it is clear of any claims whatever"; petitioner asks that error in the patent be rectified agreeable to act of General Assembly made in such cases [not signed]. May session 1801 court ordered error in John Sheffield's patent be altered according to prayer of petition; I certify above is true copy of petition & order thereon witness Archibald McBryde, clerk (signed) Sept. 2, 1801 A McBryde; fees 18/6; [on back] altered Dec. 1, 1802 D Caswell; [may be grant in grant book 22 p. 178, see shuck #1167 in Cumberland Co in Secretary's grant files].

343. petition of William H Beatty to New Hanover Co court Apr. term 1806: petition was read & proof in support of allegations in the petition were heard & understood by the court; it appears that a grant issued Dec. 5, 1805 to Wm H Beatty for 300 ac in New Hanover Co; there are the following errors: instead of running second line S60E 240 poles as described in patent it should be S86E 273 poles and instead of third line running S11W 150 poles it should be S11W 304 poles and instead of fourth line running S86W 240 poles it should be S6W 65 poles and instead of fifth line running N20W 150 poles it should be N20W 254 poles; court ordered the clerk to certify each error to Secretary of State so the same can be rectified in the patent & in the Secretary's office agreeable to act of General Assembly made in such cases; a true copy from the court minutes witness Thomas F Davis, clerk (signed) Apr. 10, 1806 Thos F Davis, clk; [on back] altered Jun. 16, 1806 [not signed]; [grant book 119 p. 227, see shuck #2682 in New Hanover

Corrections/Alterations to Land Grants

Co in Secretary's grant files].

344. petition of William Hooper to justices of New Hanover Co Pleas & Quarter Sessions Court: he is in possession of 260 ac in New Hanover Co granted in 1743 to David Dunbibin; there is an error in the grant; instead of N82E as in the grant, it should be N82W as appears by certificate of county surveyor; the petitioner asks the court to direct the error be rectified and that clerk certify the error to Secretary of State so the records in his office can be rectified according to act of Assembly made in such cases; at Sept. term 1798 court ordered prayer of petitioner be granted; a true copy of petition & court order witness Ant B Toomer, clerk (signed) Mar. 9, 1799 Anty B Toomer by James W Walker; [on back] altered Mar. 1, 1800 [not signed]; [may be 2 grants (a) grant book 10 p. 102 see shuck #938 and grant book 10 p. 51 see suck #901 or (b) grant book 5 p. 204 see shuck #249 and grant book 5 P. 260 see shuck #285 in New Hanover Co in Secretary's grant files].

345. Jan. term 1792 petition of John Miller (of New Hanover Co) to New Hanover Co Pleas & Quarter Sessions Court: the petitioner obtained a grant for "about" 120 ac in New Hanover Co; grant was signed Apr. 13, 1780 by Richard Caswell, governor of NC; on Mar. 25, 1779 James Blyth, county surveyor surveyed & returned plat for land as follows: 120 ac in New Hanover Co on E side of Long Cr, begins at a pine in Walker's "corner", runs S79W 238 poles along Mabson's line to a black oak in John Taylor's line near his corner [on] S side of a pond, S6E 95 poles along Taylor's line to Portavine's line, N75E 124 poles along "Portervine's" line to a stake, N52E 100 poles to a black jack at Portevine's S corner, & to first station; the plat is annexed to the grant; afterwards he purchased some of adjoining land from Mr. Mabson; on surveying the same petitioner discovered the courses of the survey & returned by James Blyth, county surveyor, were "manifestly" wrong & "otherwise" contained many errors which might essentially injure the petitioner; the petitioner asks that land in the patent be "clearly & completely ascertained & described"; he applied to William Houston, now New Hanover Co surveyor, who resurveyed the same on Dec. 5, 1791 and returned following plat: 120 ac in New Hanover Co on E side of Long Cr, begins at Walker's corner pine, runs S80E 238 poles along Mabson's line to a black oak in John Taylor's line ear his corner [on] S side of a pond, N80W 95 poles along Taylor's line to Portavine's line, N75W 124 poles to a stake in Portevine's line, S53W 100 poles along Portevine's line to a black jack at Portevine's S corner, & to first station; petitioner asks that, pursuant to act of General Assembly made in such cases, the court, premises being seen & understood, direct the clerk to certify the same to Secretary of State so the same can be filed in his office & errors in the patent can be corrected & also records in his office (signed) John Miller;
  2 copies of survey made Mar. 25, 1799 (signed) Wm Houston, surveyr.; [no chain carriers]; [metes & bounds same as second set above EXCEPT line is N8W 95 poles instead of N80W, as in petition];
  Jan. term 1792 petition of John Miller (of New Hanover Co) was heard; petition requests to correct errors in grant to John Miller in 1780 issued by Gov.

Corrections/Alterations to Land Grants

Richard Caswell; it appears to satisfaction of court that the errors in the grant exist; court ordered clerk to certify the facts to Secretary of State along with patent & survey so the errors can be corrected in the grant & records in his office (signed) at Wilmington Aug. 20, 1792 Geo Gibbs, deputy clerk; [grant book 37 p. 95, see shuck #1911 in New Hanover Co in Secretary's grant files].

346. petition of Edward Spearman to New Hanover Co Pleas & Quarter Sessions Court: court ordered clerk to certify to Secretary of State there appears to be an error by the surveyor in platting or making out certificate for 200 ac granted May 3, 1760 by King George II to Henry Skibbow & John Andrews; third line of the grant is stated to be S52E but it appears it should have been S52W which the court directs to be corrected according to last described direction; I certify above is a true copy from the minutes (signed) Sept. 19, 1803 Anthy B Toomer, clk; [on back] order to alter grant to "John" Skibbow & John Andrews, altered Nov. 29, 1803; [grant book 18 p. 402 see shuck #1658 and grant book 16 p. 303 see shuck #1438 in New Hanover Co in Secretary's grant files].

347. dotted plat represents courses of Ginnings' patent which is N66W 27 chains 50 links, N55W 10 chains, N33W 45 chains, N11W 34 chains to Brock's line, N55E 25 chains, S34E 88 chains, "as above delineated" to beginning and lies on only 100 ac.
    Onslow Co: being called to survey land granted Feb. 9, 1758 to Gibbin Ginnings begins at a small ash near Melton's line by little pocoson, runs N66W 27 chains 50 links, N55W 10 chains which 2 courses did not agree with the old lines that were marked, I went back to beginning and "run" S66W 27 chains 50 links and run on the old marked line, then I ran S55W 10 chains and came to the place where the old corner sassafras was always claimed to be, then I ran third course of patent N33W 45 chains and found the old lines again a dead pine Murrill had it cut into & found the old marks after examining I found the marks to be inclosed by 58 years of growth of wood, the pine was said to have been dead 4 years which I believe was & no more, on running same course we fund 2 other marked trees the distance "stopt" at a place where a number of trees had stood in a low ground, I then ran N11W 34 chains to Bock's line, run over it 18 poles as is represented by the 2 plats drawn with a black lines, I ran N55E 25 chains the fifth line of the patent which wasn't disputed, then sixth line I ran S34E and came to beginning before the distance "was gone" and covered all land that was ever claimed under the patent, the "given" line of the patent in dotted plat I found no use for the prayr. of the petitioner to the court is to give them the courses of the plat drawn with black lines which will lye on land I believe it was intended to & take the courses of "from" lying on 2 other patents Brock's & Johnson's the one older the other younger represented by the plat with dotted lines (signed) Everett Simmons, CS. Annexed plat represents the courses of "Jennings" patent in 2 different ways by running a different course on first line the black line runs S66W, the dotted lines N66W, both running the same distance; the court believes the black line is line intended by the surveyor "Skibbow" who surveyed Jennings' patent; court believes as far as their authority empowers them, that black line is

established as represented in the plat as line of Jennings' patent composed of following courses: S66W 27 chains 50 links, S55W 18 chains, N33W 45 chains, N11W 34 chains, N55E 25 chains, & S34E to beginning (signed) May 1820 James Glenn JP, Daniel Ambrose JP, & Mb Petteway; [on back] Gibbons Jennings 350 ac Onslow Co, altered Dec. 23, 1820 W H; [grant book 18 p. 432 see shuck #70 in Onslow Co in Secretary's grant files].

348. Onslow Co court Jul. term 1797: court ordered me to certify the facts in petition attached; they examined the petition and it appears true to their satisfaction (signed) R W Snead cc.   Petition of Thomas Johnston to Onslow Co court: 43 years ago, he entered 300 ac in Onslow Co on NE side of NW branch of New R in Mathew Whitfield's name; when "we" surveyed the land, Henry Skibbow was surveyor; he began at a pine near a great pond in or near John Johnston's back line, runs N35E 56 chains to a pine, N50W 57 chains to a pine, S35W 56 chains to a white oak, & to beginning; when surveyor plotted the land, he made last corner white oak the beginning & ran N75E 56 chains to a pine, N50W 57 chains to a pine, S75E 56 chains to a pine by said Johnston's back line, & with said line to first station; these courses leave the petitioner's housing & plantation & almost all the land intended in the patent to "cover vacant" & throws the patent on other patented land; the petitioner asks the court to consider the matter & grant relief by directing Secretary of State to alter the grant issued Nov. 15, 1753 to Mathew Whitfield agreeable with first beginning & courses mentioned in this petition which will "interfear" with no other person's land & secure the petitioner's land (signed) Thomas Johnston; a true copy from original in clerk's office (signed) Nov. 4, 1797 R W Snead, cc; [on back] altered patent dated Nov. 15, 1753 [not signed];
    survey: surveyed 300 ac for Thomas Johnston on NE side of NW branch of New R, the black lines represent the course & distance first surveyed agreeable to corners round the land, the dotted line represents survey agreeable to plat (signed) Nov. 26, 1795 W W Taylor, sur; [grant book 2 p. 78 see shuck #195 and grant book 10 p. 399 see shuck #417 in Onslow Co in Secretary's grant files].

349. Onslow Co court Oct. term 1808; petition of Henry Murrel was read; it appears to satisfaction of court that there is an error in patent "occasioned" by the surveyor in running first line from beginning "shand" runs S33E 556 poles to Gum Br which is called for in the patent but it now runs S33W 556 poles; court ordered clerk to certify the error to Secretary so the patent may be corrected (signed) Nathl Loomiss, cc; [on back] altered Dec. 3, 1808 [not signed]; [no grant to Henry Murrel found in Onslow Co].

350. Committee of Propositions & Grievances No. 2: petition of Edward Wortham was referred to committee: a mistake was made by Orange Co entry officer or Secretary in issuing a grant to said Wortham for 325 ac since the grant issued to Ed Northam instead of Edward Wortham; petitioner asks for legislative aid; committee reports on evidence & consideration of the case, they believe the error was committed; they recommend following resolution: Resolved that Secretary

Corrections/Alterations to Land Grants

of State alter the name fo Edward Northam to Edwd Wortham in grant No. 778 issued for 325 ac in Orange Co and make a record of the same in his office (signed) Jno M Binford, chr.   Nov. 29, 1800 in Senate: read & resolved that this house concurs (signed) Jo Reddick, SS & M Stokes, clk.   Dec. 1, 1800 in House of Commons foregoing report was read & concurred with (signed) S Cabarrus, Sp & J Hunt; [on back] grant & record altered agreeable to within Dec. 1, 1800 [not signed]; [grant book 67 p. 525, see shuck #1815 in Orange Co in Secretary's grant files].

351. Orange Co petition of Robert Dickins & William Waite: the petitioners say they obtained a grant from Secretary's office which contains an error; the certificate of surveyor made courses of land as follows: begins at Charles Horton's corner red oak, runs N55W 40 chains along his line to a hickory, E 43 chains to a stake but last course "properly by the entry" should be West; the petitioners will be greatly injured by this error; they ask the court to direct the clerk to certify the error so the same can be corrected and runs: begins at Charles Horton's red oak, runs N55W 40 chains along his line, W 43 chains to a stake, N 95.5 chains to a hickory, E 18.5 chains to Henry E McCulloch's corner gum, N85E 16.5 chains to a red oak, S 17.5 chains to a hickory, E 10 chains to Charles Horton's corner post oak "now supposed" to be William Horton's, S43E 48 chains along said line to a red oak, N88E 12 chains to a stake, & S9W 55 chains to first station; contains 640 ac surveyed Jun. 20, 1780 (signed) Robert Dickins & William Waite.   Orange Co Pleas & Quarter Sessions Court Feb. term 1799 court heard testimony about truth of allegations in annexed petition; it appears that petitioners are likely to be injured by errors in a patent mentioned in annexed petition; clerk is directed to certify and does certify to Secretary of State that an error appears in surveyor's certificate mentioned in the petition; and the error appears in the grant mentioned in the petition; so Secretary can correct the errors agreeable to act of Assembly (signed) Jul. 16, 1799 M Hart, cc. [following lined out on back of page] at Orange Co Pleas & Quarter Sessions Court held at court house in Hillsborough Feb. 24, 1799 petition of Robert Dickins & William "Wait" to correct error in surveyor's certificate was heard; [on separate sheet] altered Aug. 12, 1799; [grant book 75 p. 21, see shuck #1967 in Orange Co in Secretary's grant files].

352. Orange Co Pleas & Quarter Sessions Court held at court house in Hillsborough fourth Monday in Feb. 1798; heard petition of Barnet Troxler asking to correct error in a grant to him; grant signed by Samuel Johnston, "late" North Carolina governor; the grant describes land as follows: 166 ac in Orange Co in the fork of Stinking Quarter [Cr], joins Jacob Bosten, John Graves, John Shaley, Peter Poor, begins at Jacob Graves' corner hickory, runs N45E 20 chains to a dogwood, 45W 45 chains to a post oak, S45W 23 chains to a stake, S40E 66 chains to a spanish oak, S45W 20 chains to a stake, S45W 30 chains to a white oak, N45E 23 chains to a black oak, & N45W 11 chains to a hickory the first station; but the description "in fact contains no land"; the court considered with a majority of justices present that errors in the grant be corrected; it appeared to satisfaction of court that Andrew Gibson, who "lays or has laid some claim" to land claimed by

116

Corrections/Alterations to Land Grants

Barnet Troxler and all other adjoining land owners have been duly notified according to law; it has been made "manifest" to the court that lines of the grant should be descried in manner "hereinafter mentioned"; court ordered Secretary of State alter the land description in the grant to Barnet Troxler as follows: begins at a hickory, runs N45E 20 chains to a dogwood, N45W 45 chains to a post oak, S45W 23 chains to a stone, S45E 26 chains to a spanish oak, S45W 20 chains to a stake, S45E 30 chains to a white oak, N45E 23 chains to a black oak, & N45W 11 chains to first station; clerk to certify the same to the Secretary; a true copy from the record (signed) Morgan Hart, cc; [on back] altered agreeable to within order Aug. 6, 1798 [not signed]; [grant book 71 p. 180, see shuck #1896 in Orange Co in Secretary's grant files].

353. Orange Co Pleas & Quarter Sessions Court Nov. term 1826; petition of John Walker; grant No. 708 was issued Nov. 9, 1784 by North Carolina to Samuel Whitsell [or Whitsett] for 270 ac; grant issued due to surveyor's certificate & plat returned by Thomas Mulhollan, Orange Co surveyor, to Secretary's office & dated Jul. 27, 1782; boundaries in surveyor's certificate are as follows: on waters of Back Cr, joins James Whitsett, begins at a black oak, runs S 18 chains to a hickory, S70E 31 chains to a white oak at the ford of a branch, S45E 33 chains to a black jack, N "thrn and a half" chains to a black oak, W 20 chains to a hickory, N 48.5 chains to a post oak, E 25 chains to first station, & contains 270 acres; the petition shows surveyor made an error in the certificate and plat; the plat is drawn upside down so opposite side "of the proper on which the plat is drawn represents the figure" and from said tract and courses called for in certificate are so erroneous they don't embrace the land as will be apparent to the court on examining the plat & certificate; petitioner shows boundaries are well defined & marked during a possession of 30 years and lines have never been disputed; he shows annexed plat is true representation of the land as follows: begins at a black oak on the line "now" Joseph Armstrong's, runs S 18 chains with said line to John Campbell's corner hickory on the line, S70E 31 chains 50 links with said Campbell's line to pointers where a white oak stood, S45E 37 chains to a black jack stump & pointers, N 4 chains 25 links to a black oak, E 26 chains to pointers where a hickory stood now corner of John Walker, N 51 [or 57] chains to a post oak, & W 81 chains 50 links to first station; petitioner shows that by "sundry" mesne conveyances, the title to the land has become vested in him; he asks the court to order the clerk to certify the mistake & error to Secretary of State so the same can be corrected (signed) A D Murphey, atto. The petition was heard with petitioner's proofs to support allegations in the petition; it appears to satisfaction of court that boundaries of land in petition are ascertained by "old marked lines" and corners called for in grant & surveyor's certificate don't correspond with the marked lines nor do they truely described the land nor is the plat correct; it appears to satisfaction of court that plat & certificate annexed to the petition do represent true form & boundaries of the land; there is "a mistake" in the grant: first in fifth line course called for E 25 chains but should be W 25 chains and second seventh or last line course called for is East but should be West; court ordered clerk to certify mistake to Secretary of State so it can be corrected. John Taylor, clerk,

certifies foregoing petition was filed at Nov. session 1826 & decree was issued; foregoing is true copy of record in my office (signed) Dec. 5, 1826 J Taylor, cc; [on back] altered Jan. 2, 1827 (signed) Wm Hill, Secy; [grant book 57 p. 110, see shuck #1571 in Orange Co in Secretary's grant files].

354. Person Co Jun. court 1792; to James Glasgow, Secretary of State: George Johnston petitioned the court with his grant No. 245 issued Dec. 20, 1779 signed by Gov. Richard Caswell for 231 ac; Johnston asks for an order to direct Secretary of State t correct a mistake in the grant due to "manifest" error by Caswell Co surveyor; in second line of surveyor's certificate, he said runs N 9 chains 50 links instead of S 9 chains 50 links; this is a mistake "form the face thereof"; you are required to correct the record in your office as follows: begins at a stake on Peter Rogers' or William Stone's line, runs W 23 chains on Arthur Mitchel's line to a white oak "at B", S 9 chains 50 links on said Mitchel's line to a red oak, W 47 chains with said Mitchel's line to a pine "at D", S 13 chains on Edmd Lea's line to a white oak "at E", E 25 chains on said Lea's line to a white oak "at F", S 45 chains on said Lea's line to a white oak "at G", E 25 chains on Nathl King's line to a stake "at H", N 42 chains on Joseph Gold's line to a red oak "at J", E 20 chains on said Gold's line to a stake "at K", & N on Rogers' or Stone's line to beginning (signed) Robt Paine, cc; [grant book 41 p. 203, see shuck #247 in Caswell Co in Secretary's grant files].

355. Person Co Jun. court 1792; to James Glasgow, Secretary of State: Osborne Jeffreys petitioned the court with his grant No. 1050 issued Dec. 20, 1791 signed by Gov. Alex Martin for 400 ac; Jeffreys asks for necessary order & certificate to Secretary of State to correct mistake in the grant which appears to have been made by Caswell Co surveyor; sixth line of land from beginning in surveyor's certificate says S 4 chains with Dickins & Benton's line to a stake but it should have been S 54 chains with Dickins & Benton's line to a stake on Ragsdale's line; you are required to correct the record in your office so sixth line of the plat is correct or 54 chains instead of 5 chains as it now stands (signed) Rob Paine, cc; [grant book 75 p. 206, see shuck #1090 in Caswell Co in Secretary's grant files].

356. Person Co Jun. court 1792; to James Glasgow, Secretary of State: John Wommack, guardian of John Tapley, petitioned the court with his grant No. 25 issued Mar. 3, 1779 signed by Gov. Richard Caswell for 100 ac; Wommack asks court to issue necessary order & certificate to Secretary of State to correct mistake in the grant which appears to be a manifest error by Caswell Co surveyor; it is observed that the surveyor in his plan instead of saying runs East in third line said runs North "reverting" the same line which appears to be a mistake form the face of it; you are required to correct the record in your office as follows: begins at John Tapley's corner hickory, runs W 33 chains with his line to a white oak, S 30 chains 34 links to a pine, E 33 chains to a line on "Henery Fourd's" line, N 30 chains 34 links to first station & contains 100 ac (signed) Robt Paine, cc; [grant not identified, J Womach in grant #102 in grant book 109 p. 415, see shuck #24 in Person Co in Secretary's grant files].

Corrections/Alterations to Land Grants

357. Pitt Co, a majority of acting justices being present, heard petition of Joshua Barnes asking for clerk to be directed to certify to Secretary a mistake in a grant; court ordered clerk to certify to Secretary that there is an error in a grant issued Dec. 11, 1758 by "late" Earl of Granville to John Washington for 290 ac; error is in last line; instead of being runs down the creek to first station it should be down the creek the various courses to first station (sic); a true copy from the minutes (signed) George Evans, cc [no date]; [on back] patent altered Jun. 4, 1795; [grant not identified, John Washington mentioned in one grant for 640 ac in Johnston Co see #4990 in vol. 5 of Granville Grants by Mrs. Margaret Hofmann].

358. Pitt Co Nov. term 1801 Lydia Campbell, widow of James Campbell deceased, filed her petition to alter a grant; she proved to satisfaction of court that there is an error in a grant issued May 15, 1787 to James Campbell for 100 ac in that part of Craven Co which is "annexed" to Pitt Co; first line was left out of certificate & grant and should be E 125 poles as appears by the platt; the court believes the petitioner is likely to be injured by the error; court ordered to certify the above; I certify the same (signed) Nov. 11, 1801 George Evans, clk; [on back] altered Nov. 27, 1801; [2 grants for 100 ac to James Campbell: grant book 48 p. 295 see shuck #3789 and grant book 64 p. 93 see shuck #4025 in Craven Co in Secretary's grant files].

359. Pitt Co Feb. term 1807 petition of Furnifold Cannon; it appears to satisfaction of court that a mistake was made by the surveyor in second line of the tract on N side of Swifts Cr which was granted to Joseph Hardee for 300 ac "about" 1755; court ordered clerk to certify to Secretary of State so he can correct second line of the grant from S60E to N60E; I certify accordingly (signed) George Evans, clk by Richard Evans; [on back] altered Sept. 24, 1807; [one grant to Joseph Hardee for 185 ac in 1759 in Craven Co (crown grant), no grant identified in Granville grants].

360. Pitt Co Feb. term 1801 James S Clark filed his petition for alteration of a grant for 60 ac issued Nov. 19, 1800 to James S Clark, assignee of William Easterwood & Gideon Moye as guardians & heirs of James Quotermas; it was proved to satisfaction of court that surveyor made an error in his return; he said he surveyed land for James S Clark, guardian of heirs of James Quotermas, but it should have been James S Clark "in his own proper name" and not to his as guardian; court ordered the error be rectified; I certify the same (signed) Sept. 16, 1801 George Evans, clk; [on back] altered Sept. 30, 1801 (not signed); [only one grant found to James S Clark for 8 ac in 1782 in Pitt Co].

361. Pitt Co Pleas & Quarter Sessions Court Feb. 1837; petition of Nathan Hooker: a grant issued Aug. 25, 1786 to Thomas Hardie for survey made Aug. 1, 1785 for land in Pitt Co; a copy of grant from Secretary of State's office follows: Thomas Hardie 180 ac in Pitt Co on S side of Tar R, begins at a pine on S side of Long Br in Margaret Noble's line, runs N 160 poles with her line to a black oak,

119

Corrections/Alterations to Land Grants

W 120 poles to a pine, S 24 poles to a pine, S 60 poles on S side of Long Br to beginning; the petitioner shows by inspection of plat attached to the copy it appears one of the courses has been left out by the Secretary; after the course N 24 poles to a pine it should be W 44 poles before S 60 poles which immediately follows North in the patent; great injury may result for the petitioner who lately came into possession of the land by mense conveyance from the patentee; he asks the court, conformable to act of Assembly made in such cases, to direct the clerk to certify the fact as appear to satisfaction of court to Secretary of State so the patent can be amended to contain the land in the plat under which the patent issued; and he asks the court to make other orders as they believe fit & right (signed) Jno S Hawks, atto for Petr.   Pitt Co court Feb. term 1807: it appears to satisfaction of court, on inspection of the plat filed with Secretary of State's office, that there was an error by the surveyor in returning courses of the land and by Secretary in issuing the patent; court directed clerk to certify the whole matter to Secretary of State so patent can be corrected (signed) Archd Parker, clk. Archibald Parker, clerk, certifies foregoing is true copy of petition filed by Nathan Hooker for correcting a patent & court proceedings (signed) Feb. 17, 1837 Archd Parker, clk; [on back] record altered Oct. 4, 1837 (signed) W Hill, Secy; [grant book 61 p. 134, see shuck #865 in Pitt Co in Secretary's grant files].

362. Pitt Co Apr. term 1799 petition of Abraham Joiner was read asking for alteration of grant No. 458 issued Oct. 13, 1783 to him for 400 ac and surveyed by Jesse Procter; it appears to court that surveyor made a mistake; lines of the grant are different from lines marked by the surveyor; lines of grant agreeable to marked lines should be: begins at a white oak in Moore's line, runs S13E 231 poles "an agreed" line to a lightwood stump, W 280 poles to a pine, N 303 poles to said Moore's line, & with said Moore's line to beginning; [preceding lines] instead of courses & distances in the patent; court ordered clerk to certify these facts to Secretary of State; I certify the same (signed) Apr. 23, 1799 George Evans, clk; [on back] altered agreeable to order Nov. 20, 1799 [not signed]; [grant book 54 p. 190, see shuck #680 in Pitt Co in Secretary's grant files].

363. Pitt Co Feb. term 1801 William Lanier filed his petition for altering a grant for 640 ac to Seth Lanier deceased; court is satisfied that the survey made an error in his certificate by omitting third course which should have been: begins at William Lanier's corner pine, runs N55E 66 poles with Thomas Williams' line, N30W 178 poles to said Williams' other line "agreeable to the plat" he ought to have run E 440 poles to a pine, S34W 470 poles to a pine in William Lanier's line near "the line branch", & with his line to beginning; it appears to court that petitioner is likely to be injured by the omission; court ordered clerk to certify "as above"; I certify the same (signed) Feb. 10, 1801 George Evans, clk, to William White, Secretary; [on back] altered Nov. 9, 1801 [not signed]; [grant book 43 p. 80, see shuck #446 in Pitt Co in Secretary's grant files].

364. Pitt Co Oct. term 1796 commissioners appointed with surveyor at July term "last" to view & run lines in dispute with Shadrach Perry plaintiff & David Hatton

Corrections/Alterations to Land Grants

& others defendants; committee makes following return: we were summoned & sworn with Jesse Moye, surveyor, to correct errors in grant No. 260 issued Oct. 21, 1782 to Peter Adams for 150 ac on N side of Tarr R; land was sold by said Adams to Shadrach Perry and is now in possession of said Perry; agreeable to lines in the grant we believe it should: begin at Keley Tucer's corner poplar in Cannons Swamp, runs N60W 140 poles with the first line to a black gum, W 110 poles to a poplar "the third marked corner in the patent (patent calls for 145 poles the distance to the tree but 110 as above)", leaving the courses in the patent & runs by the marked lines along a swamp which appeared to be contract" lines when land was first surveyed "first" S30W 50 poles to a gum, S50W 80 poles to a gum, S5W 68 poles to a gum, S12W 98 poles to a white oak the patent corner in Salter's line "(the 4 last courses in this plan are to keep the marked line when the land was first surveyed which there are laid down all on one course" which is S12W 254 poles, then taking the 4 lines of the patent S60E 59 poles to William Baldwin's line, then to fifth line N 200 poles, & to beginning which is called in the patent West when it is nearly East (signed) Sept. 13, 1796 Samuel Barrow, Thos Daniel, Solomon Patrick, John Glemming, Henry Moore's mark "X", & Jesse Moye, survr; a true copy from original return filed in this office (signed) George Evans, clk cc;

Pitt Co Oct. term 1796 court ordered clerk to certify t the Secretary the return & proceedings on land dispute with Shadrach Perry as plaintiff & David Hatton & others as defendant with necessary papers relative thereto and require Secretary to alter a patent agreeable to return of the commissioners; a true copy from the minutes (signed) George Evans, clk cc; [grant book 43 p. 96, see shuck #480 in Pitt Co in Secretary's files].

365. Pitt Co court Jan. term 1799 James Robson filed his petition for alteration of 2 patents and proved to satisfaction of curt there is error in third line of a grant issued Nov. 6, 1783 to James Robson for 150 ac in Pitt Co; line now stands S22W but it should be S22E; and first line of another grant on same date to James Robson for 300 ac; line now stands S22W but it should be S22E; it appears to the court that petitioner is likely to be injured by the errors; the court ordered the clerk to certify "as above"; I certify the same (signed) Jan. 29, 1799 George Evans, clk ct to Secretary of State; [on back] altered May 14, 1799 (not signed); [150 ac grant: grant book 57 p. 301 see shuck #817 and 300 ac grant: grant book 57 p. 309 see shuck #839 in Pitt Co in Secretary's grant files].

366. Pitt Co Apr. session 1796 to justices of Pleas & Quarter Sessions Court: petition of John Salter: "before" Apr. 15, 1780 he entered 300 ac in Pitt Co on S side of Tarr R; land was surveyed for him Apr. 15 by Elias Godley, deputy surveyor of said county; a grant was obtained Oct. 21, 1782 to John Salter; but the petitioner "represents" there is a mistake in the plat of land returned to the Secretary by the surveyor; fifth line should be S68W but was erroneously described as "the reverse" of that course N68E; the error in the plott is also in the grant; due to error the petitioner's title to land is endangered & he is likely to suffer great injury; so he asks that clerk be directed to certify the error to the

121

Corrections/Alterations to Land Grants

Secretary so it can be rectified according to act of Assembly (signed) John Salter; a true copy from petition filed in this office (signed) George Evans, clk cc; [on back] patent altered [no date & not signed]; [grant book 43 p. 81, see shuck #447 in Secretary's grant files].

367. Feb. term 1820 Cannon Smith vs James Stokes: it appears to the court that James Stokes had due notice of this petition; it also appears that there is an error in grant issued May 15, 1787 to Hugh Pugh for 30 ac on N side of Neuse R & on S side of Swift Cr; one line is omitted: after the line S49W 115 poles to a stake in or near said Pugh's line there should be course N45W 200 poles and then to beginning; court ordered the clerk to certify the error to Secretary of State so the same can be rectified (signed) Alexander Evans, clk. I certify this is true copy of court order from minutes in the clerk's office (signed) at "Greensville" Nov. 8, 1820 Alexander Evans, clk; [on back] altered Dec. 8, 1820 (signed) Wm Hill, Sec; [grant No. 325 issued May 15, 1787, grant book 64 p. 100, see shuck #4043 in Craven Co in Secretary's grant files.

368. Pitt Co Pleas & Quarter Sessions Court May term 1802; George Ward filed his petition for alteration of a patent issued Oct. 13, 1783 to Israel Joiner for 200 ac in Pitt Co; it was proved to satisfaction of court that there is an error on certificate & patent by leaving out third and fourth courses, which as it now stands runs from beginning N 118 poles, N52W 68 poles, S 222 poles, & to beginning; but it should run from beginning N 118 poles, N52W 68 poles, N 68 poles, E 180 poles, S 222 poles, & to beginning; it appears to court that petitioner is likely to be injured by the error; court ordered clerk to certify "as above"; I certify the same (signed) at "Greensville" Nov. 6, 1802 George Evans, clk; [on back] altered Dec. 1, 1802 D Caswell; [2 grants for 200 ac: (a) grant book 43 p. 143 see shuck #578 and (b) grant book 54 p. 231 see shuck #750 in Pitt Co in Secretary's grant files].

369. Randolph Co Pleas & Quarter Sessions Court begun at court house in Ashboro on first Monday of Aug. 1836; petition of William Arnold to alter a state grant & deed: the petition was heard; it appeared to court that on Aug. 18, 1817 M Ward, deputy surveyor of I Elliott county surveyor, surveyed & plotted 30 ac in name of Clement Arnold due to entry No. 748 in Randolph Co entry taker's book; a state grant issued on the entry & survey to Clement Arnold for 30 ac on waters of Second Cr, begins at John Troy's corner; after hearing evidence in the case, it appeared to satisfaction of court that M Ward, deputy surveyor, made a mistake in his plot namely "begins at John Troy's corner" but it should "begin at John Taylor's corner" there being no such corner as John Troy's on waters of Second Cr; it appeared that petitioner has notified the persons owning adjoining land so the error can be corrected & grant altered to begin at John Taylor's corner instead of John Troy's corner; court ordered that clerk certify a copy of this order to Secretary for purposes aforesaid. Hugh McCain, Randolph Co clerk, certifies this is true copy of order of court on petition of William Arnold to alter a state grant (signed) at Ashboro Aug. 18, 1836 Hugh McCain, ccc; [on back] altered Oct. 6, 1840 (signed) Wm Hill, Secry; [grant book 131 p. 212, see shuck #2340

Corrections/Alterations to Land Grants

in Randolph Co in Secretary's grant files].

370. Randolph Co Sept. term 1791 William Bell esq exhibited a petition to court; he received grant No. 244 sold by the Commissioner of Confiscated Property as lot No. 12; but the courses annexed to the grant don't cover the land; court directed that a grant be made to William Bell esq agreeable to act of Assembly made in such cases with following courses: 336 ac in Randolph Co at mouth of Carraway [Cr] sold due to the confiscation act as property of Henry Eustace McCulloch, begins at a white oak corner of "No. 12 & 16", runs S 42 chains crossing Carraway [Cr] at 30 chains at mouth to a pine corner of a tract sold due to "an execution", W on said line crossing Uarie [R at] 80 chains to a red oak, N 42 chains to Fuller's corner pine, & E on his line to beginning; as by surveyor's plan may more fully appear (signed) J Harpel [or Harper], cc; [no grant found for 336 ac, W Bell received 12 grants in Randolph Co].

371. Randolph Co Nov. term 1803; heard petition of George Black filed last term stating errors in a grant issued Sept. 21, 1785 fo 150 ac on waters of Sandy Cr; Black asks that errors be rectified; court ordered that Secretary of State rectify the errors; instead of the courses in the grant "begins at a hickory in Wire's line, runs N 30 chains to a black oak, E 47 chains to a post oak, S 10 chains to a stake, "then 55 degrees East" 20 chains bounded by McCulloch & Stealey's line to a black oak, & W to beginning"; following courses to be inserted: "begins at a white oak, runs N40W 11 chains down a branch to a hickory, N 31.5 chains to a black oak, E 15.5 chains to a post oak by Harmon's Road, S68E 23 chains along Harmon's [or Herman] Road to a post oak, S7W 5 chains to a post oak, S45E 20 chains on McCulloch's line to a hickory, S 10.5 chains to a stake, & W to beginning"; Jeduthan Harper, clerk, signs (signed) J Harper Nov. 8, 1803; [on back] altered Nov. 25, 1803;
  survey included for 150 ac; surveyed Dec. 23, 1802 for George Black being old deeded land surveyed by William Millikan [metes & bounds same as second set above] (signed) B Elliott, DS; John Clay & John Black, chain carriers; [plat included]; [grant book 60 p. 306, see shuck #227 in Randolph Co in Secretary's grant files].

372. Randolph Co Aug. session 1794; petition of James Crabtree: the petitioner obtained a warrant for 250 ac in Randolph Co, begins at a black oak, runs E 18 chains to a white oak, N55E 91.5 chains to James Crabtree's line, N 67.5 chains along said line to a black oak, W 36.5 chains to a white oak saplin, & S 86.5 chains to beginning; when the grant was obtained, there were errors in the plat & courses as follows: begins at a spanish oak, runs E 28 chains to a black jack, N5E 75 chains to a black oak, W 88 chains to a black oak, & S 43 chains to beginning; the plat covers James Crabtree's old deeded land & not land he entered; the petitioner asks for an order to alter the grant agreeable to first mentioned lines; prayer of petitioner was granted; court ordered it to be transmitted to Secretary so the grant can be altered agreeable to act of Assembly made in such cases; a true copy (signed) J Harper, clk; order cost 1/, copy record 4/6, county seal 2/6, total 9/0;

Corrections/Alterations to Land Grants

[on back James Crabtree No. 471 Aug. 18, 1787 patent altered; [grant book 66 p. 141, see shuck #431 in Randolph Co in Secretary's grant files].

373. Randolph Co Nov. term 1805; on petition of Enoch Davis, court ordered that annexed grant from North Carolina to James Welbourn be altered & made conformable to within platt (signed) Nov. 5, 1805 J Harper, cc;
    survey 150 ac Oct. 21, 1805 for James "Wilburn" on waters of Bush Cr, begins at William Wilburn's NE corner black oak, runs N 150 poles on the old line to a post oak stump "the" old corner, W 160 poles on the old marked line to a spanish oak the old corner, S 150 poles to a stake, E along the old line to beginning (signed) J Elliott, CS; Joseph Bull & James Wilburn, chain carriers [plat included]; [on back] altered Nov. 29, 1805 (not signed); [grant book 82 p. 265, see shuck #795 in Randolph Co in Secretary's grant files].

374. Randolph Co; to Secretary of State: at Randolph Co court held third Monday in Feb. 1799, William Gray exhibited his petition asking court to direct alteration of grant No. 801 issued to him for 26 ac; alteration to be as follows: begins at Harper's corner stake, runs N 29 poles to Gray's corner red oak in Collet's line, E 152 poles on his line to a stake in Johnston's line, S 29 poles on his line to Harper's corner stake, & W on his line to beginning contains 26 ac; court ordered above alterations to be made agreeable to prayer of petitioner (signed) J Harper, clk; [on back] altered Nov. 22, 1799 [not signed]; [grant book 82 p. 264, see shuck #793 in Randolph Co in Secretary's grant files].

375. Randolph Co Nov. session 1800; to Secretary of State: it has been made to appear to court that the surveyor made an error in the return to Secretary's office in grant No. 580; the name should have been Joshua in place of Josiah; court directed name Josiah Hancock be altered to Joshua Hancock; I certify foregoing is true copy (signed) third Monday in Nov. 1800 J Harper, clk; [on back] altered Dec. 30, 1802; [grant book 74 p. 260, see shuck #543 in Randolph Co in Secretary's grant files].

376. Randolph Co May session 1805; it appears to court that there is an error in grant No. 546 issued to Joseph Mast for 100 ac; error is in the beginning which says begins at his father's corner pine but should say begins at his father's line near his old corner black oak; the survey is right, but surveyor mentioned beginning corner wrong; court ordered said error be certified to the Secretary of State so necessary alteration can be made; I certify above is copy of the order (signed) May 8, 1805 J Harper, clk; [on back] altered Nov. 29, 1805 [not signed]; [grant book 72 p 150, see shuck #506 in Randolph Co in Secretary's grant files].

377. to James Glasgow, Secretary of State: at Randolph Co Pleas & Quarter Sessions Court held third Monday in Aug. "last", court ordered that it be certified to you that courses in grant No. 561 issued to Jonathan McCollum for 80 ac are not agreeable with survey; he began at a black oak and ran N 11 chains to Alridge's corner "which alteration" he prays to be made; a true copy (signed)

Corrections/Alterations to Land Grants

Sept. 9, 1797 J Harper, clk; [on back] patent altered [no date & no signature]; [grant book 72 p. 154, see shuck #521 in Randolph Co in Secretary's grant files].

378. Randolph Co Pleas & Quarter Sessions Court May term 1842; petition of William Page & examination of Col. Isaac Lamb, county surveyor; it appears to satisfaction of court that a grant issued Oct. 10, 1839 to William Page for 70 ac; the county surveyor's return "sets forth" the land as situated on Fork Cr and grant issued accordingly; but the land is on Bear Cr which is an error by the surveyor; court ordered that foregoing facts be certified to Secretary of State by the clerk; Hugh McCain, clerk, certifies above is a copy of court order relating to alteration of a grant by Secretary of State to William Page (signed) at Ashboro Nov. 16, 1842 Hugh McCain, ccc; [altered Dec. 12, 1842; [grant book 146 p. 140, see shuck #2797 in Randolph Co in Secretary's grant files].

379. 100 ac surveyed for Adam Brown showing the deficiency of a former survey, begins at widow Wilborn's old corner hickory, runs W 2.5 chains to a hickory, S 14 chains 41 links to a stone, W 32.5 chains to a black gum, N 25 chains 41 links to a post oak, E 12 chains 50 links to a white oak, N 6 chains 50 links to a white oak, E 22 chains 50 links to a white oak, & S to beginning (signed) Joseph Elliott; Isaac McCollum & Timothy White, chain carriers;
    Randolph Co Nov. session 1798; to Secretary of State: it appeared to the court that there is an error in plat for grant No. 154 issued to William Wilborn for 100 ac; the survey doesn't fully describe the land; the court directed that grant be altered & made agreeable to plan enclosed signed by Joseph Elliott, surveyor; I hereby certify foregoing is true copy (signed) Nov. 25, 1798 J Harper, clk; [on back] altered Dec. 12, 1799 [not signed]; [grant book 6 p. 242, see shuck #13 in Randolph Co in Secretary's grant files].

380. Randolph Co Nov. session 1800; to Secretary of State: it appeared to court that there is an error in surveyor's return for grant No. 792 to William Wilson; courses & distances are to cover 150 ac and certificate says 100 ac; the court directs the error to be altered agreeable to courses & distances for 150 ac; I certify the above is a true copy (signed) third Monday in Nov. 180 J Harper, clk; [on back] altered Nov. 16, 1802 [not signed]; [grant book 82 p. 261, see shuck #783 in Randolph Co in Secretary's grant files].

381. Randolph Co Pleas & Quarter Sessions Court held second Monday in Sept. 1792; Zebedee Wood esquire exhibited his petition asking that it be certified to the Secretary that courses in grant No. 579 for 100 ac on waters of Sandy Cr be "reversed" to say begins at a white oak, runs North "&c"; it appears by the grant that from the white oak they runs South which runs from the land intended; the [prayer of] petition was granted & ordered certified accordingly (signed) J Harper; [on back] "done" [no date or signature]; [grant book 74 p. 258, see shuck #542 in Randolph Co in Secretary's grant files].

382. to justices of Richmond Co court at Rockingham Apr. term 1794; petition of

125

Corrections/Alterations to Land Grants

Henry Adcock; in 1772, 116 ac was surveyed for him in Richmond Co on Hitchcock Cr, begins at John Poston's corner pine on lower side of the creek, runs S25E 25 chains 14 links to a pine, N60W 51 chains 50 links to or near John Tabor's line, S38E 16 chains 40 links which last mentioned line was run N38E and is laid down in the plat with no other mistake than "South" instead of "North" owing to surveyor's mistake; the petitioner has held quiet possession of land from time "aforesaid" to the present date which is his just & equitable right or right of those to whom the petitioner has transferred the land & no one can claim any right; but he fears some doubts may arise in the future; so he asks the court to order the clerk to certify the error to Secretary of State & direct him to correct the error in the plat & grant agreeable to act of General Assembly made in such cases (signed) Henry Adcock's mark "<u>A</u>"; court ordered the clerk to certify the mistake to Secretary as appears in the plat & send a copy of the petition & order (signed) J Terry, clk; [on back] altered patent & record [no date or signature]; [grant book 26 p. 118, see shuck #3637 in Anson Co in Secretary's grant files].

383. Richmond Co Jan. session 1796; court ordered that Secretary of State be directed to insert an additional line in grant #536 issued to Archibald Carmicle for 150 ac; immediately after line marked North 240 poles the additional line to be inserted East 100 poles; copy (signed) Tod Robinson, DC for J Terry clk; [on back] patent dated 1793; [grant book 81 p. 470, see shuck #537 in Richmond Co in Secretary's grant files].

384. Richmond Co Jul. session 1805; court ordered that Secretary of State be directed to alter following courses in a grant for 250 ac to William Coleman: fourth line that is mentioned in the grant N25W to be altered to N74W, fifth line from N63E to N16E, & enter on his records "direct to beginning"; grant No. 976; copied from the minutes (signed) Nov. 14, 1805 Eli Terry, clerk [on back] altered Dec. 21, 1805; [grant book 26 p. 112, see shuck #3612 in Anson Co on Secretary's grant files].

385. Richmond Co Jun. session 1806; court ordered that Secretary of State be directed to alter the word "East" to "West" in third line of a plat of 250 ac granted to Edward Curry; a true copy from the minutes (signed) J Macalester, D clerk for Wm P Leak clk; [on back] altered Nov. 18, 1806; [grant book 83 p. 517, see shuck #704 in Richmond Co in Secretary's grant files].

386. Richmond Co Jan. term 1829; court ordered that Secretary of State be directed to alter courses of a grant issued May 18, 1789 to John Fountain for 500 ac to read as follows: begins at a pine amongst 3 pine pointers about 0.25 miles above Isaac Yates' old place, runs N89W 29 chains 50 links to a pine amongst 2 black jacks & a pine pointers, N69W 17 chains to a pine amongst 3 pine pointers to Mark Potett's beginning, N8E 80 chains crossing Drownding Cr to a corner, S77E 100 chains to a corner, S5W 26 chains to th run of the creek, up the said run to Allan Campbell's upper corner, & S5W to beginning (signed) Jan. 21, 1829 M D Crawford, cc; [on back] altered Mar. 7, 1829 (signed) Wm Hill, Secy; [grant

Corrections/Alterations to Land Grants

book 71 p. 1, see shuck #287 in Richmond Co in Secretary's grant files].

387. Richmond Co Jul. term 1808; court ordered Secretary of State be directed to alter third course or line of 100 ac granted to Norman McRae being now called "East" to that of "West"; copy from the minutes (signed) J Macalester, DC for Wm P Leak, cc; [on back] Norman McRae grant No. 1378 dated Feb. 4, 1804, altered Oct. 1, 1808 [not signed]; [grant book 118 p. 301, see shuck #1396 in Richmond Co in Secretary's grant files].

388. Richmond Co Jan. session 1796; court ordered Secretary of State be directed to alter a line of grant No. 500 issued Mar. 4, 1775 to James Poston; line marked S57W to be inserted S57E; likewise grant No. 323 issued to John Waters for 300 ac to be altered; line marked S75E to [be] N75E and line N75W to [be] S75W "dated 1790" (signed) Tod Robinson, DC for James Terry clerk; [on back] altered; [grant to Poston: grant book 25 p. 82, see shcuk #3222 in Anson Co; grant to Waters: grant book 77 p. 195, see shuck #324 in Richmond Co in Secretary's grant files].

389. Richmond Co Jul. term 1823; on petition of William Thomas, present owner of 250 ac granted Jul. 13, 1773 to William Colman; land is in said county; it appears to satisfaction of court that a mistake was made in fifth line of the patent which calls "by the lines of said patent" for N63E but should have been N6W; it is ordered by court that clerk certify the same to Secretary of State so the error can be corrected (signed) at Rockingham Mar. 17, 1824 M D Crawford, clk; [note at bottom:] grant is dated Jul. 25, 1774, survey is dated Jun. 13, 1773; [on back] altered Jul. 3, 1824 Wm Hill, Secry; [grant book 20 p. 112, see shuck #3612 in Anson Co].

390. Richmond Co Jan. session 1808; court ordered Secretary of State be directed to alter "name" of the course of second line of 300 ac granted to John Webb on both sides of Hitchcock Cr; the course of the line is called E10N but should be N80E and sixth line being the reverse of the second line to S80W; copy from the minutes (signed) J Macalester, DC for Wm P Leak clerk; [on back] certificate for alteration of grant for 350 (sic) ac issued May 25, 1757, altered Oct. 1, 1808; [grant book 2 p. 151 see shuck #428 and grant book 16 p. 82 see shuck #2198 in Anson Co in Secretary's grant files].

391. petition of Silas Adkins (of Robeson Co) to Robeson Co court: the petitioner entered 100 ac in Bladen now Robeson Co; Isaac Jones, deputy surveyor, surveyed the land; through a mistake in the plat, he inserted the name of Elias Adkins instead of Silas Adkins; the petitioner obtained a grant Nov. 9, 1784; it is "well known" to the curt that there never wan any person in the county named Elias Adkins; the petitioner asks the court to direct Secretary of State to alter the name of Elias to Silas in the grant (signed) Oct. 4, 1803 Silas Adkins. Court ordered the Secretary to correct the petitioner's patent agreeable to above copy (signed) Oct. 4, 1803 J Barnes, cc; [on back] altered Nov. 30, 1803 (not signed);

Corrections/Alterations to Land Grants

[grant not identified, Silas Adkins received 4 grants for 100 ac in Robeson Co in 1788 and 1794 and no grants for 100 ac in Bladen Co].

392. Robeson Co court Apr. term 1796; by petition, Warren Alford made it appear to satisfaction of court that he is possessed of 150 ac which was granted to Francis Falk; and he made it appear there was a surveyor's error in the plat which doesn't include any part of the intended land; the courses should be as follows: begins at a pine, runs S20E 50 chains, N70E 30 chains, N20W 50 chains, & direct course to beginning; court ordered that Secretary correct the error (signed) J Barnes, cc; [2 possible grants for 150 ac each: grant book 69 p 31 see shuck #3990 and grant book 69 p. 27 see shuck #3973 in Bladen Co in Secretary's grant files].

393. petition of Thomas Ard to Robeson Co court: the petitioner obtained a "title" for 100 ac in Robeson late Bladen Co which, on examination, if found to be platted wrong by the surveyor; the petitioner will "loose" his land due to the surveyor's error unless the court considers the case & corrects the error agreeable to an act of Assembly made in such cases; the first line of the survey runs S62E 31 chains 63 links is marked in the plat S62W 31 chains 63 links, second line runs S28W 31 chains 63 links is marked in the grant N28W 31 chains 63 links, third line runs N62W 31 chains 63 links is marked in the grant N62E 31 chains 63 links, & fourth line runs N28E 31 chains 63 links is marked in the grant S28E 31 chains 63 links (signed) Thomas Ard.   Court ordered the Secretary correct the error in the patent agreeable to above copy of petition (signed) Apr. 6, 1801 J Barnes, clk; [on back] Isaac Wolf, order to alter a grant; altered Dec. 11, 1801 (not signed); [grant #912 issued Nov. 7, 1784, grant book 69 p. 47, see shuck #4051 in Bladen Co in Secretary's grant files].

394. Robeson Co Jan. term 1797; Randal Currie made it appear to satisfaction of this court that he entered 52 ac in Bladen now Robeson Co; it appeared, due to surveyor's error, it was mentioned to be only 50 ac; and the survey didn't contain but about 41 ac due to error in platting; it should be as follows: 52 ac on S side of Middle Swamp, begins at a pine in or near MacCrainey's line, runs N55W 40 chains, N70E 15 chains 82 links, S55E 40 chains, & a direct line to beginning; court ordered that Secretary correct the error (signed) J Barnes, cc; [on back] "Runnald Curry" for 52 ac dated Dec. 20, 1791, made conformable May 31, 1797 (signed) Wm Hill; [grant book 78 p. 10, see shuck #4604 in Bladen Co in Secretary's grant files].

395. Robeson Co Pleas & Quarter Sessions Court Nov. term 1838; Archd McEachern vs Hector Currie petition to correct errors in a grant: the case was heard on testimony presented to 7 justices of court; it appeared to satisfaction of the court that 40 ac was granted to John Gilchrist in Jul. 1788; beginning corner is at 2 small pines on the side of Hurricane [Bay] "a little" below Ephraim Fennel's now "Curries"; land lies or should be between the Hurricane [Bay] & Long Swamp; by beginning as above, the courses of the grant & surveyor's certificate throw at least three-fourths of the land into the Hurricane contrary to

Corrections/Alterations to Land Grants

land marks made at time of location "to the prejudice of the claimant"; the errors complained of should be corrected by running the second line North instead of South as stated in the grant & surveyor's certificate which will restore the claimant to his right; court ordered that clerk certify the above facts to the Secretary of State with accompanying survey of the premises made in this case to be filed by Secretary in his office so he can correct the errors in the certificate & grant according to law. Shadrach Howell, clerk, certifies foregoing case, order, & decree are correctly copied from minutes & records in my office (signed) Dec. 15, 1838 Shadrach Howell, clerk cc. Shadrach Howell, clerk, certifies a copy of annexed plat & survey are filed in office of clerk of Robeson Co court (signed) Dec. 15, 1838 Shadrach Howell, ccc;

Jan. 2, 1839 to William Hill, Secretary: I expect that Mr. Blount or Mr. Tuton will pay you your fee for the alteration of before mentioned grant; Mr. Blount & Mr. Tuton are representatives now in Raleigh from Robeson Co (signed) Sdh Howell; [on back] to be altered when the grant is presented (signed) W H;

at Robeson Co Pleas & Quarter Sessions Court begun at court house in Lumberton fourth Monday in Aug. 1839; Wednesday Aug. 28, 1839 court met present Charles Moore, John Drake, & Thomas A Norment; Archd McEachern vs Flora Currie & Hector Currie petition to correct courses in a grant for 40 ac: it appeared to satisfaction of this court that original grant is lost by "time and accident"; court ordered this fact be certified to Secretary of State so he can correct the copy in his office agreeable to former decree of this court and similar correction be made in Register's office in this county. Shadrach Howell, clerk, certifies foregoing order was truly copied from minutes & records in my office (signed) Nov. 16, 1839 Shd Howell, clerk cc. Robeson Co clerk of court's office Nov. 16, 1839 to William Hill, Secretary of State: on your examining foregoing order of Robeson Co court concerning case of Archd McEachern vs Flora & Hector Currie for correction of grant about 1788 to John Gilchrist, if you recollect, I sent my mail last Winter about time or rise of the Legislature a certified copy of a decree of this court made Nov. term 1838 about this case; the order authorised you to make the correction requested; I requested Messers Tuton & Blount, who "was" them members of the Legislature, to speak to you about the alteration; I think Mr. Blount informed me since that you could not legally make the correction without the original grant; but it appears the original is lost; so the plaintiff has taken the "present plan" to have the correction made; it appears the original grant was registered agreeable to law in Robeson Co Register's office; I have enclosed 40 cents as your fee for making the correction; when this comes to hand & you discover there is anything more necessary to carry the case into effect, please inform me by letter as soon as convenient (signed) Shad Howell; [at bottom] answd. "Nov. 25 Nov. 18, 1839";

survey with plat: above plat begins at the index [finger mark] and is 40 ac in Robeson Co between Huricane Bay & Long Swamp granted to John Gilchrist sr Jun. 12, 1788, begins at 2 small pines on the side of Huricane Bay below "Faniel's" now Curries improvement, runs due E 25 chains to a stake, due S 16 chains to a stake, due W 25 chains to a stake, & a direct line to beginning; in surveying the 40 ac I find marked lines running due E and due N from beginning corner and beginning trees marked on E & N sides; word "South" inserted by the surveyor at second corner should be "North" to agree with original marked lines & beginning corner trees; double lines in above plat are courses which the land was laid out agreeable to marked lines; single lines are land agreeable to original courses; dotted lines are lands of Currie in 4 surveys; zig zag lines are Faniel's improvement (signed) Nov. 19, 1838 James McAlpin, CS; [on back] altered the record of the grant Nov. 25, 1839 (signed) W Hill, Secy; patent not presented said to be lost or destroyed (signed) W H; [grant No. 13 issued Jul. 12, 1788 to John Gilchrist, grant book 68 p. 214, see shuck #75 in Robeson Co in Secretary's grant files].

396. the plat [drawn at top of page, "W Ashley 200 ac" (sic) written in plat] is 200 ac in Robeson Co on W side of Drowning Cr & N of Coward Swamp; land granted in year [blank] to Andrew Griffin; begins at a pine in Flowers' line agreeable to the course in the patent first line runs S30W 28 chains "mentioning" a black jack for second corner, then "&c" running parallel with marked lines; but agreeable to the marked lines, the first line runs S60W 28 chains to a black jack original marked corner, then as in the patent S35E 31 chains to a stake 3 pines & a white oak, S55W 50 chains to a pine, S20E 21 chains to a pine, N70E 29 chains to a pine, due S 15 chains to a pine, N55E 38 chains to a pine, & a direct line to beginning [N20W 88 chains--lined out]; surveyed Sept. 16, 1817 for Andrew Griffin [William Ashley esq--lined out] (signed) D MacAlpin, CS; Robe Hills esq & John G Ashley, chain carriers.   Jul. term 1808 Robeson Co agreeable to court order, the Secretary of State is authorized to alter the lines in patent No. 1521 to Andrew Griffin agreeable to "enexed" plat (signed) Sept. 17, 1808 Rt Haills, DS; [on back] altered Sept. 20, 1808 (not signed); [grant to A Griffin not identified, William Ashley received 6 grants in Bladen Co and 4 in Robeson Co, but none with number 1521, grant not identified].

397. Jan. term 1808 Robeson Co; on petition of John Humphrey, it appears to satisfaction of court that an error was made by the surveyor in "location or certificate" in "his" grant for 200 ac; one line of the survey was omitted being "thence East 254 poles" which comes after the word "oak" in eleventh line of the grant; court ordered the grant be altered according to act of Assembly made in such cases; a true copy (signed) Rt Haills, cc; [on back] alteration of grant No. 413 to John Oliphant, claimant John Humphry; altered Sept. 9, 1808 (not signed); [grant book 30 p. 461, see shuck #2898 in Bladen Co in Secretary's grant files].

398. Robeson Co Pleas & Quarter Sessions Court Feb. term 1822; court ordered Secretary of State correct an error in grant No. 750 to David MacColl for 100 ac so that words "and running East" from beginning corner will read "and running West" and words "and runs East" from third corner will read "and runs West"; a true copy from minutes (signed) Richd C Bunting, clk; [on back] altered Dec. 7, 1822 Wm Hill, Secry; [2 grants to D McColl in Robeson Co, but not No. 750, grant not identified].

Corrections/Alterations to Land Grants

399. Robeson Co Pleas & Quarter Sessions Court Aug. tern 1821; Archibald McLachlan vs John McBryde & heirs of Jno McLachlan petition to correct error in a grant & mesne conveyances: it appeared to satisfaction of court that an error was committed by the Secretary of State in recording grant No. 137 issued Nov. 18, 1771 to Aaron Strickland for 150 ac in Bladen now Robeson Co; error is in first line of the grant; those claiming under the patentee are liable to be injured by the error; the court "considered" the error be corrected and said line as amended to run S15E 38 chains 73 links as it stands in the surveyor's plat appended to the grant; court ordered likewise that clerk certify these facts to Secretary of State to be filed & to correct the record in his office; and the same "amendment" be made to all mesne conveyances from the patentee to the petitioner; a copy of this judgment be recorded in the Register's books (signed) J Wood sr, "chearman", & Richd C Bunting, clk. A true copy from the records in my office (signed) Aug. 29, 1821 Richd C Bunting, clk. (Robeson Co) Mar. 28, 1822 Archibald McLauchlan, the petitioner in whose favor the within judgment was entered, before Duncan McBryde, justice of peace, swore he has never seen the original grant to Aaron Strickland and doesn't know if it exists; William Overstreet sold the land to the petitioner and told McLauchlan "about the time of the purchase" that the grant was consumed by fire (signed) Archd McLauchlan's mark "X" & Duncan McBryde. Richard C Bunting, clerk, certifies Duncan "MacBryde" is acting justice of peace in Robeson Co (signed) Mar. 30, 1822 Richd C Bunting, clk; [on back] altered Jan. 3, 1826 (signed) Wm Hill, Secry; [grant No. 137 issued Nov. 18, 1771 to Aaron Strickland, grant book 20 p. 710, see shuck #2035 in Bladen Co in Secretary's grant files].

400. Robeson Co Oct. term 1796; by a petition & "other proofs", Daniel Matthews made it appear to satisfaction of court that he is possessed of 300 ac granted to Jacob Alford; there is a surveyor's error in plating the land & Matthews doesn't hold all the intended land; the courses should be: on Big Marsh, begins at a pine on upper side of "the" road, runs N20E 54 chains 78 links, S70E 54 chains 78 links, S20W 54 chains 78 links, & a direct line to beginning; court ordered Secretary to correct the error (signed) J Barnes, cc [at top of page] "No. 1692, Dec. 15, 90"; [grant book 75 p. 147, see shuck #4557 in Bladen Co in Secretary's grant files].

401. Robeson Co court; petition of William Moore: he obtained a grant for 150 ac in Robeson late Bladen Co; on examination, the grant contains only 125 ac which will cause the petitioner to lose 25 c due to surveyor's error unless the court considers this case and corrects the error agreeable to act of Assembly made in such cased; first line of the survey runs S48W 50 chains but should be 60 chains and third line runs N48E 50 chains but should "be attended to" 60 chains; by this attention the petitioner will have what is justly entitled or 150 ac (signed) Jan. 8, 1800 Wm Moore. Apr. term 1800 court ordered Secretary to correct an error in a patent agreeable to prayer of above petition; certified by Josiah Barnes, clerk (signed) Apr. 7, 1800 J Barnes, cc; [on back] altered agreeable to within Dec. 6, 1800 (not signed); [two possible grants (a) grant book 75 p. 186 see shuck #4559

Corrections/Alterations to Land Grants

and (b) grant book 75 p. 187 see shuck #4560 in Bladen Co in Secretary's grant files].

402. petition of Lewis Powell to justices of Robeson Co court: the petitioner made an entry Nov. 26, 1778 for 100 ac in Bladen now Robeson Co; at direction of the petitioner, the surveyor surveyed the land as follows: begins at a large pine in Caleb Bigg's line, runs S70E 90 poles with said line to a pine, N20E 180 [190--lined out] poles to a stake, N70W 90 poles to a stake, & a direct line to beginning as appears by marked trees in above described lines; but surveyor made an error in describing the courses in the plat as follows: begins at a large pine in Caleb Bigg's line, runs S70W 90 poles with said line to a pine, N20W 180 poles to a stake, N70E 90 poles to a stake, & a direct line to beginning; agreeable to this "representation" the Secretary of State issued a grant Nov. 12, 1799 whereby the petitioner "looses" the land he had surveyed; the patent "turned over on" old patented land and greatly damages the petitioner; he hopes the court will see the justice of his claim and asks them to direct the clerk to certify the same to Secretary of State so the petitioner can be "releived" under an act made in such cases by having the patent altered agreeable to actual survey as first described (signed) Lewis Powell's mark "P"; a copy (signed) J Barnes, cc. Oct. 5, 1802 court ordered the Secretary to correct the error in the above patent agreeable to above "copy" (signed) J Barnes; [on back] altered Dec. 14, 1802 (not signed); [grant book 33 p. 270, see shuck #2944 in Bladen Co in Secretary's grant files].

403. Robeson Co Pleas & Quarter Sessions Court Nov. term 1819; on petition of Joseph Regan esq, court ordered that Secretary of State be directed to correct an error in grant No. 992 issued Nov. 7, 1784 to Ralph Regan in such a manner so that beginning corner will read "to a pine in Joseph Regan's line" instead of "Joseph Regan's corner" (sic); a true copy from the minutes (signed) Richd C Bunting, clk; [on back] altered Nov. 22, 1823 (signed) Wm Hill; [grant book 69 p. 67, see shuck #4130 in Bladen Co in Secretary's grant files].

404. petition of Robert Sims to justices of Robeson Co court: he entered 100 ac in Bladen Co before it was divided; he obtained a patent in 1779; courses of the grant should have been: begins at a stake in "the" marsh, runs S31E 180 poles to a pine, N59E 90 poles to a stake, N31W 180 poles to a stake, N31W 180 poles to a stake, & S59W 90 poles to beginning; the petitioner says the surveyor made a mistake in making out the certificate of survey; he certified the first line to run S21E instead of S31E; the Secretary made an error in second line of the grant which differs from the plat & certificate of survey; instead of being N59E 90 poles to a stake it is said to run N 59 poles to a stake which means the lines in the patent don't join and the petitioner may be materially injured; petitioner asks that clerk be directed to certify the "mistake" to Secretary of State so the errors in the patent can be rectified (signed) Jul. term 1800 Robert Sims. Robeson Co court Oct. term 1800 court ordered Secretary to correct the error in the petitioner's patent agreeable to above copy (signed) Oct. 6, 1800 J Barnes, cc; [on back] altered Dec. 18, 1801 W W; [4 possible grant for 100 ac in Bladen Co to Robert Sims, see

Corrections/Alterations to Land Grants

shucks 3044, 3186, 3205, & 3264 in Secretary's grant files].

405. Robeson Co Jan. session 1807; court ordered Secretary of State be directed to correct an error in grant No. 1054 to Peter Smith for 152 ac; in first "written" line instead of "So East" insert "North East" and in second course instead of S22W insert N22W to make the grant conformable to the plat thereunto annexed; copy from the minutes (signed) J McQurrll, clk; [on back] altered Nov. 27, 1807; [grant book 86 p. 109, see shuck #1059 in Robeson Co in Secretary's grant files].

406. I certify that James Stephens made it appear to satisfaction of Robeson Co court that there was an error in a patent to him for 150 ac on "Contrary" Branch; it appeared there was a material difference between the plat made by the surveyor and the grant issued by the Secretary due to mistake in the latter; court ordered that Secretary correct the error [error not described] (signed) J Barnes, cc; [on back] John "Stevens" order of Robeson Co court to alter patent; altered Dec. 20, 1798 (not signed); [two grants to John Stephens in Bladen Co, but not for 150 ac, grant not identified].

407. Robeson Co Pleas & Quarter Sessions Court Oct. session 1797; James "Steven" petitioned the court saying Elias "Barns", deputy surveyor, surveyed land for John Cain which has since become property of said Steven; [land] begins at a red oak about 20 yards from "the" Great Swamp, runs W 160 poles to a stake among 3 pines, S 219 poles to a stake among 3 pines, E 219 poles to a persimmon tree, N 219 poles to a stake, & a direct line to beginning; the deputy surveyor made a mistake in describing the land in his return to Secretary's office as follows: begins at a red oak 20 yards from the Great Swamp, runs W 160 poles to a stake among 3 pines, S 219 poles to a stake among 3 pines, E 219 poles to a persimmon tree & a direct line to beginning; Steven asks that courses of the grant be made agreeable to first mentioned courses; court ordered that the Secretary make such alteration agreeable to prayer of petition; I certify the above is taken from records in my office (signed) Jan. 3, 1798 J Barnes, cc; [on back] Oct. 3, 1799 W W; [only one grant to John Cain in Robeson Co, grant book 77 p. 5, see shuck #342 in Robeson Co in Secretary's grant files].

408. petition of Thomas "Towsend" to Robeson Co court: the petitioner obtained a patent Oct. 23, 1782 from the Secretary of State for 300 ac then in Bladen Co on E side of Horse Swamp; the survey made out the plat of survey & certified first line to run S70W 106 poles instead of N70W 106 poles; the petitioner asks that clerk be directed to certify the mistake to Secretary of State so the error can be rectified (signed) Thomas Townsend; copy (signed) James Macqueen, ccc. Robeson Co Oct. term 1804 court ordered that Secretary of State correct the error in petitioner's patent agreeable to above copy (signed) James Macqueen, ccc; [on back] altered Nov. 23, 1804 (not signed); [300 ac grant in Bladen Co issued to Thomas Townsend jr, grant book 47 p. 261, see shuck #3427 in Bladen Co in Secretary's grant files].

Corrections/Alterations to Land Grants

409. Robeson Co court Apr. term 1793; I certify John Willis esq. made it appear by certificate from William Singletary, Bladen Co entry taker, that it appeared on books of Thomas Robeson, former Bladen Co entry taker, that on Dec. 20, 1784 John Willis & Griffith J McRee entered 300 ac on Saddletree Swamp joining John Blount, John Clibourn, George Willis, Thomas Owens, & includes said swamp "and both sides"; John Willis also made it appear by petition & affidavit that a grant issued for the land to Abraham Tatam "in the plan of said John Willis" (sic); he never authorized such alteration (signed) J Barnes, cc; [on back] patent No. 1692 dated in 1791; altered patent [no date or signature]; [grant not identified in Bladen or Robeson Co].

410. I certify Simon Willis made it appear to satisfaction of Robeson Co court that there is an error in a patent to him for 100 ac on N side of Saddletree Swamp, begins in Blount's line but it appeared it should run West instead of East; court ordered that Secretary correct the error (signed) Jul. term 1794 J Barnes, cc; [on back] No. 1699; "p" altered Mar. 16, 1795 (not signed); [grant book 78 p. 16, see shuck #4621 in Bladen Co in Secretary's grant files].

411. petition of Jonathan Wishart to Robeson Co court: in 1793 the petitioner purchased land from Isom Ivey of Robeson Co; Ivey had obtained the land by patent from Secretary of State for 100 ac in Robeson "then" Bladen Co on W side of Great Swamp, begins at a stake at lower corner of said Wishart's "plantation", runs N18W 10 chains to a lightwood stake, N72E 20 chains to a stake, N17W 9 chains to a stake, N73W 20 chins to a stake, N29W 20 chains to a stake, N61W 3 chains 50 links to a stake, S15E 8 chains 50 links to a stake & 3 pines, S72W 19 chains 5 links to a small lightwood tree, S7W 25 chains to a pine, S43E 16 chains to a pine, & a direct line to beginning; the petitioner says by a mistake the patent indicates fifth line instead of N29W 20 chains to a stake as S25W 20 chains to a stake, sixth line instead of S61W 3 chains 50 links as S17E 10 chains, seventh line instead of S15E 8 chains 50 links as S67W 20 chains, eighth line instead of S72W 19 chains 50 links as S 20 chains, ninth line being entirely left out which runs S43E 16 chains to a pine & direct line to beginning; by these means the petitioner may be materially injured; the petitioner asks that clerk be directed to certify the mistake to Secretary of State so the "error" can be rectified (signed) Oct. term 1800 J Wishart. Robeson Co court Jan. term 1801 court ordered that the Secretary correct the error in petitioner's patent agreeable to above copy; certified by Josiah Barnes, clerk (signed) Jan. 7, 1801 J Barnes, cc; [on back] Jonathan Wishart petition to alter grant; altered Dec. 19, 1803; [grant book 89 p. 157, see shuck #4894 in Bladen Co in Secretary's grant files].

412. Rowan Co Nov. 7, 1807 I certify that at Aug. session 1807 Mathew Brandon esq filed his petition, in Rowan Co Pleas & Quarter Sessions Court, to amend various errors in grant No. 1224 issued Oct. 25, 176 to Andrew Bostian for 278 ac; it appeared to court that Mathew Brandon complied with requisites of act of Assembly made in such cases; court ordered Mathew Brandon had leave to amend all errors in said grant agreeable to annexed platt & certificate of lines &

boundaries of the tract made by William Moore esq, county surveyor; clerk to certify the same to Secretary of State (signed) Ad Osborn, cc; [on back] altered Dec. 7, 1807;

pursuant to directions of Rowan Co court, I surveyed boundaries of 278 ac originally granted in grant No. 1224 Oct. 25, 1786 to Andrew Bostian "deceased"; actual situation of the land is as follows: begins at a post oak on W side of Crane Cr, runs E 5 chains crossing the creek to a post oak on the line of a tract formerly John Bellah's but now Moses Bellah's land, N with his line crossing the creek 14 chains to said Bellah's corner black jack, N30E 37 chains 75 links with his line to a black jack on what was formerly called Anne but now Matthew Brandon's line, N65W with "it" crossing "the" great road leading from Salisbury to Concord Charlotte "&c" in all 42 chains to his corner black jack, N 30 chains 50 links with his line to a red oak on what was formerly Richard but now is Matthew Brandon's line on N side of N fork of Panther Run, W 13 chains 50 links with it crossing Panther Run below the forks to a black oak formerly William Alexander's but now John Stirewalt's corner, S 5 chains 75 links with his line to his corner black jack, S70W 25 chains 50 links with his line to said Stirewalt's corner dead black oak on the timber ridge, N53W 37 chains 50 links with his line crossing Grants Cr to a dogwood on what was formerly John Cathey's but now Richard Trottor's line on N side of said Trotter's spring Br, S5E with his & what was formerly William Cathey's but now Bernard Crider's line crossing Grants Cr in all 44 chains to a sassafras about 4 chains S of said Criders SE corner and 2 chains W of a marked black oak corner of John Liliker's and another tract belonging to estate of Paul Barringer deceased, then runs past said black oak along the lines of last mentioned tract the 4 following courses first E 41 chains 50 links to a small post oak, S 15 chains to a dead black oak, E 34 chains 50 links to a "B" gum, & S to beginning; surveyed Sept. 12, 1807 W Moore, CS; Moses Bellah & Daniel Shuford, chain carriers; [grant book 67 p. 61, see shuck #2009 in Rowan Co in Secretary's grant files].

413. [caveat of land entry or grant suspension, not grant alteration] Rowan Co Nov. session 1789 Jane Cathey vs James Gay; caveat tried on premises by Hugh Terrence then Iredell Co sheriff returned to court that a jury of "good & lawful men" tried above disputed claim of land on the premises in Iredell Co being Rowan at constitution of the "cavay"; jury find a general verdict for caveatee James Gay which verdict is confirmed by court; certified (signed) Ad Osborn, cc;

Rowan Co Nov. session 1789 Jane Cathey vs James Gay caveat: the sheriff returned to court the "pannel" of a jury summoned on the premises and their general verdict in "favour" of James Gay; the verdict was confirmed by court (signed) Ad Osborn, cc;

Jane Cathey before Jas Brandon, one of Rowan Co justices of peace, swore James Gay "run" into her land across a conditional line between them and returned the works to Secretary's office; if a deed issues on the works it will greatly damage the deponant (signed) Sept. 21, 1786 Jas Brandon [Jane doesn't sign]; [copy of entry] No. 821 May 19, 1778 James Gay enters 300 ac in Rowan Co on waters of Yadkin R & Fourth Cr, joined on S by James Porter, on E by

Corrections/Alterations to Land Grants

James Dickey, SW of widow Cathey, runs down "the" branch, joins Jane Cathey, & his other entry "a copy" (signed) Jas Brandon; [on back] issued Dec. 9, 1786, Jane Cathey widow vs James Gay; to "lodg a caviat" in the Secretary's office; [grant to James Gay: grant #2292 issued Dec. 31, 1793 on entry #821, grant book 81 p. 354, see shuck #3112 in Rowan Co in Secretary's grant files].

414. Rowan Co Pleas & Quarter Sessions Court Feb. term 1793; it was made to appear to satisfaction of the court that James Dobbins is likely to be injured in his land title due to error by surveyor in platting the same; it appears James Dobbins exhibited his petition to the court & complied with act of Assembly made in such cases; court ordered that clerk certify the error in grant No. 646 to James Dobbins of Rowan Co by Gov. Alexander Martin at Hillsborough issued Oct. [hole in page] 10, 1783 for 280 ac; the surveyor omitted ninth line in the plat; correction to be made by inserting words "N 78 chains to a" between words "Lock's corner" and word "hickory" agreeable to duplicate survey herewith introduced [annexed--lined out]; (signed) Feb. session 1793 Ad Osborn, cc; [on back] altered the patent [no date & no signature]; [grant book 51 p. 194, see shuck #1263 in Rowan Co in Secretary's grant files].

415. Rowan Co Nov. session 1797; it appears to court that a grant issued Oct. 25, 1786 to John Gaither for 150 ac should have been to "Johnsey" Gaither; the name "John" has been inserted by the Secretary by mistake instead of "Johnsey"; court ordered the same be certified to Secretary of State who is required to rectify the error by altering the name of John to Johnsey (signed) Ad Osborn, cc; [on back] No. 1429 dated 1786; patent altered [no date or signature]; [grant book 67 p. 134, see shuck #2214 in Rowan Co in Secretary's grant files].

416. Rowan Co May session 1793; at preceding session Alexander Hughes presented his petition to alter a state grant for 438 ac in Rowan Co made to John Hughes; it appeared to court that the same should have been made to Alexander; it appears to court that due notice was given according to law; it appears to satisfaction of court that name of "John" was an error in the grant & should have been Alexander; court ordered Secretary to alter the name of John to Alexander (signed) May 11, 1793 Ad Osborn, cc; [on back] No. 1952, 438 ac [dated] 1789, patent altered [no date or signature]; [grant book 71 p. 154, see shuck #2661 in Rowan Co in Secretary's grant files].

417. Rowan Co Aug. session 1793; pursuant to petition of James McMahan sr presented to court due to act of Assembly to amend errors in grants & "mean" conveyances, it appears to court that due notice was given to every person who held or claimed adjoining land or in anyways interfered; it appears to court that by certificate of all such persons, they were "contented" the prayer of McMahan's petition should be granted; court ordered that clerk certify to Secretary of State to make following amendment to a deed from Earle Granville, by "Corven & Bodly" to James Jones for 422 ac "to wit" instead of E 65 chains to a red "o" then W 65 chains to "wh o" then to first station amend "viz" runs E 65 chains to a white oak,

Corrections/Alterations to Land Grants

S 65 chains to a black "o", W 65 chains to a "w o", & to first station; above deed dated May 11, 1757 (signed) Ad Osborn, cc; [grant book 6 p. 167, see shuck #298 in Rowan Co in Secretary's grant files].

418. Rowan Co May session 1795; petition of William Nesbett asking to correct error in deed dated Mar. 25, 1752 by Earle Granville to John Nesbett for 648 ac; the petitioner is now proprietor of the land; it appeared to court that due notice was given as required by law; by proof & inspection of the deed, it appears to court that survey made an error in beginning the survey at a white oak on E side of Grants Cr but it "most clearly" should have been on W side of the creek; I am directed to certify the same to the Secretary so the above error can be rectified by him by altering East side to West side of Grants Cr in said deed (signed) Ad Osborn, cc; [on back] altered May 27, 1795 [not signed]; [may be grant issued Apr. 20, 1753 in book 6 p. 199, see shuck #452 in Rowan Co in Secretary's grant files].

419. Rutherford Co Apr. court 1802; Harbert Hawkins petitioner the court complaining about a mistake made by the Secretary of State in a grant by inserting name of Robert Hawkins in the grant instead of Harbert Hawkins; it appears to satisfaction of court by the petition & patent that the mistake was made; court ordered clerk to certify to Secretary that issuing the grant in name of Robert was a mistake; Secretary is directed, agreeable to act of Assembly, to insert name of Harbert in place of Robert agreeable to the plat annexed to the grant (signed) R Lewis, cc; [on back] altered Dec. 4, 1802; [grant book 96 p. 271, see shuck #1454 in Rutherford Co in Secretary's grant files].

420. Rutherford Co Oct. court 1806; 7 justices present in court; Joseph King petitioned the court for alteration of grant No. 1144 issued by the State to him for 150 ac; it appears to court that legal notices have been given to "parties conserned" and sufficient testimony before the court by the surveyor who surveyed the same; court believes error was made agreeable to prayer of petitioner; court ordered clerk to certify to Secretary of State that the error was made so the Secretary can rectify the same agreeable to act of Assembly made in such cases; alteration is as follows: S60E 220 to N30W 228 poles, N60E 110 poles to N60E 126 poles, N60W 220 poles to S30E 230 poles; a true copy of order of court which I certify to Secretary of State (signed) R Lewis, cc; [on back] altered Sept. 19, 1807 [not signed]; [grant book 91 p. 361, see shuck #1269 in Rutherford Co in Secretary's grant files].

421. Rutherford Co Oct. court 1806; 7 justices on the bench; John McCurry petitioned court for alteration of grant No. 983 issued to him for 400 ac; it appears to court that legal notice has been given and sufficient testimony before the court by the surveyor who surveyed the same; the error was committed as follows: instead of running as called for in the patent, it should be altered agreeable to prayer of petition as follows: begins at a black oak by Trout's corner, N35E 121 poles to a pine, N88W 16 poles to a pine, N10W 17 poles to a maple, N80W 78

poles to a stake, S10W 37 poles to a stake, S86W 12 poles to a black oak, W 128 poles to a black oak, N10E 241 poles to a stake "or pine", W 115 poles to a post oak, S10W 200 poles to a maple, E 66 poles to a stake, S 182 poles to a red oak, S78E 150 poles to a hickory, & N30E 100 poles to beginning; Secretary of State is directed & authorized, under act of Assembly for rectifying patents when errors appear to be made, to make out the patent agreeable to prayer of petition which is the order of court (signed) R Lewis, cc; [on back] altered Sept. 19, 1807; [John McCurry received 3 grants in Rutherford Co, but not this number].

422. Rutherford Co Jul. court 1800; petition by Martha Morgan to court under act of Assembly for amending & correcting mistakes in surveying or granting patents: court ordered the clerk to certify a mistake was made by the surveyor and inserted in a grant issued May 15, 1772 to Aaron Biggerstaff signed by Jo Martin, governor & countersigned by J Parrott, P Sec; following alterations to be made: instead of N73E 200 poles to a stake, N17W 200 poles to a hickory, S73W 200 poles to a white oak, & to beginning the following alterations be made: begins at white oak & black gum, runs N15E 200 poles to a black oak, N75W 200 poles to a black oak, S15W 196 poles to a post oak, & S75E 200 poles to beginning (signed) R Lewis, clk; [on back] altered Dec. 10, 1801 [not signed];

survey due to petition of Martha Morgan to Rutherford Co court for land on Robinsons Cr granted to Aaron "Bigerstaff" for 250 ac; first course in grant called N73E on tracing the line it is N15E the courses now & boundaries as follow: begins at a white oak & black gum near where the old corner stood, N15E 200 poles to a black oak, N75W 200 poles to a black oak, S15W 196 poles to a post oak, & S75E to beginning; all the way I found the old lines inside of which has been "allway" understood to be land granted to Aaron Biggerstaff (signed) Oct. 20, 1800 D Dickey; John Harder & John Norrel, chain carriers; [grant book 22 p. 23, see shuck #473 in Tryon Co in Secretary's grant files].

423. Rutherford Co Jul. court 1806; 7 justices on the bench; Thomas Whiteside, by Joseph Grayson, petitioned the court for alteration of grant No. 435 to Thomas Whiteside and sold by said Whiteside to said Grayson; it appears to court that lawful notice has been given & sufficient testimony before the court that an error was committed by surveyor in running out "the same" and grant doesn't cover the 100 ac of land intended to be taken; lines weren't run long enough to contain the compliment; court ordered Secretary of State be directed & authorized, under act of Assembly made in such cases, to alter the grant by extending the lines from beginning "so as to make 100 ac" agreeable to intention of surveyor & prayer of petitioner [no more details] (signed) R Lewis, cc; [on back] altered Sept. 19, 1807; [grant book 71 p. 331, see shuck #471 in Rutherford Co in Secretary's grant files].

424. Rutherford Co Superior Court Apr. term 1820 "Wiliam" P Mangum, one of the judges for the state presided; following petition was heard: Jul. session 1813 petition of John Murry to Rutherford Co Pleas & Quarter Sessions Court; petition for alteration of a grant; on Nov. 16, 1790 William Monrow, "late" of said county, obtained grant No. 551 from North Carolina for 100 ac in Rutherford Co; the

surveyor made an error in the plat & certificate for this grant; land was surveyed as follows: begins at an old post oak "the" old corner, runs W 121 poles to a post oak saplin on Lowry's line, N10E 132 poles to a black oak saplin, E 121 poles to a chesnut bush, & S10W 132 poles to beginning; this is altogether different from courses & distances in the grant; the petitioner asks that error be corrected by "asertaining the proper" courses agreeable to the original survey as set forth before pursuant to act of Assembly made in such cases (signed) Jno Paxton, atto. On examination of the petition, grant, & all papers relative to suit of John Murry plaintiff against Richard Martin defendant, court ordered that courses & distances, instead of running as in the grant to William "Munrow" under whom Jabus Murry claims title in Rutherford Co on Camp Br of Duncans Cr begins at a red oak above Lewis Price's line, E 100 poles to a post oak, S 160 poles to a red oak, W 100 poles to a pine in Lewis Price's line, N 160 poles along said line to beginning, [lines] should run pursuant to courses in the patent as follows: begins at an old post oak "the" old corner, runs W 121 poles to a post oak saplin in Lowrey's line, N10E 132 poles to a black oak saplin, E 121 poles to a chesnut bush, & S10W 132 poles to beginning; the error in the grant was committed by the surveyor in making out the plat as appears by evidence of John Price, one of the original chain bearers, & "Frances" Alexander, the present Rutherford Co surveyor; court ordered that courses mentioned in original grant in first part of this decree be altered and made conformable to courses in petitioner's petition and agreeable to "last" courses in this decree (signed) Willie P Mangum, JSCLE. James Morris, clerk of Rutherford Co Superior Court, certifies foregoing is transcript of plaintiff's petition and court decree in said suit (signed) Jul. 3, 1820 James Morris, clk; [on back] altered Dec. 4, 1821 (signed) Wm Hill, Sec; [grant not identified, only one grant to W Munrow in Rutherford Co No. 234].

425. Sampson Co Aug. term 1809; Sampson Co court order about a grant issued Oct. 9, 1783 to Jesse Darden deceased; it appears there is a surveyor's error in the tract "to wit" begins at an old pine stump & lightwood stake in John Sykes' line, runs N76E 286 poles along his line to a pine in John Chesnut's line, N20W 168 poles along said Chesnut's line to his corner 2 water oaks & a bay tree in a pond, N65W 20 poles to Joshua Bass' corner stake, S34W 226 poles to said Bass' other corner, N78W 82 poles along his other line to a stake in Murphey's Br, & up the meanders of the branch to first station (signed) John McKenzie, DC for H Holmes cc; [on back] altered Dec. 23, 1809 [not signed]; [no grant to Jesse Darden found in Sampson Co, 2 grants to Joseph Darden].

426. I certify on examination of lines of a grant to Nicholas Sessums for 200 ac in Sampson Co on N side of Cow Br, there has been an error by setting down the wrong courses not agreeable to the marked lines of the survey; courses agreeable to marked lines follow: begins at a pine & white oak in edge of said branch, runs N15W 152 poles to a poplar in edge of Cabbin Br near Saml Faircloth's "plantation", W 210 poles to a stake on W side of Great Swamp, S15E 152 poles to a stake, & to the beginning; (signed) Jan. 13, 1797 E Herring, survr. Sampson Co Feb. term 1797 this certifies that the certificate annexed to "the" patent was

exhibited in Sampson Co court; court ordered clerk to certify the same to Secretary of State "as the error mentioned" may be rectified as the law directs (signed) Apr. 13, 1797 H Holmes, cc; [onback] altered agreeable to order Oct. 13, 1797 (signed) Wm Hill D Sec; [grant book 66 p. 219, see shuck #143 in Sampson Co in Secretary's grant files].

427. Stokes Co Jun. term 1799; petition of Seth Coffin, agent for Henry Drinker & Josiah Hughes of "Philedelphia": surveyor made an error in the plat for land surveyed by William Thornton for John Hailey for 300 ac in grant No. 1225 issued May 18, 1789; the patent doesn't contain the number of acres called for "by a deficiency" of "100 & large odd acres"; there is sufficient land within the lines actually run; the errors appear as follows: first on second line running N40W with "Mendenghall's" line where it says 12.5 chains it should be 42.5; second in third line running N35E where it says 12 chains it should be 10.5 chains; third in eighth line running N70E with Harrold's line it says 38 chains but should be 33 chains "only"; fourth in ninth & last line in the original plat it is due South but it should be S28E to beginning; reference being made to plat of resurvey accompanying this [not found]; a copy from the records (signed) Robt Williams, cc by Jo Williams DC. Stokes Co Jun. term 1799 Robert Williams, clerk certifies Charles Banner esq swore in court about substance of errors mentioned in within order and that within is true copy from the records (signed) Jun. 7, 1799 Robt Williams, cc by Jo Williams DC. Sept. term 1800 court ordered Secretary of State to alter & correct errors in a certificate issued from the clerk Jun. 1799 stating the errors in a survey made for John Hailey in grant No. 1225 issued May 18, 1789 for 300 ac (signed) Sept. 8, 1800 Robt Williams, cc by Jo Williams DC; [grant not identified in Stokes or Surry Co, no grant to John Hailey found].

428. Stokes Co; Joseph Cloud, Stokes Co surveyor, came to court & swore an error was made in certificate of a survey to Joseph Cox for 150 ac on N Double Cr of Dan R, begins at a white oak on N side of the creek, runs W 50 chains to a white oak, S 30 chains crossing the creek to a black oak, E 50 chains to a post, & N 30 chains crossing the creek to first station; survey was made Dec. 10, 1779 in Surry now Stokes Co; the mistake was inserting name of Joseph which should have been Joshua; the mistake appears in the grant from Secretary's office (signed) Robt William, cc (sic). Robert Williams, clerk of Stokes Co court, certifies Joseph Cloud, surveyor of said county, came to court & swore an error was made in a return to Secretary's office for survey to Joshua Cox; he inserted word "Joseph" instead of word "Joshua" agreeable to his annexed deposition (signed) Sept. 5, 1794 Robt Williams, cc; [on back] patent No. 700 Nov. 3, 1784, patent altered [no date or signature]; [grant book 55 p. 3, see shuck #701 in Surry Co in Secretary's grant files].

429. Stokes Co Pleas & Quarter Sessions Court held at court house in Germantown on first Monday in Jun. 1803; petition of Richard Goode: "testamony was had"; it appears to court that "sundry" errors were made by the surveyor in his return for land warrant No. 131 entered Nov. 13, 1792 for 100 ac;

there wee only 47 ac returned by the surveyor and Goode obtained grant No. 584 Oct. 14, 1800 at Raleigh; it also appears that within the lines of the patent are 67 ac 144 perches; error is as follows: (a) the patent mentions begins at Thomas Flynt's corner white oak at Perkins' grave but it should begin at a pine 9.5 chains N of Perkins' grave and run N 14 chains instead of 23 to a pine in Thomas Good's line "also" Flynt's N & S line; (b) line running East calls for only 20.5 chains to a white oak in Isaac Garrison's line but it should be 27.5 chains to the corner white oak; (c) line running South with said line calls for only 23 chains to a stake in Thos Flynt's line but it should be S 28 chains to a spanish oak & white oak Murray's old corner "said Flynt's land being 27.5 chains W of said corner"; (d) line running West calls to run to beginning which would run through John Cooley's land but it should be West 21 chains to a white oak in Cooley's line, then N 14 chains on his line to his corner pine, & W with his line to first station containing 67 ac 144 "pearches"; the court ordered Secretary be directed to alter the errors in the patent agreeable to foregoing (signed) Robt Williams, cc by Thos Armstrong; [on back] altered Nov. 22, 1803 [not signed]; [grant to Richard Goode "jr" in grant book 109 p. 312, see shuck #614 in Stokes Co in Secretary's grant files].

430. Stokes Co; above plat represents land resurveyed for John Haley of 300 ac in grant No. 1225 issued May 18, 1789; it appears from certificate of survey annexed to the grant, that there is not the complement of land called for in the patent; deficiency is "100 and large odd" acres; certificate also doesn't agree with original marked lines; there is land sufficient within the original lines actually run to satisfy the patent as follows: begins at a persimon tree "the" old beginning corner, runs S70W 71 chains to an old corner post oak, N40W 42.5 chains with Mendinghall's line to an old corner white oak, N35E 10.5 chains to pointers in Walker's line, E 4 chains on his line to a "B" oak, N 5 chains on "Do" to a black oak, E 29 chains on "do" to a white oak, N 15 chains on "do" to pointers, N70E 33 chains with Harrold's line to a post oak, S28E with "do" to beginning; resurveyed Apr. 1799 (signed0 Charles Banner, DS; Jonathan Sell jr & William Williams, chain carriers; [on back] altered Nov. 25, 1800; [goes with #427 above].

431. Stokes Co Pleas & Quarter Sessions Court held at court house in Germanton second Monday in Sept. 1810; petition of William "Whickur": an error was made by William Thornton, deputy surveyor of Surry Co, in his certificate for 200 ac on waters of Muddy Cr in Surry now Stokes Co surveyed for Jesse Sapp [or Lapp]; certificate was annexed to grant No. 1222 issued May 18, 1789 to Joseph Sapp; certificate follows: begins at Mills' corner "B" jack, runs N20W 38 chains on his line to pointers, S20W 15.5 chains to pointers, S57W 8.5 chains to a "P" oak on Toms Creek Road, S 30 chains to a white oak, N 58 chains to a stake, & W to beginning; error is only in 2 last lines where it says N 58 chains & W to beginning but it should be E 58 chains instead of N and N to beginning instead of W to beginning; court ordered Secretary of State to correct the error by erasing word "North" and inserting word "East" and word "West" and inserting "North" in its place in the grant and make the same alterations in surveyor's certificate annexed

thereto in the records in his office (signed) Sept. 12, 1810 Robt Williams, cc by Thos Armstrong DC; [on back] William Whicker's certificate for alteration of grant to Jesse Sapp, altered Dec. 10, 1810 [not signed]; [grant book 78 p. 135, see shuck #1204 in Surry Co in Secretary's grant files].

432. Surry Co Pleas & Quarter Sessions Court held at court house in Rockford second Monday in May 183; petition of John Allen, by Zachariah Sugart, about errors in grant No. 1013 to said Allen for 400 ac; he has proved that notice was given as required by law in such cases; court heard testimony concerning the matter; it appears to court that an error was made by surveyor in following manner: at end of third line from beginning, he says runs N 87 chains to a post oak but it should say W 23.5 chains and N 87 chains to a post oak and E 42 chains to a black oak in Lindsay's line and to beginning; court ordered clerk to certify the facts accordingly. May term 1803 Joseph Williams, clerk, certifies above is true copy from minutes of said court (signed) May 14, 1803 Jo Williams, cc; [on back] altered Dec. 7, 1804 [not signed] "for Zachariah Sugart 5/ due paid by Lutes to MCC"; [grant book 65 p. 274, see shuck #1021 in Surry Co in Secretary's grant files].

433. Surry Co Pleas & Quarter Sessions Court Nov. term 1824; petition of Jacob Bails was filed asking to correct error in survey attached to a grant agreeable to an act of Assembly made in such cases; it appeared to satisfaction of court that error is in writing after word "oak South" in fifth line and in sixth line after word "stake" in writing word "South" but it should be in each case "North" instead of "South"; court ordered clerk to certify the same to Secretary of State; Joseph Williams, clerk, certifies that at Nov. session 1824 Surry Co court ordered above correction to be made in the survey attached to the grant accompanying this certificate "in altering" the words "South" to words "North" in fifth and sixth lines of the survey (signed) Jo Williams, cc. Nov. 1824 Jonathan Hains, chairman of Surry Co court, certifies Joseph Williams who attested above certificate is and was clerk of Surry Co Pleas & Quarter Sessions Court (signed) Nov. 13, 1824 Jonth. Haines, chr; [on back] altered Nov. 24, 1824 Wm Hill, Sec; [2 possible grants see shucks #2173 and #2643 in Surry Co in Secretary's grant files].

434. Surry Co Nov. session 1803; it appears to satisfaction of court with 7 justices present that there is an error in grant No. 2288 issued to Benjamin Bledsoe in following word: on face of grant & certificate of survey, the grant issued for 50 ac instead of 100 ac; court ordered that clerk certify the same to secretary of State and he is directed to insert 100 in place of 50. Nov. term 1803 Joseph Williams, clerk, certifies above is true copy from the records (signed) Nov. 16, 1803 (signed) Jo Williams, cc; [on back] altered Dec. 7, 1803 [not signed]; [grant book 117 p. 16, see shuck #2351 in Surry Co in Secretary's grant files].

435. Surry Co Pleas & Quarter Sessions Court at court house in Rockford on second Monday in Nov. 1804; petition of William Bond in behalf of James Lindsay, to have some errors corrected in grant No. 973 issued Aug. 9, 1787 to

Corrections/Alterations to Land Grants

James Lindsay for 640 ac; petition was produced in court, and it was proved by oath of William Sugart that adjoining neighbors have been notified; the "error" follows: from a "certain" maple it mentions runs N21W to beginning but it should have been W 36 chains to a white oak and N21W to beginning as appears by examining the plat "although" it appears line should be 25 degrees W to cause the same to close; court ordered with 7 justices present that clerk certify the same to Secretary of State; Secretary is to correct the errors agreeable to act of Assembly; Joseph Williams, clerk, certifies foregoing is true copy from records of said court (signed) Nov. 19, 1804 Jo Williams, cc; [on back] altered Dec. 7, 1804 [not signed]; [grant book 65 p. 265, see shuck #981 in Surry Co in Secretary's grant files].

436. [copy of grant] No. 1593 for 50 shillings per 100 ac granted 640 ac to William McBride in Surry Co on Reed Cr a draft of Yadkin R; begins at a white oak S 5 poles from Peter Eaton's SE corner, runs N 83 chains to said corner along his line cross the creek to a black oak, S 35 chains to a post oak, W 5 chains to John Martin's corner post oak, S 48 chains to a chesnut stake, & to beginning; McBride to pay yearly sums required by General Assembly and record grant in Surry Co Register's office within 12 months otherwise grant is void (signed) Richard Dobbs Spaight & Rd Sheppard, D Sec at New Bern Jul. 9, 1794. Nov. 14, 1803 Surry Co Register's office, I certify above is true copy from books in this office (signed) Wm Thornton, P Reg. Surry Co May 14, 1806 this day William McBride came & swore grant No. 1593 is "alluded to" in annexed "instrument of writing" and is lost or mislaid and he cannot "command it" (signed) Wm McBride & J Franklin, JP.

   Surry Co Nov. session 1803; it appears to satisfaction of court with 7 justices present that there is an error in grant No. 1593 issued Jul. 9, 1794 to William McBride for 640 ac in leaving out second course & distance; court ordered Secretary to be directed to alter the grant to make it read as follows: begins at a white oak 5 poles S of Peter Eaton's SE corner, runs N 83 chains to said corner "so" along his line crossing the creek to a black oak, E 75 chains, S 35 chains to a post oak, W 5 chains to Jno Martin's corner post oak, S48 chains to a chesnut stake, & to beginning. Nov. term 1803 Joseph Williams, clerk, certifies above is true copy from records of the court (signed) Nov. 16, 1803 Jo Williams, cc; [on back] altered Nov. 21, 1806 [not signed]; [grant book 85 p. 17, see shuck #1578 in Surry Co in Secretary's grant files].

437. Surry Co Pleas & Quarter Sessions Court at Rockford second Monday in Feb. 1821; court ordered with 7 justices present that clerk certify to Secretary of State that there is an error by the surveyor in the certificate for survey for Gotlieb Shober for 1,000 ac in grant No. 2841; instead of words "North on Poindexter's line & passing his corner [or concer] 87 chains to a stake" it should read "N 32 chains to a black oak, W 45 chains to a hickory sapling, & N 80 chains to a stake"; the grant is to be amended accordingly; Joseph Williams, clerk, certifies above is true copy of minutes (signed) Feb. 15, 1821 Jos Williams, cc; [on back] altered Mar. 5, 1821 Wm Hill, Sec; [grant book 134 p. 442, see shuck #2883 in Surry Co

Corrections/Alterations to Land Grants

in Secretary's grant files].

438. Surry Co Pleas & Quarter Sessions Court at court house in Rockford on second Monday in May 1800; petition of Henry Speer; it is the unanimous opinion of court with 7 justices on the bench that clerk certify to Register of Rowan Co to alter a deed by James Innis & Francis Corbin, agents of Earl Granville & for Earl Granville, to Morgan Bryan for 510 ac dated Oct. 27, 1772 in following manner: deed to be altered to read begins at a white oak on S side of Deep Cr, runs N 340 poles to a post oak, E 240 poles to a spanish oak, S 340 poles to a stake, & W 240 poles to beginning; it appears to court that land originally intended to be sold by Earl Granville to Morgan Bryan by the said deed provided the line trees marked as by witnesses introduced to this court; clerk is to certify to said Register to alter the conveyance from Morgan Bryan to John Kimbrough registered in his office; and certify to Surry Co Register to alter deed of conveyance from John Kimbrough to John Bruce dated Feb. 25, 1783 and deed from John Bruce to Robert Adams dated Jul. 3, 1788 to make them read & describe the same lines to be altered in original deed to Morgan Bryan agreeable to "several" acts of General Assembly made in such cases; it appears to court that those persons claiming adjoining land were "regularly" notified agreeable to said acts; court ordered clerk to certify these alterations to Secretary of State agreeable to acts of General Assembly made in such cases; Joseph Williams, clerk, certifies to the Secretary that above is true copy from records of said court (signed) May 16, 1800 Jo Williams, cc; [on back] certificate from Surry Co clerk in favor of Henry Speer for alteration of deed to Morgan Bryan from Earl Granville for 510 ac in Rowan Co, not found in Secretary's office W H, the deed produced & altered Jul. 10, 1800 W H; [may be grant in book 10 p. 2, see shuck #979 in Anson Co in Secretary's grant files].

439. Tyrrell Co Oct. term 1792; petition of Edmund Blount jr & Thomas Mackey, under act of Assembly passed at Fayetteville 1790 "CXV S1" [chapter 65 ?], was read to court; Hezekiah Spruill esq, Tyrrell Co surveyor, made an error in a certificate to the Secretary's office for 1,400 ac; error was in words "situated on eastward & southward of Long Acre" instead of northward & westward; so petitioners are likely to receive no benefit from patent No. 520 for land they entered [granted] May 18, 1789 and signed by [Gov.] Samuel Johnston; on motion, it appears to satisfaction of court that due notice was "regularly" given to all parties interested or concerned "particularly" to Josiah Collins, Nathaniel Allen, & Samuel Dickinson under firm of Lake Company, & Edward Van Daniel who own adjacent land; the mistake was the surveyor's by inserting "word" eastward & southward instead of northward & westward "by consent" of the Lake Company who were present by themselves & their council and Edward Van Daniel; court ordered that clerk certify above facts & mistake of county surveyor to Secretary of State so error can be "amended & corrected" agreeable to act of Assembly made in such cases. Tyrrell Co Nov. 13, 192 a true copy from the docket (signed) J(?) Macbey, CTCt; [on back] "done"; [grant book 70 p. 228, see shuck #713 in Tyrrell Co in Secretary's grant files].

Corrections/Alterations to Land Grants

440. Tyrrell Co Apr. term 1796 petition of John Fitzpatrick was heard; he sets forth that there is a surveyor's mistake in his patent No. 639 for 9 ac; mistake is in a course: instead of running N75W he platted it N 75E; court ordered that prayer of petition be granted and clerk to certify the above facts to Secretary of State so "his" patent can be corrected; a true copy from the docket (signed) Aug. 24, 1797 J Clleson [or H Nesson] clk; [on back] altered patent & record [no date or signature]; [grant book 86 p. 523, see shuck #887 in Tyrrell Co in Secretary's grant files].

441. petition of John Liverman (of Tyrrell Co), planter, to Tyrrell Co justices: in 1778 John Gibson & the petitioner made an entry in Tyrrell Co entry taker's office for 200 ac on S side of Richard Woods' line, joins John Gibson's line, runs E along his line & Seth Woods' line, S to Niel's line, joins his line to Cherry ridge Swamp, & up the swamp to first station; see copy of entry No. 94 dated Aug. 18, 1778 signed by the entry taker; the petitioner shows that surveyor made a mistake and Secretary of State issued the patent for land on which the entry was taken; the patent issued to John Gibson & John Liverman for 183 ac on W side of great Alligator R, begins at a maple in Woods' line, runs E 211 poles, S 15 poles to a beach, S40W 204 poles, W 80 poles to a pine, & N 172 poles to first station; this is contrary to the original entry, and the petitioner has "in a great measure" lost the benefit of the first entry since it falls short 20 ac "in first instance" and 23 ac in "the next" by a survey made & not being agreeable to actual boundaries of the land; patent is dated Aug. 18, 1783 and the entry, & "other" evidence can be produced; due notice was given agreeable to law to all persons concerned or interested in the premises; petitioner asks court to inquire into the premises & do justice allowed by act of Assembly (signed) J Hamilton.   Tyrrell Co court Jan. 1794 petition was heard & notice was proved; a majority of justices were on the bench; it appears that an error was made by the surveyor in his return to Secretary for a survey different from the location as described in the petition; court directs Secretary to correct the patent agreeable to location of 200 ac; it appears location according to the boundaries will contain land petitioned for & no more; petitioner suffering(?) on the other hand a loss of 32.5 ac by patent differing from location; court ordered clerk, agreeable to "act", to forward the above judgment to Secretary of State so the patent can be corrected; [on back] No. 321, filed Jan. term 1794, patent altered [no date or signature];

[copy of entry] No. 94 Aug. 18, 1778 John Gibson & John Liverman enter 200 ac in "Tyrrel" Co on S side of Richard Woods' line, joins John Gibson's line, runs E along his line & Seth Woods' line, S to "Neels" line, joins his line to "Cherrey" Ridge Swamp, & up the swamp to first station; a true copy from Mr. Peter Wyn's book (signed) Ben. Spruill, ET; [grant book 45 p. 220, see shuck #200 in Tyrrell Co in Secretary's grant files].

442. Tyrrell Co Apr. term "93"; Samuel Mann, Edward Mann, Solomon Ashbee petition the court for alteration of courses of a patent in Tyrrell Co; petition was read; all interested parties were duly notified according to law; evidence was heard to support allegation in the petition; following facts were established &

proved to satisfaction of court: survey made a mistake in courses of a patent by running back the second course in the patent almost to the beginning and exclude almost "the whole land" intended to be covered by the patent; patent should be altered to begin at a pine on lower end of Croatan [Sound], runs N15W 320 poles up the sound, S65W 270 poles to Spencers Cr, S60E 350 poles down various courses of the creek, & N65E 30 poles to first station instead of the courses mentioned in the grant issued Nov. 4, 1727 to John Mann; court ordered clerk to certify this to the Secretary; Tyrrell Co Apr. 25, 1793 a true copy from the docket (signed) J Mackey, CTCt; [on back] "done"; [grant book 3 p. 236, see shuck #74 in Currituck Co in Secretary's grant files].

443. Tyrrell Co Apr. term 1793 petition to alter courses of a grant in Tyrrell Co; petition was heard; all interested parties were duly notified according to law; evidence heard in support of allegations in the petition; following facts were established & proved to satisfaction of court: the surveyor made a mistake in courses of a patent; courses as laid down in patent would run directly into Croatan Sound & give the patentee nothing but land covered with water; course as laid down in the patent should be reversed to run as follows: begins at a pine on the sound side, runs S25E 320 poles along the sound to a chinkapin post, S65W 320 poles, N25W 320 poles, & N45E 320 poles to first station instead of courses in the patent dated Jan. 15, 1728 to John Boyd; court ordered clerk to certify the same to the Secretary; Tyrrell Co Apr. 25, 179 a true copy from the docket; petition of Samuel Mann & Solomon Mann to the court (signed) J Mackey, CTCt; [on back] "done"; [2 possible grants: book 2 p. 225 see shuck #46 and book 2 p. 228 see shuck #47 both in Bath Co in Secretary's grant files].

444. Tyrrell Co Pleas & Quarter Sessions Court Oct. term 1803; John A Patrick petition to court: petition of John A Patrick "and" Joseph White was heard along wit testimony; it appears to court that grant No. 936 issued to John A Patrick & Joseph White for 200 ac; survey for the grant contains no more than 100.5 ac; petitioners are injured by the surveyor's error in platting the grant or by Secretary's error in making out the grant in that "he" is made to pay for 99.5 ac more that is contained in the survey; court ordered that the error be made a record of this court and clerk to certify to Secretary of State the said facts & the order of this court. Tyrrell Co Joseph Halsey, clerk, certifies foregoing is true copy from original order in my office (signed) at Columbia Nov. 8, 1830 Jos Halsey, clk; [on back] altered Dec. 16, 1831 W Hill, Sec;
[survey] above plat (in shape of triangle) is 200 ac of juniper swamp surveyed for John A Patrick & Joseph White SW of Endless Bay on great Alligator R in "Tyrrel" Co, begins at a black gum in their own line on W side of patent No. 878, runs W 340 poles, S37E 210 poles, & N 51E 270 poles to first station; surveyed Oct. 10, 1831 by Chas McClees, surveyor; Sal C Patrick & Jno White, chain carriers; [grant book 135 p. 472, see shuck #1083 in Tyrrell Co in Secretary's grant files].

445. Tyrrell Co Jul. term 1793 petition of Revd. Charles Pettigrew to court asking

Corrections/Alterations to Land Grants

for alteration of a name in grant No. 474 issued May 18, 1789 to him; the name of Revd. Charles Pettigrew is misspelled in the grant; petition was read and granted; court ordered clerk to certify the same to Secretary of State so alteration can be made agreeable to act of Assembly made in such cases; a true copy (signed) J Mackey, CTCt; [grant book 70 p. 201, see shuck #661 in Tyrrell Co in Secretary's grant files].

446. Warren Co court; petition of Philemon Hawkins jr: petitioner has a grant from Secretary's office for land in Warren Co on head of Fishing Cr; the surveyor made an error in the courses in the grant as follows: begins at a pine in the county line at letter "A", runs E 143 poles to a pine in "widdow" Basket's line, S 231 poles by said line across Fishing Cr to a pine, E 230 poles across the creek to a stake, N 98 poles by Duke's line across the creek to a red oak, E 108 poles by his other line to a pine, N 206 poles by James Basket's line, W 200 poles to Callers Road, S52W 52 poles up said road to county line, & by said line to first station; in lieu thereof, the following courses should have been mentioned in the grant: begins at a pine in the county line at letter "A", runs E 143 poles to a pine in "widdow" Basket's line, N 231 poles by said line across Fishing Cr to a pine, E 230 poles across the creek to a stake, N 98 poles by "Duties" line across the creek to a red oak, E 108 poles by his other line to a pine, N 206 poles by James "Basketts" line, W 200 poles to Callers Road, S52W 52 poles to the old county line, & by said line to first station; the petitioner can make the error appear by testimony and asks the court to direct the clerk to send a certificate to the Secretary's office as law directs in such cases (signed) May 26, 1794 Phil Hawkins jr; a true copy (signed) M Duke Johnson, CWC. May court 1794 Warren Co petition of Philemon Hawkins jr to rectify error in a grant in Warren Co on head of Fishing Cr; grant issued Sept. 20, 1779; petition stated an error in one of the courses: said line should be N 231 poles across Fishing Cr but line is called "South" in the grant; court ordered the same be certified to the Secretary (signed) M Duke Johnson, CWC; [on back] Jun. 14, 1796 altered (signed) J Speight; [may be grant book 39 p. 336, see shuck #15 in Warren Co in Secretary's grant files].

447. Watauga Co "special" Jul. term 1883 Superior Court; H H Hardin ex parte petition to correct mistake in a grant; case was heard; it appears that W H Hardin, the petitioner, is entitled t relief demanded; court ordered that his grant issued in 1879 for land in Watauga Co on waters of Buckeye Cr of Watauga R be corrected by establishing his beginning corner a wild cherry tree; court ordered clerk to certify to Secretary of State that "the fact" that a wild cherry tree is found to be correct corner of his grant so the error can be corrected and records in office of Register of Deeds of Watauga Co to be corrected; clerk is also directed to notify Register of Deeds to make said correction (signed) J C L Gudger, judge presiding. Joseph B Todd, clerk, certifies foregoing is true copy of judgment in the above case (signed) at Boone, NC, Oct. 11, 1883 Joe B Todd, CSC; [grant book 169 p. 587, see shuck #982 in Watauga Co in Secretary's grant files].

448. Watauga Co Pleas & Quarter Sessions Court Aug. term 1850; court ordered Secretary of State is directed to correct grant No. 11 issued Oct. 16, 1849 "owing to" a new survey which reads as follows: begins at 2 gums, runs S10W 165 poles to Allen Mitchell's corner ashe, S 40 poles to a stake in Joseph Shull's line, S70E 125 poles to a stake, N10W 248 poles to a stake, & to beginning; "entered" Aug. 15, 1847 in Ashe Co (signed) Aug. 20, 1850 A W Penly, clk. The Secretary of State will make out the grant according to above described courses as certified by me (signed) Aug. 16, 1850 A W Penly, clk; [on back] David Sands 100 ac Watauga Co, order of court to alter grant, altered Dec. 16, 1850 W Hill, Sec; [grant book 153 p. 34, see shuck #8 in Watauga Co in Secretary's grant files].

449. [2 copies of the following] Watauga Co; by warrant No. 147 entered Jan. 19, 1850, surveyed 100 ac for Wriley Tribet on Fork Ridge, begins at Alfred Hilyard's [or Hilliard] corner beach, runs S 126 poles to a buckeye, E 127 poles to a stake, N 126 poles to a stake, & W to beginning (signed) Apr. 20, 1850 L J Mast, CS; Solomon Tribet & John Johnson, chain carriers [plat in shape of a square]. Watauga Co Pleas & Quarter Sessions Court Aug. term 1853; court ordered Secretary of State to correct errors in grant No. 141 to "Wrily" Tribet for 100 ac issued Jan. 5, 1853 to make it read as follows [repeat of above metes & bounds]; certified by Henry Blair, clerk (signed) third Monday in Aug. 1853 H Blair, clk; [on back] altered Sept. 24, 1853 W H; [grant book 157 p. 32, see shuck #155 in Watauga Co in Secretary's grant files; grant to "Riley" Tribet].

450. Wayne Co Pleas & Quarter Sessions Court Aug. term 1802; Jesse Ammons petition for alteration of grant issued Sept. 21, 1785 to David Jernigan; petition was heard; it appears to satisfaction of court that there is an error in third, fourth, & fifth lines of certificate & grant which should be: begins at Pollok's corner on the bank of Little R, runs W 180 poles with Walden's line to Walden's corner pine, N 83 poles with Walden's other line to Hardy Jones' corner hickory, W 160 poles with Jones' line to Theophelus Jones' line, S 160 poles to a stake, E [no distance] to said Jernigan's corner of another tract, with the line of said tract to Little R, & up the river to beginning; the surveyor made an error in platting the third, fourth, & fifth lines; instead of as described in the grant they should have been as above which is according to lines actually run out & marked by the surveyor & intended to be secured by the grant to Jernigan; court ordered the clerk to certify the same to Secretary of State which I do (signed) Sept. 14, 1802 Jas Lasser, "c"; [on back] altered Nov. 26, 1802 [not signed]; [7 grants issued in 1786 to David Jernigan sr and jr in Wayne Co, no grant found in 1785].

451. Wayne Co Pleas & Quarter Sessions Court Aug. term 1802; Ethelred Boyet vs Robert Crawford, Isham Rogers, & Stephen Lasser: petition to alter a patent; this suit began in presence of all the parties; it appears that legal notice was served; the court heard the petition and examined the grant & other testimony was "adduced"; court believes the surveyor made an error in the plat & certificate of the grant alluded to in the petition "viz" a grant for 140 ac issued Mar. 17, 1756 to Thomas Jernigan; error is in second & third lines; second line read S54E instead of N54E and third line read N36E instead of S36E the way it appears to have been

run by the surveyor; the court believes the petitioner is likely to be injured; so court ordered that clerk certify these facts to the Secretary of State which I hereby do (signed) Sept. 22, 1802 Jas Lasser, cc; [on back] altered Oct. 8, 1802 [not signed]; [grant book 15 p. 124 see shuck #907 and grant book 13 p. 100 see shuck #54 in Johnston Co in Secretary's grant files].

452. Wayne Co Pleas & Quarter Sessions Court Feb. term 1819; on third Monday in Nov. 1818 Barna Cox by Moses Mordecai his attorney came before the justices of the court to present his petition against Thomas Kennedy, John McKinne, & David McKinne as follows: petition of Barna Cox to justices of Wayne Co Pleas & Quarter Sessions Court: on Jul. 1, 1758 a patent issued from the government of the province of North Carolina signed by Gov. Arthur Dobbs to Richard Cox for 160 ac within that part of Johnston Co which is now in Wayne Co; in the grant, the land is described as: on S side of Neuse R, on "the" Roundabout, joins his own land, begins at his upper corner "read" oak, runs S62W 162 poles to a pine, S79E 80 poles to a black jack, S12E 120 poles to a pine, N61E 72 poles to a white oak on the river, 80 poles with the river to Cox's corner pine, & with the "several" courses of his own line to beginning; but the patent should begin at a corner pine on a tract granted to Richard Cox on Oct. 8, 1748 as will appear not only from the plats annexed to the patent but "ancient" boundaries which the petitioner can establish; he also shows that Thomas Kennedy, John McKinee, & David McKinne "who are infants under guardianship of John McKinne jr" have adjoining land granted in 1758 "which is now the petitioner's property"; he asks that notice be given to said persons to appear & show cause why the patent should not be altered to conform with true location & that alteration be ordered by the court (signed) M Mordecai, for petr.   7 justices present, the court has proof that due notice was given to defendants; court is satisfied that error stated in petition does exist; court ordered clerk to certify the same to Secretary of State so the same can be corrected (signed) P Hooks, clk; [on back] altered Dec. 15, 1819 W H; [grant book 2 p. 207 see shuck #180 and grant book 16 p. 231 see shuck #1176 in Johnston Co in Secretary's grant files].

453. Wayne Co Jan. term 1779 to William White, Secretary of State: petition of Richard Cox to alter a patent for 300 ac; land was "expressed" to run S4E but should be S40E, its true course; it appears to satisfaction to court [that this is true]; court ordered clerk to certify the same which I hereby do witness James Sasser, clerk (signed) Jan. 17, 1799 Jas Sasser, ccc; [on back] grant altered agreeable to within order Dec. 5, 1800 the record of same cannot be found (signed) P H; [Richard Cox received 2 grant in Dobbs Co but not for 300 ac, grant not identified].

454. Wayne Co Pleas & Quarter Sessions Court May term 1803; Daniel Croom petition to alter a patent issued Apr. 27, 1767 to Jesse Croom; petition was heard; it appears to satisfaction of court that there is an error in first, second, third, fourth, & fifth lines of the certificate & patent which should be as follows: begins at John West's corner post oak, runs S53W 4 poles with his line to a stake in Charles

Corrections/Alterations to Land Grants

Holmes' line, S36E 103 poles with his line to a red oak, S8E 12 poles to a poplar in a branch, S36E 168 poles to a stake, N40E 178 poles to a pine, & to beginning; the error was made by the surveyor in platting & describing first, second, third, fourth, & fifth lines which instead of being platted & described as in the grant should have been as described above according to lines actually run out & marked by the surveyor and intended to be patented to Jesse Croom; the court ordered clerk to certify the same to Secretary of State which I hereby do (signed) Jun. 11, 1803 (signed) Jas Sasser, "c"; [on back] altered Nov. 22, 1803 [not signed]; [grant book 23 p. 67, see shuck #829A in Dobbs Co in Secretary's grant files].

455. Wayne Co Jan. term 1796 to James Glasgow, Secretary of State: petition of Isaac Crow, guardian of Charles Hines & David Hines sons & heirs of Charles Hines sr, for alteration of a patent of 70 ac; land was "expressed" in patent as N40E 80 poles to a hickory in Joseph Shaw's line, N55E 40 poles with his line to a red oak, S70E 62 poles with Shaw's line to Shaw's corner pine, S 100 poles to a stake, & to first station; but it should have been on Falling Cr, begins at a pine on N side of the creek & on W side of Brads Br being said Hines' beginning tree "a poplar being marked by it", runs S43E 80 poles to a black gum in the swamp, N80E 24 poles to a maple in the swamp, S1E 46 poles across the creek to a sweet gum, S75W 105 poles to Willis Wiggan's & Arthur Parker's corner black jack, W 70 poles with Parker's line to a stake in said Hines' own patent line, & with his own lines to beginning "its true course it appears to satisfaction of court"; court ordered clerk to certify the same which I hereby do witness James Sasser, clerk (signed) Mar. 15, 1796 Jas Sasser, clk; [Charles Hines received grants for 68 ac in shuck #308 and 75 ac in shuck #826A in Dobbs Co in Secretary's grant files; 70 ac grant not identified].

456. petition of Thomas Edgerton, an infant by James Edgerton his guardian, to justices of Wayne Co court; the petitioner is proprietor of 125 ac granted Sept. 13, 1785 to James Boyet in Wayne Co on N side of Little R & on Buck Swamp; in the certificate of the patent, the surveyor made following mistakes: in fourth line described N55E 50 poles but should be S45E 52 poles, in fifth line described S45E 130 poles but should be S45W 152 poles, & in sixth line described S50E 98 poles to a "brack" gum in Robert Hooks' & John Tilton's lines but should be S68E 147 poles to said gum; due to the errors, the petitioner is liable to be injured; he asks that allegations of petition be inquired into and errors certified to Secretary of State so the same may be corrected (signed) May term 1800 John Stanly, atto. for petitioner; a true copy from original petition filed in my office (signed) Jas Sasser, "C";

Wayne Co Pleas & Quarter Sessions Court at court house in Waynesborough Nov. 22, 1804 [following] justices present: Josiah Jernigan, John C Pender, John Everett, Laurence Wood, Joseph B Boyet, Stephen Sasser, & Richard Croom; Thomas Edgerton, by his guardian, petition for alteration of patent; petition was heard with proofs of the petitioner; court is satisfied that errors stated in the petition do exist in the grant and should be rectified as stated in petition; court ordered that clerk certify the same to Secretary of State so the same can be rectified; I certify the same (signed) Dec. 3, 1804 Jas Sasser "C"; [on back] altered Dec. 11, 1804 W W;

 [survey] above plan represents a patent for 125 ac to James "Boyd"; dotted lines are courses of the patent; black lines are way it ought to run: begins on S side of Jumping Run at Wm Hooks' corner red oak, runs N45W 99 poles along his line to a pine in his own line, S 50 poles with the same to a corner pine, course continued 47 poles to a pine in John Wigg's line, S45E 52 poles with the same to a corner red oak, S45W 152 poles with his other line to a gum in Buck Swamp on Robert Hooks' line, S68E 147 poles with the same to a black gum in said line & John Tilton's line, N94 poles with his line to Wm Hooks' corner pine, & a straight line to beginning (signed) Britton Hook, surv [no chain carriers mentioned]; [following written in pencil at bottom of page:] Wm Hooks, John Wiggs, Robt Hooks dead, Jno Tilton dead, Hannah & Henry Wilson, John Tilton & Wm Tilton heirs of John Tilton, Washington(?) Philip, Hillary & Betsey infants of Robt Hooks, & Arthur Crawford guardian; [grant not identified in Wayne Co or Dobbs Co].

457. Wayne Co Pleas & Quarter Sessions Court at court house in Waynesborough third Monday in Nov. or Nov. 17, 1806; present: Ezekiel Slocumb, Isaac Handley, John C Pender, Stephen Cooke, John Dunn, Abraham Sims, Joseph B Boyet, & Stephen Sasser esqs; Robert Fellow sr & Samuel Elliot and wife petition to correct error in grant issued Oct. 10, 1748 to John Page for 300 ac; petition was heard; it appears to satisfaction of us that there is an error in first line of the patent; patent erroneously described to run N24W 160 poles instead of N24E 160 poles; court ordered clerk to certify the same to Secretary of State which I do (signed) Dec. 3, 1806 Jas Sasser, cc; [on back] altered Mar. 20 [or 26], 1807 [not signed]; [grant book 5 p. 436, see shuck #52 in Johnston Co in Secretary's grant files].

458. Wayne Co April term 1795; to James Glasgow, Secretary of State: I certify John Herring sr petitioned the justices of Wayne Co court showing on Oct. 27, 1779 he obtained a grant entered in Dobbs now Wayne Co for 200 ac; the survey in plating the land expressed the fourth course to run S55W 174 poles but true course was S35W 174 poles; this error appears to satisfaction of court to be "truley" stated; court ordered clerk to certify the same to Secretary of State; I hereby certify the same (signed) M McKinne, clk Co; [on back] record altered [no date or signature]; [closest is grant #157 in grant book 29 p. 357, see shuck #1302 in Dobbs Co in Secretary's grant files].

459. Wayne Co Jan. term 1796 to James Glasgow, Secretary of State: petition of executors of Charles Hines deceased for alteration of a patent for 71 ac; land was expressed to run N40E 80 poles to a hickory in Joseph Shaw's line, N55E 40 poles with his line to a red oak, S70E 2 poles with Shaw's line to Shaw's corner pine, S 80 poles, E 9 poles to a pine, S 100 poles to a stake; but it should have been S43E 80 poles to a black gum in the swamp, N80E 24 poles to a maple in the swamp, S1E 46 poles across the creek to a sweet gum, S75W 105 poles to Parker's corner black jack, W 70 poles with his line to a stake in his own line, & with the

same to beginning; which are the true courses as it appears to satisfaction of court; court ordered clerk to certify the same which I do (signed) Mar. 15, 1796 Jas Sasser, CC; [on back] altd. [no date or signature]; [grant book 76 p. 87, see shuck #396 in Wayne Co in Secretary's grant files].

460. Wayne Co Pleas & Quarter Sessions Court May term 1802; Hardy Hines vs Joseph Green [or Grun] & Jacob Herring: petition to alter the line of a grant; suit commenced in presence of all parties; it appears that legal notice "had him" served; court proceeded to hear petition (sic) and examined the grant, plat, & other testimony was adduced; court believe the surveyor made an error in the certificate of the grant alluded to in the petition "vizt" a grant issued Dec. 5, 1761 to William Hines; error is in second line from beginning; course was N80E instead of N80W the way it appears to have been run by the surveyor; court believes petitioner is likely to be injured thereby; court ordered clerk to certify these facts to Secretary of State agreeable to law which I hereby do (signed) Jul. 12, 1802 Jas Sasser, CC; [on back] altered Dec. 14, 1802 [not signed]; [2 possible grants: (a) 42 ac in grant book 13 p. 314 see shuck #503 and (b) 112 ac in grant book 15 p. 389 see shuck #1058 in Johnston Co in Secretary's grant files].

461. Wayne Co Jan. term 1796 to James Glasgow, Secretary of State; petition of Ezekiel Hollamon for alteration of grant for 300 ac; land was expressed to run S62E 180 poles to a stake in Solomon Thomas' line but it should have been N62E 180 poles to a stake in Solomon Thomas' line its true course it appears to satisfaction of court; court ordered clerk to certify the same which I do (signed) Mar. 5, 1796 Jas Sasser, clk Co;
    Wayne Co Jan. term 1796 to James Glasgow, Secretary of State; petition of Ezekiel Hollamon for alteration of patent for 3000 ac; land was expressed to run S62E 180 poles to a stake in Solomon Thomas' line but it should have been N62E 180 poles to a stake in Solomon Thomas' line its true court [as] it appears to satisfaction of court; court ordered clerk to certify the same   which I hereby do (signed) Apr. 14, 1796 (sic) Jas Sasser, cc; [on back] altd Jan. 1, 1799 [not signed]; [grant book 65 p. 33, see shuck #257 in Wayne Co in Secretary's grant files].

462. Wayne Co Oct. term 1796 to James Glasgow, Secretary of State; petition of Charles Holmes for alteration of grant issued "some time" in Mar. 1761 to John Dickson for 100 ac; land was expressed as follows: begins at his corner hickory, runs N30E 38 poles to a pine, N70W 38 poles, S28W 160 poles to a pine, S62E 140 poles, N28E 96 poles to his own line, & with the same to beginning; but it should have been described in fourth line "omitting a figure" making the course S2E instead of S62E which is the true course it appears to satisfaction of court; court ordered clerk to certify the same which I hereby do (signed) Nov. 22, 1796 Jas Sasser, cc; [on back] altered Dec. 16, 1798; [grant book 15 p. 27 see shuck #200 and grant book 13 p. 297 see shuck #63 in Dobbs Co in Secretary's grant files].

Corrections/Alterations to Land Grants

463. Wayne Co Pleas & Quarter Sessions court Nov. term 1805; petition of Richard Bass was heard along with evidence in support; it appears a grant issued Sept. 13, 1785 to David Miles [or Mills] for 56 ac in Wayne Co with errors stated in the petition "vizt" patent should begin at John Brogdon's corner black jack, run N65E 120 poles with his line to a corner white oak, N49E 192 poles with his other line to a corner pine, N81W 126 poles to a pine on the side of Little Br, S70W 68 poles down the same to a lightwood tree, S 10 poles to a pine in Caleb Mustgrave's line, E 20 poles with the same to a corner pine, S19E 35 poles with his other line to a corner pine, & with his other time to beginning; court ordered clerk to certify the same to Secretary of State so the same can be corrected; I hereby certify the same (signed) Nov. 27, 1805 by Jas Sasser, CC; [on back] altered Dec. 13, 1805 [not signed]; [grant #114 issued Sept. 30, 1785, grant book 58 p. 49, see shuck #115 in Wayne Co].

464. Wayne Co May term 1806; James Mustgrave petition for alteration of grant issued in 1798 to James Mustgrave for 50 ac; it appears to satisfaction of court that there is an error due to mistake in the survey describing fifth line as N77E but should have been S77E its true course; court ordered that clerk certify the same to Secretary of State which I hereby do (signed) Jul. 19, 1806 Jas Sasser, CC; [on back] James "Mustgrove" certificate to alter grant, altered Aug. 3, 1806 [not signed]; [grant book 99 p. 189, see shuck #711 in Wayne Co in Secretary's grant files].

465. Wayne Co Pleas & Quarter Sessions Court Nov. term 1802; Tabitha Coor Pender & others vs George Jernigan & others petition for alteration of grant issued Mar. 2, 1775 to Thomas Coor for 640 ac in Dobbs now Wayne Co; this cause was argued before Richard "Croone", William "Ecum", Ezekiel Slocumb, Richard McKeane, & Joseph B Boyet, justices of Wayne Co court; it appears that all persons owning or claiming adjoining land described in the petition have been duly notified and were willing to have the petition tried at this term; court proceeded to hear testimony about truth of allegations in the petition; court is satisfied that survey made errors in his certificate as set forth in petition; real courses originally surveyed & intended to be patented are: begins at a red oak, runs N82E 270 poles to a red oak, N23W 375 poles to a pine, N84W 258 poles to a stake, N60E 84 poles to a pine, N65W 157 poles to a pine, S18E 213 poles to a hickory on his own line at an old survey, & to first station instead of courses laid down by surveyor in certificate annexed to the grant which were: begins at a red oak, runs N22W 348 poles to a pine, S87E 400 poles to a stake, N39W 120 poles, E 120 poles to a pine, S28E 180 poles to a hickory on his own line of an old survey, & to first station; court ordered clerk to certify these mistakes to Secretary of State which I hereby do (signed) Nov. 23, 1802 Jas Sasser, cc; [on back] altered Dec. 14, 1802 [not signed]; [grant #312 issued Mar. 2, 1775, grant book 25 p. 19, see shuck #1016 in Dobbs Co in Secretary's grant files].

466. Wayne Co Apr. term 1796 to James Glasgow, Secretary of State; petition of Winkfield Pope for alteration of a patent for 320 ac to John Holland; land was

expresses in patent as 184 poles but should have been 284 poles its true "course" [as] it appears to satisfaction of court; court ordered clerk to certify the same [to Secretary] which I hereby do (signed) Jun. 20, 1796 Jas Sasser, cc; [at bottom of page:] No. 138 dated 1785; [on back] altered Nov. 26, 1797 W H; [grant book 58 p. 74, see shuck #139 in Wayne Co in Secretary's grant files].

467. Wayne Co Pleas & Quarter Sessions Court Feb. term 1819; on third Monday of Feb. 1819 before justices of the court, John Smith by John Stanly his attorney, petitioned against Joel Grantham & James Grantham in following words: petition of John Smith to justices of Wayne Co Pleas & Quarter Sessions Court; Smith is proprietor of land in Wayne formerly Johnston Co on Marsh Br & Falling Cr granted Apr. 6, 1749 to Robert Hatcher for 250 ac; [land] begins at a white oak proved by John Brown; third line of the patent is wrong described to run S84E 33 chains from a hickory to a stake but in "North" [truth] the line was actually run N84W 33 chains to a stake; the grant joins land held by Joel Grantham & James Grantham to whom the petitioner has given notice of this petition; the petitioner asks that facts of the petition be "enquired" into and truth appearing that the same be certified to Secretary of State so the same can be corrected (signed) Feb. term 1819 J Stanly, atto for petitioner.   7 justices present, the court has proof that notice [was given] agreeable to law to the defendants; court is satisfied of error in the grant as stated in the petition; court ordered clerk to certify the same to Secretary of State so he an correct the same (signed) P Hooks, clk; [on back] altered Dec. 18, 1819 (signed) Wm Hill, Sec; [no grant in Johnston Co, closest is grant in 1748 in Craven Co in shucks #355 & 1183 in Secretary's grant files].

468. Wayne Co Apr. term 1795 to James Glasgow, Secretary of State; I certify James Thompson petitioned justices of Wayne Co court showing he owns a tract in Wayne Co granted to John Thompson; in plotting the land, surveyor expressed second line as N5E 30 poles but it should be N5E 90 poles and fifth line S6E 21 poles but true course was S60E 21 poles; these errors appear to satisfaction of court to be truely stated; court ordered clerk to certify the same to Secretary of State which I hereby do (signed) M McKinne, clk Co; [on back] altered Nov. 4, 1795 [no signature]; [no grants in Wayne Co, but 3 grants to John Thompson in Dobbs Co in shucks 455, 599, & 1002 in Secretary's grant files].

469. Wayne Co court Apr. term 1793; John West petitioned court about error in Wayne Co surveyor's return in a plan dated Jan. 25, 1787 for 100 ac to Secretary's office; grant issued Jul. 11, 1788 conformable to the return; courses are as follows: on the branch of Stony Cr, begins at his own corner post oak near Ready Br, runs N43E 56 poles with his line to Roberts' line, N80W 60 poles with his line to a spanish oak corner on Ready Br, S15E 27 poles with his own line to Jesse Croom's line, S48E 100 poles to another of his own lines, N15W 246 poles with that line to his corner post oak, N15E 40 poles to a pine, & to beginning; it appears to court that the line that runs S15E 27 poles is an error and should run S15E 270 poles to Jesse Croom's line; it appears to court that Jesse Croom had legal notice f the petition and "does not" appear to make any objections to prayer of petition; court

Corrections/Alterations to Land Grants

ordered clerk to certify the same to Secretary of State so mistake can be rectified (signed) Jas Cobb, clk Co, to James Glasgow; [on back] "done" [no date & no signature]; [grant book 68 p. 192, see shuck #305 in Wayne Co in Secretary's grant files].

470. petition of Moses Westbrook & Solomon Grantham to justices of Wayne Co court: they are proprietors of 600 ac in Wayne Co on Horse Swamp granted Sept. 5, 1761 to John Grantham; fourth line is described to run N75E 228 poles to a hickory but should be N75W 228 poles to a hickory; the petitioners are likely to be injured by this error; they ask that allegations of their petition be inquired into and error certified to Secretary of State so the same can be corrected [not signed] May term 1804.   Notice of petition was given to Nancy Bizzell guardian of John Bizzell an infant, Needham Grantham, Sumner Tadlock, John Reaves, Laurence Wood, Joel Grantham, & Jacob Grantham.   At Wayne Co Pleas & Quarter Sessions Court at court house in Waynesborough on third Monday in Feb. 1805; following justices present: B Robin Hood, William Bizzell, Ezekiel Slocumb, John Everett, Richard McKinne, Stephen Sasser, & Abraham Simms; Moses Westbrook & Solomon Grantham petition to alter a grant to John Grantham; it appears to satisfaction of court that fourth line of the grant N75E 228 poles to a hickory should be N75W 228 poles to a hickory; court ordered that the error be certified to Secretary of State so the same can be corrected which I hereby do (signed) Mar. 10, 1805 Jas Lasser, CC; [on back] altered Nov. 29, 1806 [not signed]; [grant book 13 p. 314 see shuck #71 and grant book 15 p. 389 see shuck #208 in Dobbs Co in Secretary's grant files]

471. Wayne Co court Apr. session 1792; petition of Lewis Whitfield asking court direct clerk to certify to the Secretary the facts stated in the petition relative to mistake in a patent described therein; it appears to satisfaction of court that a legal entry was made by said Whitfield for land in Wayne Co; land was surveyed Dec. 18, 1786 and described as follows: on N side of Neuse R & waters of Mill Br, begins at Uzzel's beginning corner pine near "the" dead pond, runs N2W 388 poles with Uzzel's line to his other corner, E 179 poles to his other corner, S60E 320 poles, S50E 15 poles to another of Uzzel's lines, N40W 412 poles with said line to said Whitfield's corner, W 179 poles with his line to his corner pine, S5E 350 poles, & to beginning; it also appears that there was a mistake in the surveyor's certificate to Secretary in describing last line "except one"; surveyor said line runs N5E but agreeable to survey the line should run S5E; said Whitfield was ignorant of the mistake on Nov. 17, 1790 when grant issued agreeable to surveyor's mistake; this injures Whitfield and error should be rectified; certified to Secretary by order of the court (signed) Jas Cobb, clk Co; [on back] Lewis Whitfield cert. to alter patent No. 336 dated 1790, "done" [not signed]; [grant book 76 p. 90, see shuck #404 in Wayne Co in Secretary's grant files].

472. to James Glasgow, Secretary of State: petition of Lewis Whitfield to Wayne Co court; there is an error in first line of survey in Wayne Co on E side of Walnut Cr; grant No. 377 issued Nov. 17, 1790 to him for 12 ac; first line in grant runs

Corrections/Alterations to Land Grants

S7tW 58 poles but it should be S75E 58 poles; it appears to satisfaction of court that first line is in error and should run S75E 58 poles its true course; court ordered clerk to certify the same to Secretary of State; certified (signed) Jas Cobb, Clk Co; [grant book 76 p. 102, see shuck 445 in Wayne Co in Secretary's grant files]

473. Feb. 3, 1791 Wilkes Co surveyed 560 ac for John Brown, surviving executor of Hugh Montgomery deceased in trust for use of Hugh Devizees; land on S side of Yadkin R above mouth of Mervin Cr; begins at a large walnut in a small island at mouth of the creek, runs S 62 poles up the creek to Andrew Moore's line at a white walnut on N bank of the creek, S60W 180 poles on a conditional line with Mr. Moore to 2 spanish oak saplings, S 122 poles to a chesnut, W 254 poles to a chesnut, N 42 poles to a gum in Jno Brown's line, N46W 40 poles with him down a dividing branch to a black walnut at mouth of the branch, & down various courses of the river to first station (signed) Ben Elledge, DS for Jos Herndon CS; John Nelson & Isaac Elledge, chain carriers; plat included].

474. Wilkes Co Nov. term 1833 Thomas Earp vs State of North Carolina petition to amend a grant; testimony was heard; court ordered that third line of the plat of the survey for a grant to Aquilla Low to be amended to read "and instead" 196 poles instead of 296 poles as at present described by original plat identified by county surveyor accompanying grant No. 130 issued in 1780. I William Mastin, clerk of Wilkes Co Pleas & Quarter Sessions Court, certify above is true copy from record in this case (signed) Nov. 13, 1833 Wm Mastin, clerk; [on back] altered Dec. 7, 1833 (signed) Wm Hill, Secry; [grant book 100 p. 62, see shuck #1517 in Wilkes Co in Secretary's grant files].

475. to Wilkes Co court now "setting" petition of Ebenezer Fairchild; the petitioner had 200 ac surveyed by Jonathan Hughes, deputy surveyor "under authority" of Col. Jos Herndon county surveyor; land is on Howards Cr; petitioner obtained a grant; on inspecting the grant, petitioner finds "the field works" made out by deputy surveyor are wrong; from the beginning they run courses agreeable to his return which throws the survey "immediately" off the land the petitioner claimed and which was actually surveyed; so petitioner asks the court to take legal methods pointed out by law to rectify the same by directing the Secretary to make out a grant in following manner: instead of beginning at a white oak on a ridge and running N 140 poles to a "white", E 26 poles to a white oak in a swamp, S 140 poles to a forked white oak on a branch, & W 226 poles to beginning; it should begins at said white oak on a ridge on N side of Howards Cr, runs "first" E 226 poles to a spanish oak in a swamp, S 140 poles crossing the creek to a forked white oak, W 226 poles, & to beginning being the true "manner" in which the survey was made (signed) May 3, 1796 Ebenezer Fairchild. May term 1796 it has been made known to the court by petition of Ezenezer Fairchild that he is likely to be injured by mistake in surveyor's return of the works for a piece of land entered by said Fairchild; a grant has come to his hand not expressing the courses of the land he expected but quite the reverse; court ordered clerk to certify the same to Secretary of State; I certify within petition & court order "has" been

granted & ordered to be certified (signed) Hs Gordon, cc; [on back] altered patent platt & record Jun. 10, 1796 [not signed]; [grant book 83 p. 15, see shuck #1098 in Wilkes Co in Secretary's grant files].

476. Wilkes Co court to James Glasgow, Secretary: it has been made to appear to us that an error was made by the surveyor in "putting" 200 ac "in the face" of a plat for Benjamin Herndon instead of 320 ac; the grant has come out for 200 ac; so grantee might suffer considerable injury; we certify the mistake to you so the same can be corrected agreeable to law (signed) Wm B Lenoir, CC; [on back] No. 795 dated 1787 altered W H; [grant book 64 p. 135, see shuck #798 in Wilkes Co in Secretary's grant files].

477. Ashe Co court to North Carolina Secretary: it has been made to appear to us by James Williams that there is an error is his grant; it appears to be a surveyor's mistake in following manner: where it mentions running South from a black gum the word "North" should be inserted because that line runs North "in fact" and in last line where it mentions running West it should be East 120 poles to beginning as that is the course marked; we certify the same to you so the grant & records of it may be corrected agreeable to act of Assembly made in such cases; land was entered in Wilkes Co by Jams Mechan and grant No. 371 issued Oct. 23, 1782 to him; witness John McMillan, clerk. (signed) Nov. 8, 1803 Jno McMillan, cc; [on back] altered Dec. 6, 1803; [grant not identified in Yancey Co or Burke Co].

478. Yancey Co Pleas & Quarter Sessions Court Fall term 1854; court ordered clerk to make out a certificate to the Secretary of State "as set forth here to fore" by Thomas Gibbs as follows: begins at a dogwood tree on said Gibbs' old line on a ridge, runs S 160 poles with said line to a stake in or near David Ballew's line, E 20 poles to a stake in said Thomas Gibbs' own line of another survey, S 160 poles with said line to a "state" in his old line, & W 20 poles with said line to beginning; David McCanles, clerk of said court, certifies above is an order of said court (signed) at Burnsville Oct. 26, 1854 David McCanles, clerk of Yancey Co court; [on back] altered Dec. 8, 1854 W H; [Thomas Gibbs received 5 grants in Yancey Co in Secretary's grant files].

479. "Yancy" Co Pleas & Quarter Sessions Court Jun. term 1834; Isaac Grinstaff the younger & David Baker jr petition ex parte to correct errors in a grant; the case was heard ex parte on the "petition grant original certificate of survey" testimony of one of original chain carriers and county surveyor; court ordered that grant issued Apr. 5, 1798 from Secretary of State's office ot Joseph Dobson for 640 ac in Burke now Yancey Co on Mine Fork of Cane Cr, begins at a chesnut in a conditional line between Isaac Grinstaff & Joseph Thomas, runs S 160 poles to a large poplar & gum between 2 branches, E 320 poles to a chesnut oak, N 320 poles to a chesnut & spanish oak in Nathaniel [Thomas--lined out] Armstrong's line, S 320 poles with said line to a chesnut, & S 160 poles to beginning; lines to be corrected & extended to make an offset at the chesnut & spanish oak "off" 22 poles West to a chesnut, N 101 poles to a chesnut, & then according to other calls

157

in the grant; it appears to satisfaction of court that the Secretary committed an error "and mistake" in making the North(?) line of the grant terminate at the chesnut & spanish oak and the offset of 22 poles West and N 101 poles to a chesnut which is also in Nathaniel Armstrong's line added to the 264 poles North from the chesnut & spanish oak "the chesnut" is the true North line and without which the grantee will not have his compliment of land called for in the grant nor reach the lines called for in the survey; court further orders clerk to certify this order to Secretary of State. Amos L Ray, clerk, certifies foregoing is a true copy from records in my office in foregoing case and certifies there is no seal of office and for want of which I have annexed my private seal [private seal not evident] (signed) Jul. 1, 1834 A L Ray, clk; [on back] altered Nov. 24, 1834 Wm Hill, Sec; [may be grant book 95 p. 289, see shuck #2453 in Burke Co in Secretary's grant files; J Dobson received lots of grants in Burke Co but this is the only one in 1798 for 640 ac].

480. Yancey Co Pleas & Quarter Sessions Court Fall term 1840; 7 justices resent; petition of James Medcalf was presented to court to correct error in state grant No. 54; following order was made by the court; court ordered James Medcalf has leave for an order to issue to Secretary of State to correct error in state grant No. 54 "to wit" begins at a hickory, runs N 50 poles to a black oak, N40W 96 poles to a hickory on top of a ridge, N67E 84 poles to a white oak, S53E 42 poles to a white, S30W 40 poles to a white oak, S 61 poles to a "state", & to beginning; warrant is No. 527 entered May 2, 1835 "Joel B Jews, D surveyor"; John Crawford & R B Crawford, chain carriers; foregoing are lines intended to be established (signed) J W Garland, clk. J W Garland, clerk, certifies above transcript & "exhibits" are true copies of records in the above case (signed) at Burnesville Nov. 14, 1840 J W Garland, clk; [on back] altered Dec. 1, 1840 (signed) Wm Hill, Secry of State, grant No. 54 dated Dec. 17, 1836; [grant book 143 p. 340, see shuck #54 in Yancey Co in Secretary's grant files].

481. Claiborne Co, TN Mar. session 1804; petition of Thomas Henderson filed at Sept. term 1802 was taken up & examined; it appears to court that errors have been made by surveyor in plating the survey & making out certificate of survey to Secretary of State's office; court "considers" the errors to be corrected and grant made as follows: begins at a small "hycory" a dogwood & 2 white oak pointers on E side of "saide" creek, runs W 116 poles crossing said creek to a chesnut, N 398 poles to a spruce pine white oak & poplar on "the" Indian boundary, N77E 286 poles with said boundary & Colonel William Herd's line to a double beech & red oak, S 90 poles to a black oak, E 60 poles to a white oak & dogwood, S 248 poles to a poplar, W 60 poles to a white oak, S61W 280 poles to 2 beeches, N50W 193 poles to a stake, N58E 210 poles to a pine, & N17E 124 poles to beginning; more than 5 justices are present; court ordered clerk to certify the same to North Carolina Secretary of State; Walter Evans, clerk of Claiborne Co Pleas & Quarter Sessions Court, certifies foregoing is true copy from records in my office; certified under my hand & private seal having no public seal (signed) Mar. 7, 1804 Walter Evans, Clk CC. Claiborne Co, TN Isaac Lane, presiding justice of Claiborne Co

Corrections/Alterations to Land Grants

Pleas & Quarter Sessions Court, certifies foregoing attestation is in due form of law (signed) Mar. 9, 1804 Isaac Lane; [on back] altered Sept. 10, 1804 [not signed]; [grant not identified, Thomas Henderson received 6 grants in Tennessee].

482. Claiborne Co, TN Sept. term 1803; pursuant to order of county court this term, Walter Evans, clerk, certifies to North Carolina Secretary of State that the court, this term, "took before them" the petition of Thomas Jeffers filed last Jun. term 1803 for correction of errors by the surveyor in a certificate for 650 [640-- lined out] ac to Secretary of State's office; court examined the petition; court finds a manifest error was committed by the surveyor in his certificate; court believes the error should be corrected & grant made out as follows: begins and runs as expressed in original grant for 650 ac to a stake & 3 white oak pointers, then N13E 314 poles to a stake, then as called for in the grant to the beginning (signed) Sept. 24, 1803 Walter Evans, Clk CC; [on back] Thomas "Jeffries" altered Nov. 22, 1804; [grant book 112 p. 360, see shuck #5 in Grainger Co Eastern Dist in Secretary's grant files].

483. Claiborne Co Sept. term 1803 petition of John Miller filed at last term of court was taken up & examined; it appears to court there were manifest errors by the surveyor in platting a survey & making certificate of survey to North Carolina Secretary of State's office; court "considers" that errors ought to be corrected & grant made as follows: begins at a red oak & black oak called for in patent, runs S 180 poles on the patent line to a poplar, S57W 390 poles passing a marked beech ash & "hycory" near a drean at 360 poles to a stake near the creek, N 194 poles to a stake, & a direct course to beginning; 5 justices are present; court ordered clerk to certify the same to North Carolina Secretary of State; Walter Evans, clerk, certifies foregoing is true copy of John Miller's petition recorded in my office and signs with private seal having no seal of office (signed) Dec. 8, 1803 Walter Evans, clk C; [on back] court order to alter grant to John Blair, altered Sept. 10, 1804 [not signed], old balance due 10 cents this copy 60 cents due 70 cents; [grant not identified, John Blair received 17 grants in Tennessee].

484. Davidson Co, TN; Jacob Cassellman petitioned Davidson Co court Oct. session 1797 and "suggested" to the court that surveyor made an error in a certificate of survey for 640 ac on both sides of Stoners Lick Cr; he returned the same as lying on N side of Cumberland R but it does lie on S side of Cumberland R; all of which appears to satisfaction of the court; court ordered clerk to certify the same to North Carolina Secretary of State "to the intent" that the error may be corrected by inserting the word "South" instead of "North"; I hereby certify aforesaid to the Secretary (signed) Oct. 19, 1797 Andrew Ewing; [on back] grant altered Jan. 23, 1800 W W; [grant book 63 p. 206, see shuck #604 in Davidson Co in Secretary's grant files, grant due to assignment of military bounty warrant].

485. Davidson Co, TN, to James Glasgow, North Carolina Secretary of State: Thomas Cox petitioned Davidson Co court Jan. session 1797; he was a chain carrier for laying off the military boundary line and became entitled, for his

services, to 640 ac; "afterwards" he entered the land in Davidson Co joining Samuel Wilson's preemption on W fork of Stones R on upper side; he had the land surveyed: begins at said Wilson's SW corner and runs S & E for quantity; but surveyor Barkley William P[page torn] made an error in the certificate of survey: begins at said Wilson's SE corner which is wrong; all this appeared to satisfaction of the court; court ordered the same be made a record and the same to be certified to said Secretary so the error can be corrected; I do now certify this (signed) Jan. 17, 1797 Andrew Ewing.   Davidson Co James Robertson, presiding justice of said county court, certifies Andrew Ewing was at time of the record clerk of county court "duly elected & qualified" (signed) [blank] 1797 [no signature]; [on back] altered agreeable to within order Mar. 6, 1797 (signed) Wm Hill; [2 possible grants see shuck #1209 and 2120 in Davidson Co in Secretary's grant files].

486. Davidson Co, TN, to North Carolina Secretary of State: Andrew Ewing, clerk of said county court, certifies David Earhart petitioned Davidson Co Pleas & Quarter Sessions Court Oct. session 1797; petition describes a surveyor's error in the return to the Secretary's office for 480 ac surveyed for said Earhart on Hays Cr waters of big Harpeth R; return says: begins at William Marshall's NE corner but he should have said begins at said Marshall's SE corner as per the survey; all of this was made to appear to satisfaction of court; court ordered clerk to certify the same to North Carolina Secretary of State so error can be corrected by inserting in said Earhart's grant the words "begins at SE corner of said Marshall's land" instead of NE corner (signed) Jan. 15, 1801 Andrew Ewing.   Davidson Co James Robertson, presiding justice of Davidson Co court, certifies Andrew Ewing was at time of signing clerk of said county court (signed) Jan. 15, 1801 Jas Robertson; [on back] altered Feb. 4, 1801 (signed) W Hill, D Sec; [see shuck #05 in Davidson Co in Secretary's grant files; also see item #1233 in Tennessee Land Warrants Volume 4 for grant].

487. Secretary & Comptroller, to whom were referred petition of John King of Halifax Co, report it appears to them the surveyor made an error in surveying land alluded to in the petition; error is in certificate that accompanied the plat; grant was made conformable thereto instead of being conformable to the plat; they believe the Secretary [should] by directed to alter the record of the grant and make it contain the quantity of land intended; Comptroller is "induced" to recommend following resolution: Resolved that Secretary be directed to alter record or copy of grant to John King of Halifax Co to make it conformable to plat accompanying surveyor's certificate filed in this office noting the alteration in the margin of the book (signed) Dec. 21, 1797 J Craven, compt; in Senate Dec. 21, 1797 foregoing report read & resolved this house concurs (signed) Benja Smith, Spkr, & J Haywood; in House of Commons Dec. 22, 1797 read & concur (signed) M [Musendine] Matthews, Spkr & J Hunt, CHC; [on back] resolve to alter grant to John King for 547 ac in Davidson Co; [grant book 81 p. 168, see shuck #2063 in Davidson Co in Secretary's grant files].

Corrections/Alterations to Land Grants

by petition of Thomas Thompson that Thompson is assignee of John Step and made an entry Jan. 28, 1786 in "the" entry taker's book for 640 ac on E side of Stones R & on the first creek above Stoners Lick Cr on right hand fork of said creek and joins upper end of an entry made by William Nash for Robert Nelson; the surveyor made a mistake in making out the certificate & plat of survey; instead of saying the first creek above Stoners Lick Cr he said "below" but there is no such creek; court ordered clerk to certify the same to the Secretary so the error can be corrected agreeable to act of Assembly made in such cases; pursuant to the order Andrew Ewing, clerk, certifies to James Glasgow, Secretary, that above is "of record" (signed) Oct. 20, 1796 Andrew Ewing. No. 1451 Jan. 28, 1786 Thomas Thompson, assignee of Step, 640 ac on E side of Stones R, on the first creek above Stoners Lick Cr, & on right hand fork of the creek, joins upper end of an entry made by William Nash for Robt Nelson of 640 ac and runs up both sides of the creek (signed) Wm Nash; [on back] patent altered [no date or signature]; [grant book 81 p. 17, see shuck #1864 in Davidson Co in Secretary's grant files].

493. Grainger Co, TN, May session 1801; petition of George Bean presented in court asking court to send order to North Carolina Secretary of State to alter and amend a mistake by the surveyor in a survey "in favour" of Jesse Bean for 2,000 ac on German Cr; grant No. 739 issued Jul. 11, 1788 to Jesse Bean on the plot; court ordered Secretary of State to alter grant #739 agreeable to annexed plat (signed Jun. 10, 1801 Am Yancey, clerk Grainger Co; [metes & bounds on plat:] begins and runs S 140, S54W 105, S 60, W 200, S 60, W 490 poles, S 40, W 100, N 470 poles, E 916 poles, & S 104 poles to beginning; land on both sides of German Cr [not signed]; [on back] altered Jun. 26, 1801; [grant book 63 p. 256, see shuck #756 in Davidson Co in Secretary's grant files].

494. Grainger Co, TN "Eastern District" Sept. court 179; petition of John Brown esq was produced in court; court ordered North Carolina Secretary of State to be "requested" to alter a mistake made by Thomas King, deputy surveyor of Eastern Dist, in courses of a plat for grant No. 625 in name of James King for 100 ac; mistake to be amended to agree with annexed plat; it appears to satisfaction of court that the purchaser is Mr. John Bowin who is now in possession of the land "intended to be covered" by the grant as appears by a conveyance "inclosed herein"; said Bowin has fulfilled every requisite required by law; a copy from the records (signed) Sept. 14, 1796 Am Yancey, CGC; [on back] No. 625 Jas King 1794 Hawkins Co to be altered; [grant book 82 p. 221, see shuck #785 in Hawkins Co in Secretary's grant files].

495. Grainger Co, TN "Eastern District" Sept. court 1796; petition was preferred to court by Nichlas Countz; court ordered North Carolina Secretary of State be requested to alter a mistake made by Thomas King, deputy surveyor of Eastern Dist, in the courses of a plat; grant #607 issued on the plat to the petitioner; mistake to be amended agreeable to annexed plat; a true copy from the records and given under my private seal for want of seal of office (signed) Sept. 14, 1796

Corrections/Alterations to Land Grants

Am Yancey, CGC;

[2 copies of survey] Territory S of Ohio R; pursuant to warrant No. 1311 I surveyed 200 ac for Nicholas "Counce" in Hawkins Co on Richland Cr; includes the improvement where John King jr formerly lives; begins at 3 sycamores on the bank of the creek, runs N55E 254 poles to 2 white oaks, S20E 127 poles to a hickory & dogwood, S5W 254 poles to a stake, & a direct line to beginning (signed) James McCarty, DS; John Muckelhany & Josiah Smith, chain carriers; [grant book 82 p. 214, see shuck #767 in Hawkins Co in Secretary's grant files].

496. Grainger Co, TN, Feb. session 1800; agreeable to act of General Assembly providing for alteration & rectifying mistakes in land surveys & pursuant to which Nicholas Perkins petitioned for alteration of grant No. 178 issued Dec. 26, 1791 for 400 ac on Holston R in Grainger Co; grant has following courses: begins at 2 spanish oaks linn & a beach marked "R" just above a small clift of rocks, runs up the river 462 poles to a stake on the river bank, S140 poles to a stake, & S69W to beginning; but courses should be: begins at 2 spanish oaks linn & a beach marked "R just above a small clift of rocks, runs up the river 492 poles to a stake on the river bank, S256 poles to a stake, & a direct line to beginning; petition was allowed & court ordered that clerk certify the mistake "so make" to North Carolina Secretary of State. To North Carolina Secretary of State, "peasuance" to a court order before recited, you are directed & authorized to alter & rectify a mistake in said grant & make it conformable to courses before recited & make the record conformable thereto (signed) Apr. 21, 1800 Am Yancey, cc; [on back] altered Nov. 13, 1800 [not signed];

[survey with plat] persuant to order of Grainger Co court formerly part of "Hackings" Co, I resurveyed 400 ac granted to Nicholas Pirkins on S side of Holston R [metes & bounds same as second mentioned above] (signed) [no date] J Chamberlain; James Carmichael & Duncan Carmichael, chain carriers; [grant book 75 p. 174, see shuck #144 in Hawkins Co in Secretary's grant files].

497. Grainger Co, TN, Eastern District Sept. court 1796; petition of Mr. John Ward to this court; court ordered North Carolina Secretary of Sate be requested to alter & rectify a mistake made by Wm Payne, deputy surveyor of Eastern Dist, in making courses & plat on which grant #147 issued to the petitioner; mistake to be amended agreeable to annexed plat; a copy from the records given under private seal for want of seal of office (signed) Sept. 14, 1796 Am Yancey, CGC;

[survey & square shaped plat] Sept. 16, 1796 due to order of Grainger Co court, I resurveyed 200 ac for John Ward on N side of Holsteins R & on waters of German Cr; being the same where he lives; begins at a red oak on W side of a spring, runs N 200 poles along a conditional line made by said Ward & Daniel Robertson to a post oak, E 160 poles to a stake & red oak, S 200 poles to a stake, & W 160 poles to beginning (signed) Wm "Paine", DS; John Horner & George Russell, chain carriers; [on back] No. 147 service "write" 1795 to be altered on record Sept. 14, 1796 (sic) [not signed]; [grant book 89 p. 145, see shuck #887 in Hawkins Co in Secretary's grant files].

Corrections/Alterations to Land Grants

498. Grainger Co, TN, Feb. session 1799; to North Carolina Secretary of State: agreeable to act of General Assembly providing for alteration of mistakes in land surveys, petition of Thomas West, by his attr. Absolem Hayworth, was presented to said county court; his grievance is a mistake in 300 ac as appears by original grant No. 276 issued Jan. 14, 1793; Secretary is hereby requested to alter first North course to a South course and the distance of second North line from 165 poles to 238 poles and make the record conformable thereto (signed) Feb. 22, 1799 by Am Yancey, CGC; [on back] altered May 29, 1800 [not signed]; plat attached on a small sheet but beginning corner not well identified; may show 2 adjoining tracts (a) 192.5 ac and (b) 300 ac; [5 grants to Thomas West, but none for 192.5 ac].

499. Greene Co, Territory of United States of America South of Ohio River, May session 1792; justices of Greene Co court to James Glasgow, North Carolina Secretary of State; Thomas Brown exhibited his petition to our court; the petitioner has a tract surveyed by Jeremiah Chamberlain on N side of Holstein R; through mistake, the surveyor calls for S side of the river; we direct & order our clerk to certify these facts to you so the error may be corrected agreeable to prayer of petitioner; enclosed plat is sent; "a copy" (signed) Danl Kennedy, CGC;
    [survey with plat] Feb. 18, 1785 surveyed, due to warrant No. 949, 300 ac for Thomas Brown in "Green" Co on N side of Holston R above mouth of Flat Cr; beings at a white oak on the river bank, runs 161 poles down the river to a stake, includes "different meanders as appears by the draft annexed", N150 poles to a stake, & S79E 265 poles to beginning (signed) J Chamberlain, DS; Andrew Chamberlain & Wm Robertson, chain carriers; [on back] altered agreeable to order for that purpose [not signed]; [grant book 65 p. 486, see shuck #403 in Greene Co in Secretary's grant files].

500. Greene Co, TN, justices to James Glasgow, North Carolina Secretary of State: Abraham Carter exhibited his petition to our court; there is an error in a grant by North Carolina to him; he has certified to us he has given legal notice to all adjoining land owners; we directed our clerk to certify following are true courses of his survey agreeable to annexed plat: on Lick Cr, begins at a stake below a lick, runs N20W 177 poles to a stake & white oak, S60W 31 poles to a white oak in Daniel Carter's line, N11W 88 poles to a white oak on the bank of Lick Cr, & runs up the creek various meanders to a marked ash on the creek bank now John Melone's formerly John Carter's corner, S45E 150 poles with said Melone's line to a marked white oak, the same course 220 poles "in all" to a stake, & a straight line to beginning (signed) second Monday in Nov. 1797 Dan Kennedy, CGC; "NB" my it please your Honour "who ever may be Secretary of State", that however frauds may have taken place in "the" office "geting" new grants, I am "consious" there is none intended by this (signed) Joseph Brown "S";
    [survey with plat] surveyed Jan. 4, 1795 due to warrant No. 256 dated Oct. 22, 1783; surveyed 275 ac for Mr. Abraham Carter to correct error in patent No. 347 on "main" Lick Cr [metes & bounds same as above except "Melone" is spelled "Millone"] (signed) Joseph Brown, DS; John Millone & Daniel Carter,

Corrections/Alterations to Land Grants

chain carriers; [on back] patent dated Sept. 28, 1787 altered Mar. 18, 1799 [not signed]; [grant book 65 p. 471, see shuck #345 in Greene Co in Secretary's grant files].

501. Grainger Co, TN, Eastern Dist Feb. session 1801; to North Carolina Secretary of State; persuant to act of Assembly for correcting mistakes in land surveys, by order of court, you are directed to alter & amend grant No. 665 to William Coche for 640 ac dated Jul. 8, 1788; in the line from the "T K" oak to the beginning walnut corner from that "of" N70½E to N66E; make your records conformable thereto (witness) Ambrose Yancey, clerk (signed) Feb. 21, 1801 Am Yancey, CGC; [on back] altered this Mar. 13, 1801; [grant book 66 p. 448, see shuck #624 in Greene Co in Secretary's grant files].

502. Hawkins Co, Territory of United States of America South of Ohio R, Sept. court 1795; petition of William Cocke esq to the court; court ordered North Carolina be requested to alter a mistake by David Stuart, deputy surveyor of Green Co, in the courses & plat on which grant No. 665 issued to the petitioner; mistake to be "amenede" agreeable to annexed plat [not in shuck]; a true copy from the records (signed) Sept. 20, 1795 Richd Mitchell, clk; [grant book 66 p. 448, see shuck #624 in Greene Co in Secretary's grant files].

503. Greene Co, TN, Pleas & Quarter Sessions Court to North Carolina Secretary of State: due to act of General Assembly entitled "an act making provision for mistakes in surveys of land", it among other things provided that where there has been an error by the surveyor in platting or making our certificates to Secretary's office so the claimant is injured, the injured claimant shall prefer a petition to county pleas & quarter sessions court where the land is situated describing the injury he, she, or they might sustain due to the error or mistake & court shall hear testimony about truth of allegations in the petition; if it appears from testimony or from surveyor's return that patentee is liable to be injured, the court is required to direct the clerk to certify such facts as appears to their satisfaction to North Carolina Secretary of State; Greene Co Pleas & Quarter Sessions court held fourth Monday in Apr. 1806 heard petition of Matthew Cox for Benjamin Goodin; in 1787 Benjamin Goodin obtained a grant from North Carolina for 400 ac on Roaring Fork of Lick Cr in Greene Co; in the survey, the surveyor erred by leaving out a "considerable" part of the land intended; petitioner asks for relief; petition was ordered to be filed & set for hearing at next court; petition has first proved to satisfaction of court he duly notified all persons holding adjoining land; at Greene Co court fourth Monday in Jul. 1806, petition was heard; petitioner produced to court his testimony supporting allegations in the petition; this was examined and fully understood by the court; it appears "manifest" from the surveyor's return that an error was committed by surveying the land and the petitioner is liable to be injured; no opposition was made to granting the petition; court ordered clerk to certify to North Carolina Secretary of State the facts in the petition so the error can be corrected; to correct errors in Benjamin Goodin's grant insert the following: begins at a white oak near a pine tree, runs S 157 poles to a hickory on

Corrections/Alterations to Land Grants

Rachel Anderson's line, E 76 poles with the same to her corner beech, S 167 poles with said line to a stake near a white oak "service" & Hickory on said line, E 104 poles to a stake on a conditional line, S 31W 127 poles with the conditional line to a dogwood red oak beech & sourwood on the side of a hill corner of Peter Harmon & on "the" patent line, E 205 poles on with said line to a corner stake of the patent in a hollow near a hickory, N 146 poles to first corner beech of said Harmon, N40E 28 poles to an old corner white oak, "last line of patent calls for N64W" insert N62 degrees 15 minutes W 105 poles to Harmon's corner stake opposite a small sycamore on S bank of the creek, N24E 13 poles to a stump near a small black walnut pointer by an elm on the side of a hill, N62W 93 poles along said hill a "condition" with Daniel Carter to a white oak & poplar, N36W 37 poles to a small slippery elm, N55W 37.5 poles to a black walnut, N59W 26 poles through part of the creek to a mulberry, N73W 26 poles to a white oak & small beach on corner of a hill, N 36 poles along the hill to an ash white oak & hickory in a hollow, & N64W 76 poles with the patent line to beginning; contains 400 ac (witness) Valentine Sevier, clerk (signed) at Greeneville Sept. 13, 1806 V Sevier. Benjamin McNutt, chairman of Greene Co court, certifies Valentine Sevier is clerk (signed) Sept. 13, 1806 B McNutt, CH;

[survey & plat] surveyed Feb. 1, 1806 for Mathew Cox 400 ac to correct errors of Benjamin "Goodwin's" patent No. 337 issued Sept. 20, 1787 for 400 ac on Roaring Fork of Lick Cr [metes & bounds same as above] (signed) Jas Temple, Greene Co surveyor; Isaac Armitage & Isaac Herman, chain carriers; [on back] grant altered Jan. 12, 1807 [not signed]; [grant book 65 p. 468, see shuck #335 in Greene Co in Secretary's grant files].

504. Greene Co, Territory of United States of America South of Ohio R, Nov. session 1795; justices of the court to James Glasgow, North Carolina Secretary of State; William Donelson has exhibited his petition to our court; in 1783 a survey was made by Isaac Taylor, Greene Co surveyor, for 250 ac; in platting the survey, a considerable error has been made; the petitioner's grant includes "other" patented land not claimed by the petitioner; the error was running E 17 poles but line intended should have run W 17 poles; so intended line would not have includes land of any person; petitioner says his grant when corrected will contain no more that 250 ac agreeable to his warrant; the facts appears to satisfaction of this court; we directed our clerk to certify to you so th error can be corrected [agreeable] to prayer of petitioner (witness) Daniel Kennedy, clerk (signed) second Monday Nov. 1795 Dan Kennedy, CGD; [on back] altered, done [not signed & no date];

[survey with plat] surveyed for Wm "Donaldson": begins at a stake on John Moor's line, runs N9½W 165 poles with said line to a white oak on E side of "Littel" Linking Cr, W 17 poles to a small hickory on said Moor's line, N16E 117 poles on "Samual" Moor's line to a stake, S55E 56 poles to Thomas Mitchal's [line ?] to a beech on E side of a branch, E 163 poles to a white oak on Joseph Eatton's line, S 69 poles to a red oak, S 27W 265 poles to a stake, & W 110 poles to beginning [not signed]; [grant book 65 p. 421, see shuck #217 in Greene Co in Secretary's grant files].

Corrections/Alterations to Land Grants

505. VERY fragile copy of grant #321 issued Sept. 2, 1787 to Robert Gentry for 475 ac in Greene Co; copy of survey included dated Oct. 22, 178[page missing]; by James Houston; George Fry & John Gentry, chain carriers; land on [page missing] of Kelseys Mill Cr waters of French Broad R;

Greene Co Nov. session 1792; justices of Greene Co court to James Glasgow, North Carolina Secretary: Robert Gentry & James Houston exhibited their petition at our last court as law directs; "his" patent No. 321 doesn't cover the land said Houston was directed to run; Gentry has notified all owners of adjoining land; we direct clerk to certify the same to you so you will be able to correct the grant agreeable to the enclosed plat dated Oct. 22, 1782; warrant No. 210 (signed) Dan Kennedy, CGC; [on back] altered record [not signed & no date];

[second survey] survey due to warrant No. 210 dated Oct. 22, 1783; Dec. 10, 1788 surveyed 475 ac for Robert Gentry on N side of French Broad R & on head of Kelseys Mill Cr, begins at an elm, runs S44W 318 poles to a black oak & hickory, S 220 poles to a post & pine, E 60 poles to a stake, N44E 389 poles to 2 pines, & a direct course to beginning (signed) John Hackett, DS; Jes Gentry & Luke Kimborland, chain carriers;

May 5, 1795 to James Glasgow, North Carolina Secretary of State: Dear Sir, My old & very perticular friend Mr. Gentry comes to get a "deed" altered so as to rectify errors by the surveyor agreeable to order of Greene [Co] Court persuent to act of Assembly made in such cases; he has complied with all requisites of the law; the order says the mistake will be easily rectified; your friend the "Govournour" of this country & his family together with your good friend Col. Donelson are all well; any civilities my from Mr. Gentry who is a good old man may receive from you will be acknowledged by your real friend & esteemed as if done himself (signed) Wm Cocke;

"Jonesbo" Sept. 16, 1795 to James Glasgow, Secretary of State: Dear Sir, This will be handed to you by Mr. Bartly Gentry who is about to apply to your office to obtain a patent for land entered by his father Robert Gentry; permit me to inform you that I made the entry for Mr. Gentry in 1783 at "Hillsbo" when the office first opened on "Kelsys" Creek, including Duke Kimbrough's improvement [entry] No. 210; it has turned out that Mr. Gentry never got a patent for the land occasioned as I suggest by some neglect of the surveyor; I am well assured Mr. Gentry has the prior & best claim to the land; neither have I ever understood any one set up a claim to it either by occupancy or entry; Mr. Gentry is a man of repute & respectability always conducting himself as an orderly citizen and good member of society but is aged & infirmed and not capable of looking after his own business; therefore is obliged to send his son; could the Secretary with propriety make out the grant for Mr. Gentry it would oblidge him in a very particular manner as he has sold the land and is in danger of a suit should he not soon make a title; also greatly oblidge your friend who is with sincere & great esteem your most obedt. & very hbl. servant (signed) John Sevier; [grant #321 issued Sept. 20, 1787 due to warrant 210 dated Jun. 7, 1784 (from John Armstrong's office), grant book 65 p. 464, see shuck #319 in Greene Co in Secretary's grant files].

Corrections/Alterations to Land Grants

506. Greene Co Oct. term 1798; at Greene Co Pleas & Quarter Sessions Court fourth Monday in Jul. 1798, Joseph Hardin sr filed his petition asking to correct errors in grant No. 345 issued Oct. 21, 1783; land is in Greene Co on Lick Cr; court heard testimony about the allegations in the petition; court ordered clerk to certify the errors pursuant to a plat annexed to Honble. North Carolina Secretary of State so the same can be corrected accordingly (witness) Daniel Kennedy, clerk (signed) Oct. 24, 1798 by Dan Kennedy, CGC; [on back] altered Dec. 26, 1798 [not signed];
[survey with plat] black lines are the way the return was made to Secretary's office: begins at a black oak, runs E 140 poles to a hickory, N 175 poles to a white oak, W 224 poles to a stake, & S25E 195 poles to beginning; dotted line are courses of land the way survey was "first made" & marked: begins at the same corner black oak of the "other", runs E 242 poles to a hickory, N 178 poles to a white oak, N68W 121 poles to a black oak, & S29W 256 poles to beginning [not signed & no date]; [grant book 43 p. 316, see shuck #55 in Washington Co].

507. justices of Greene Co, TN, court to North Carolina Secretary: Joseph Hardin sr exhibited his petition to our court; there is an error in grant No. 814 issued Dec. 10, 1789 by North Carolina "at Fairfield" to him; it is certified to us that owners of all adjoining land have been notified to attend agreeable to law; court ordered clerk to certify the errors in the grant to you accordingly which you will correct by inserting the true courses from annexed plat (witness) at Greenville fourth Monday in Oct. 1799 Daniel Kennedy, clerk (signed) Dan Kennedy, CGC; [on back] grant altered Mar. 13, 1800;
[survey with plat] Jul. 25, 1799 surveyed 200 ac for Joseph Hardin in Green Co on waters of Roaring Fork of Lick Cr, joins a tract said Hardin formerly lived on & sold to David Purkins, William McAmos' line, & Samuel Blair's line, begins at a white oak & dogwood, runs E 78 poles to a black oak in said Hardin's former line, S68E 75 poles to a black oak "along" said Hardin's line to William McAmos' line, N3E 75 poles along said line to a poplar, N34E 44 poles [on] said McAmos' line to a black oak, N454W 100 poles [on] said Blair's line to a white oak, N18E 100 poles to a white oak, W 116 poles to a stake, & to beginning (signed) Joseph Hardin "S" [no chain carriers mentioned]; [grant book 75 p. 17, see shuck #864 in Greene Co in Secretary's grant files].

508. Greene Co court Nov. term 1791; petition of Michael Woods asking to correct errors in a grant; court ordered following facts to be certified to North Carolina Secretary of state; the same were first authenticated by oath of James Woods Lackey sworn in open court as law directs: said James says the land survey by Isaac Taylor [or Teeylor], surveyor of said county, for Michael Woods on Meadow Cr is on S side of Noluchucky R and that North side of the river is certified in the plat & grant from North Carolina; a copy (signed) Dan Kennedy, CGC; [grant book 66 p. 152, see shuck #555 in Greene Co in Secretary's grant files].

Corrections/Alterations to Land Grants

509. Greene Co, TN, Oct. term 1798; justices of county court to North Carolina Secretary of State: Elizabeth Telfair has exhibited her petition to our court; there is an error in grant No. 1863 [or 5863] issued Nov. 27, 1795 at Raleigh by North Carolina to her; it has been certified to court that the petitioner notified all persons having adjoining land; the court directed the clerk to certify to you following true courses to be inserted in alterations of the grant "viz" begins at a white oak, runs W 201 poles to a black oak, S 80 poles to a stake, E 80 poles to a black oak, N72E 26 poles to a white oak, N48E 96 poles to a white oak, N58E 30 poles to a white oak, N60E 94 poles to a white oak, N45W 115 poles to a stake, & S 127 poles to beginning; contains 100 ac (signed) Dan Kennedy, CGC; [on back] altered Mar. 27, 1801 [not signed]; [grant book 89 p. 287, see shuck #1687 in Greene Co in Secretary's grant files].

510. Greene Co, TN, Oct. session 1798; justices of Greene Co court to North Carolina Secretary of State: Jonathan Trippet petitioned our court fourth Monday in Jul. 1798; there is an error in grant No. 1253 by North Carolina to him; court heard allegations; court ordered clerk to certify to you following courses agreeable to annexed plat [not in shuck] as true courses of the survey: begins at a black oak & hickory, runs N27E 185 poles to a white oak & ash corner of Jonathan Evans & William Magill's surveys, S52W 150 poles to a corner hickory of said Evans' survey, N70W 100 poles to a stake, & a direct course to beginning (witness) Daniel Kennedy, clerk (signed) Oct. 26, 1798 Dan Kennedy, CGC; [on back] altered Mar. 27, 1801 [not signed]; [grant not identified].

511. Greene Co Pleas & Quarter Sessions Court to North Carolina Secretary of State: George Wells of our county petitioned our court; he "represented" that an error was made by the surveyor in platting & or making out his certificate to your office for land "calling for" 200 ac S of Nolichcky R on Lick Br in grant No. 1226 issued Jan. 12, 1793 to Daniel "Niilson"; petitioner asks for relief; court is satisfied that error happened and petitioner may be injured; due to power granted to it, the court directed the clerk to certify the errors to you for corrections; courses inserted in patent are: begins at a marked corner white oak of Johnson Nelson, runs E 200 poles to a chesnut, N 160 poles to a black oak, W 200 poles to a stake, & S 160 poles to beginning; in place thereof for correcting the errors insert the following: begins at a marked corner white oak of Johnson Nelson, runs N59E 200 poles with his line to 2 post oaks & a black oak, N 100 poles to a black oak, W 200 poles to a stake, S 220 poles to 2 white oaks on George Wells' lie, & N59E 36 poles to beginning as represented by the dotted lines in "subjoined" plat; the black lines are the form described in the grant [plat at bottom of page] (witness) Valentine Sevier, clerk (signed) Jul. 30, 1805 V Sevier; Oct. 18, 1806 Benjamin McNutt, chairman of Greene Co Pleas & Quarter Sessions Court, certifies Valentine Sevier is clerk (signed) Bn McNutt; [on back] grant altered Jan. 12, 1807; [grant book 79 p. 505, see shuck #1511 in Greene Co in Secretary's grant files].

Corrections/Alterations to Land Grants

512. Greene Co, TN, Oct. term 1798; justices of Greene Co court to North Carolina Secretary of State: Thomas Wyatt exhibited his petition to our court; there "is" errors in grant No. 1234 issued Jul. 12, 1794 at New Bern by North Carolina to him; Thomas Wyatt has complied with the directions of the act of Assembly made in such cases; pursuant to [authority] invested in us, we directed the clerk to certify to you the following errors: in first line instead of 134 poles insert 124 poles on a West line, in second line instead of N43W 62 poles insert "the same course" 82 poles, in fourth line instead of N62W 56 poles insert "the same course" 44 poles, in eighth line instead of S10E 225 poles insert "the same course" 260 poles; corners mentioned in the grant are all right "also the lines as they are marked" (signed) Dan Kennedy, CGC; [on back] altered Mar. 26, 1801; [grant book 81 p. 572, see shuck #1470 in Greene Co in Secretary's grant files].

513. Hawkins Co, TN, Sept. session 1795; on application of Jessee Bean, administrator of estate of Robert Bean deceased, & James Orr for alteration of grant No. 238 issued Dec. 26, 1791 agreeable to a plat produced by them in court, it appears to the court that the lines in the grant & survey don't interfer with lines on any other persons whatsoever; court ordered that clerk certify to North Carolina Secretary of State that said application was made in due form so the grant & survey can be altered agreeable to a plat produced in court which is annexed; Richard Mitchell, clerk of Hawkins Co Pleas & Quarter Sessions Court, certifies above is true copy of court order obtained by James Orr & Jesse Bean for purposes mentioned therein & annexed plat was produced by them to court to obtain said order (signed) Jun. 10, 1801 Richard Mitchell, clerk by Edward Scott his deputy; [on back] altered Jun. 26, 1801 [not signed];
    [survey & plat] Territory of United States of America South of Ohio R, Hawkins Co; due to order of Hawkins Co court to resurvey land belonging to Robert Bean deceased on N side of Holstiens R & on German Cr for which grant No. 238 issued Dec. 26, 1792 to him; 640 ac begins at 2 ashes poplar dogwood & "cheritree" on W side of the creek just below the forks, runs S75W 108 poles along a conditional line between Robert & Jesse Bean to a chesnut & maple, N41W 140 poles to 2 post oaks along said conditional line, N41E 40 poles to 2 black walnuts, N40W 275 poles along a conditional line between Robert & Jesse Bean to a post oak, N55E 280 poles to a stake, S71E 114 poles to a white oak & maple, & S3.5E 425 poles to beginning; surveyed Aug. 7, 1795 [not signed]; Jesse Bean & David Small, chain carriers; [grant book 77 p. 326, see shuck #250 in Hawkins Co in Secretary's grant files].

514. Hawkins Co Nov. session 1799; petition of Thomas Jackson to this court; a mistake was made by North Carolina Secretary of State by issuing grant No. 41 in 1789 for 200 ac to the petitioner; in the body of th grant it is "filled up at" 50 shillings per 100 ac but it should be £10 per 100 ac and the month and day of month on which the grant issued "is inserted"; court ordered the clerk to certify the mistakes to North Carolina Secretary of State and request him to alter the grant "that is" insert £10 in the place of 50 shillings and insert day of issuing grant No. 41 (signed) Richard Mitchell, clk; [on back] altered agreeable to order filed Jan.

171

Corrections/Alterations to Land Grants

12, 1800 [not signed]; [grant book 72 p. 252, see shuck #56 in Hawkins Co in Secretary's grant files].

515. Hawkins Co, TN, Feb. court 1799; petition of Robert Koyle for a survey; court ordered that clerk certify to North Carolina Secretary of State that there has been a resurvey made; it appears to satisfaction of court that a mistake was made in plating the land for grant No. 276 issued Nov. 10, 1784 to Robert Koyle for 400 ac; whereby Robert Koyle is much injured; North Carolina Secretary of State is requested to alter the grant agreeable to annexed plat which includes the land entered & is surveyed agreeable to the location; Richard Mitchell, clerk, certifies foregoing is true copy from the records (signed) Apr. 26, 1799 Richard Mitchell, clk; [on back] Robert "Coyle" certificate for alteration of grant, Hawkins formerly Sullivan Co, May 24, 1799 [not signed];
      [copy of warrant] No. 1861 Oct. 7, 1779 Washington Co, "NC", Robert "Koil" entered 400 ac on head waters of Caney Cr, joins Cashbrooks & Peter Anderson's land, includes a cove known as Hickory Cove; a true copy from records certified Feb. 14, 1799 (signed) John Carter, ET; [on back] No. 752 of land warrant supposed to be a supernumery;
      [survey & plat] Jan. 2, 1799 due to order of Hawkins Co court, resurveyed 400 ac for Robert Koyle on which he obtained a grant Nov. 10, 1784, but by surveyor's mistake the lines would not include the land surveyed "which is" agreeable to above plat; begins at a mulberry tree & walnut on William Bruce's line "heir of Cash Brooks deceased", runs S42W 378 poles along the line of a 200 ac survey for said Koyle to a stake, S70E 222 poles along Joel Gillenwater's line to a stake, N35E 315 poles to said Bruce's line, & along the same to beginning (signed) Wm Paine, DS [no chain carriers mentioned]; Jan. [lost in edge of page] 1799 Cornelius Carmack, William Brice, Stephen Richards, Joel Gillenwater, & John Cridner consider the survey agreeable to spirit & meaning of the entry; [grant book 69 p. 169, see shuck #397 in Sullivan Co in Secretary's grant files].

516. to Hawkins Co court "now sitting", petition of David Larkins; petitioner is injured by mistake in land survey made by James Ford; a plat of land is presented; land is 300 ac on S side of Holston R opposite the "plantation" were the petitioner lives; the petitioner was present at the surveying & personally directed said Ford to run down meanders of the river which the surveyor actually did; but in making out "the works" he didn't observe to call for the meanders of the river and called a certain course which leaves out the best part of the land surveyed; so the petitioner is greatly injured and asks that an order be "passed" by the court directing the North Carolina Secretary to alter the grant so as to cover the land actually surveyed; a copy (signed) David Larkins [page torn] 1803(?). Aug. session 1803 Hawkins Co on foregoing petition filed at May court 1803, the court ordered the clerk to certify the error to the North Carolina Secretary of State and request him to alter the mistake agreeable to prayer of petition; this order to be his authority for doing so (signed) Dec. 13, 1803 Richard Mitchell, clk. Following "is" the courses by which the petitioner's grant is to be altered: begins at 3 beaches, runs N75W 44 poles, N67W 33 poles, N55W 23 poles, N52W 18 poles,

Corrections/Alterations to Land Grants

N74W 14 poles, N53W 53 poles, N70W 40 poles, N82W 41 poles, S83W 36 poles, S54W 24 poles, S36.5W 22 poles, S18W 18 poles, S6E 22 poles, S31E 20 poles, S51E 30 poles, S53E 20 poles, S49E 24 poles, S32.5E 21 poles, S22E 20 poles, & a strait line to beginning (signed0 for Richard Mitchell, clerk [by] Jon Spyker(?); [one course: N79W 280 poles, shown on plat]; [on back] courses must be inserted on which this grant is to be altered before it can be done (signed) RWG, grant altered Feb. 25, 1805 [not signed]; [grant book 79 p. 488, see shuck #371 in Hawkins Co in Secretary's grant files].

517. Hawkins Co Dec. term 1797 petition of David Looney for a resurvey; court ordered clerk to certify to North Carolina Secretary of State that there has been a resurvey; it appears to the court that a mistake was made in the plat on which grant No. [blank] issued to David Looney much to his injury; North Carolina Secretary of State is requested to alter the grant agreeable to annexed plat; foregoing is true copy from the records (signed) Apr. 16, 1799 Richard Mitchell, clk; [on back] altered Sept. 10, 1801;

Sept. court 1797 court ordered Wm Hord be appointed to resurvey land in grant issued Nov. 10, 1797 to David Looney and rectify "such" mistakes as appears to have been made by the former surveyor; James Forgey, Arthur Galbraith, John Waddle, John Hannah, & Walter Beaty to be a jury to attend the survey & report to our next court (signed) Richd Mitchell, clk;

[survey & plat] pursuant to order of Hawkins Co court, I surveyed 560 ac for David Looney on waters of Possom Cr & in Stanley Valley: begins at a white oak in the valley knobs, runs N45W 140 poles across the valley on an old line to a "w" oak on Looney's line, N59E 92 poles to a poplar & gum, S28E 8 poles to a red oak, S87E 34 poles to a red oak on a ridge, N65E 150 pes to a chesnut oak, S57E 8 poles to a white oak, N69E 80 poles to a white oak & gum, N5E 8 poles to a hickory, N70E 116 poles to a stooping white oak, S35E 20 poles to a poplar, N70E 232 poles to a white oak, N 14 poles to "a", N70E 52 poles to a maple, E 30 poles to a "w" oak, N64E 38 poles to a white oak corner of Thomas Larkin, S35E 92 poles on his line crossing Pompom Cr to a line & white oak, S68W 200 poles to a sugar tree & beach, S80W 68 poles to a beach, due S 10 poles to a beach, S61W 120 poles to 2 white oaks, S75W 54 poles to a "w" oak, S50W 40 poles to a buckeye & hickory, & a straight line to beginning; surveyed Nov. 10, 1797 (signed) W Hord, DS; [no chain carriers mentioned]; Nov. 11, 1797 pursuant to court order, we caused David Looney's survey to be made as above; we consider it to be agreeable to spirit & meaning of the entry (signed) James "Foyey", Arthur Galbreath, John Waddle, John Hanna, & Walter Beaty; [grant book 69 p. 167, see shuck #390 in Sullivan Co in Secretary's grant files].

518. Hawkins Co, United States of America South of Ohio R, Mar. court 1792; petition of Francis Mabury, Tho Jackson, & Thomas Hutchings presented to court; they have been much injured by mistake or error by surveyor in making out a plat for land on SE side of Clinch R about one or 2 miles above mouth of Bull Run & surveyed by said Hutchings; the plat was sent to Secretary's office and grant No. 30 issued Jul. 11, 1788 to Francis Mabury; court ordered that Secretary alter the

mistake agreeable to annexed plat (signed) Mar. 22, 1794 Richd Mitchell, clk;

Territory of USA south of Ohio R; justices of Hawkins Co Court to James Glasgow, North Carolina Secretary of State: Francis Maybury & Thomas Jackson exhibited their petition to this court saying there is a surveyor's mistake in 640 ac on SE side of Clinch R about one or 2 miles above mouth of Bull Run surveyed by Thomas Hutchings; the grant doesn't cover the land it calls for nor do the courses include any part thereof; they pray that a new grant issue according to the plats enclosed with said "deed"; I certify above was proved & allowed in open court first Monday in Mar. 1792 (signed) Jas Maybury, DC;

grant No. 30 included; grant issued Jul. 11, 1788 to Francis Mabury for 64 ac in Eastern Dist; survey attached; surveyed Dec. 14, 1784 by Thomas Hutchings George Brooks & Wm Reid, chain carriers; on SE side of Clinch R, begins at a beach on the river bank, runs N45W 240 poles to a red oak, S45W 400 poles to a stake, S45E 240 poles to a sycamore on the river bank, & down the river to beginning; [on back of grant] grant registered "Feb. 23" in book E folio 26 in Hawkins Co Register's office (signed) Jas Mayberry, "C";

[resurvey & plat] due to warrant No. 693, surveyed 640 ac for Francis Maybury & Thomas Jackson on SE side of Clinch R about one or 2 miles above mouth of Bull Cr, begins at a spanish oak ash & mulberry on the river bank, runs N45E 150 poles to a red oak, N45W 454 poles crossing a small creek to a stake, S45W 350 poles to a stake on the river bank, & down the river to beginning; surveyed Nov. 8, 1791 (signed) Js Maybury, DS; Andw Reid & Stephen Bishop, chain carriers; [grant book 67 p. 352, see shuck #30 in Eastern Dist in Secretary's grant files].

519. Hawkins Co, United States of America South of Ohio R, Dec. court 1793; court ordered clerk to certify to North Carolina Secretary of State that there is an error in grant No. 91 issued to James Cain; but it should have issued to James McCain; the error was made by the surveyor; the Secretary is requested to alter the mistake; a copy from the records (signed0 Richd Mitchell, clk.   Dec. 14, 1793 Thomas Amis, presiding justice pro tempore for Hawkins Co, certifies Richard Mitchell is clerk (signed) Thos Amis, JP; [on back] altered patent [no date or signature]; [grant book 43 p. 281, see shuck #80 in Sullivan Co in Secretary's grant files].

520. Hawkins Co, TN, Aug. term 1798; petition of John McKee for resurvey of land; Stockley Donelson, surveyor, made a "very great" mistake either in surveying or platting land for Daniel Grant on which grant No. 37 issued Oct. 23, 1782 signed by Gov. Alexander Martin; court ordered clerk to certify the same to North Carolina Secretary & request him to alter the grant agreeable to annexed plat; foregoing is true copy from the records (signed) Nov. 9, 1798 Richard Mitchell, clk; [on back] alteration of Daniel Grant's grant No. 37 for 350 ac Sullivan Co;

[survey & plat] begins at a white oak on the creek bank, runs S40E 120 poles to a gum on the side of a nob, N42E 46 poles to a white oak elum poplar & walnut, N34W 20 poles [to] McMurry's corner lin, the same course 315 poles along McMurry's line to a stake, S42W 194 poles to a stake, S40E 215 poles to beginning; surveyed Oct. 17, 1798 (signed) Ballard Caldwell; David Caldwell & Henry Turney, chain carriers; [plat in shape of rectangle, doesn't match metes & bounds]; [grant book 43 p. 255, see shuck #26 in Sullivan Co in Secretary's grant files].

521. Hawkins Co, TN, Sept. court 1796; petition was preferred to this court; court ordered clerk to order North Carolina Secretary of State to alter a surveyor's mistake in making out plot of survey for Saml McPheeters on which grant No. 309 issued to said McPheeters; grant to be amended agreeable to annexed plat; a copy from the records (signed) Richd Mitchell, clk. [plat & following description for 640 ac to Samuel "McFuters":] S line mentioned in the grant runs 320 poles to a spanish oak to be altered to N 320 poles to the spanish oak and next 2 lines to stand as they are in the grant and "the rest" to be altered to following courses: from Lamberd Lain's corner white oak runs S80E 90 poles with said Lain's line to his corner 2 pine trees & a stake on James Paterson's line, S 24 poles with said Paterson's line to his corner dogwood & hickory, E 32 poles to a stake, S 276 poles to a stake, & straight line to beginning [not signed]; [written on plat:] W 240 poles, N 320 poles, E 140 poles, S 4 poles, S80E 90 poles, S 24 poles, E 32 poles, & S 276 poles; [on back] altered agreeable to order Apr. 24, 1797 W H; [grant to Samuel McFeeters, grant book 69 p. 179, see shuck #430 in Sullivan Co in Secretary's grant files].

522. Hawkins Co, TN, Feb. session 1800; complaint made by Constant Purkins by his attorney to this court that grant No. 179 issued Sept. 26, 1791 by State of North Carolina for 400 ac to [omitted]; Secretary of State made a mistake by inserting 50 shillings per 100 ac instead of £10; court ordered clerk to certify the above complaint to North Carolina Secretary's of State and request him to search his office & see if the mistake exists; if it does, he is to rectify the same (signed) Nov. 1, 1800 Richard Mitchell, clk; [on back] Constant Perkins certificate for alteration of grant, altered Nov. 13, 1800 [not signed]; [grant not identified; C Perkins received 3 grants in Tennessee].

523. Hawkins Co, United States of America South of Ohio [R], Mar. court 1795; petition of Clisba Riggs & Thomas Jackson to this court asking for an order to North Carolina Secretary of State for alteration of a mistake by a surveyor in a plat for grant No. 493 issued to the petitioners; order to be for alteration of the mistake agreeable to annexed plat [not in shuck]; [prayer of] petition was granted (signed) Mar. 13, 1795 Richd Mitchell, clk; [on back] altered Apr. 18, 1795 [not signed]; [grant book 80 p. 359, see shuck #431 in Hawkins Co in Secretary's grant files].

524. [plat & resurvey] pursuant to order from Hawkins Co court Feb. term 1803 directing me to resurvey land in the order; begins at a sugar tree elm & buckeye at "the" river bank, runs S37E 12 poles along Bays Mountain to a sugar tree, S44W 50 poles to a sugar tree, S79W 160 perches along the mountain "or" natural

boundary to a poplar, N557W 310 perches to an ash 2 beeches & sugar tree along said natural boundary, N62W 398 [310--lined out] to 2 hickorys & a beach, S81W 58 perches to a beech & poplar, N32W 26 perches to a hickory & buckeye on the river bank "along" said natural boundary, along up the river the several courses as the plat directs to beginning; includes 420 ac surveyed May 24, 1803 (signed) Absalom Looney, Hawkins Co surveyor;

Hawkins Co, TN, May session 1803 petition of Isaac Shelby, executor of Evan Shelby deceased by his attorney, filed at Feb. session 1803 asking for correction of a mistake by the surveyor in calling for N60E instead of N60W in a grant issued to Evan Shelby; court ordered clerk to make out a certificate to North Carolina Secretary of State requesting him to correct the mistake agreeable to prayer of petitioner; Richard Mitchell, clerk, certifies above is true copy from the records Nov. 28, 1803 [not signed]; [on back] altered Dec. 20, 1803 [not signed]; [grant not identified; closest are: 425 ac in shuck #059, 400 ac in shuck #060, & 396 ac in shuck #061 in Sullivan Co in Secretary's grant files].

525. Hawkins Co, United States of America S of Ohio R, Sept. term 1795; petition of James Short to the court asking that court issue an order to North Carolina's Secretary of State to alter a surveyor's mistake in plat for 150 ac returned to North Carolina Secretary of State; plat was returned for grant No. 316 issued Jun. 5, 1793 to James Short; the petitioner is greatly injured by the mistake; North Carolina Secretary of State to alter the mistake agreeable to annexed plat; a true copy from the records (signed) Sept. 8, 1795 Richd Mitchell, clk; [on back] patent altered Nov. 21, 1795 [not signed];

[plat & survey] Territory of United States of America S of Ohio R, due to a "sparael" warrant to me, I surveyed 150 ac for James Short in Hawkins Co between head of Germon Cr & head of Richland Cr "in the barriens"; begins at a post oak, runs N68E 192 poles along William Bean's line to a post oak & black oak, N20W 138 poles along Jesse Bean's line to a pine, S68W 192 poles to a stake, S20E 138 poles to beginning; surveyed Jul. 16, 1795 (signed) Jos Cobb, DSED, & Stockley Donelson, SED; George Bean & Isaac Standly, chain carriers; [grant book 80 p. 156, see shuck #427 in Hawkins Co in Secretary's grant files].

526. Hawkins Co, United States of America S of Ohio R, Dec. court 1793; petition of Robert Lock Stubblefield to the court about a mistake by the surveyor which much injures the petitioner; grant No. 291 for 300 ac on N side of Holstons R; agreeable to courses mentioned in the grant, it doesn't contain the land the petitioner claims; court ordered the Secretary to alter the mistake and issue a grant agreeable to annexed plat (signed) Mar. 22, 1794 Richd Mitchell, clk;

[survey & plat] due to warrant issued [date blank] No. [blank], I surveyed for Robert "Locly" Stubblefield 300 ac in Hawkins Co on N side of Holston R and joins & below William Cocke on said river; begins at a small poplar & beech at mouth of a branch, runs 200 poles on a conditional line between William Cocke & said Stubblefield to a post oak & hickory, W 52 poles along a conditional line between "Right Bend" & said Stubblefield to 3 pines, N30W[? page torn] 100 poles along said conditional line to 2 hickorys, S77W 100 poles along foot of a

Corrections/Alterations to Land Grants

ridge to a pine, S 152 poles along a conditional line between Wyatt Stubblefield & Robert Locly "Subblefield" to a post oak at top of a ridge, S17E 180 poles to a stake, S54E 40 poles to a cucumber & mulberry near the river bank, & up the several meanders thereof to beginning (signed) Dec. 9, 1793 Henry Rowan, DS; Joseph Crab & Martin Subblefield, chain carriers; [grant book 78 p. 342, see shuck #280 in Hawkins Co in Secretary's grant files].

527. Jefferson, formerly Greene, Co, Territory S of Ohio R; William Headly preferred his petition of Jefferson Co court for correction of errors in a grant No. 1201 issued to William Headly; court "considered" the clerk to certify to North Carolina Secretary the following errors: begins at end of first line at a stake on a line of a tract originally surveyed for Edward Seaborne, runs N40W 110 poles to a corner stake "thereof", S59W 123 poles to "ditto to a stake", N 50 poles to a stake near foot of Bays Mountain, N 48 degrees 45 minutes E 105 poles to a stake, & by a "right" line to beginning; includes 100 ac (witness) Joseph Hamilton clerk (signed) Nov. 5, 1795 J Hamilton, clk; [on back] Wm Headly 1210 (sic) Green Co 100 ac 1793, altered patent Nov. 5, 1795 [not signed]; [grant No. 1201, grant book 74 p. 289, see shuck #891 in Greene Co in Secretary's grant files].

528. Jefferson Co, TN, at Jefferson Co Pleas & Quarter Sessions Court on third Monday in Apr. 1802, William Kerr filed his petition to have certain errors corrected in a grant issued Jul. 12, 1794 at New Bern by state of North Carolina to William Kerr for 89 ac; court has heard allegations of the petition and had "mature deleberation" thereon; court ordered clerk to certify errors contained in the grant to North Carolina Secretary of State so the same can be corrected; in annexed plat, the black lines represent the courses of original grant & dotted lines represent courses which th petitioner prays may be inserted and which the court has "commanded" me to certify (signed) Apr. 24, 1802 by Joseph Hamilton CJC; [on back] grant altered Dec. 22, 1802 but not found on record "of course" there is alteration of the records W W;
    [survey & plat] plats represent situation of land on S side of "Holsteins" R in Jefferson Co and joins Adam Meek's claim below & Joseph McCullah above; a mistake was made by surveyor in the survey; for rectification of mistake, application was made & order obtained from said court by William Kerr; black line are courses of the grant as follows: begins at a beech & 2 white oaks on the river bank, runs N80E 40 poles up the river to a white oak, N50E 60 poles to a hickory, N25E 82 poles to a stake on said McCullah's line, due E 82 poles along said line to a stake, S44W 224 poles to a stake, & to beginning; contains 98 ac. The dotted line are courses which the petitioner prays to have the patent lines altered to: begins at a beech & 2 white oaks on the river bank, runs 182 poles up the river "as it meanders" to a white oak near said McCullah's line, S82E 98 poles to a patent corner stake, & with the same to beginning [not signed]; [grant No. 1270, grant book 81 p. 585, see shuck #1509 in Greene Co in Secretary's grant files].

529. Jefferson Co May session 1794; James W Lackey exhibited his petition to

court to correct courses in grant No. 111 issued to John Henry; it "also" appeared that land adjoining the grant are vacant & not claimed by any person; the court heard the matter contained in the petition; court directed me to certify those errors in the grant to North Carolina Secretary of State; first line of the survey to be altered by running 40 poles to a stake, then E 60 poles, N 60 poles, & W 160 poles to Suding's line; (witness) Joseph Hamilton, clerk; (signed) May 20, 1794 J Hamilton, CJC; [grant book 78 p. 370, see shuck #1261 in Greene Co in Secretary's grant files].

530. Jefferson Co, United States of America S of Ohio R, to North Carolina Secretary, James Glasgow; James W "Lacky" exhibited his petition to Jefferson Co court about a warrant for 400 ac which was to be laid on a tract surveyed for Andrew Henderson; but by surveyor's mistake it contains no more than 330 ac; it appears to court that notice was given to those who claim land contiguous thereto; "we" require you to correct the errors in the survey by extending a line of the survey that runs N10E so far as may be sufficient to make the compliment of 400 ac by running W on the next line & closing it to a corner of the survey formerly made (witness) Joseph Hamilton, clerk (signed) May 24, 1793 J Hamilton, CJC; [grant book 79 p. 286 see shuck #157 in Eastern District in Secretary's grant files].

531. Jefferson Co, TN, Oct. term 1798; James Lea filed his petition heretofore in our court asking to correct errors in a grant issued to James Lea; correction to be made pursuant to an act of Assembly made in such cases; testimony respecting allegations of the petition was heard; court ordered clerk to certify said errors to North Carolina Secretary of State; I certify annexed plat contains lines as corrected by survey on the premises agreeable to prayer of petitioner & order of court; (witness) Joseph Hamilton, clerk (signed) Oct. 16, 1798 J Hamilton, clk; [on back] altered Dec. 26, 1798 [not signed];

    [survey & plat] pursuant to order from Jefferson Co court to me, I resurveyed grant No. 11 issued Nov. 1, 1786 by North Carolina to James Lea for 218 ac; resurvey under inspection of 5 free holders: William Horner, David Coffman, James Forrest, George Horner, & William Rash; begins at a post oak on Britain Smith's line, runs due W 110 poles to a red oak on said line, S63W 34 poles to a post oak on George Evans' line, S52W 66 poles to a locust & black oak on said line, N31W 38 poles to a post oak on said line, N20W 73 poles to a dogwood & poplar on John Smith's line, E 168 poles to a locust & stake, N9E 38 poles to a hickory on Wm Horner's line, E 292 poles with said line to a stake in Wm Horner's little field, S 50 poles to a stake, S35E 40 poles to a stake on Wm Horner's line, W 60 poles to a stake, S 64 poles to a white oak & pine on David Coffman's line, & W 110 poles to beginning; surveyed Sept. 22, 1798 (signed) Luke "Lees", DS; George Horner & James Lea, chain carriers; [grant book 59 p. 372 see shuck #53 in Greene Co in Secretary's grant files].

532. Knox Co, TN, Jan. session 1801; "heretofore" Amos Bird preferred a petition saying Thomas King, a deputy surveyor for Eastern District, made a mistake in plotting 1,000 ac granted Dec. 16, 1791 by North Carolina to Amos Bird; Bird

Corrections/Alterations to Land Grants

conceives himself liable to be greatly injured due to the mistake and ask that the grant be altered & made to cover the land actually surveyed; at this term, the petition was taken up; on examination, it appears to court that there has been an error committed in platting the survey; the error should be corrected & grant made as follows: begins at a sugar tree & elm the original corner, runs up the river including various meanders thereof to a swamp white oak, N45W 140 poles to a white oak small black oak & dogwood, N41E 52 poles to a hickory, N45W 40 poles to a post oak corner of Samuel "Holmesferth" & John Swan, N48W 57 poles to a stake, & a direct to beginning; court ordered clerk to certify the same to North Carolina Secretary of State; Charles McClung, clerk, certifies foregoing is a copy of proceedings on Amos Bird's petition (signed) Jan. 19, 1801 by Chas McClung; [on back] patent altered Feb. 10, 1801 W H; [see shuck #010 in Hawkins Co (no grant, sic) in Secretary's grant files].

533. Knox Co, TN, Jul. session 1797; David Campbell petitioned Knox Co court saying Stockley Donelson made a mistake in plotting 640 ac on E fork of Turkey Cr & on N of Holston R; David Campbell supposes himself liable to be greatly injured by the error; at same time plot of survey by John McClellan was presented; request was made that grant to be made conformable to John McClellan's survey; Oct. session 1797, a majority of acting justices present, court is satisfied that the plot contains the land intended to have been surveyed by Stockley Donelson; court is satisfied that due notice was given agreeable to law; court considered th petition and believe the grant issued to David Campbell should be altered & made conformable to plat of survey made by John McClellan; the clerk to certify the same to North Carolina Secretary of State; Charles McClung, clerk, certifies foregoing is a copy of proceedings had on David Campbell's petition and annexed plot of survey is plot presented to the court (signed) Nov. 4, 1797 Chas McClung using private seal not having a seal of office; [on back] altered May 29, 1800 [not signed];
    [survey & plat] Hawkins Co 1787 (sic) surveyed 640 ac for David Campbell on E fork of Turkey Cr & N side of Holsten R; known as the "plesent" forrest; begins at 5 post oak on Archibald McCalob's line, runs N35W 244 poles with his line crossing the creek to a black oak, S55W 420 poles to a stake, S35E 244 poles to a stake, & N55E 420 poles to beginning (signed) John McClellan, DS [no chain carriers mentioned]; above survey was made Aug. 20, 1787 by Stockley Donelson & run over again by me Oct. 28, 1797 (signed) John McClellan; [grant book 80 p. 291, see shuck #583 in Hawkins Co in Secretary's grant files].

534. Knox Co, TN, Jul. session 179; at Knox Co Pleas & Quarter Sessions Court "heretofore", Alexander McMillin petitioned the court saying Adam Meek, deputy surveyor, made a mistake in surveying or platting 250 ac on Turkey Cr; Alexander McMillin "supposed" himself liable to be greatly injured by the error; at same time McMillin presented a plat of survey made by Robert Houston, deputy surveyor, and asked that the grant be made conformable to said plat; at this term with majority of acting justices present, court is satisfied that the plat contains

land intended to have been surveyed; court is satisfied that due notice was give agreeable to law; court considered the petition & are were of opinion that grant No. 213 issued Dec. 26, 1791 to Alexander McMillin should be made conformable to the plat of survey; clerk is to certify the same to North Carolina Secretary of State; Charles McClung, clerk, certifies foregoing is a copy of the proceedings had on Alexander McMillin's petition and annexed plat of survey is plat presented in court (signed) Aug. 28, 1799 Chas McClung; [on back] grant altered Oct. 1, 1799 [not signed];

[survey & plat] I resurveyed 250 ac for Alexander "McMullin" on Turkey Cr; begins at Ashburn's corner, runs N118 poles to 3 hickory saplings, S50W 65 poles crossing the creek at 50 poles to a horn beam, W 20 poles to a black oak, S 270 poles to 2 black oaks, E 183 poles crossing the creek at 170 poles to a black oak & pine, N 190 poles to a dogwood, & W 110 poles to beginning; surveyed May 30, 1799 (signed) R Houston, DS: Tos Gower & John McMullin, chain carriers; [grant No. 211(?), grant book 77 p. 317, see shuck #224 in Hawkins Co in Secretary's grant files].

535. Knox Co, TN, Jan. session 1799; "heretofore" James "Millar" preferred a petition to Knox Co court saying a mistake in surveying or plotting was made for 640 ac in Knox Co on Fourth Cr; James Millar "supposed" himself liable to be greatly injured by the error; he holds the land by deed under Thomas King under whom the grant issued; at same time Millar presented a plot of survey and asked that the grant be made conformable to the plat of survey presented; at this term of court with majority [of justices] being present, court was satisfied that the plot contains the land intended to have been surveyed; a grant was obtained for the land; court is satisfied that due notice was given agreeable to law; court considered the petition and believe the grant to Thomas King, under which James Millar claims, should be made conformable to the plat of survey; clerk is to certify the same to North Carolina Secretary of State; Charles McClung, clerk, certifies foregoing is true copy of proceedings on James Millar's petition and annexed plat of survey was presented to court (signed) Jul. 22, 1800 Chas McClung; [on back] altered Dec. 28, 1801 W W;

[survey & plat] on Fourth Cr, begins at 2 pines on N side of the creek, runs N60W 320 poles to 2 black oak corner of James White's 320 ac survey called Virgin Spring survey, S30E 342 poles along a conditional line to a post oak in a grassey valley, N74E 370 poles to a stake, & a direct line to beginning (signed) R Houston, DS [no chain carriers or date mentioned];

[second copy of petition] petition of James "Miller" to Knox Co court: Miller claims under Thomas King; on Jul. 15, 1785 Thomas King surveyed for himself 640 ac; in making the certificate & plat of survey, the courses were said to be: 640 ac for Thomas King on Fourth Cr, begins at 2 pines on N side of the creek, runs E 320 poles to 2 black oaks a corner of James White's 320 ac survey called Virgin Spring survey, S30E 340 poles along a conditional line to a post oak in a grassey valley, S74W 370 poles to a stake, & to beginning; in truth the survey was made and land intended was for land in following bounds: [metes & bounds of Houston's survey repeated]; the petitioner says he claims under Thomas King;

due to the surveyor's error, the patent doesn't cover land intended and which the petitioner purchased; petitioner asks that his petition be heard & facts be certified to the Secretary so the error can be corrected and the patent issue in conformity with "original actual" survey and cover land as intended which the petitioner purchased from Thomas King (signed) at Knoxville Jan. 10, 1798 Jas Miller; Jan. session 1799 on John Miller's petition for alteration of a grant on Fourth Cr for 640 ac, court ordered petition "granted" agreeable to prayer of petition; clerk to certify the same to North Carolina Secretary; Charles McClung, clerk, certifies foregoing is a copy of James Miller's petition and order by court thereon (signed) Sept. 27, 1802 Chas McClung; [on back] second certe. see first [not signed]; [grant No. 1219, grant book 82 p. 165, see shuck #1554 in Greene Co in Secretary's grant files].

536. Knox Co, TN, "heretofore" James Tennan petitioned Knox Co court saying Thomas King, deputy surveyor for Greene Co, made a mistake in plotting 500 ac; James Tennan "supposed" himself liable to be greatly injured by the error; the court directed a resurvey of the land so they could be satisfied of h error; at Oct. session 1800, Robert Houston, deputy surveyor, returned annexed plat & certificate of survey to court; James Tennan by his attorney asked that grant might be made conformable to the plat of survey returned by Robert Houston; court is satisfied that the plat by Robert Houston contains land originally surveyed for James Tennan; court is satisfied that due notice was given agreeable to law; court considered the petition and believe grant No. 828 issued Nov. 27, 1789 to James "Tenan" should be altered & made conformable to Robert Houston's plat of survey; court ordered the clerk to certify the same to North Carolina Secretary of State so their order can be carried into effect; Charles McClung, clerk, certifies foregoing is a copy of proceedings on James Tenan's petition and annexed plat of survey is the plat presented to the court (signed) Oct. 18, 1800 Chas McClung; [on back] altered agreeable to within order Feb. 10, 1801 (signed) Wm Hill, D Sec;

[survey & plat] agreeable to order of Knox Co court, I resurveyed 500 ac on the second creek below mouth of French "Brawd" [R]; being same that appears to have been surveyed Apr. 3, 1785 for James Tennan; begins at a pine & post oak the original corner as shown by James White one of the chain carriers on first survey and on NE side of the creek, runs S50W 200 poles to a stake & pointers near where a sowerwood & white oak stood the sowerwood being cut down & white oak dead, N50W instead of S50E 400 poles along "the" marked line to a stake pine & post oak "not found", N50E 200 poles to a stake, S50E 400 poles to beginning (signed) Oct. 1, 1800 R Houston [no chain carriers mentioned]; [grant not identified].

537. Robertson Co, TN, Pleas & Quarter Sessions Court at town of Springfield on third Monday in Jul. 1800; John Russel McShehee preferred his petition to court asking to correct errors in grant issued on warrant No. 1087; correction to be made agreeable to act of General Assembly made in such cased; petition follows: petition of John Russel McShehee to Robertson Co, TN, Pleas & Quarter Sessions Court: the petitioner's father Miles McShehee was a lieutenant in North

Corrections/Alterations to Land Grants

Carolina Line; Miles McShehee is dead; the petition is son & heir of Miles and is entitled to 2,560 ac within th military boundary of "this" state in consideration of military services of Miles McShehee; warrant No. 1087 was issued by North Carolina Secretary of state for surveying land which was located Aug. 30, 1785 in entry taker's office; Martin Armstrong, surveyor by his deputy Anthony Foster, surveyed the entry; said Martin, by his deputy, committed an error in making the certificate by leaving a blank in the certificate immediately preceding words "heir of Miles McShehee" which should have been filled up with name of John Russel McShehee, the petitioner; the petitioner also shows a grant was issued by North Carolina due to said warrant, entry, & certificate; in the grant the Secretary of State was guilty of an error by leaving a blank in the grant for name of grantee which should have been filled with name of the petitioner John Russel McShehee; this mistake is still more fatal than surveyor's mistake; words "heir of Miles McShehee" are in the certificate but totally omitted in the grant; petitioner shows he is in danger of total loss of the land in the patent which is without a grantee "and of consequence of no effect" and the certificate is so vague that it doesn't specify who is the heir of Miles McShhee; petitioner asks court to direct the clerk to certify above facts to North Carolina Secretary so the mistakes can be corrected (signed) Jul. 22, 1800 John Russel McShehee.   On hearing the petition & proofs supporting the allegations therein contained, court ordered [prayer of] the same be "granted".   Thomas Johnson, clerk, certifies foregoing is true transcript from records of said court (signed) Jul. 25, 1800 Thos Johnson, clk RC; [on back] altered & corrected Sept. 17, 1800 WW; [grant No. 2094 issued May 20, 1793, grant book 81 p. 148, see shuck #331 in Robertson Co in Secretary's grant files].

538. Sullivan Co, Territory of United States of America S of Ohio R, May session 1795; petition of George Vincent esq, surveyor of said county, & John Anderson, acting executor of William Anderson deceased; court ordered following course in a grant: fourteenth course which is "crossed in the platt" and calls S64E 116 poles to a stake to be altered to S64W 116 poles to a stake and beginning corner which mentions 2 "black" to [be altered] to 2 black oaks; grant is No. 641 in name of William Anderson deceased; the same to be notified to Honble. James Glasgow, North Carolina Secretary (signed) Matthew Rhea, CSC; [on back] patent altered [not signed]; [grant book 81 p. 635, see shuck #693 in Sullivan Co in Secretary's grant files].

539. [Sullivan Co], Territory of United States of America S of Ohio R, Sept. session 1794; to "Colonel" James Glasgow, North Carolina Secretary: agreeable to order of Sullivan Co court in favour of Moses Cavitt, heir of Alexander Cavitt, the clerk is directed to certify to James Glasgow, North Carolina Secretary of State, to admit following alteration, pursuant to "order" of George Vincent, surveyor of said county: in grant No. 46 to Moses Cavitt heir of Alexander Cavitt for 348 ac in Washington, now Sullivan, Co: instead of running N8E 21 poles alter to S8E up the river as it meanders to upper corner white oak on said river and alter last line in grant which is "East" to a straight line to beginning; a copy (signed) Oct. 14, 1794 Mattw Rhea, CSC; [grant to Alexander Cavitt, grant book

Corrections/Alterations to Land Grants

47 p. 21 se shuck #178 in Washington Co in Secretary's grant files].

540. Sullivan Co, TN, Aug. session 1797; court ordered clerk to certify to North Carolina Secretary that there are errors in courses of grant No. 566, as described in a petition, issued to John Gentry for 240 ac; errors to be altered as follows: third course mentions W 264 poles to be altered to S84W 238 poles to a stake, fourth line is right only the distance which mentions 148 poles to be altered to 162 poles, fifth line mentions a straight line to beginning to be altered to E 210 poles to a stake & then a straight line to beginning; (witness) Matthew Rhea, clerk of Sullivan Co (signed) Nov. 24, 1797 Matthew Rhea, CSC; [on back] altered Aug. 10, 1803 [not signed]; [grant book 77 p. 308, see shuck #611 in Sullivan Co in Secretary's grant files].

541. Sullivan Co, Territory of United States of America S of Ohio R, Nov. session 1795; petition of George Vincent, surveyor of said county, & Matthias Little (of "the same"); court ordered following amendments of grant No. 598 to said Little for 90 ac: for course N70E 244 poles to a stake to be altered to N70E still on Jacob Flunor's [or Flernor] line 96 poles to a pine & white oak and also N42E 154 poles still on Flunor's line to a stake, S 164 poles to a stake, & a straight line to beginning; contains 150 ac; which "fills up" the warrant mentioned in the grant; the same to be notified to James Glasgow, North Carolina's Secretary (signed) Feb. 9, 1795 Matthew Rhea, CSC; [on back] patent altered [no date or signature]; [grant book 80 p. 383, see shuck #650 in Sullivan Co in Secretary's grant files].

542. Sullivan Co, TN, Aug. session 1801; petition of David Ross filed in Sullivan Co clerk's office May session 1800 to correct errors in a land grant from North Carolina Secretary's office issued Aug. 9, 1787 to Christian Roads & John Manifee for 1,280 ac and sold by them by deed to David Ross; Sullivan Co court at Aug. session 1801 ordered clerk to certify to North Carolina Secretary that there is an error as mentioned in the petition; court ordered grant to be altered agreeable to prayer of petition; error is that in first course surveyor said N60W 160 poles but it should have been S60W 160 poles; certification to Secretary is hereby done by Matthew Rhea, clerk (signed) Aug. 18, 1801 Mattw Rhea, clerk Sullivan Co; [on back] altered Oct. 14, 1801; [grant issued to Christian "Rhodes" & John Manifee, grant book 61 p. 425, see shuck #267 in Sullivan Co in Secretary's grant files].

543. Sullivan Co, TN, Aug. session 1798; petition of Martin Wirick; court ordered at this session that North Carolina Secretary be notified to correct errors in a grant issued from his office to said Wirick for 150 ac; errors appear to have been committed in the Secretary's office as follows: "in surveying the distance" in the second course is 160 poles and third course is 80 poles "in lieu there of in the grant"; it appears the distance of second line & course of third is entirely left out of the grant which will plainly appear by reference to plot & grant; "in order" a new deed can issue agreeable to the original plot (signed) Aug. 25, 1798 Matthew Rhea, clerk; [on back] altered Nov. 27, 1799 [not signed]; [grant book 67 p. 487,

Corrections/Alterations to Land Grants

see shuck #342 in Sullivan Co in Secretary's grant files].

544. Sumner Co, TN, Apr. term 1797; Thomas Stokes preferred a petition to this court saying an error was committed by the survey in returning a certificate of survey for 1,000 ac on which grant No. 283 issued; error was in inserting in the certificate on N side of Cumberland R instead of S side of Cumberland R; court considered the petition and allegations set forth; court ordered clerk to certify to North Carolina Secretary of State that it appears "plain & evident" that the word "North" in surveyor's certificate which precedes words "side of Cumberland R" was inserted in error by the surveyor and word "South" should be substituted in lieu thereof by Secretary of State agreeable to act of Assembly of "this" state entitled an act making provision for mistakes in land surveys; I testify foregoing is true extract from Sumner Co court records (signed) Apr. 10, 1797 David Shelby, CSC; [on back] order for alteration of grant in 1787 to Jas Cole Montflourance; altered agreeable to within order Oct. 30, 1797 (signed) Wm Hill, DS; [grant due to military warrant #2149, grant book 63 p. 104, see shuck #297 in Davidson Co in Secretary's grant files].

545. Tennessee Co, Territory of United States S of Ohio R, court Apr. term 1796; Matthew McCauley exhibited his petition to this court saying a mistake was made by Joseph Brock, deputy surveyor for North Carolina Continental Line; it appears by petition & platts laid before court "of" Capt. Campbell's & said McCauley's lands on Spring Cr that "by" beginning at SE corner of James Campbell's survey but in fact "he" begins at SE corner and runs agreeable 'to law"; by laying down plat beginning at SW corner, it runs altogether in Campbell's claim so said McCauley will loose his land; court ordered clerk certify to North Carolina Secretary that it is their opinion that he issue a grant to "Mathew" McCauley for land intended for him & called for by his location; Anthony Crutcher, clerk of Tennessee Co Pleas & Quarter Sessions Court, certifies above is taken from the minutes (signed) Apr. 28, 1796 A Crutcher; [on back] altered & "done with" [no date or signature]; [may be grant for shuck #18 or #19 in Davidson Co in Secretary's grant files].

546. Washington Co, TN, Nov. session 1799; agreeable to court order, North Carolina Secretary will alter errors in grant No. 1076 issued Jul. 12, 1794; instead of running 80 poles in second line run 89, in third line 44 poles instead of 84, in seventh line run 164 poles instead of 160, in ninth line S70E instead of S7E and instead of 100 poles run 104, in tenth line 168 poles instead of 146, in eleventh line 129 poles instead of 130, in twelfth line 32 poles instead of 33, in thirteenth line instead of 110 poles run 130, in fourteenth line S13W instead of S22 W, in fifteenth line instead of 40 poles run 48, in sixteenth line 56 poles instead of 48, in seventeenth line instead of 112 poles run 114, in eighteenth line run S53W 162 poles instead of S47W 215 poles, and instead of 200 ac 190 ac (signed) No. 4, 1799 Jas Sevier, CWC;

[survey & plat] due to order of Washington Co, TN, Pleas & Quarter Sessions Court Nov. 1799, surveyed 190 ac for Joseph "Britten"; begins at David

184

Corrections/Alterations to Land Grants

Denham's corner hickory, runs N 57 poles crossing Sinking Cr to a black oak & post oak, W 89 poles to a black oak on Chapman's line, N33E 44 poles to a red oak, N 120 poles to a hickory, E 42 poles to a white oak, N 100 poles to a red oak, W 164 pols to a hickory, N 53 poles to a cestnut, S70E 104 poles to a locust, N20E 168 poles to a hickory, S129 poles to a black oak, E 32 poles to a post oak, S 130 poles to a white oak, S13W 80 poles to a red oak, E 48 poles to a small hickory, S 46 poles to a white oak, E 114 poles to a poplar, & S53W 162 poles to beginning (signed) Nathan Shipley, DS [no chain carriers mentioned]; [grant book 81 p. 561, see shuck #1117 in Washington Co in Secretary's grant files].

547. Washington Co, TN, May session 1799; court ordered North Carolina Secretary of State to correct errors in grant No. 882 issued to Joseph Brown for 150 ac, begins at the same corner as the old grant at a large black oak, runs N55E 18.75 poles with land purchased by David Deaderich to a locust stake & white oak, N30W 114 poles with said Deaderich's line to a stake, N42E 175 poles with widow Young's line to a spanish oak & white oak, S45E 128 poles with John Smith's line to 3 sowerwoods, S 38.5 poles to a small black oak, W 71 poles to a sasafras, S 139 poles with James Delaney's line to a stake on Edward Smith's line, & to beginning (signed) May 11, 1799 Jas Sevier, cc; [on back] altered Jun. 10, 1799 (not signed);
　　　[survey & plat] due to warrant No. 2794 issued Feb. 20, 1781, I surveyed, on Apr. 26, 1799, 150 ac in Washington Co for Joseph Brown due to court order to correct error in grant No. 882; land on waters of Cherokee Cr; [same metes & bounds as above] (signed) Joseph Brown, DS; John Smith & James Harvey, chain carriers; [grant book 76 p. 138, see shuck #905 in Washington Co in Secretary's grant files].

548. [survey & plat] due to warrant No. 2451 issued Feb. 28, 1780 by Washington Co entry taker, surveyed 400 ac for John Carter; land on S side of Lynn Mountain & joins said Carter's 640 ac survey; begins at a black oak & forked dogwood corner of said survey & Emanuel Carter's survey, runs N19E 440 poles along line of said 640 ac survey to a red or spanish oak on the bank of "Wataugah" R corner of said 640 ac survey, N68E 50 poles up the river to a white oak on the river bank corner of William Cocke, S29E 315 poles to a stake, & S65W to beginning; surveyed May 28, 1780 (signed) James Stuart, CS; [on back] Washington Co, Territory S of Ohio R, agreeable to court order, the Secretary is requested to alter lines of grant agreeable to within plat (signed) Feb. 21, 1795 Jas Sevier, CWC; John Carter No. 634 grant altered (not signed); [grant book 69 p. 147, see shuck #820 in Washington Co in Secretary's grant files.

549. Washington Co, Territory S of Ohio R; agreeable to order of said county court, the Secretary is requested to alter lines of a grant agreeable to within plot (signed) Feb. 21, 1795 Jas Sevier, CWC;
　　　[survey & plat] due to warrant No. 603 issued Nov. 23, 1778 by Washington Co entry taker, surveyed 640 ac for John Carter on S side of Wataugah R and joins William Cocke, Thomas Houghton, & Emanuel Carter;

185

Corrections/Alterations to Land Grants

begins at a black oak & forked dogwood corner of Emanuel Carter, runs N73W 80 poles with his line to a black oak, N38W 70 poles with his line to a black oak, W 18 poles to a spanish oak on the bank of Doe R corner of Thomas Houghton, N45W 54 poles with said Houghton's line to a spanish oak, N35W 64 poles with said line to a forked post oak, N16W 60 poles with said line to a red oak, N12W 20 poles with said line to a small red oak, N7E 62 poles with said line to a chesnut white oak standing in a hollow, N20W 70 poles along said line to a hickory on S bank of Wataugah [R] corner of said Houghton, E 80 poles up the river to a sycamore, N62E 66 poles to a black walnut on lower point of an island, N49E 34 poles along the river bank to a white hickory, N80E 22 poles along the river bank to a white hickory, E 45 poles along the river bank to a forked poplar, N50E 42 poles to 2 black walnuts on the river bank, N85E 20 poles to a white walnut on the river bank, S80E 20 poles to a lyn on the river bank, S59E 56 poles along the river bank to head of Island Cr, N70E 10 poles to a hickory, N85E 46 poles to a red or spanish oak on the river bank, & S19W 440 poles to beginning; surveyed Feb. 18, 1780 (signed) James Stuart, CS; [on back] Jno Carter No. 96, grant altered 1782 [not signed]; [grant book 47 p. 47, see shuck #228 in Washington Co in Secretary's grant files].

550. Washington Co, Territory S of Ohio R, Nov. session 1795; agreeable to court order, North Carolina Secretary is requested to alter & correct errors in grant No. 306 issued Oct. 7, 1782; instead of running 200 in first [line] run 214 poles, instead of W 134 poles run S80W 108 poles in second line, in third line run 264 poles instead of 206, and instead of N85E 194 poles run N64E 180 poles in fourth line to beginning (signed) Nov. 6, 1795 Jas Sevier, cc; [on back] David Hughs 200 ac, altered Jun. 17, 1803;

[survey & plat] due to order of Washington Co court Nov. session 1795, surveyed 200 ac for David Hughes Jan. 2, 1796; land on Coopers Cr; begins at a large white oak, runs S17W 214 poles along Jacob Headrich's line to a hickory, S80W 108 poles to a white oak, S 264 poles to a spanish oak, & N67E 180 poles to beginning (signed) Nathan Shipley, DS; Wills Jones & Jas Chance, chain carriers; [4 grants to David Hughes (or Hughs), but none for 200 ac; grant not identified].

551. [survey & plat] in order to correct errors in grant No. 781, resurveyed 170 ac for John Hunter on Dec. 12, 1799; land in Washington Co, TN; begins at first corner of original grant at a white oak "called" Taylor's line, runs N70W 21 poles to a beech ash & maple, S35W 20 poles to a stone, S82E 38 poles to a white oak, N50E 12 poles 17 links to a white oak, E 220 poles to a post oak & stake, S 42 poles to a stake, E 92 poles to a stake, N 92 poles to a large black oak, N40W 103 poles to 2 walnuts, S62W 166 poles to a stake, N30W 46 poles to 3 lyns, & a direct line to beginning (signed) Joseph Brown, DS; Anthony Brily & [blank], chain carriers. Washington Co, TN May session 1800 petition was filed by John Hunter sr for correcting errors in grant No. 981 (sic) for 170 ac; court ordered that North Carolina Secretary of State alter & correct errors in the grant to true courses described in within certificate (signed) May 5, 1800 Jas Sevier, cc; [on back]

Corrections/Alterations to Land Grants

altered Aug. 21, 1800 [not signed]; [grant No. 781, grant book 64 p. 146, see shuck #518 in Washington Co in Secretary's grant files].

552. [survey & plat] in order to correct errors in grant No. 1068 issued Dec. 18, 1793 to John Kenady, surveyed 200 ac on waters of Nolachuckey [R]; begins at a stake & black oak formerly James Logan's line now Thomas Messey's land, runs W 217.5 poles to a white oak, N 148 poles with or near Alexander Matthews' line to a stake & white oak, E 217.5 poles with Joseph Messer's line to a large black oak, & with "Simons Hunts" line a direct course to beginning (signed) Joseph Brown, surveyor; surveyed Nov. 9, 1802; Thomas Ball & Edward Millon, chain carriers; (signed) James Stuart, county surveyor. Washington Co, TN, May session 1803; agreeable to court order in favour of John "Kennedy", the petitioner claiming land mentioned on within plat, North Carolina Secretary of State is required to alter the grant agreeable to courses of within plat (signed) May 7, 1803 Jas Sevier, clerk of Washington Co Court; [on back] altered Jun. 17, 1803 [not signed]; [grant not identified].

553. [survey & plat] in order to correct errors in grant No. [blank] due to warrant No. 511, resurveyed on Feb. 7, 1800 300 ac for James Moore in Washington Co formerly North Carolina now Tennessee; land on Little Limestone [Cr] & includes Joseph Fowler's improvement; begins on N side of the creek formerly James Pierce's now Thomas Embree's corner 2 hicorys & 2 white oaks, runs S21E 140 poles crossing the creek & a road that leads to Embree's Mill formerly Pierce's to a white oak in a flat, N88E 255 poles to Daniel Brown's formerly Alexander Campbell's & Brunk's corner at a hickory & 2 white oaks, N25W 232 poles with said line crossing a branch of said [Little ?] Limestone Cr to a white oak sour wood & gumb now Daniel Brown's formerly said Campbell's corner, S52W 61 poles with said line to 2 hickory saplins said Campbell's now David Brown's corner, N11W 86 poles crossing [Little ?] Limestone [Cr] to a stake, & a direct line to beginning (signed) Joseph Brown, DS; Daniel Brown & William Shannon, chain carriers. Washington Co, TN, Feb. session 1801; agreeable to order of Washington Co court, North Carolina Secretary of State is authorized to correct errors in a grant to James Moore for 300 ac agreeable to within courses (signed) Feb. 7, 1801 Jas Sevier, CWC; [on back] altered Nov. 30, 1801 [not signed]; [grant book 47 p. 49, see shuck #232 in Washington Co in Secretary's grant files].

554. [survey & plat] in order to correct errors in grant No. 1201, on Apr. 8, 1800 resurveyed 150 ac for Ephraim Murry & James "Moor" in Washington Co on waters of Cherokee [Cr]; begins at a chesnut & white oak on a line of said Murry's land, runs W 184 poles to a white oak, S5W 54 poles with said Moor's line to a forked chesnut & white oak corner of Mr. James "Stewart's" land, S82E 28 poles with said Stewart's line to a stake & white oak, S 52 poles 10 links to a stake, N80E 5 poles to a chesnut & white oak corner of Peter Ruble's land, N74E 268 poles with his line to a stake & white oak, N "forty fifty" West 134 poles to a stake, & direct line to beginning (signed) Joseph Brown, DS; Ephraim Murry & John Gregg, chain carriers. Washington Co, TN, May session 1800; agreeable

to petition filed in my office, court ordered that North Carolina Secretary correct errors in grant No. 1201 for 15 ac to Ephraim Murry agreeable to within courses (signed) May 7, 1800 Jas Sevier, cc; [on back] altered Aug. 21, 1800 [not signed]; [grant book 89 p. 325, see shuck #1263 in Washington Co in Secretary's grant files].

555. [sheet in pieces; survey & plat] due to order of Washington Co Pleas & Quarter Sessions Court, resurveyed 250 ac for Charles Robertson in Washington Co; begins at a corner popler of Col. Charles "Robison's" survey, runs N34E 120 poles to a white oak, S39E 12 poles to a chesnut, S83E 30 poles to a popler, N21E 58 poles to a stake, E 264 poles to a red oak, S10W 132 poles to a black oak, N89W 220 poles to a hickory, & S 86 degrees 18 minutes W 155 poles to beginning (signed) N Shipley, DS [no chain carriers mentioned]. Washington Co, TN, May session 1800; agreeable to petition filed in my office by Chas "Robison" for correcting errors in grant No. 631 for 300 ac, court ordered that North Carolina Secretary of State correct errors in the grant agreeable to true courses in within certificate (signed) May 5, 1800 Jas Sevier, CWC; [on back] altered Aug. 21, 1800 [not signed]; [grant not identified].

556. [survey & plat] in order to correct errors in grant No. 927, on Feb. 1, 1797 resurveyed 190 ac for "Collonel" Charles Robertson of Washington Co agreeable to order of Washington Co court Aug. term 1796; land on N side of Nolachuckey R; begins at a hickory & 2 spanish oaks, runs N170 poles to a chesnut in David Huffman's line, S76W 35 poles with the same to 2 gumbs James McAdams' line, W 156 poles with said line to Jacob Brown's corner black oak & 2 white oaks, S 160 poles crossing a branch of Cherokee [Cr] to 2 white oaks, & with meanders of Nolachuckey R to beginning (signed) Joseph Brown, DS; Charles Robertson jr & Samuel King, chain carriers. Washington Co, TN, May session 1800; agreeable to petition filed in my office by Chas "Robison" to correct errors in grant No. 927 for 190 ac, court ordered that North Carolina Secretary of State correct errors in the grant agreeable to true courses in within certificate (signed) May 5, 1800 Jas Sevier, cc; [on back] altered Aug. 21, 1800; [grant book 76 p. 153, see shuck #950 in Washington Co in Secretary's grant files].

557. [survey & plat] due to order from Washington Co, TN, Pleas & Quarter Sessions Court Aug. 1796 [Feb. 1797--lined out], resurveyed 500 ac for Col. Charles Robison on Nolechucky R on N side; begins at a hickory, runs S20 degrees 30 minutes W 82 poles to a white oak, S5W 147 poles to a poplar, S17W 24 poles to a white oak, S79E 108 poles to a sycamore, S6E 14 poles to a white oak, E 30 poles to 2 white oaks, S 58 poles to an ash, S56W 180 poles along foot of Buflow Mountain to a white oak on the river bank, down meanders of the river to a black oak on the river, N 170 poles to a stake, N53E 137 poles to a "fell down" poplar, & N 86 degrees 18 minutes E 155 poles to beginning (signed) N Shipley, DS; Andrew Lilburn & David Huffman, chain carriers. Washington Co, TN, May session 1800; agreeable to petition filed in my office by Charles Robison to correct errors in grant No. 643 for 500 ac, court ordered that North Carolina

Corrections/Alterations to Land Grants

Secretary of State correct errors in the grant agreeable to true courses in within certificate (signed0 May 5, 1800 (signed) Jas Sevier, cc; [on back] altered Aug. 21, 1800 [not signed]; [grant book 69 p. 150, see shuck #829 in Washington Co in Secretary's grant files].

558. Washington Co, TN, Feb. session 1799; agreeable to order of court, North Carolina Secretary of State will correct errors in grant No. 604 issued Nov. 9, 1784 and instead of 62 poles in third line run 236 and in fifth line run N10E instead of 10W (signed) Feb. 19, 1799 Jas Sevier, CWC; [on back] altered Dec. 19, 1799 [not signed];

[survey & plat] due to order of Washington Co court dated Feb. 19, 1799, surveyed 486 ac for William Stone on S side of Boons Cr; begins at a stone in the creek, runs S33E 58 poles to a post William Bean sr's corner, S44W 100 poles to a black oak, S20E 236 poles crossing a branch to a black oak, N76E 180 poles to a hickory & spanish oak on N side of Indian Ridge, N10E 270 poles to a white oak & black oak, N33W 71 poles to a stake in the creek, & up meanders of the creek to beginning (signed) Nathan Shipley, DS [no chain carriers mentioned]; [grant book 69 p. 139, see shuck #790 in Washington Co in Secretary's grant files].

559. Washington Co, Territory S of Ohio R, Aug. session 1794; agreeable to order of Washington Co court in favor of William Ward, clerk is directed to certify to James Glasgow, North Carolina Secretary of State, to "admit" alteration of 2 lines in grant No. 713 to said Ward for 200 ac; instead of running N76W to be N26W 86 poles to at white and in place of 49 degrees W 34 poles to beginning [insert] a straight line to beginning; a true copy (signed) Oct. 10, 1794 Jas Sevier, clerk; [grant book 66 p. 202, see shuck #624 in Washington Co in Secretary's grant files].

560. petition to Washington Co Pleas & Quarter Sessions Court: the petitioner represents he had 100 ac surveyed by Isaac Taylor, [deputy] for James Stuart Washington Co surveyor; a grant issued from North Carolina to the petitioner on the survey; the courses & "instances" of the survey follow: begins at John McGlaughlin's corner white oak, runs due W 140 poles to a black oak on Thomas Rogers' line, N55E 144 poles to a white oak on McBride's line, N60E 221 poles to a stake, & S39W 228 poles to beginning; instead of the first course running W 140 poles to a "black" on Thomas Rogers' line it should run 139 poles to said black oak on said Rogers' line, instead of second line running n55E 144 poles it should run N55.5 W 150 poles to a white oak on William McBride's line, & instead of third line running N60E 221 poles to a stake it should run N65E 130 poles to a stake & white oak & to beginning; the petitioner asks the court to take his case into consideration and grant that the errors be certified to North Carolina Secretary of State so justice may be "own" in the premises as the law directs (signed) Jun. 27, 1803 Joseph Willson.   Washington Co, TN, May session 1804 I certify within is true copy of petition filed in my office; court ordered at May session that clerk certify to North Carolina Secretary of State to correct errors in

189

the grant agreeable to true courses mentioned in the petition (signed) May 28, 1804 Jas Sevier, clerk Washington Co court;

[survey & plat] In order to correct errors in grant No. 457 issued to Joseph Willson for 100 ac & agreeable to proceedings of Washington Co court, I surveyed 100 ac for John Willson: begins at first corner white oak of the original grant & John McLaughlin's corner on waters of Mill Cr, runs W 139 poles to a black oak on Thomas Rodgers' line, N55.5W 150 poles to a white oak on William McBride's line, N65E 130 poles with the same to a stake & white oak, & a direct line to beginning; (signed) Jun. 13, 1804 Joseph Brown, surveyor; James Kennedy & Thomas Bidle, chain carriers; [on back] altered Nov. 26, 1804 [not signed]; [grant book 52 p. 292, see shuck #465 in Washington Co in Secretary's grant files].

561. [survey & plat] pursuant to order of Washington Co court to correct errors in grant No. 899, on Dec. 20, 1798 I surveyed 200 ac for Mr. Charles Young on waters of Brush Cr; begins at William Meek's corner white oak black oak & hickory, runs S70E 78 poles crossing a spring branch to a red oak & 2 elms, N31E 278 poles with William Young jr's line to a stake, N78E 20 poles to said Wm Young's corner mulbery, N8E 4.5 poles to a large spanish oak corner of Robert Young, S78W 379 poles with his line to a white oak & black oak, S11E 10 poles to a white oak, N 78 degrees 45 minutes E 89 poles to a dogwood, & to beginning (signed) Joseph Brown, DS; Daniel Baley & Robert Cashady, chain carriers. Washington Co, TN, Nov. session 1798 agreeable to order of Washington Co court Nov. session 1798, North Carolina Secretary of State will correct errors in grant No. 899 to Charles Young for 200 ac agreeable to within courses (signed) Jul. 27, 1799 Jas Sevier, cc; [on back] grant altered Aug. 12, 1799 [not signed]; [grant book 76 p. 144, see shuck #922 in Washington Co in Secretary's grant files].

562. to correct errors in grant No. 956 issued to Charles Young for 240 ac, insert "begins at a stake on corner of said Young's entry [survey--lined out] No. 1140 for 200 ac, run S3E 286 poles "Do" to a stake on corner "thereof" & on Meek's line; second: in place of second line, insert N56E 224 poles to a white oak mentioned in the patent; third: "irraze" the third line & insert in its place the following: N73W 71 poles to a black oak N32E 154 poles to "Treble" white oak S64E 16 poles to a chesnut & white oak; and "lastly" insert fourth line 150 poles to beginning and "erase" fifth line out; the above errors made in surveying "corrected Sept. 1798 by John [Johnson ? faint] (signed) John Shield, DWC. Washington Co, TN, Nov. session 1798 agreeable to order of Washington Co court Nov. session 1798 North Carolina Secretary of State will correct errors in grant No. 956 issued to Charles Young for 240 ac agreeable to within courses (signed) Jul. 27, 1799 Jas Sevier, cc; [on back] grant altered Aug. 12, 1799; [grant book 76 p. 164, see shuck #979 in Washington Co in Secretary's grant files].

563. Wilson Co, TN, Sept. term 1805; Thomas Stokes vs John Buchannan & John Gray Blount: petition to rectify a grant; petition was filed at last court; case was

Corrections/Alterations to Land Grants

heard this term in presence of 6 acting justices of peace: Andrew Donelson, William Steele, William Bartlett, William Gray, William Babb, & Phillip Koonce esqs; it was proved that petitioner had notified John Buchannan 30 days prior to preferring the petition and said John Gray Blount by his attorney John Strother has acknowledged John Gray Blount received legal notice; John Buchannan & John Gray Blount have separately been called to come forward & show cause against granting the petition; each of them failed to appear; court heard testimony respecting allegations contained in the petition; it appeared to court that patentee is laible to be injured by surveyor's mistake in making his certificate of survey as stated in the petition; court ordered that clerk certify to North Carolina Secretary that Robert Ewing "mistook" in making out his certificate of survey on warrant No. 2149 for James Cole Mountflorence for 1,000 ac on which grant No. 283 issued Mar. 22, 1787 pursuant thereto; the mistake was that surveyor began at NE corner of a 1,600 ac survey at a small sugar tree & elm but should be beginning at a small sugar tree & elm being NW corner of said 1,600 ac survey; [mistake to be certified] so the mistake in surveyor's certificate & error in the grant can be rectified.   John Allcorn, clerk, certifies foregoing is true copy of record in above case (signed) Sept. 27, 1805 Jno Allcorn, CWC; [on back] grant altered Dec. 5, 1805 WW; [grant book 63 p. 104, see shuck #297 in Davidson Co in Secretary's grant files].

Index to Corrections/Alterations to Land Grants

Index to Corrections/Alterations to Land Grants

Index to Corrections/Alterations to Land Grants

Index to Corrections/Alterations to Land Grants

Index to Corrections/Alterations to Land Grants

Index to Corrections/Alterations to Land Grants

Index to Corrections/Alterations to Land Grants

Index to Corrections/Alterations to Land Grants

Index to Corrections/Alterations to Land Grants

200

Index to Corrections/Alterations to Land Grants

Index to Corrections/Alterations to Land Grants

Index to Corrections/Alterations to Land Grants

Index to Corrections/Alterations to Land Grants

Index to Corrections/Alterations to Land Grants

Index to Corrections/Alterations to Land Grants

Index to Corrections/Alterations to Land Grants

Index to Corrections/Alterations to Land Grants

Index to Corrections/Alterations to Land Grants

Index to Corrections/Alterations to Land Grants

Index to Corrections/Alterations to Land Grants

Index to Corrections/Alterations to Land Grants

Index to Corrections/Alterations to Land Grants

Index to Corrections/Alterations to Land Grants

Index to Corrections/Alterations to Land Grants

Index to Corrections/Alterations to Land Grants

216

Index to Corrections/Alterations to Land Grants

Index to Corrections/Alterations to Land Grants

Index to Corrections/Alterations to Land Grants

Index to Corrections/Alterations to Land Grants

Index to Corrections/Alterations to Land Grants

Index to Corrections/Alterations to Land Grants

Index to Corrections/Alterations to Land Grants

Index to Corrections/Alterations to Land Grants

Index to Corrections/Alterations to Land Grants

Index to Corrections/Alterations to Land Grants

Index to Corrections/Alterations to Land Grants

Index to Corrections/Alterations to Land Grants

Index to Corrections/Alterations to Land Grants

Index to Corrections/Alterations to Land Grants

Index to Corrections/Alterations to Land Grants

www.ingramcontent.com/pod-product-compliance
Lightning Source LLC
Chambersburg PA
CBHW021900020426
42334CB00013B/407